Extreme Sustainability Rhetoric and Sustainable Development

Mauro Fracarolli Nunes and Camila Lee Park

Routledge
Taylor & Francis Group
LONDON AND NEW YORK

earthscan
from Routledge

First published 2023
by Routledge
4 Park Square, Milton Park, Abingdon, Oxon OX14 4RN

and by Routledge
605 Third Avenue, New York, NY 10158

Routledge is an imprint of the Taylor & Francis Group, an informa business

British Library Cataloguing-in-Publication Data
A catalogue record for this book is available from the British Library

Library of Congress Cataloging-in-Publication Data
A catalog record for this book has been requested

ISBN: 978-0-367-64478-9 (hbk)
ISBN: 978-0-367-64479-6 (pbk)
ISBN: 978-1-003-12471-9 (ebk)

DOI: 10.4324/9781003124719

Typeset in Times New Roman
by Apex CoVantage, LLC

To our children, the love of our lives.

Acknowledgements

To God.

To all the masters, educators, and colleagues that contributed to our path.

To our editor, Annabelle Harris, who believed in our project, and Jyotsna Gurung, who supported us along the way.

Contents

Illustrations

Figures

Tables

Preface

How does the way arguments for and against sustainability are presented influence the beliefs and attitudes of those who hear them? How does using the environmental cause to promote political and economic interests contribute to the polarization and to the interruption of dialogue? What are the origins of extreme positions on sustainability, and what can be done so that they do not ruin the possibility of sustainable development? The book seeks to answer these and other related questions through its 16 chapters. Issues as diverse as the nature of rhetoric, the roots of ideological thinking, and the emotional use of marketing tools are addressed, offering readers a holistic and contextualized view of the main challenges present in the public debate on sustainability. This involves an understanding of the different interests that sometimes employ the environmental cause as a pretext, as well as the troubled relationships maintained between environmentalists, academics, politicians, businessmen, celebrities, voters, and consumers, among other social actors.

The complexity of the topics addressed, however, does not allow for the proposition of definitive answers, nor even for the exhaustion of all aspects that refer to them. Despite these limitations, the authors seek to offer insights so that important aspects of the sustainability debate are better understood, mainly those that – despite their relevance – are often ignored, neglected, disguised, or intentionally hidden. Thus, the book seeks to shed light on some of these themes, in such a way that interests behind the environmental discourse come to be more easily recognized. In this sense, the contamination of the sustainability debate by political and economic ideologies is proposed as one of the main causes of radical thinking. The association between sustainability and idealized worldviews ends up importing passions that are typical of the latter, usually making the debate about the environment irrational. In this set, various forms of environmental tribalism may be formed, contributing to radicalism on both sides of the here proposed *sustainability spectrum*. Still, the misuse and distortion of empirical outputs combined with militant behaviours on the part of professors and researchers compromise the belief in scientific data and, in a way, the credibility of science. In particular, the perception that the urgency and timing of climate issues are conveniently suited to electoral calendars or to the launch of new products raises doubts about the seriousness of the arguments.

Originally aimed at an audience interested in these issues, the book should be useful to academics and students from a wide range of fields, including sustainability studies, economics, political science, management, psychology, philosophy, sociology, and linguistics. Evidently, the multitude of topics covered conditions the level of depth with which the specific issues of each area are dealt. This, however, is in line with the book's objectives, which are not to educate specialists but rather to allow those who dedicate themselves more intensely to a certain aspect to have contact with others that are often unknown. The main contribution of this work resides in the fact that it articulates different issues, so that themes normally restricted to the fields mentioned earlier are approached in light of the many other issues with which they relate. In this sense, the discussions should collaborate so that many strictly academic matters escape from their limited circles to invade public debate (or at least come to arouse the interest of academics from other areas). This search for the integration of different visions is not an end in itself – on the contrary, this effort aims to allow for dialogue on sustainable development to be enriched and, ultimately, to become increasingly productive.

Despite its ambitious goals and its original focus on the academic community, the debates offered here are by no means elitist. The objective and direct language adopted in most of the book allows readers who are initially unfamiliar with the topics covered to follow them without further difficulties. The employment of practical examples and illustrations is particularly useful in this regard, also contributing to the applicability of the points covered. This search for a greater interface with different audiences does not translate, however, into a vulgarization or discredit of the issues dealt with here. Instead, by allowing academics from the most diverse areas and non-academics to have access to a common content, the book contributes to its main mission, which is precisely to promote the re-establishment of an honest, fair, comprehensive, and effective dialogue on the different aspects that make up sustainable development.

As previously mentioned, the discussion of political and economic ideologies is one of the main raw materials of the arguments proposed here. Among other things, this means that the positions defended throughout the book will necessarily be polemical, opposing, in most cases, the reader's beliefs, as they are not likely to agree with all the points presented. Therefore, tolerance is asked, especially from those who tend not to admit ideas that do not coincide with their own, or with those of the group with which they identify. It must be noted that the acceptance of divergent thinking is a fundamental condition for maintaining dialogue. Anyone sincerely interested in establishing a path of exchange and in advancing sustainable development should find in the ideas presented here – especially the ones they disagree with – an opportunity to exercise a much-needed tolerance. In this sense, the authors recognize the limitations of what they propose, not intending, under any circumstances, to present their ideas as absolute truths. The authors hope, then, that the readers who disagree with their views will see them as an invitation to dialogue. The acceptance that the ideas presented here have the right to be conveyed (regardless of one's disagreement with them) serves as a thermometer of intellectual tolerance, as an evidence of a taste for the diversity of ideas and, undoubtedly, as an indication in the belief that freedom of expression is unnegotiable. In a world that seems to be moving fast towards the adoption of 'official truths', the questioning of views considered mainstream represent important instruments in the fight against any attempt to normalize totalitarianism. For this reason, tolerance of contradictory thinking must be not only exercised but also encouraged.

This work is the result of many years of study, research, and dedication. If it is true that we are often transformed by reading a book, it is also true that we are much enriched by writing one. When putting their ideas on paper, authors are faced with something new. This is because ideas come to life and grow as they converse with literature. Ideas have power. Ideas have consequences. Pronouncing them demands responsibility and prudence. And, also, some courage. It cannot be claimed, however, that a single work will solve all the problems of the world. Nor that it will validate or invalidate everything that has already been said or done. Even so, each contribution has its value, especially when understood in conjunction with what precedes and follows it. In essence, a book is the result of a dialogue. It is also an open door. May everyone be welcome.

Mauro Fracarolli Nunes
Paris, France
Camila Lee Park
Paris, France

Part I

The Nature of Extreme Sustainability Rhetoric

1 Sustainability Rhetoric

Introduction

The sustainability debate has become extremely complex in the last decades (Swilling, 2020). In addition to relying on a multitude of data, arguments seem to be increasingly dependent on the way they are presented. In this sense, emotional appeals are common (Kals and Maes, 2002), as well as exaggerations (Garnett et al., 2016) and metaphors (Larson, 2011). The involvement of politicians and celebrities with social and environmental causes makes the way their ideas are exposed even more relevant (Willis, 2017; Doyle et al., 2017; Friedlander and Riedy, 2018). In view of these and other transformations, the study of rhetoric applied to sustainability and sustainable development gains relevance (Van der Leeuw et al., 2012). Among other things, understanding the techniques used in messages sent to the public may allow for the identification of their real intentions. Just as a frame can value or devalue a painting, rarely will the content of an argument be immune to the way it is exposed. Along with appreciation of rhetoric on its own, the investigation of its uses and misuses is critical. More than an intellectual exercise, it reveals dynamics of power and influence. In addition to occasionally enchanting the ears of those it addresses, rhetoric can arouse extreme feelings and ultimately influence attitudes of armies and crowds. Seeking to develop ideas that contribute to a better understanding of the nature, uses, and misuses of sustainability rhetoric, this chapter presents a multidisciplinary and contextualized discussion on the main issues related to this theme.

As sustainability discussions leave the scientific orbit to be directed to consumers (White et al., 2019) and voters (Rootes and Carter, 2010), one may expect it to be 'packaged' like a product, with the use of sustainability as an ideological instrument (Borland and Lindgreen, 2013) possibly contributing to its wear. Social and environmental topics might be very convenient for communicating with crowds as, beyond having a universal appeal, they are often difficult to assess (Bragança et al., 2010). From this initial observation, two important conclusions follow: The first refers to the great adaptation of environmental themes to mass consumption, with messages associated with the lowering of environmental impacts often well regarded by final customers. The universality of such approaches allows companies to implement unified messages across countries that, in addition to reducing

DOI: 10.4324/9781003124719-2

the costs of advertisement, can be an important element in the construction of international brands. The second, in turn, relates to the use of sustainability-linked communication in support of political goals, as messages with environmental appeal favour candidates' interactions with diverse segments of society. The fact that basically everyone is affected by climate matters, for example, shall lead to a natural agglutination.

This convergence around environmental messages is expected to increase as voters perceive the questions treated as serious (e.g., threats to their well-being or survival). In addition, messengers' ability to present themselves as the solution to the problems they herald should increase the effectiveness of such speeches. In both cases, rhetoric plays a prominent, and sometimes dangerous, role. As approached throughout the book, the political use of environmentalism seems to be among the main causes of distortions, with the opportunism of those who dispute power often causing confusion. Attempts to frame climate change in the electoral calendar, for instance, result in the creation of panic among voters so that their intentions are influenced. These irresponsible attitudes end up fuelling various forms of environmental skepticism.

The universal nature of sustainability-related themes also seems to act as a magnet for celebrities who seek to have their names associated with environmental protection. While many may be sincerely interested in advancing the environmental agenda, the behaviour of others suggests that they are on the opposite path, that is, seeking to benefit from this association. As environmental causes tend to have a positive evaluation among the most diverse audiences, this works as an additional element in the attraction of musicians, actors, and comedians interested in projecting themselves in an equally positive way. This behaviour can be advantageous from a financial point of view, since the notoriety arising from association with environmental causes may increase box office numbers, as well as accredit these celebrities to represent the products of companies that seek to position themselves as 'good ventures'.

The fact that environmental issues are difficult to measure favours the use of hyperbolic arguments, as they are unlikely to be questioned or denied. It is possible, therefore, that the environmental benefits of products and services have disproportionately increased, as well as the effects of the initiatives adopted by companies in this regard. Similarly, the veracity of environmental problems advertised by politicians can hardly be verified, which can contribute to unconfirmed information or mere hypotheses being used as if they were evidence of a parallel reality. As discussed in greater detail in Chapter 11, in many cases these dynamics end up having the support of scientists, which can significantly damage the validity of their work. As a result, the indiscriminate use of environmentalist rhetoric can distort facts at the mercy of secondary interests. As inconsistencies between discourses and reality are perceived, however, the credibility of the environmental cause deteriorates, which can have a negative effect on the progress of sustainable development. Continuing this brief introduction to the topics covered in the chapter and throughout the book, the concept of rhetoric is discussed more comprehensively. The various topics related to the theme serve as a basis for discussions on both pro- and anti-sustainability rhetoric.

Rhetoric

Pragmatically, rhetoric may be seen as a source of clout. One who is able to persuade has her/his force multiplied as, beyond her/his own, s/he count on the voices, arms, and energy of others, of as many people as s/he convince of the justice of her/his cause, or of its logic. Or, by any reason, of its merit to be defended. One that convinces can do things. Can move things. Big things. Those capable of making good use of rhetoric shall claim their share of influence. For some, this is a gift (e.g., Mifsud, 2007). For others, it is a technique, or a competence that may be acquired (e.g., Bliese, 1977). In any case, rhetoric seems to be associated with the constitution of power, both formal and informal. Not by chance, some of the greatest leaders are reported to have found in rhetoric a path to their success.

Winston Churchill's rhetoric, for example, is often argued to be a powerful example of a patriotic and inspirational voice. Among other things, it allowed him to rise above the fray of general politics, with the expression of deeply felt common values unifying his audiences around the defence of principles (Martin, 2013). Margaret Thatcher, in turn, is claimed to have based her persuasion on her personal credibility as well as emotional responses (Crines et al., 2016). Likewise, Napoleon's achievements are partially attributed to his capacity to coin dramatic phrases in a vibrant manner (Guggenheim, 1961). Rhetoric is also art – the construction of valid and convincing arguments may be as arduous as the building of a cathedral, as everything must be in equilibrium. This dual nature of rhetoric (power and beauty) makes it interesting, and relevant. Maybe that is why it has attracted the attention of brilliant minds throughout history. Coherent with these views, Martin (2013) proposes that 'rhetoric is the art of speech and persuasion, the study of argument and, in Classical times, an essential component in the education of the citizen' (p.i).

From a historical viewpoint, the development of rhetorical theory reflects the conjunction of several contributions. As pointed out by Bitzer (1988), for instance, earlier works like *The Rhetoric* by Aristotle, *De Oratore* by Cicero, *Institutes of Oratory* by Quintilian, and *On the Sublime* by Longinus are among the most the important. Likewise, Whately's *Elements of Rhetoric* and Campbell's *The Philosophy of Rhetoric* also brought important elements to the literature. Although all these texts are recognized as important, Aristotle's Rhetoric is often seen as key. In discussing the architecture of Aristotle's work, Rorty (1996) points out that 'despite having been written at different times, patched together of different pieces, and being far from the most elegant or perspicuously organized of Aristotle's writings, the Rhetoric forms a relatively coherent and familiar structure' (p.1). Still, per Rorty, in preparing his 'handbook for the rhetorician', Aristotle would not have engaged in any special effort, or at least not effort that could indicate a different approach from that usually dedicated to his work. Yet, this does not mean that he did not build something of great value. Instead, the fact that he was faithful to his style becomes evident as the reader perceives the articulation of theory and practices through locating the first in a field of related activities.

For Rapp (2010), well beyond its intrinsic contribution, the value of the concepts and ideas developed in the text can be perceived in the influence they exerted right after appearing, as well as later in time. As Rapp discusses, if Aristotle's teachings are still vivid today, this is due also to subsequent input, with input from authors more closely linked to Aristotle being of particular importance. Along with many additions within the peripatetic tradition, famous Roman teachers of rhetoric (e.g., Cicero, Quintilian) usually built on elements from the Aristotelian doctrine. Furley (2016) clarifies that the peripatetic school refers to a series of philosophers initiated by Aristotle himself, of whom he would be – by far – the most significant. Geographically located in the Lyceum (i.e., a sanctuary dedicated to Apollo outside Athens), the school was a gathering of people, not a building. Among its most prominent members is Theophrastus (371–287 BC), who, beyond being Aristotle's immediate successor, led his philosophical school for 35 years (Pertsindis, 2018).

Sharples (2003) adds that the school's early activities consisted of the collection and interpretation of information issued from every field, as well as by raising and attempting to solve theoretical complications. Examples of the different themes approached include Theophrastus' *Characters*, understood as 'a series of sketches of more or less imperfect personality types' (p.147), as well as his botanical writings, among which the *Historia Plantarum* (Research on Plants) and *De Causis Plantarum* (Explanations of Plants). While the former has been 'variously interpreted as material for a study of comedy, for the presentation of character in rhetoric, or for the study of character which the ancients called 'ethics' but we might rather classify as psychology', the latter represent the 'earliest systematic botanical texts to survive'. For Fortenbaugh (1994), Theophrastus' interest in rhetoric would be evident, with both Cicero and Quintilian acknowledging his contributions to the field. Along with following Aristotle's distinction between deliberative, judicial, and epideictic oratory, he would have also recognized several parts of an oration. Still, after the author, *Characters* would be the best known among all of Theophrastus' surviving works, having influenced both English and German literatures. Organized in sketches, it discusses 30 types of unattractive behavioural patterns, without, however, addressing the reasons one behaves in a given manner. In approaching the differences between *Characters* and Aristotle's *Ethics*, Furley (1953) points out Immisch's (1898) work. Accordingly, while *Ethics* treats the concept and has a scientific outlook, *Characters* focuses on the man and is aesthetic in nature.

In this set, Fortenbaugh (1994) stress three features relating Theophrastus' work on rhetoric. The first is the fact that the sketches are constructed in a well-defined style, combining the rhetorical figure of synathroismos with polysyndeton (i.e., 'the sketches are composed of a string of different actions brought together under a single heading and linked by the conjunction and"', p.19). Second, the content of the sketches is immediately linked to the portrayal of character, meaning that, based on selected pieces of behaviour, one could build a depiction of a person initially perceived as fitting a specific character (e.g., an overly religious person discussed on the basis of *deisidaimonia*, or the sketch of superstition). Later, the humorous nature of the sketches would become of interest to both pupils and professional rhetoricians, who were often more interested in entertaining than in instructing.

More recently, authors such as Corbett and Connors (1999) have devoted attention to the dissemination of rhetoric as an important tool in the construction of texts today. Works such as *Classical Rhetoric for the Modern Student* have served as a guide for those interested in the topic, with the three basic components of classical rhetoric – argument, arrangement, and style –presented according to their practical utility. Likewise, Sloane's (2001) *Encyclopedia of Rhetoric* stresses that, from the earliest times, teachers have insisted that both the nature and identity of rhetoric were best learned through practice (rather than by reading). Despite the fact that rhetoric has proved to be an extremely interesting object of study – which is reflected in the multitude of works dedicated to it – its applications in different spheres of practical life give it an even greater value. In this sense, it is possible to talk about several subdivisions of its applications, according to purpose. McCloskey (1983), for instance, speaks of 'The Rhetoric of Economics', an idea equally embraced by several other authors (e.g., Klamer et al., 1988; Stettler, 1995). Krebs and Jackson (2007), in turn, point to a political rhetoric, arguing that, differently from what is usually believed, rhetoric would not be limited to persuasion, with its expression in the political world being more aggressive. Determining the place of rhetoric in politics is particularly important for the purposes of this book, as are the applications of sustainability rhetoric, discussed next.

Sustainability Rhetoric

In a very broad way, *sustainability rhetoric* can be defined as the set of techniques and methods used in the public debate on sustainability that aims both to convince recipients of the validity of certain arguments and to incite concrete actions that change the state of things. Among other things, this implies the identification and study of the different ways in which issues related to sustainable development can be presented, ranging from the display of eminently objective data (e.g., variations in temperature, levels of pollutants) to messages of an essentially emotional nature. The first group includes the results of academic and scientific research that generally point to different ways of measuring or predicting certain environmental impacts. The communication of these data can be understood as being naturally objective.

From a philosophy of science perspective, this would be equivalent to classifying the presentation of scientific data within an objectivist perspective and, according to the criteria discussed by Burrell and Morgan (1979), ontologically realistic and epistemologically positivist. This is equivalent to the recognition of the existence of a reality and the possibility of it being accessed and known. This gives great credibility to the arguments built on these bases, with the research outcomes that follow scientific methods being reproducible and auditable. Despite these strengths, it is rare for scientific data to cause a stir on its own, as the complexity of the topics covered and the high degree of specialization that their understanding demands usually restrict access to this type of data to a small group of people within the scientific community. This means that the conclusions presented are not expected to have an immediate impact on society unless they are communicated in a more vehement way and addressed to the general public. Examples of this type of communication can be seen in academic articles that seek to build their arguments on eminently empirical data.

At the other extreme are narratives constructed from an emotional angle. Inversely to the first group, the latter seems to be more committed to the effects of arguments than to their validity. Here, the various exaggerations and even the lies presented to the public aim to condition their behaviour. Inserted in a constructivist perspective, the use of rhetoric detached from reality can be quite harmful to sustainable development. In addition to potentially serving secondary interests – mainly political and economic – the detection of its use can have the opposite effect, leading those who suspect the misuse of environmental issues to develop different levels of skepticism. As discussed throughout the book, this possibility can seriously damage the reputation of those who in any way contribute to the development of exaggerated or radical views. This category includes the various advertising pieces created by environmental groups that, in general, seek to draw the public's attention to a specific issue. Typically, this involves the creation of videos and reports in which a company known to the general public is identified as responsible for a certain environmental damage, even if the offenses have been committed by its suppliers. Some of the most famous cases refer to the campaigns that Greenpeace enacted against multinational companies such as Nestle, Unilever, Procter and Gamble (Fracarolli Nunes, 2019), and Dove. In the first case, the use of palm oil in the manufacture of Kit Kat chocolate bars is pointed out as one of the main factors leading to the deforestation of tropical forests and, consequently, to the increase in the change of extinction of endangered species. In the promotional video for the campaign, chocolate is replaced with parts of an animal's body, with a consumer spilling his blood when he bites into it (Greenpeace France, 2010).

Adopting milder language, but no less forceful, the issue of palm oil is also addressed in the form of a cartoon, in a format that seems to be aimed at an audience of children. Developing a story in which a baby orangutang causes disorganization in a young girl's room, the work defends the message that the consumption of products containing palm oil is responsible for the destruction of this animal's natural habitat (Greenpeace France, 2018). In another video, the environmental group points to the use of palm oil in the manufacture of Dove soap (produced by Unilever) as an important driver of deforestation. Similar to the previous videos, the material is quite forceful in its statements and does not shy away from blaming the companies in question for the situation (Greenpeace International, 2009). In addition to these and other videos released on the internet, Greenpeace also promoted several campaigns, using the most diverse forms of *sustainability rhetoric* to accuse large companies for contributing to the deterioration of the environmental situation around the world. This includes protests in front of organization headquarters (Greenpeace USA, 2014) and reports in which the paper used in packages by companies like KFC are pointed to as causes of deforestation (Greenpeace, 2012).

Sustainability rhetoric with radical overtones also seems to be common among politicians. One of the best-known examples of the use of this tool comes from the numerous speeches of former American Vice President Al Gore (1948–) who, through lectures (TED, 2007), films (Algore.com, 2022a), and books (Algore.com, 2022b), promoted the idea that, within a relatively short period of time, the effects of global warming would become devastating. Among other things, this would include melting of the polar layers and the inundation of coastal cities due to rising sea levels. Likewise, American congresswoman Alexandra Ocasio-Cortez did not hesitate to declare that 'the world is going to end in 12 years if we don't address climate change' (Cummings, 2019). It is not difficult to imagine the impact that a public statement of this nature can have on those who listen to it, especially for younger people.

Swedish activist Greta Thunberg (2003–) may be among those most affected by statements such as this. In one of her most famous speeches, the teenager professed her own version of extreme sustainability rhetoric. In her participation at the 2019 World Economic Forum, she declared:

> Our house is on fire. I am here to say, our house is on fire. According to the IPCC (Intergovernmental Panel on Climate Change), we are less than 12 years away from not being able to undo our mistakes. . . . Adults keep saying: 'We owe it to the young people to give them hope.' But I don't want your hope. I don't want you to be hopeful. I want you to panic. I want you to feel the fear I feel every day. And then I want you to act. I want you to act as you would in a crisis. I want you to act as if our house is on fire. Because it is.
>
> (*Guardian*, 2019)

Chapter 12 deals with some of the most important aspects in developing such an attitude, with so-called eco-anxiety debated as one of the most likely causes. French President Emmanuel Macron (1977–) appears to have adhered to a similar rhetoric. When referring to fires in the Amazon rainforest, he declared 'our house is burning' as a way of drawing the attention of other members of the group of the seven richest countries in the world to the issue (NPR, 2019). These and other applications of using extreme *sustainability rhetoric* are taken up later in the book.

Companies also often present their own versions of sustainability rhetoric, with the disclosure of sustainability reports being one of the most common expressions. Undoubtedly, this type of expression seems to be not only a way of communicating with the various actors with which organizations maintain an interface (i.e., stakeholders), but rather a kind of protection against possible damage to their reputational assets that may arise from their own operations (Kang et al., 2016) or those of its supply chain partners (Fracarolli Nunes et al., 2020, 2021b). These measures may actually be necessary, as the products and services offered by organizations have been blamed for much of the environmental damage. The use of products such as diesel, for example, has been identified as an important factor for air pollution, receiving severe attacks from diverse sources (Fracarolli Nunes and Lee Park, 2021b). This dynamic has been unfolding for decades; some of the most important works in the current debate on sustainability were written in the 1960s. In her famous book, *Silent Spring*, biologist Rachel Carlson (1962) pointed out the environmental problems arising from indiscriminate use of pesticides and other chemicals.

Maintaining a constant dialogue therefore seems to be one of the only alternatives available to companies as they seek to protect themselves from accusations. These efforts seem to be even greater when companies seek to get rid of environmental scandals. Cases such as the Volkswagen Dieselgate (Fracarolli Nunes and Lee Park, 2016, 2021a), for example, tend to lead the companies involved to seek an increase in their transparency levels as a way of regaining the trust of their stakeholders. As discussed by Robinson (2016), dialogue plays an important role in establishing trusting relationships, especially when seeking to regain the trust of those with whom one interacts after failures of integrity. The discussion about *sustainability rhetoric* cannot, nevertheless, be restricted to the rhetoric debate. A broader discussion of the main concepts and visions of the modern perspectives on sustainability and sustainable development must be incorporated. The following section seeks to fulfil this mission, presenting an overview of the main lines of reasoning in the area.

The Sustainability Part of Sustainability Rhetoric: Lessons From Management Literature

From the perspective of the relationship between companies, the environment, and society, sustainability is commonly understood as the simultaneous achievement of social, environmental, and economic performance (i.e., triple bottom line in business; Elkingon, 1997), failing to seek one of these goals results in sacrifices for the others (i.e., sustainability trade-offs, Fracarolli Nunes et al., 2020). Conceptually, the triple bottom line in business (Elkington, 1997) seems to be supported by the precepts of stakeholder theory (Freeman, 1984), with the adaptation of business models to a broader reality being critical in this sense. In particular, the transition from the input–output model to the stakeholder model encompasses the main changes (Donaldson and Preston, 1995).

The traditional input–output model is based on the hierarchy of stakeholders, with companies' basic function being reduced to serving the interests of a specific group in the most efficient way possible. In that path, resources from other stakeholders are gathered and organized so that the final objective is achieved. In the specific case of the traditional input–output model, the consumer assumes the role of principal, with investors, suppliers, and employees acting as mere factors of production. Investors, for example, are responsible for financing operations. This includes the money needed for the purchase of machinery, the construction of fixed assets (e.g., warehouses, buildings), and working capital, as well as any other matters that are necessary for the company to function.

Suppliers, in turn, guarantee the necessary inputs for the production process (e.g., raw material), while employees offer their workforce (e.g., physical strength, skills, know-how, experience). All these resources are gathered by the company that manages them in the direction of delivering to the consumer something for which he is willing to pay. These relationships can be understood by the direction of the arrows in the model. While the other stakeholders 'donate' something to the company, only the consumer receives something. Evidently, the model is subject to much criticism and is far from explaining the complexities of how companies operate, to say nothing of their interfaces with the different groups with which they relate. One of the possible criticisms is that all stakeholders are somehow remunerated for what they deliver. Employees receive salaries, suppliers are paid, and investors are entitled to the profits generated by the operation. However, these payments are based on the amounts collected from consumers when they choose to buy the products and services offered to them. The recognition that the consumer is the major funder of all this gear explains the fact that it is placed at the centre of organizations' objectives.

The Sustainability Cause

The sustainability cause, in turn, may be understood as the set of beliefs that position sustainable development as the only viable alternative to the future. Within this view, the implementation of socially and environmentally responsible initiatives would be seen as not only necessary but also fair and urgent. Among other things, these pursuits are portrayed as the sole viable paths to the salvation of both the planet and mankind itself. From a philosophical approach, these perspectives seem to be anchored in a sort of reformed Marxism, in which the traditional class struggle is reinterpreted. In place of the old dispute over the value generated in the capitalist mode of production (i.e., surplus value), the mechanisms of domination and oppression began to be applied to other social relations that go beyond economic dynamics. Thus, so-called minorities took the place of the oppressed, with the figure of oppressor being exercised, in most cases, by white and heterosexual men. The concept of minority came to be used in reference to any group that did not fit into this oppressive category, even if they outnumbered them. Thus, the concept of minority loses its quantitative aspect (i.e., number of individuals) and is applied in reference to those who, in principle, would find themselves in a less favoured situation. It is possible that this reframing of the concept has the objective of reinforcing the idea that these groups are fragile and therefore susceptible to victimization. Among the reasons for this Marxist transition towards new groups may be the perception that the original oppressed class (i.e., workers) would not have the necessary characteristics to lead the dreamed revolution. Throughout history, it seems to have become clear that, instead of seeking to subvert the system, workers sought to associate themselves with it. This perception is based on the fact that most trade union movements focused on the demand for salary increases and not on taking power. In the view of a more rigorous Marxist, this dynamic sounds like a betrayal since, instead of seeking to turn the table on which capitalists organize their banquet, workers would only be claiming the bigger bucks that fall from it.

Along with conditioning moral assessments of companies', governments', and individuals' actions, adherence to the sustainability cause may end up justifying reprovable initiatives. It is possible, for example, that people come to operate within a logic of hierarchization, with things being assessed by not only their intrinsic value but also their comparative ones. As a result, causes would be classified from worst to best. Depending on the position something occupies in this sort of ranking, it risks being sacrificed in the name of arguably more noble matters. With the sustainability cause being seen as the antidote to apocalypse, it inevitably ends up being placed in a very high position (possibly in the highest). Among other consequences, this means that defence of the sustainability cause may justify disrespect to nearly anything. This may include disrespect to individual freedoms, the adoption of protectionist measures, the raising of taxes, and the banishment of products, for instance. Defence of the sustainability cause seems to grant superpowers to those supporting it. Within this view, it would assume attributes similar to those of religions. Issues such as feelings of belonging, perception of a moral superiority, and provision of a cause to defend would justify the existence of those who adhere to this belief, providing them with an explanation for the current state of affairs and a reason for living (i.e., altering the course of human activities towards what they perceive as correct). It is possible that this religious character is at the origin of radicalism. More than that, these characteristics may actually explain its success. In the context of diminished religiosity, people seem more open to this sort of idea. While religion might be an important component of the human psyche, as it allows one to live without fear (living in fear can be very harmful to the psyche) and to find meaning in life (including solutions to fundamental philosophical questions – where we came from, who we are, where we are going), it plays an important role in enabling human experience from a psychic point of view. This perception often translates into actions directed to the viability of social and environmental agendas of sustainable development.

Pro-Sustainability Rhetoric

Pro-sustainability rhetoric is here defined as the ensemble of methods, techniques, and forms used to convince an interlocutor of the fairness, justice, urgency, and/or correctness of the sustainability cause. That includes all the arguments in favour of the necessity of practical actions to fight sustainability-related issues (e.g., deforestation, global warming and climate change, social inequalities, modern slavery, child labour). As discussed in greater detail throughout the book, *pro-sustainability rhetoric* seems to have found shelter in the most diverse social sectors, to the point that it can be considered a type of mainstream discourse. Among the groups that adhered more strongly to this form of expression, academics, politicians, journalists, and celebrities can be highlighted. The reasons leading each of these groups to adopt this stance may be diverse, ranging from a sincere and honest concern about socio-environmental issues, to simple conformity with the official discourse. Whether for fear of reprisal, or for the perspective that the adoption of the majority's views can yield some kind of dividend (e.g., career progression, admiration of peers), people seem to be more prone to assume pro-sustainability postures, contributing to spreading pro-sustainability rhetoric more quickly. In the case of academics, for example, it is possible that the pressure to publish pushes them to address 'hot topics', or those that, in their evaluation, are more likely to convert manuscripts into articles. Thus, the perception that the topic of sustainability gained momentum might influence their research. Likewise, the increase in research grants for topics related to sustainable development can lead many academics to convert to the field. In these cases, it is possible to recognize what appears to be a certain type of opportunism in seemingly environmentally friendly behaviour.

In the case of politicians, it is possible that the adoption of social and environmental discourses is associated with electoral pragmatism or even with a kind of sense of survival. With the exception of those who defend well-defined causes supported by strong programmatic bases, politicians seek, in general, to be in line with the popular will, in the hope that the consonance of their speech with what they understand to be the desire of the masses comes to guarantee their needed votes. Still, it may be argued that the overall characteristics of sustainability-related themes make them particularly attractive to politicians. Generally linked to long-term goals that are difficult to measure, social and environmental issues allow them to evade more forceful demands during their terms of office. The abstract essence of many of the issues related to sustainability also favour this dynamic. On the other hand, the nobility of the causes serves as an important justification for tax increases. Altogether, these qualities seem to make sustainable development a very convenient cause for immoral politicians.

Regarding journalists, it is possible to point to marketing aspects as, perhaps, the main trigger of their eventually non-sincere engagement. If in fact the majority of society is convinced of the need to defend social and environmental causes, it should be more open to news and comments that meet these views. Likewise, topics such as ocean pollution offer plenty of material for sensationalist vehicles that present them as irrefutable evidence of a near and inevitable apocalypse. Without judging the merit of these relationships, it can be argued that they often capture the attention of readers and viewers, who, probably out of panic, end up consuming these contents. For traditional media outlets driven by the search for profits, increases in audience numbers are certainly welcome. Unfortunately, social and environmental issues are sometimes misused for this purpose. For celebrities (e.g., actors, singers, writers, artists), adherence to social and environmental causes seems to be one of the most effective ways to obtain or consolidate a positive image with the public. In this set, the concept of social value (Sheth et al., 1991) is particularly interesting, as the demonstration that one is concerned with noble causes may have a direct effect on her/his social status. This greater public approval can guarantee greater exposure in the media, which, in addition to consolidating fame itself, helps to promote products and services in the form of advertising. When seen from this perspective, the adhesion of celebrities to the defence of nature or of the less favoured people can be understood as an important profit instrument for them, with the maintenance of a positive image being fundamental in this sense.

The fact that these groups have great influence with the public seems to have been essential for the creation of a more generalized sustainability mindset, contributing to the dissemination of environmental and social causes by the most diverse segments. In a way, it may be said that the adoption of *pro-sustainability rhetoric* became a synonym for good conduct and, in some cases, even a prerequisite for someone to be considered a good citizen. This seems to explain the intensity with which visions considered socially and environmentally responsible are displayed by those thirsty for social approval. This seems to be a common attitude for both members of the groups mentioned above (e.g., celebrities) and the general public. While in the first demonstrations of social and environmental correctness also occur in traditional media vehicles, in the second they are restricted to social media (e.g., Facebook, Instagram, Twitter).

Anti-Sustainability Rhetoric

Anti-sustainability rhetoric can be defined as any form of communication aimed at questioning, denying, or even ridiculing pro-sustainability rhetoric. From the definition follows that, discourses against the sustainability cause are, in general, reactive, meaning that their emergence is intended to confront previously stated visions. Thus, *anti-sustainability rhetoric* can be understood as a kind of counterpoint that opposes the proposed changes and/or the speed with which it is intended to implement them. These characteristics bring it closer to a more conservative view of the world. Regarding its philosophical origins, it may be argued to be rooted in what came to be known as skepticism. Simplistically understood as a lack of belief or non-adherence to other ideas, skepticism developed mostly in the 16th century in France, with authors such as Michel de Montaigne (1533–1592) being some of its main representatives (Pondé, 2016). As discussed in greater detail later in the book, this philosophical root seems to be common to political thinking positioned more to the right.

More recently, however, anti-sustainability discourse has echoed in the words of authors like Milton Friedman (1912–2006). Nobel Prize Laureate in Economics (strictly speaking, the prize given by the Swedish central bank) and considered one of the main exponents of the Chicago School of Economics, Friedman's views on the relationship between economic activities and the generation of well-being for society has offered arguments for *anti-sustainability rhetoric* for decades. In his famous article, 'The Social Responsibility of Business Is to Increase Its Profits' (Friedman, 1970), Friedman defends the idea that the improvement of social standards should be seen as a positive externality from economic performance, not as a company's main goal. Friedman's ideas, however, seem to have been misinterpreted over the years, being pointed out as exponents of petty and individualistic thinking that promotes the generation of profits for shareholders as the only objective that must be pursued by organizations. In a sense, these interpretations have served as a basis for stereotyping and even stigmatizing liberal economic thought.

A more detailed discussion of the text may be helpful in demystifying these more closed views. In fact, it does not seem to be true that Friedman is against the idea that all of society should benefit from corporate activities. The difference between Friedman's positions and those of the most arduous defenders of the notion of corporate social responsibility seems to be more related to the path towards achieving the common good, which essentially involves the establishment of priorities. While more progressive visions propose that companies should work to serve the interests of all their stakeholders equally – thus offering their share of the value generated by the company – the more liberal visions, among which is that defended by Friedman, argue that the benefits to society will be offered indirectly, as the company is efficient in achieving its primary objective (i.e., generating profits). In competitive environments, this would be done by fulfilling the needs of customers in the most efficient way possible, which, in itself, would already represent a generation of value to society. Second, taxes generated by economic activities – whether they are levied on the ownership of the means of production, on transport, or on income – would finance social programs related to health, education, public security, or any other matter associated with social welfare that must be administered by governments. Another current of *anti-sustainability rhetoric* is based on a hypothetical logical impossibility of simultaneously meeting all the objectives presented by both Elkington's (1997) triple bottom line in business and stakeholder theory. These ideas are presented in the work of Jensen (2010), among others.

References

Algore.com. (2022a). *An Inconvenient Truth* (movie). Available at https://www.algore.com/library/an-inconvenient-truth-dvd

Algore.com (2022b). The Assault on reason: 2017 edition. *Algore.com*. Available at https://www.algore.com/library/the-assault-on-reason-2017-edition

Bitzer, L.F. (1988). Editor's introduction. In: G. Campbell (Ed.). *The Philosophy of Rhetoric*. Southern Illinois University Press.

Bliese, J. (1977). The study of rhetoric in the twelfth century. *Quarterly Journal of Speech*, Vol.63, No.4, pp.364–383.

Borland, H., and Lindgreen, A. (2013). Sustainability, epistemology, ecocentric business, and marketing strategy: Ideology, reality, and vision. *Journal of Business Ethics*, Vol.117, No.1, pp.173–187.

Bragança, L., Mateus, R., and Koukkari, H. (2010). Building sustainability assessment. *Sustainability*, Vol.2, No.7.

Burrell, G., and Morgan, G. (1979). *Sociological Paradigms and Organizational Analysis*. Heinemann.

Carson, R. (1962). *Silent Spring*. Houghton Mifflin.

Corbett, E.P.J., and Connors, R.J. (1999). *Classical Rhetoric for the Modern Student*, 4th edition. Oxford University Press.

Crines, A.S., Heppell, T., and Dorey, P. (2016). *The Political Rhetoric and Oratory of Margaret Thatcher*. Springer.

Cummings, W. (2019). 'The world is going to end in 12 years if we don't address climate change', Ocasio-Cortez says. *USA Today*, January 22. Available at https://eu.usatoday.com/story/news/politics/onpolitics/2019/01/22/ocasio-cortez-climate-change-alarm/2642481002/

Donaldson, T., and Preston, L.E. (1995). The stakeholder theory of the corporation: Concepts, evidence, and implications. *Academy of Management Review*, Vol.20, pp.65–91.

Doyle, J., Farrell, N., and Goodman, M.K. (2017). Celebrities and climate change. In: *Oxford Research Encyclopaedia of Climate Science*. Oxford University Press.

Elkington, J. (1997). *Cannibals with Forks: The Triple Bottom Line of 21st Century Business*. Oxford: Capstone.

Fortenbaugh, W.W. (1994). Theophrastus, the characters and rhetoric. In: W.W. Fortenbaugh and D.C. Mirhardy (Eds.). *Peripatetic Rhetoric After Aristotle*, Vol.6, pp.15–35. Rutgers University Studies in Classical Humanities.

Fracarolli Nunes, M. (2019). The impact of negative social/environmental events on the market value of supply chain partners. In: L. De Boer and P. Andersen (Eds.). *Operations Management and Sustainability*, pp.151–178. Palgrave Macmillan.

Fracarolli Nunes, M., and Lee Park, C. (2016). Caught red-handed: The cost of the Volkswagen dieselgate. *Journal of Global Responsibility*, Vol.7, No.2, pp.288–302.

Fracarolli Nunes, M., and Lee Park, C. (2021a). Dieselgates: VW, FCA, Renault, and PSA. In: M. Fracarolli Nunes and C. Lee Park (Eds.). *Business Ethics and Environmental Fraud: Improper Competitive Advantage in the Age of Green*, pp.131–157. Palgrave Macmillan.

Fracarolli Nunes, M., and Lee Park, C. (2021b). Is diesel dead? In: M. Fracarolli Nunes and C. Lee Park (Eds.). *Business Ethics and Environmental Fraud: Improper Competitive Advantage in the Age of Green*, pp.251–277. Palgrave Macmillan.

Fracarolli Nunes, M., Lee Park, C., and Paiva, E.L. (2020). Can we have it all? Sustainability trade-offs and cross-insurance mechanisms in supply chains. *International Journal of Operations & Production Management*, Vol.40, No.9, pp.1339–1366.

Freeman, R.E. (1984). *Strategic Management: A Stakeholder Approach*. Pitman Publishing Inc.

Friedlander, J., and Riedy, C. (2018). Celebrities, credibility, and complementary frames: Raising the agenda of sustainable and other 'inconvenient' food issues in social media campaigning. *Communication Research and Practice*, Vol.4, No.3, pp.229–245.

Friedman, M. (1970). The social responsibility of business is to increase its profits. *The New York Times Magazine*, September 13. Available at https://www.nytimes.com/1970/09/13/archives/a-friedman-doctrine-the-social-responsibility-of-business-is-to.html

Furley, D.J. (1953). The purpose of Theophrastus's characters. *Symbolae Osloenses*, Vol.30, No.1, pp.56–60.

Furley, D.J. (2016). Peripatetic school. In: *Oxford Classical Dictionary*. Available at https://oxfordre.com/classics/view/10.1093/acrefore/9780199381135.001.0001/acrefore-9780199381135-e-4870

Garnett, S.T., Lawes, M.J., James, R., Bigland, K., and Zander, K.K. (2016). Portrayal of sustainability principles in the mission statements and on home pages of the world's largest organizations. *Conservation Biology*, Vol.30, No.2, pp.297–307.

Greenpeace (2012). *Greenpeace Calls Out Procter and Gamble to Clean Up Its Supply Chain*. Available at https://www.youtube.com/watch?v=bw8yZ9bx7lM

Greenpeace France (2010). *Greenpeace dénonce Nestlé, qui contribue à la déforestation en Indonésie*. Available at https://www.youtube.com/watch?v=hgcHTHGu5tA

Greenpeace France (2018). *Rang-Tan: Les ravages de l'huile de palme*. Available at https://www.youtube.com/watch?v=7lM0HLdDmXc

Greenpeace International (2009). *Dove onslaught(er)*. Available at https://www.youtube.com/watch?v=odI7pQFyjso&t=7s

Greenpeace USA (2014). *Greenpeace Calls Out Procter and Gamble to Clean Up Its Supply Chain*. Available at https://www.youtube.com/watch?v=bw8yZ9bx7lM

The Guardian (2019). 'Our house is on fire': Greta Thunberg, 16, urges leaders to act on climate. *The Guardian*, January 25. Available at https://www.theguardian.com/environment/2019/jan/25/our-house-is-on-fire-greta-thunberg16-urges-leaders-to-act-on-climate

Guggenheim, M. (1961). Review of 'the literary culture of Napoleon' by Frank George Healey (1959). Librairie Minard, Paris. *Modern Language Notes*, Vol.76, No.3, pp.276–279.

Immisch, O. (1898). Ueber Theophrasts Charaktere [On Theophrastus's characters]. *Philologus*, Vol.57, pp.193–212.

Jensen, M.C. (2010). Value maximization, stakeholder theory, and the corporate objective function. *Journal of Applied Corporate Finance*, Vol.22, No.1, pp.32–42.

Kals, E., and Maes, J. (2002). Sustainable development and emotions. In: *Psychology of Sustainable Development*, pp.97–122. Springer.

Kang, C., Germann, F., and Grewal, R. (2016). Washing away your sins? Corporate social responsibility, corporate social irresponsibility, and firm performance. *Journal of Marketing*, Vol.80, No.2, pp.59–79.

Klamer, A., McCloskey, D.N., McCloskey, D.N., and Solow, R.M. (Eds.) (1988). *The Consequences of Economic Rhetoric*. Cambridge University Press.

Krebs, R.R., and Jackson, P.T. (2007). Twisting tongues and twisting arms: The power of politica rhetoric. *European Journal of International Relations*, Vol.13, No.1, pp.35–66.

Larson, B. (2011). I. Metaphor and sustainability. In: *Metaphors for Environmental Sustainability*, pp.1–30. Yale University Press.

Martin, J. (2013). *Politics and Rhetoric: A Critical Introduction*. Routledge.

McCloskey, D.N. (1983). The rhetoric of economics. *Journal of Economic Literature*, Vol.21, No.2, pp.481–517.

Mifsud, M. (2007). On rhetoric as gift/giving. *Philosophy & Rhetoric*, Vol.40, No.1, pp.89–107.

NPR (2019). *Macron Urges G-7 Members to Put Amazon Fires at Top of Agenda*, August 23. Available at https://www.npr.org/2019/08/23/753639869/macron-urges-g7-members-to-put-amazon-fires-at-top-of-agenda

Pertsinidis, S. (2018). *Theophrastus' Characters: A New Introduction*. Routledge.

Pondé, L.F.C.S. (2016). *Ceticismo*. Available at https://www.youtube.com/watch?v=-DBTwK1axGs

Rapp, C. (2010). Aristotle's rhetoric. In: E.N. Zalta (Ed.). *The Stanford Encyclopedia of Philosophy*, Spring 2010 Edition. Available at https://plato.stanford.edu/cgi-bin/encyclopedia/archinfo.cgi?entry=aristotle-rhetoric

Robinson, S. (2016). Trust me, I'm a businessman: Integrity, trust, corruption and counterfeits. In: *The Practice of Integrity in Business*. Palgrave Studies in Governance, Leadership and Responsibility. Palgrave Macmillan.

Rootes, C., and Carter, N. (2010). Take blue, add yellow, get green? The environment in the UK general election of 6 May 2010. *Environmental Politics*, Vol.19, No.6, pp.992–999.

Rorty, A.O. (Ed.) (1996). *Essays on Aristotle's Rhetoric*, Vol.6. University of California Press.

Sharples, R.W. (2003). The peripatetic school. In: D.J. Furley (Ed.). *Routledge History of Philosophy Volume II – From Aristotle to Augustine*, pp.147–175. Routledge.

Sheth, J.N., Newman, B.I., and Gross, B.L. (1991). Why we buy what we buy: A theory of consumption values. *Journal of Business Research*, Vol.22, No.2, pp.159–170.

Sloane, T.O. (2001). *Encyclopedia of Rhetoric*, Vol.1. Oxford University Press on Demand.

Stettler, M. (1995). The rhetoric of McCloskey's rhetoric of economics. *Cambridge Journal of Economics*, Vol.19, pp.391–391.

Swilling, M. (2020). *The Age of Sustainability: Just Transitions in a Complex World*. Taylor & Francis.

TED (2007). *Averting the Climate Crisis | Al Gore*. Available at https://www.youtube.com/watch?v=rDiGYuQicpA

Van der Leeuw, S., Wiek, A., Harlow, J., and Buizer, J. (2012). How much time do we have? Urgency and rhetoric in sustainability science. *Sustainability Science*, Vol.7, No.1, pp.115–120.

White, K., Habib, R., and Hardisty, D.J. (2019). How to SHIFT consumer behaviors to be more sustainable: A literature review and guiding framework. *Journal of Marketing*, Vol.83, No.3, pp.22–49.

Willis, R. (2017). Taming the climate? Corpus analysis of politicians' speech on climate change. *Environmental Politics*, Vol.26, No.2, pp.212–231.

2 Sustainability and Dialogue

Introduction

Starting from the etymology of the word, the idea of dialogue may be understood as the potential for something to be communicated through words. In this sense, Bohm (1996) clarifies that the construct originates from the Greek (*dialogos*), with the union of the prefix *dia* (through) with the suffix *logus* (word) explaining this idea. In its most everyday use, however, the concept of dialogue refers to the idea of an interaction between two parties in which points of view are presented and debated. From a merely functional perspective, this exchange can take place with the aim of solving a problem or creating something of general interest, with all participants interacting to achieve this objective. At the end of this process, the sharing of such appreciations would ideally progress to truth, which would emerge unannounced (regardless of one's choice to do so), and this shared meaning would stand as the glue that keeps people and societies attached to each other. In this perspective, Isaacs (1999) proposes dialogue as a conversation with a centre but not sides, while Kabat-Zinn (2005) reinforces that dialogue presupposes equity between the parties involved. Among other things, this means that one part should not overlap the other, with interactions that move in this direction not qualifying to be classified as dialogues anymore, from the very moment an imbalance is established.

Despite being consistent with the origins of the construct, these views and definitions seem to express a very optimistic view of dialogue, with it being proposed as a useful instrument in the construction of something productive and peaceful (Bolaños, 2016). If, on the one hand, this can occur in many cases, it is possible that in others the dialogue is established due to different factors, which may not even be spontaneous. Dialogue can, in reality, have several causes and objectives, taking place in the most diverse ways, with a brief discussion of these variables providing the basis for the development of further debates. Regarding the causes, the motivations of dialogues can be separated into two large groups: random and specific. The first group includes interactions that occur due to occasions when the parties meet not because they wanted to, but because of any reason that leads them to be in each other's presence (Gilmartin et al., 2018). This is the case of encounters between neighbours who leave their homes at the same time, or acquaintances

DOI: 10.4324/9781003124719-3

that recognize each other in a queue at the supermarket. As these circumstances may suggest, there is generally no prior agenda for the meeting, so there is no topic to be addressed at first. On these occasions, it is common for a random dialogue to be established, with topics such as the results of sports games or weather conditions being among the most popular (Perinbanayagam, 2015; Mattar and Wachsmuth, 2012).

In other cases, dialogue does not result from casual encounters but is rather desired between the parties (Forester, 2006), when one or more specific issues should be discussed, which usually makes the exchange more objective. In some instances, however, the establishment of dialogue is unilateral, with one party determining that it should take place, while the other is limited to participating. This situation is common in interactions that occur within hierarchical structures, when a superior demands that a subordinate come forward to deal with an issue (Kuroda and Yamamoto, 2018). In any case, the fact that there is a predetermined agenda – even if only by one of the parties – makes this type of dialogue fit into the category of specific. In situations like this, it can be said that the premise proposed by Bohm (1996) does not hold up, as dialogues of this type are not usually egalitarian, as the opinions of one of the parties (i.e., superior) overlaps those of the other (i.e., subordinate) from the beginning. Despite the establishment of an imbalance from the beginning, it is difficult to imagine arguments against the idea that exchanges carried out under these conditions constitute a dialogue.

This initial classification allows for a better analysis of the objectives of dialogues, with those classified as random being generally associated with little more than the fulfilment of a social norm or the maintenance of minimum levels of civility between people who are linked by relatively weak relational ties (Coupland, 2003). As discussed in the examples cited earlier, this includes neighbours or acquaintances, among other groups with whom more superficial relationships are maintained. In a casual encounter between two people who share stronger relational ties (e.g., close relatives, friends, co-workers, clients), dialogues on common topics between the parties can be initiated or resumed, even if they had not been previously planned. In these cases, they cannot be considered random, despite having occurred due to chance.

Regarding the objectives of a specific dialogue, one can separate them into those that seek to (1) solve a problem, (2) prevent a problem from occurring or intensifying, and (3) seize opportunities. The first group deals with situations in which something is not happening in the desired way, demanding, therefore, adjustments for it to return to a situation of normality (Blaylock and Allen, 2005). It can be expected that the type of dialogue established in these circumstances will basically depend on the type of problem in question, its seriousness, and the ability or willingness of the parties to resolve it. It is common for dialogues aimed at solving a problem to occur amid moments of tension and may involve old acquaintances, or people who end up getting to know each other precisely because of the occurrence of the problem.

For illustration purposes, it is possible to imagine a dialogue between two drivers who were involved in a traffic collision. The problem in question was not expected, so that both are faced with a breakdown of normality that they need to resolve. Depending on factors such as the mood of each, their respective financial situations (as a collision between vehicles will involve additional costs), whether or not they have insurance coverage, the level of commitment of the vehicles, the different levels of emotional attachment that each driver can have with their respective cars, and the availability of time of those involved (it is possible that they were just riding around on a sunny day or heading to an important meeting for which they were already late), the type of dialogue that develops will vary. It is also possible to imagine that this collision took place on an expressway, and that the cars involved are occupying two of the three available lanes for traffic. The situation should generate a traffic jam so that the dissatisfaction of the other drivers is reflected in the sound of their horns. The context will add yet another element of stress, with the sense of urgency possibly influencing the development of dialogue between drivers.

The second and third objectives of specific dialogues (i.e., to prevent a problem from occurring or intensifying, and to seize opportunities) will demand some form of collaboration between the parties. In the case of problem prevention, it is important, for example, that both parties are convinced that something undesirable might occur. This may require a previous form of dialogue aimed at convincing one of the parties if it is not able to reach such a conclusion on its own. In this sense, rhetoric can play a key role. In the case of seeking to seize opportunities, a similar dynamic can unfold, with the difference that the rhetoric can focus on something positive (i.e., the benefits that can be obtained if the opportunity is seized). It is likely that this function of specific dialogues takes place when the capabilities or resources of the parties involved are complementary.

Regarding the form, it is possible to classify the dialogues as verbal or nonverbal. This division goes against the etymological origins of the word, which, as discussed earlier, refers to something that can be expressed through words. Strictly speaking, only verbal dialogues would meet these initial criteria. However, the extension of the idea to other forms of communication is necessary due to the multitude of ways in which human beings communicate (Buxton, 1989). Along with words, dialogues can develop through a series of more subtle forms such as looks (Poggi et al., 2000), postures, and body expressions (Matsumoto and Hwang, 2012), among others. In a slightly more extended analysis of the subject, it can be considered that, at the limit, all social interactions represent forms of dialogue, even if the parties involved do not have the direct intention of communicating. This argument is based on the idea that the way we behave or dress (Gibbins, 1969) in public sends signals to those who observe us and, from the messages received, they make interpretations about our financial situation (Oh et al., 2020), age (König, 2008), and social position (Piacentini and Mailer, 2004), among others. In this sense, it is possible to say that all those who live in some outside society where social contact is inevitable (even if limited to the look) are involved in a constant dialogue with all the other individuals that make up the environment in which they are inserted. In addition to seeking to develop understandings around the concept of dialogue itself, the preceding discussions provide the basis for the debates that form around themes related to sustainability and sustainable development. For practical purposes, the characteristics of the different types of dialogue proposed will be addressed in the light of these interactions.

Small Talk, Apocalypse, and Other Forms of Environmental Dialogue

As discussed, random dialogues usually develop around trivial topics or topics that at least do not have a greater underlying interest. Throughout history, discussions about weather conditions seem to have served as one of the most useful forms of 'small talk', with comments like 'it has been hot these days' or 'maybe it is going to rain tomorrow' used to avoid the awkward silence that can develop in an encounter between two people who share weak relational ties and who do not usually deal with specific subjects. Most of these conversations do not seem to evolve into something more elaborate, serving only as a background for a social interaction of little importance or interest. However, given the growing environmental awareness that has developed over the past few decades (Chen et al., 2019), these light-hearted conversations about the weather can easily turn into heated debates on topics such as global warming and climate change (Meierding, 2013). Depending on the participants' intimacy with these issues, dialogues started at random can quickly migrate to a more conflicting form, bringing up issues related to the participation of politicians in the search for solutions (Brulle, 2010) or the individual responsibility of consumers in adjusting their habits (Wells et al., 2011). These possibilities are discussed next, together with other expressions of the different objectives of the sustainability dialogue.

According to the classification proposed, specific dialogues can have three basic types of objective. When applied to the perspective of exchanges aimed at the progress of sustainable development, the first of these objectives (i.e., problem solving) can result in quite complex dialogues, mainly because there is no consensus on the best way to solve environmental problems. Disagreements tend to predate this phase; the very recognition of the existence of environmental problems or the role played by human activity in their development are objects of great disagreement (Thompson, 2009). These questions form the basis of the environmental skepticism and are discussed in greater detail in Chapter 5. For practical purposes, it is considered that the dialogue between environmental skeptics and those who actually believe in the existence of serious environmental problems in some cases may be classified as unfeasible (i.e., impossible dialogues), since the exchange of ideas depends on a minimum level of agreement between a given subject. Thus, it is argued here that an accord on the definition of basic premises is necessary for the evolution of the dialogue, a condition without which it cannot be expected that there will be real gains in this regard.

In this way, discussions on different dialogue objectives at the environmental level can only focus on a later stage, in which all parties not only agree that environmental problems are real but also that humanity has the capacity to treat them. Before advancing on this issue, however, a disclaimer is necessary. The fact that dialogue on sustainability is only possible when the parties agree with the premises does not necessarily mean that these premises are true. As discussed in several passages throughout the book, there is no scientific consensus on the exact impact of human activities on the environment (Happer, 2018), or even on the nature of documented climate change (Lindzen, 2016). In this sense, many argue that they are a consequence of the planet's natural cycles (Ring et al., 2012) or other circumstances arising from issues that are far beyond our understanding, such as the different levels of radiation from solar activity (Trenberth and Fasullo, 2009). One of the reasons why an analysis of the dialogue between those who believe in climate change processes and environmental skeptics is difficult is the fact that, in many cases, the parties distrust each other's technical capacity as well as their suitability. Added to this is the great politicization of the theme, which, as discussed throughout the book, works as an additional factor for the repulsion that these different sides have for each other's arguments.

Impossible Dialogues

Given the degree of contradiction and incompatibility of some ideas, it is possible that, in some cases, dialogue between individuals and groups that identify with the opposite side becomes close to impossible. Attempts to reconcile incongruous worldviews seem, in fact, to be a recurring concern. In a looser interpretation, French motto of 'freedom, equality, fraternity' (*liberté, égalité, fraternité*) can be understood as an attempt to appease the inherently divergent thoughts that were consolidated during and after the historical process that led to the French Revolution. With the concepts of right and left still incipient at that time, the destruction of an ancient monarchical system and the instabilities generated by the power disputes that followed represented fertile ground for different ideas to be suggested and experienced (Tocqueville, 2010). In this sense, it can be argued that those who sympathized more with freedom represent the embryo of right-wing thinking, while those who were most enthusiastic about the possibility of equality among citizens would represent the relief of leftist thinking. Thus, the question of fraternity would be a call for the proponents of these apparently incompatible worldviews to see themselves all as coming from the same homeland (i.e., brothers) and, as such, not to be divided. The French flag itself can be interpreted in this sense, with each of its colours representing a part of the motto. While blue and red would refer to the right and left respectively (i.e., freedom and equality), white between them would be a proposition where peace and harmony between these parts (i.e., fraternity).

In a large sense, it can be said that the establishment of a dialogue presupposes the recognition of a common desire between two parties. This may indicate the existence of a minimal degree of agreement in terms of diagnosis, at least concerning the existence of a problem that deserves to be treated. From a utilitarian perspective, the main motivator of dialogue would, therefore, be the possibility that the exchange between the parties allows the development of a solution to a certain issue common to both, with the exchange of information and collaboration acting as facilitators for the achievement of the expected results. Despite probably being favoured by a greater degree of affinity between those who seek to solve a given problem, it is possible that the understanding of its seriousness and the fact that its consequences will not be limited to one of the parties is the main vector in willingness to dialogue.

Regarding the debate on sustainable development, it is possible to identify this dynamic in companies' search for improvement in their social and environmental performance. In this set, discussions around sustainable supply chain management (Seuring and Müller, 2008) are probably one of the best illustrations of the functionalist aspect of dialogue. As discussed throughout the book, the commercial dynamics that accelerated from the second half of the 20th century resulted in the strengthening of competition based on the reduction of production costs (Christopher, 2016). Much of this objective was pursued through the geographical redistribution of production processes, with many stages being transferred to areas offering advantages such as lower labour costs (Quinn and Hilmer, 1994; Lau and Zhang, 2006). Issues linked to a large number of people willing to exchange their time and energy for a livelihood would negatively pressure wages, favouring the establishment of industrial operations in these locations (Rani and Belser, 2012).

Factors such as a relatively low cost of energy, construction of an adequate infrastructure, and even more aggressive fiscal policies can also be pointed out as motivating decisions regarding the location of factories. This has resulted in companies having less control over the processes of producing and distributing goods and services (Kang et al., 2012), with individual organizations contributing with progressively smaller shares of the whole. As each company focused on a few tasks, the activities previously performed by these same entities began to be acquired from third parties. Thus, the atomization of production processes would have given rise to the formation of what is now classified as supply chains. Understood as the alignment of three or more companies that contribute to a common objective (Mentzer et al., 2001), these formations have established themselves as the basis of many current business models.

While they allowed companies to specialize in a few activities, the cost savings resulting from the strategic outsourcing process was translated into competitive advantages, allowing consumers to have access to increasingly complex products at decreasing prices (Ikumapayi et al., 2020). The biggest profits generated by the supply chains built around this rationale were distributed among its many participants. Although there were imbalances in the appropriation of the generated value – usually due to significant differences in the bargaining power of buyers and suppliers (Porter, 1979, 1980) – most actors involved in these processes seem to have benefited from their greater efficiency. On the other hand, the division of industrial activities by a large number of companies significantly increased the complexity of managing the material flows involved in the transformation, storage, and transport processes, as well as the management of transfers of financial resources and information (Christopher, 2012).

The optimization of these issues involved strengthening the collaboration between the many parties involved, with the dialogue between buyers and suppliers being perhaps what developed the most in this sense (Ballantyne, 2004; Wynstra et al., 2006). As companies began to be increasingly pressured to act in a socially and ecologically responsible manner, the lessons learned in the search for profit maximization were progressively adopted in the management of issues related to the sustainability of production processes. The quest for transparency in all the stages comprising these dynamics (Sodhi and Tang, 2019) resulted in the search for a greater exchange between the different companies that make up the supply chains, with their lead firms typically taking the lead in these movements. The adoption of more open positions to dialogue would thus denote the understanding that the exchange of ideas is one of the most efficient means by which two parties can achieve a common objective. This perception is part of the previously proposed view according to which the benefits of dialogue would be inserted in a utilitarian perspective.

Still in relation to the various manifestations of dialogue as an instrument of pursuit of a common good, one can point to the cooperative relationships maintained by competing companies. It is not uncommon for companies that produce similar goods and services and that compete in the same market segment to work in partnership if they perceive that they can obtain mutual benefits. This is the case, for example, when two competing organizations use the same component as raw material. The organization of a joint purchase would therefore result in lower costs for both, as they could benefit from scale gains (e.g., discounts, transport optimization). Co-opetition (Nalebuff and Brandenburger, 1996) would, therefore, be one of the most sophisticated forms of relationship between companies. In extreme cases, however, excessive dialogue between competitors can result in negative situations from an ethical perspective, with significant damage being caused to economic systems. It is possible, for example, that competing companies reach agreements on the prices to be charged for their products, thus constituting one of the most common practices of cartels. Among the main consequences of this practice is the fact that it allows competitors to escape from a price-based competition, a process by which their profit margins tend to zero, mainly in the relation between products that present little or no differentiation (Porter, 1996). Cartel formation through immoral dialogue between competitors would primarily harm consumers (Laitenberger and Smuda, 2015), with the practice running counter to the entire free market pricing mechanism and the economy as a whole (Ivaldi et al., 2016). These practices should be more common in markets that have a reduced number of competitors, with duopolies (Stiglitz, 1987) and oligopolies (Huck et al., 2004) possibly being the formations most prone to this type of intervention. Despite being used in a harmful manner, price alignment represents yet another example of the utilitarian character of the dialogue.

Conversely, dialogue must be difficult to maintain when at least one of the parties sees the other as an obstacle to achieving their objectives. This behaviour seems to be common among the most radicalized individuals, especially with regard to their political and ideological positions. As elaborated in later chapters, people identified with conservative thinking tend to perceive those more aligned with a left-wing mindset as enemies, as they come to understand that their worldviews are incompatible. The idea that right and left visions cannot occupy the same space feeds the notion that the advance of one implies the disappearance of the other. This tends to lead extreme groups to develop defensive attitudes within a logic of survival. Among the different ways in which these feelings are expressed is the aggressiveness between the parties that, while repelling contrary ideas, can serve as a powerful stimulant of cohesion. The most immediate result of the interruption of dialogue is the strengthening of modern forms of tribalism.

Dialogue may also be hampered in the absence of minimum levels of trust between the parties (Head, 2012). This issue is of particular relevance to the debate on sustainable development, with the association made between environmentalism and political ideologies being particularly damaging. The connection of the environmental movement to leftism seems to have been reinforced in the period of the Cold War, with a significant part of the political and intellectual production of the 1970s and 1980s showing a tendency to identify in the capitalist mode of production the main reasons for the deterioration of environmental conditions (Fracarolli Nunes and Lee Park, 2021). Accordingly, the term sustainability itself was used for the first time in the text 'A Blueprint for Survival', published by *The Ecologist* in 1972, which would have had a clear leftist bias. These associations would have had an impact on the development of the discussions that followed, with the propositions present in this and other texts attracting individuals who somehow sympathized with leftist ideas.

Even in the 1970s, social causes were also associated with socialist and communist ideas, with some of the most relevant academics of the time defending this hypothesis. Among the most famous is American economist and Nobel Prize winner Milton Friedman (1912–2006). In his article entitled 'The Social Responsibility of Business Is to Increase Its Profits', Friedman (1970) argues that companies should focus on generating profits, which is the way in which they contribute to the well-being of society. The reasoning is based on the idea that, by producing goods and services that meet the needs of the market, organizations would be providing the means for a better functioning of society, increasing its efficiency and comfort levels. Paying taxes and creating jobs would also be included in the category of benefits generated by companies. Attempts to reverse this order through the concept of a corporate social responsibility would be, according to Friedman, nothing more than an expression of socialism. Friedman's positions and the impact they had on the development of the sustainability debate are taken up in later chapters.

The association made between sustainability and leftism was very harmful to the development of a purposeful dialogue. As individuals most identified with right-wing thinking perceived social and environmental causes as a pretext for advancing collectivist ideas, a natural resistance was formed, with the same repulsion they felt for socialism and communism extending to topics such as the need to protect natural resources and rationalize consumption, among others. While the confusion between sustainability and leftism reflects a kind of myopia, it cannot be entirely attributed to a failure of interpretation. This is because sustainability actually seems to have been instrumentalized by political and economic interest groups, having served as a basis for electoral and commercial disputes. The first case favours the formation of ideological resistance blocs. The second, in turn, feeds the idea that sustainable development would be nothing more than a marketing instrument, not worthy of trust.

The search for the creation of corporate social and environmental reputations (Fracarolli Nunes and Lee Park, 2017) really seems to be one of the main objectives of companies that try to present themselves as promoters of environmental peace and social justice. This phenomenon seems to have accelerated in recent decades, with some of the world's largest companies dedicating much of their resources to building a positive brand image among their stakeholders. Nevertheless, the perception that messages sent to the public are not sincere can have the opposite effect, helping observers to develop an unfavourable judgment. The feeling of being faced with a case of corporate hypocrisy (Wagner et al., 2009) may even lead them to avoid products and services associated with a specific company. This brief discussion of the difficulties that organizations may encounter when seeking to establish positive contact with their stakeholders shows the fragility of the pillars that sustain the dialogue. Add to this the considerable increase in the complexity of information exchanges, with the transformation from one representation system to another in which the contact between the parties is usually hybrid or direct. An example of this metamorphosis concerns the forms of dialogue traditionally maintained between sportsmen, politicians, and celebrities.

References

Ballantyne, D. (2004). Dialogue and its role in the development of relationship specific knowledge. *Journal of Business & Industrial Marketing*, Vol.19, No.2, pp.114–123.

Blaylock, N., and Allen, J. (2005, September). A collaborative problem-solving model of dialogue. *Proceedings of the 6th SIGdial Workshop on Discourse and Dialogue*, pp.200–211.

Bohm, D. (1996). *On dialogue* (L. Nichol, Ed.). Routledge. https://doi.org/10.4324/9780203180372

Bolaños, P.A. (2016). Between struggle and peaceful dialogue: An overture to Honneth and Ricoeur on recognition. *Budhi: A Journal of Ideas and Culture*, Vol.20, No.2, pp.85–117.

Buxton, B. (1989). The 'natural' language of interaction: A perspective on non-verbal dialogues. *INFOR: Information Systems and Operational Research*, Vol.27, No.2, pp.221–229.

Brulle, R.J. (2010). From environmental campaigns to advancing the public dialog: Environmental communication for civic engagement. *Environmental Communication*, Vol.4, No.1, pp.82–98.

Chen, X., Huang, B., and Lin, C.T. (2019). Environmental awareness and environmental Kuznets curve. *Economic Modelling*, Vol.77, pp.2–11.

Christopher, M. (2012, January). Managing supply chain complexity: Identifying the requisite skills. *Supply Chain Forum: An International Journal*, Vol.13, No.2, pp.4–9.

Christopher, M. (2016). *Logistics & Supply Chain Management*. Pearson.

Coupland, J. (2003). Small talk: Social functions. *Research on Language and Social Interaction*, Vol.36, No.1, pp.1–6.

Forester, J. (2006). Making participation work when interests conflict: Moving from facilitating dialogue and moderating debate to mediating negotiations. *Journal of the American Planning Association*, Vol.72, No.4, pp.447–456.

Fracarolli Nunes, M., and Lee Park, C. (2017). Self-claimed sustainability: Building social and environmental reputations with words. *Sustainable Production and Consumption*, Vol.11, pp.46–57.

Fracarolli Nunes, M., and Lee Park, C. (2021). The age of green. In: M. Fracarolli Nunes and C. Lee Park (Eds.). *Business Ethics and Environmental Fraud: Improper Competitive Advantage in the Age of Green*, pp.87–104. Cham: Palgrave Macmillan. https://doi.org/10.1007/978-3-030-73800-6_4

Friedman, M. (1970). The social responsibility of business is to increase its profits. *The New York Times Magazine*, September 13. Available at https://www.nytimes.com/1970/09/13/archives/a-friedman-doctrine-the-social-responsibility-of-business-is-to.html

Gibbins, K. (1969). Communication aspects of women's clothes and their relation to fashionability. *British Journal of Social and Clinical Psychology*, Vol.8, No.4, pp.301–312.

Gilmartin, E., Cowan, B.R., Vogel, C., and Campbell, N. (2018). Explorations in multiparty casual social talk and its relevance for social human machine dialogue. *Journal on Multimodal User Interfaces*, Vol.12, No.4, pp.297–308.

Happer, W. (2018). *Can Climate Models Predict Climate Change?* Available at https://www.youtube.com/watch?v=qZN2jt2cCU4

Head, N. (2012). Transforming conflict: Trust, empathy, and dialogue. *International Journal of Peace Studies*, Vol.17, No.2, pp.33–55.

Huck, S., Normann, H.T., and Oechssler, J. (2004). Two are few and four are many: Number effects in experimental oligopolies. *Journal of Economic Behavior & Organization*, Vol.53, No.4, pp.435–446.

Ikumapayi, O.M., Oyinbo, S.T., Akinlabi, E.T., and Madushele, N. (2020). Overview of recent advancement in globalization and outsourcing initiatives in manufacturing systems. *Materials Today: Proceedings*, Vol.26, pp.1532–1539.

Isaacs, W. (1999). *Dialogue and the Art of Thinking Together: A Pioneering Approach to Communicating in Business and in Life*. Broadway Business.

Ivaldi, M., Jenny, F., and Khimich, A. (2016). Cartel damages to the economy: An assessment for developing countries. In: F. Jenny and Y. Katsoulacos (Eds.). *Competition Law Enforcement in the BRICS and in Developing Countries*, pp.103–133. Springer.

Kabat-Zinn, J. (2005). *Coming to Our Senses: Healing Ourselves and the World Through Mindfulness*. Hachette.

Kang, M., Wu, X., Hong, P., and Park, Y. (2012). Aligning organizational control practices with competitive outsourcing performance. *Journal of Business Research*, Vol.65, No.8, pp.1195–1201.

König, A. (2008). Which clothes suit me? The presentation of the juvenile self. *Childhood*, Vol.15, No.2, pp.225–237.

Kuroda, S., and Yamamoto, I. (2018). Good boss, bad boss, workers' mental health and productivity: Evidence from Japan. *Japan and the World Economy*, Vol.48, pp.106–118.

Laitenberger, U., and Smuda, F. (2015). Estimating consumer damages in cartel cases. *Journal of Competition Law & Economics*, Vol.11, No.4, pp.955–973.

Lau, K.H., and Zhang, J. (2006). Drivers and obstacles of outsourcing practices in China. *International Journal of Physical Distribution & Logistics Management*, Vol.36, No.10, pp.776–792.

Lindzen, R. (2016). *Climate Change: What Do Scientists Say?* Available at https://www.youtube.com/watch?v=OwqIy8Ikv-c

Matsumoto, D., and Hwang, H.S. (2012). Nonverbal communication: The messages of emotion, action, space, and silence. In: *The Routledge Handbook of Language and Intercultural Communication*, pp.146–163. Routledge.

Mattar, N., and Wachsmuth, I. (2012). Small talk is more than chit-chat. In: *Annual Conference on Artificial Intelligence*, pp.119–130. Springer.

Meierding, E. (2013). Climate change and conflict: Avoiding small talk about the weather. *International Studies Review*, Vol.15, No.2, pp.185–203.

Mentzer, J.T., DeWitt, W., Keebler, J.S., Min, S., Nix, N.W., Smith, C.D., and Zacharia, Z.G. (2001). Defining supply chain management. *Journal of Business Logistics*, Vol.22, No.2, pp.1–25.

Nalebuff, A., and Brandenburger, B. (1996). *La Co-Opétition, une Révolution dans la Manière de Jouer Concurrence et Coopération*. Village Mondial.

Oh, D., Shafir, E., and Todorov, A. (2020). Economic status cues from clothes affect perceived competence from faces. *Nature Human Behaviour*, Vol.4, No.3, pp.287–293.

Perinbanayagam, R.S. (2015). *Games and Sport in Everyday Life: Dialogues and Narratives of the Self*. Routledge.

Piacentini, M., and Mailer, G. (2004). Symbolic consumption in teenagers' clothing choices. *Journal of Consumer Behaviour: An International Research Review*, Vol.3, No.3, pp.251–262.

Poggi, I., Pelachaud, C., and De Rosis, F. (2000). Eye communication in a conversational 3D synthetic agent. *AI Communications*, Vol.13, No.3, pp.169–181.

Porter, M.E. (1979). How competitive forces shape strategy. *Harvard Business Review*, pp.21–38.

Porter, M.E. (1980). *Competitive Strategy: Techniques for Analyzing Industries and Competitors*. Free Press.

Porter, M.E. (1996). What is strategy? *Harvard Business Review*, November–December.

Quinn, J.B., and Hilmer, F.G. (1994). Strategic outsourcing. *MIT Sloan Management Review*, Vol.35, No.4, pp.43–55.

Rani, U., and Belser, P. (2012). The effectiveness of minimum wages in developing countries: The case of India. *International Journal of Labour Research*, Vol.4, No.1, pp.45–66.

Ring, M.J., Lindner, D., Cross, E.F., and Schlesinger, M.E. (2012). Causes of the global warming observed since the 19th century. *Atmospheric and Climate Sciences*, Vol.2, No.4, pp.401–415.

Seuring, S., and Müller, M. (2008). From a literature review to a conceptual framework for sustainable supply chain management. *Journal of Cleaner Production*, Vol.16, No.15, pp.1699–1710.

Sodhi, M.S., and Tang, C.S. (2019). Research opportunities in supply chain transparency. *Production and Operations Management*, Vol.28, No.12, pp.2946–2959.

Stiglitz, J.E. (1987). Competition and the number of firms in a market: Are duopolies more competitive than atomistic markets? *Journal of Political Economy*, Vol.95, No.5, pp.1041–1061.

Thompson, A. (2009). Responsibility for the end of nature: Or, how I learned to stop worrying and love global warming. *Ethics and the Environment*, Vol.14, No.1, pp.79–99.

Tocqueville, A. (2010). *The Old Regime and the French Revolution*. Anchor.

Trenberth, K.E., and Fasullo, J.T. (2009). Global warming due to increasing absorbed solar radiation. *Geophysical Research Letters*, Vol.36, No.7, p.L07706.

Wagner, T., Lutz, R.J., and Weitz, B.A. (2009). Corporate hypocrisy: Overcoming the threat of inconsistent corporate social responsibility perceptions. *Journal of Marketing*, Vol.73, No.6, pp.77–91.

Wells, V.K., Ponting, C.A., and Peattie, K. (2011). Behaviour and climate change: Consumer perceptions of responsibility. *Journal of Marketing Management*, Vol.27, No.7–8, pp.808–833.

Wynstra, F., Axelsson, B., and Van Der Valk, W. (2006). An application-based classification to understand buyer-supplier interaction in business services. *International Journal of Service Industry Management*, Vol.17, No.5, pp.474–496.

3 Right Thinking, Left Thinking

> The conservative has long been marked, whether he knows it or not, by long-run pessimism: by the belief that the long-run trend, and therefore Time itself, is against him.
>
> (Rothbard, 1979, p.5)

Philosophical, Political, and Economic Traditions

From a broad perspective, it can be said that right and left thinking are distinguished by presenting radically opposing views on the notions of freedom and equality (Rokeach, 1973; Braithwaite, 1994). While classical conservative and liberal views value liberty above nearly all things (Rothbard, 1979), the various currents of leftism (e.g., Marxism, Trotskyism, Leninism, Stalinism) defend that inequality between men is an issue to be fought (Jackson, 2013). These different approaches must be related to the distinct ways in which leftists and right-wing ideologues conceptualize mankind. While the former tend to perceive man as a naturally good being (Singer, 2000), the latter seem more inclined to distrust the idea of innate kindness (Phillips, 1956), with control mechanisms (e.g., monitoring, punishment) being necessary to avoid opportunistic behaviour (Muris, 1980). As discussed before, these differences can be seen from the earliest philosophical roots of both left-wing and right-wing thinking, with allegories such as Jean-Jacques Rousseau's (1712–1778) good selvage and Thomas Hobbes' (1588–1679) description of man as being the wolf of man (*Homo homini lupus* in its original form as a Latin proverb) illustrative of these distinct views. In this set, it must be argued that leftist thinking deals with the ideal man, while right wing is centred on the real one. The basic division of the political spectrum places on opposite sides the worldviews that have been conventionally called right and left. Although the philosophical origins of these denominations are linked to much more remote schools of thought, the origins of a more formal division go back to the course of the French Revolution (Fukuyama, 2011).

Although useful for the classification of the basic worldviews to which individuals and groups may be attached, this binary division between left and right is no longer sufficient to accommodate the changes that ideologies have absorbed

DOI: 10.4324/9781003124719-4

over the years (Arter, 2002). The construction of the theoretical bases on which political thought is built has undergone major changes as the economies, customs, and relations between countries have changed over time (Flynn, 1979; Strugnell, 2012). The inadequacy of the original forms of ideologies to deal with issues of the present is probably due to the fact they were developed within specific historical and technological contexts. The views developed by Karl Marx in *Capital*, for example, are the result of the author's observations of a particular moment when a profound change in social relations was taking shape (Hughes and Southern, 2019). The same is true for Engel's famous book, *The Condition of the Working Class in England in 1844* (Jones and Charlot, 1996). The changes brought about by the industrial revolution changed labour relations quickly and forcefully, putting the immense mass of workers who moved from the countryside to the city (Mays et al., 2008) in a situation of apparent fragility in relation to the owners of the means of production (Clark, 2005). The long working hours to which these workers were subjected (Hopkins, 1982), as well as the unhealthy conditions in which they lived (Schwarz, 1992), contributed to the development of the idea that Marx was facing a blatant exploitation relationship that could only be interrupted through a revolt of the dominated class (i.e., workers) against the dominant class (i.e., capitalists).

In addition to his own interpretations, it is possible that Marx was influenced by the characteristic malaise of the 19th century, which is expressed, for example, in the development of Romanticism as a literary, musical, and even philosophical genre (Berlin, 2013). The idea that the world was undergoing rapid changes and that these changes are not necessarily positive would be responsible for this collective discomfort, which, among other things, would result in the idealization of the past (Garside, 1972). Large mass migrations from the countryside to cities, for example, would be among these changes (Long, 2005). The unfavourable living conditions that former farmers faced in growing urban centres would lead them to value the life they previously enjoyed, with rural habits being revered. As discussed by Brazilian historian Fernando Novais (2012), these sudden changes in societies would be at the origin of some of the most celebrated social sciences. Accordingly, the advent of sociology and economics as a discipline segregated from its philosophical roots would be an attempt to understand the rapid changes that societies were experiencing.

The Problem With Ideologies

Despite starting from observations of reality and attempts to explain or predict the functioning of something concrete, the development of these reasonings – which are often logical – ends up flowing into a series of prescriptive measures that aim to correct the faults detected. Prior to this process, however, is the definition of what society should be in the eyes of those who observe it, with this aesthetic and flawless vision being the essential raw material of ideologies. Many political and economic tensions arise from the conflict between ideological visions and reality, with agents' initiatives turning in most cases to attempts to change reality. Since the ideological vision is perfect – at least in the minds of those who propose it – the reality must conform to it, not the other way around. This often leads to exaggerations and absurdities, which stem from an irrational attempt to demonstrate the applicability of an ideology often developed from the comfort of an office or beside a fireplace. These same ideologies are used to explain human relationships and sensations that their authors often do not even imagine exist, giving rise to some of the incongruities of ideologies.

Even if, to some extent, they are able to provide explanations for the dynamics of power at a given moment – albeit in a simplistic and often short-sighted way – these conjectures (i.e., ideologies) quickly lose value when the bases on which they stand undergo the mutations that are typical of social bodies (Heath, 2009). Accordingly, in discussing the intellectual foundations of analytical Marxism, John Roemer (1945–), for example, argues that 'it is bound to be primitive by modern standards, wrong in detail, and perhaps even in some basic claims' (Heath, 2009, p.1). Added to this is the infinite complexity of human relationships. The attempt to summarize them in theoretical constructions contributes to their discredit, as the reality is often different from what was initially imagined. Thus, the set of flaws in ideologies leads their heirs to seek to repair them so that they apply in some way to new contexts and remain alive. Among other results, this constant adaptation of inadequate original thoughts generates a sort of patchwork where there is always room for one more piece. At the same time that this dynamic allows the accommodation of different perspectives, it can lead to the creation of a misshapen conceptual framework that will hardly serve to explain or anticipate social dynamics.

In a certain sense, it can be argued that the blocks created to lay down intermediate ideas between what is meant by the original left and right are attempts to bring these overly conceptual views to something closer to reality (e.g., centre-left, centre-right). From this perspective, these attempts may be quite worthwhile, although they are likely to be seen by the adherents of the corner views only as badly stitched scraps. While understandable from the point of view of the originality of ideas, such a judgment does not seem to do justice to the intermediate forms, since they themselves developed their own theoretical and conceptual bases (e.g., social democracy). If, on the one hand, it is true that they are based on previous ideas, they also bring something original (Arter, 2002). This more pragmatic bias seems to explain, at least in part, the greater electoral success of the views seen as more moderate (Tomasson, 1969). While these seem to address the daily concerns of ordinary people, the most extreme views are limited to controlled environments such as universities, political parties, academic centres, and think thanks, among other. Evidently, this does not mean that extreme views occupy only the underground of society. Although they seem to be more easily adopted by a minority, they generally occupy positions that allow them not only to be in contact with a large number of people, but also to influence them (Hayek, 1949). Thus, a professor at a journalism school who shares her/his extreme views with her/his students will end up, even if indirectly, reaching a significant portion of public opinion, with her/his students possibly reproducing part of the views and opinions to which they were exposed. This power of dissemination will be even greater when these students start to exercise their professions in traditional media vehicles (e.g., radio, television, newspapers, magazines).

While planned economies result from a great deal of intellectual effort, the idea of market economies would reflect something that actually exists (Murrel, 1991). From this, three main consequences seem to follow: the first is the idealistic essence of the socialist/communist economic systems, meaning that the theoretical efforts in that direction are dedicated to building what economies should be. In this set, the allocation of resources would not be directed by the market (i.e., by mechanisms of demand and supply) but rather by a higher entity seeking to maximize the common good (Moroney and Lovell, 1997). This system invariably presupposes control over the means of production, as well as over the distribution of what is produced. By contrast, the conceptual structures supporting capitalist economies are focused on understanding and/or explaining the economy as it is. This includes the reality and nature of incentive mechanisms, as well as the actual way in which exchanges between economic agents take place.

The second consequence stems from the artificiality of planned economies itself. Since these are not natural – just as free market economies would be – they would not adapt to the real dynamics of societies, being thus destined to collapse. While the notion of socialist/communist economics results from the work of several thinkers, one cannot point to an inventor of capitalism. Some erroneously indicate Adam Smith (1723–1790) as the creator of this system, with his work *The Wealth of Nations* being commonly determined as the origin of the free market. In particular, the concept of the *invisible hand* is sometimes referred to as the cornerstone of economic liberalism. It should be noted that, although fundamental to the development of economics as a science, Adam Smith's valuable work cannot be seen as purposeful, but rather as a description of a reality that has its own dynamics. From a practical point of view, the third consequence is perhaps the most important. In addition to the points already explored, the fact that the planned economies are artificial means that the seizure of power appears as a *sine qua non* condition for its prosperity (Moroney and Lovell, 1997). It is not by chance that the implementation of planned economies usually takes place in dictatorial regimes established through armed struggles. This is the case with the Russian, Chinese, and Cuban revolutions, as well as the recent history of several Central American, African, and Southeast Asian countries. These episodes provide several arguments to those who argue that the implantation of planned economies is incompatible with a democratic regime.

Dissemination of Right and Left Ideas

The academic community's strong adherence to leftist ideologies stands out (Hayek, 1949). As discussed by Jesús Huerta de Soto (2010) in his lecture, entitled '¿Por qué los intelectuales odian el capitalismo?' (Why do intellectuals hate capitalism; our translation), it is possible that this apparent propensity of professors and researchers to associate themselves with socialist/communist views is originally linked to a resentment on their part, with some seeing the financial success of others as a sort of injustice towards them. With social status often associated with economic power (Zou, 1998), it is not uncommon for a person who has not received formal academic training to have more prestige than a writer, a chronicler, a university professor, or than anyone who exercise an intellectual activity. The fact that academic careers usually require great intellectual effort and a long and arduous training (e.g., bachelor's, master's, doctorate) also contributes to the perception that the value attributed to intellectuals in practice is less than deserved. Altogether, these factors construct a perception by academics that market dynamics (i.e., capitalism) are unfair.

Another characteristic of leftist movements worth mentioning is its greater tendency towards organization. In fact, while individuals more identified with right-wing thinking seem to remain dispersed, leftists seem to have greater opportunities to associate themselves with orderly movements, which range from unions (Andretta and Reiter, 2009) to so-called collectives (Batarce, 2019) (i.e., groups of people who organize themselves around common themes in order to promote debates, literary production, and demonstrations). The fact that they are organized can explain the political power that the leftist groups have, even when they represent a minority of the population. In this sense, the generation and systematic dissemination of ideas contributes to the electoral success of socialist ideologies. It is possible that among the reasons for this difference is the very nature of basic thinking that supports the views on the right and on the left. While the first is based on individualism, the second is clearly inserted in a collectivist perspective. Thus, individuals more aligned with right-wing thinking seem, in general, to be more concerned with their own well-being, while, theoretically, the individual most accustomed to left-wing ideas perceives society as a set of different classes that, in the end, overlaps the individual. As a result, it is likely that the individual who identifies with the right will remain busy in the pursuit of her/his specific goals, while the one who perceives her/himself as left will place her/himself as a part of a larger gear. This usually translates into the individual on the right dedicating her/himself to economic activity and the left on dedicating himself to promoting the revolution.

Professors' ideological positions are, perhaps, among the most important aspects in the dissemination of ideas (Hayek, 1949), whether they represent left- or right-wing thought. This stems from basically three interrelated factors. The first is that teachers have a captive audience. Among other things, this means that students cannot choose not to hear her/his preaching, especially when it is disguised as a lesson. Unlike a radio or television program that can be silenced by the listener/viewer, the teachers' messages will have to be heard and assimilated, as in many cases they form the basis for the course evaluations. The second factor concerns the power that is intrinsic to the position of teacher. The fact that they evaluate students can have a significant impact on their lives, ranging from simple failure to delay in the job market, or even the loss of their jobs. This power is often used in a kind of intellectual intimidation, in which students feel constrained to confront the ideas presented to them. This dynamic is particularly damaging with regard to solidification where extreme positions and the consequent interruption of dialogue. As discussed in Chapter 2, the lack of coexistence with adverse positions coupled with the continuous reinforcement of ideas by peers who think in a similar form results in the creation of tribal dogmas and, ultimately, in isolation.

One must also consider the relative power that the position grants those who occupy it, particularly in the eyes of students. With grading systems often relying in subjective evaluations, it is possible that students will end up agreeing with teachers' ideas, even if they are at odds with their individual values. Thus, for fear of seeing their school performance impaired – and possibly their chances of success in the job market – students may end up not only absorbing the ideas transmitted by their masters but also professing them to their colleagues. This process seems to be associated with the establishment of hegemonic ideas in academic communities (i.e., teachers, professors, students, employees). The creation of intellectual clusters can favour feelings of ideological tribalism and even the creation of dogmas. In both cases, one may experience an interruption or at least a greater difficulty in maintaining the dialogue between the opposing parties. Along with the various forms of intellectual intimidation, teachers and professors can also count on an important social capital arising from the admiration that their students may come to nurture for them. In fact, some courses seem to be formed by a mixture of content transmission and entertainment, with the classroom sometimes representing a form of theatre for more performative teachers. The display of their intellectual skills may increase the admiration of students, which, in general, contributes to their being more likely to absorb the opinions and views expressed by teachers. It may be said, then, that professors may profit from considerable doses of soft power.

In view of all these issues, the value of teachers and professors as disseminators of ideologies is clear. It is not by chance that the Italian Marxist Antonio Gramsci (1891–1937) already prescribed the occupation of space in universities as a fundamental factor for the spread of leftist ideologies. Although this mechanism is useful in the coexistence of professors with students enrolled in the most diverse courses, the absorption of left-wing ideas by students in the journalism course is particularly interesting, since they themselves can act as disseminators of ideologies when they occupy their professional positions in radio and television stations, newspapers, magazines, or in any other vehicle of traditional media. Once again, the occupation of spaces defended by Gramsci seems to have been successful, with the journalistic class apparently having a strong adherence to the ideologies of the left. Evidently, the occupation of spaces by professionals aligned with leftist ideologies leads to a hegemony of discourse, which can also contribute to the interruption of the dialogue (see Chapter 2). This process of dominating public discourse seems to have been successful for decades until the emergence of social networks. With users exchanging information directly with each other, the ideological filter that seems to have formed in many media outlets is not applicable, which may favour the emergence of ideas hitherto repressed. However, breaking the hegemony does not contribute to the creation of a constructive dialogue between the opposing parties. On the contrary, it appears to have exacerbated polarization, as discussed previously.

Resentment as Left's Origins

The argument that resentment is the driving force of left-wing ideologies is not exclusive to academics, although they represent, perhaps, the best-finished example of this feeling as a collective class. In reality, the feeling that one has less than one deserves, or that other people have more than they should, seems to affect all social strata, without distinction. Usually this resentment – which is often accompanied by envy – occurs around the possessions of others. This obsession with objects and things is in line with the materialist aspect that, in general, is present in all leftist ideology. Thus, the supposed search for equality would be nothing more than a smokescreen for these feelings, with the redistribution of income and the collectivization of property being the most effective way to remedy the resentment generated by the perception that the other has more. In this sense, although many leftist ideologies present themselves as kind and loving, their root would be hatred, with the ideology being disguised as social justice. Obviously, these premises cannot be generalized, since there are left-wing individuals genuinely concerned with the world's ills.

Although apparently noble at a first glance, the idea that all human beings have the same right to enjoy material goods demands some ethical considerations. The premise seems to ignore that access to material resources is, in general, a direct consequence of individual merit. Thus, the accumulation of capital would be the result of labour, or more precisely, of the value that each individual generates for society, and not of usurpation. In this sense, admitting that all human beings must have equal rights to material goods is equivalent to saying that those who work and produce must support those who do not. In the extreme, the idea that a part of society has the right to appropriate the fruit of another party's work is comparable to the logic that supports slave production systems. Brought to the reality of communist/socialist thinking, the issue can be illustrated by the famous fable of the ant and the cicada.

In general, left-wing ideologues seem to harbour the idea that the agenda they advocate is virtuous. Among other factors, this perception would result from an alleged search for the correction of what they classify as social injustices, which materialized in the different forms of inequality between human beings. Thus, the idea that societies need to be solidly reformed so that we all move towards 'a better world' would be the basis of what is understood today as progressivism. Given the elasticity that is common to social constructs, the idea of progressivism serves as a huge umbrella where the most diverse flags defended by the left today are inserted. This includes issues related to gender, race, and sexual orientation, for example. The defence of equality has guaranteed leftist ideologists a kind of monopoly on virtues. More broadly, this means that leftists see in defending their ideas the path to 'good', placing the rightmost views on the opposite pole (i.e., the path to 'evil'). This dichotomy contributes a lot to the radicalization of the parties and, consequently, to the interruption of the dialogue between them.

Selfishness as Right's Origins

The set of convictions and ideas traditionally classified as right-wing may have their origin in an excessive concern of individuals with themselves, so that the pursuit of their personal interests occupies the highest place in their hierarchy of priorities. These individuals will dedicate their efforts, therefore, to creating a situation that is as favourable as possible for them, without the conditions of the other individuals causing them, at first, great concerns. This search for individual well-being would be expressed in the most diverse spheres of life, the economic being perhaps the most evident, with the right-wing individual probably the most adapted to the capitalist mode of production. Entrepreneurship, for instance, seems to concentrate much of this search, with the creation and management of businesses by individuals being a means by which they seek financial returns and, therefore, an improvement in their living conditions from a material point of view. Participation in the economy through the sale of their labour would have a similar logic since the salary is the main objective. As discussed earlier, this focus on improving individual conditions would be one of the main reasons why leftist thinkers have chosen over the years to gradually remove the proletariat from the position of the main agent of an eventual revolution, attributing this role to other groups seen as oppressed. This change would be based on the perception that the struggle for better working conditions – mainly better wages – would denote the agreement of the proletariat with the system that, in theory, would oppress them. Thus the proletariat would no longer be focused on destroying the system, but on maximizing the benefits workers collects from it.

From a moral point of view, the selfishness of the right-wing individual can be discussed from the most diverse perspectives. Initially, it is necessary to consider the means by which this individual seeks to maximize their well-being. In general, these means can be separated according to the eventual benefits and losses they may cause to society, which are important drivers for the classification of these actions from the angle of their ethicality. On the one hand, one can put personal effort and risk-taking. On the other, all the ways in which the individual can seek to corrupt free market mechanisms. Each of these positions is discussed in more detail next.

Personal Effort

The idea that the fruits of labour belong to those who have put in the personal effort to obtain it seems to form the basis of right-wing economic thinking. From this premise, several others arise that, together, give rise to arguments that support the most varied perspectives regarding individual freedom, the individual's relationship with society, and, more specifically, between the latter and the State. Regarding the first, the guarantee that the results of the work will belong to those who dedicate effort to this end solidifies a virtuous incentive mechanism from an economic perspective, from which, for example, emerge the tendencies towards entrepreneurship as a way to improve the living conditions of those who so desire. As the investment of personal effort can represent different forms of sacrifice (e.g., time, energy, financial resources), it is necessary that the individual considering undertaking an endeavour be sure that the eventual results of these efforts will not be entirely taken from them, nor intended for those who chose not to incur such sacrifices. Otherwise, there seems to be no logical reason for the economic initiative, since the acceptance of pain arising from personal effort only seems to make sense from the perspective of something positive later on. This issue also seems to be associated with the individual's willingness to compose the workforce as an employee, albeit in a less direct way. As discussed in greater detail in Chapter 13, this perception would lead to the typical economic views of individuals on the right, especially in relation to the size and functions of the State. This includes mainly criticism of the mechanisms for distributing the wealth generated by society, with tax collection at the heart of the issue. The social programs promoted by governments would be, in the view of these individuals, a form of usurpation of the fruit of their work, since a part of the result of their sacrifice – which is individual – is directed to a collective without it having necessarily deserved it.

From a point of view restricted to meritocratic issues, the distribution of income through the collection of taxes would constitute an injustice, fuelling the repulsion of individuals on the right for this system. Criticism of the size and scope of the State is based on the perception of inefficiency in public services, which are generally considered inferior to those promoted by the private sector. Among other factors, this lower efficiency would be due to the lack of incentive mechanisms typical of market economies, with the prerogative of the state monopoly over certain activities being an important factor in this regard. The lack of competition combined with the impossibility of state actors to benefit directly from the result of their work would thus be at the origin of the lack of this incentive mechanism and, therefore, of the inefficiency. Faced with this scenario, right-wing individuals tend to defend what they call a minimal state, that is, a state that abstains from participating in economic activities as much as possible, and that is limited to functions such as guaranteeing law and order. These would, however, be second-order arguments, as they are somehow a consequence of the perception that the allocation of results to those who did not work for them is inherently unfair. The role of the State as a distributor of the wealth generated ends up being, therefore, based on what can be understood as the simple desire of individuals to enjoy what results from the sweat of their faces, which is sometimes pejoratively classified as a form of selfishness.

In the last decades, several mechanisms have been put into practice in an attempt to counteract the idea that the results of work should, in justice, belong to those who made the effort to produce them. In this sense, the reinterpretation and application of Marxist ideas to current times has been particularly notorious, in which the supposed mechanisms of social oppression would have generated privileges for certain classes. According to this view, the redistribution of the value generated by the classes considered privileged would represent a form of rebalancing the system. Added to this is the idea of historical debt, in which the classes understood as privileged would benefit from not only current oppressions but also those arising from the past. Once again – according to the Marxist perspective – the redistribution of generated value would represent a way of remedying oppression. Despite being very popular among adherents of leftist thought, Marxist views are sometimes criticized for their lack of empirical evidence and for their evident simplification of reality, reducing the complexity of human life and social relations to an alleged mechanism of oppression that it would serve to explain not only the past but also present and future realities. For these and other reasons, Marxism is usually classified as a form of magical thinking, which would approach a form of pseudo-scientific literature. These and other issues are discussed in greater detail throughout the book.

Risk Taking

If, on the one hand, personal effort seems to be a fundamental condition for generating value, it is not the only one for an individual to achieve higher-than-average returns for any activity. In this sense, the finance literature has been, in general, consistent in defending the idea of a form of parallelism between the notions of risk and return. At the base, this means that the search for higher returns implies the acceptance of higher levels of risk, just as tolerance of lower levels of risk would imply lower returns. Associated with uncertainty about a particular outcome, risk can be understood as a measure of possible variability. In other words, the concept of risk translates the possibility of something not happening as expected, deviating from what was planned or naturally anticipated. Although most commonly used in the study of asset prices, projected cash flows, and consequent investment returns, this definition applies to virtually everything that refers to future events. The concept of volatility, in turn, represents the generally observed degree of deviation from expectations. In general, these conjectures support the idea that the results of any economic activity are subject to variation in such a way that the same capital that can give rise to profit can be lost.

In the same way that it seems logical that the results of personal effort should be directed to those who employed it, the fruits of economic activities – both profit and capital erosion – belong, in fairness, to the one who chose to accept the inherent risks of the activity performed. This understanding seems to have been accepted by the vast majority of legislation dealing with business and labour rights, with the liabilities assumed by the entrepreneur not extended to employees. Among other issues, this perception separates the interests of those who chose to assume the risks of the business (i.e., entrepreneurs) from those who chose to appropriate only the result of their personal effort in the form of a salary (i.e., employees). Business law also seems to deal with the separation of the typical risks of the firm's core activities from those specific to the different operations that compose it. Thus, while the final result of business activities (i.e., profit or loss) should be destined for the entrepreneur, creditors would only assume the specific risk of their decisions (e.g., default risk). As a result, the entrepreneur must honour her/his commitments to employees and creditors, regardless of the end result of the company they command. Added to market and competition variations, this separation of rights and responsibilities forms the basic tripod of business risk. Considering that the individual who accepts taking risks in the search for economic returns is aware of these issues – even if s/he does not elaborate in detail the arguments that support her/his views – s/he will feel that s/he will be entitled to the fruits of this risk.

Despite the apparent logic of the cause-and-effect relationship discussed (i.e., the economic return is caused by the union of personal effort and risk taking) and its natural consequence (i.e., the economic return belongs to the one who applied personal effort and took risks), several theories defend opposing views, contending collectivist and distributive views of the value generated by individuals or groups of individuals (e.g., companies). Among the most used is stakeholder theory (Freeman, 1984), which, among other elements, proposes that the interests of all those who may affect or be affected by the activities of a company should be equally considered and attended to. The theory is positioned in the debate on the objectives of organizations, questioning the pursuit of profit as a priority and the hierarchy of different groups of stakeholders (typically the consideration of the interests of consumers or investors as superior to those of other groups such as employees, governments, and local communities).

This view has received harsh criticism over decades, with the most prominent ones drawing attention to the lack of applicability and even usefulness of such reasoning (e.g., Jensen, 2010). Despite predating the development of the most elementary aspects of stakeholder theory, Milton Friedman's criticisms of the so-called corporate social responsibilities in the early 1970s (Friedman, 1970), seem to suit his arguments. According to the Nobel Prize laureate in Economics and one of the most prominent figures of the Chicago School, the social objectives of companies should be restricted to the pursuit of profit, since, in addition to generating employment and income, financial returns would be the result of the value generated for society. Thus, for Friedman, attempts to incorporate social responsibilities into companies would represent an effort towards a 'pure and inadultered socialism'. With these words, the author makes it clear that the collectivist and distributive views of the value generated in society (by individuals or groups of individuals) are associated with leftist thinking, and not, therefore, part of the worldview of those identified with the right.

Corruption of Free Market Mechanisms

As anticipated, while the pursuit of profit through personal effort and risk-taking can be considered ethical means – therefore justifying the allocation of results to those who do so – the same cannot be said of the different ways by which free market mechanisms can be corrupted. In general, these deviations occur in the form of corruption of state agents, precisely those who should guarantee justice in competitive processes. Corrupting economic agents can have undue advantages over others, which can range from non-payment of fees and taxes to access to privileged information. However, deviations from free competition do not always occur through illegal methods. Depending on the political power of the groups that seek undue competitive advantages, the deviations they apply can be validated under the law. This seems to be precisely the work of parliamentarians who either form part of these economic groups or are elected with their direct support.

In these cases, attacks on free competition end up being incorporated into the country's own legislation, which comes to undermining its economic capacity in the long run. As a result, it is common to observe the formation of monopolies, duopolies, and oligopolies. The costs of these deviations can be quite high for populations, especially when the State is the only agent authorized to explore a certain economic activity. Regardless of the form in which it takes place (i.e., legal or illegal), the corruption of free competition represents an injustice to the affected economic agents and a serious threat to the development of the societies where they occur. Among the main negative consequences of these schemes is the decrease in the quality of goods and services offered to consumers, and more broadly in the value generated. Based on the above, it can be argued that the more respectful and appropriate to the current mode of production are the means by which individuals seek to maximize their well-being, the more ethical they will be.

Evidently, this does not imply the automatic judgement of the morality of the mode of production itself, but the conclusion that observance of the rules of the game – here understood as the de facto respect for the democratic state of law – is probably the most efficient way to show respect to a society that has forged its laws over the centuries. The preceding discussions serve as a basis for designing a basic political-economic spectrum, which in turn supports the development of the sustainability spectrum. It is necessary to point out that, given the complexity of the possible political and economic convictions that each individual may have, as well as their own psychologies, the political/economical spectrum proposed here is not exhaustive. On the contrary, it seeks to focus on the main features that are common to the different groups discussed, presenting them in a simplified and useful way for the purposes of the book.

References

Andretta, M., and Reiter, H. (2009). Parties, unions, and movements: The European left and the ESF. In: D. Della Porta (Ed.). *Another Europe*, pp.193–223. Routledge.

Arter, D. (2002). 'Communists we are no longer, social democrats we can never be': The evolution of the leftist parties in Finland and Sweden. *The Journal of Communist Studies and Transition Politics*, Vol.18, No.3, pp.1–28.

Batarce, M.S. (2019). A Tragédia da Esquerda Acadêmica e o Mal-Estar na Universidade Brasileira. *HIPÁTIA-Revista Brasileira de História, Educação e Matemática*, Vol.4, No.2, pp.189–205.

Berlin, I. (2013). *The Roots of Romanticism*. Princeton University Press.

Braithwaite, V. (1994). Beyond Rokeach's equality-freedom model: Two-dimensional values in a one-dimensional world. *Journal of Social Issues*, Vol.50, No.4, pp.67–94.

Clark, G. (2005). The condition of the working class in England, 1209–2004. *Journal of Political Economy*, Vol.113, No.6, pp.1307–1340.
Flynn, T.R. (1979). The political thought of Jean-Paul Sartre: Three essays: I. L'Imagination Au Pouvoir: The evolution of Sartre's political and social thought. *Political Theory*, Vol.7, No.2, pp.157–182.
Freeman, R.E. (1984). *Strategic Management: A Stakeholder Approach*. Pitman Publishing Inc.
Friedman, M. (1970). The social responsibility of business is to increase its profits. *The New York Times Magazine*, September 13. Available at https://www.nytimes.com/1970/09/13/archives/a-friedman-doctrine-the-social-responsibility-of-business-is-to.html
Fukuyama, F. (2011). *The Origins of Political Order: From Prehuman Times to the French Revolution*. Farrar, Straus and Giroux.
Garside, P.D. (1972). Scott, the romantic past and the nineteenth century. *Review of English Studies*, Vol.23, No.90, pp.147–161.
Hayek, F.A. (1949). The intellectuals and socialism. *The University of Chicago Law Review*, Vol.16, No.3, pp.417–433.
Heath, J. (2009). Habermas and analytical Marxism. *Philosophy & Social Criticism*, Vol.35, No.8, pp.891–919.
Hopkins, E. (1982). Working hours and conditions during the industrial revolution: A re-appraisal. *Economic History Review*, Vol.35, No.1, pp.52–66.
Hughes, C., and Southern, A. (2019). The world of work and the crisis of capitalism: Marx and the fourth industrial revolution. *Journal of Classical Sociology*, Vol.19, No.1, pp.59–71.
Jackson, B. (2013). *Equality and the British Left: A Study in Progressive Political Thought, 1900–64*. Manchester University Press.
Jensen, M.C. (2010). Value maximization, stakeholder theory, and the corporate objective function. *Journal of Applied Corporate Finance*, Vol.22, No.1, pp.32–42.
Jones, G.S., and Charlot, M. (1996). Voir sans entendre: Engels, Manchester et l'observation sociale en 1844. *Genèses*, Vol.22, pp.4–17.
Long, J. (2005). Rural-urban migration and socioeconomic mobility in Victorian Britain. *The Journal of Economic History*, Vol.65, No.1, pp.1–35.
Mays, S., Brickley, M., and Ives, R. (2008). Growth in an English population from the industrial revolution. *American Journal of Physical Anthropology*, Vol.136, No.1, pp.85–92.
Moroney, J.R., and Lovell, C.A.K. (1997). The relative efficiencies of market and planned economies. *Southern Economic Journal*, Vol.63, No.4, pp.1084–1093.
Muris, T.J. (1980). Opportunistic behavior and the law of contracts. *Minnesota Law Review*, Vol.65, pp.521–690.
Murrell, P. (1991). Can neoclassical economics underpin the reform of centrally planned economies? *Journal of Economic Perspectives*, Vol.5, No.4, pp.59–76.
Novais, F. (2012). *Materialismo histórico e historiografia*. Available at https://www.youtube.com/watch?v=6cRfan3LMfI&t=5s
Phillips, N.R. (1956). The conservative implications of skepticism. *The Journal of Politics*, Vol.18, No.1, pp.28–38.
Rokeach, M. (1973). *The Nature of Human Values*. Free Press.
Rothbard, M.N. (1979). *Left, Right, and the Prospects for Liberty*, Vol.1. Ludwig von Mises Institute.
Schwarz, L.D. (1992). *London in the Age of Industrialisation: Entrepreneurs, Labour Force and Living Conditions, 1700–1850*, Vol.19. Cambridge University Press.

Singer, P. (2000). *A Darwinian Left: Politics, Evolution and Cooperation.* Yale University Press.

Soto, J.H. (2010). *¿Por qué los intelectuales odian el capitalismo?* Available at https://www.youtube.com/watch?v=S1Ta0zxdXJE

Strugnell, A. (2012). *Diderot's Politics: A Study of the Evolution of Diderot's Political Thought After the Encyclopédie*, Vol.62. Springer Science & Business Media.

Tomasson, R.F. (1969). The extraordinary success of the Swedish social democrats. *The Journal of Politics*, Vol.31, No.3, pp.772–798.

Zou, H.F. (1998). The spirit of capitalism, social status, money, and accumulation. *Journal of Economics*, Vol.68, No.3, pp.219–233.

4 The Sustainability Spectrum

Spectrums

The idea of a spectrum refers to a gradation, in such a way that eventual nuances might be more clearly perceived (e.g., Akiskal and Pinto, 1999). Just like a rule branched into infinite divisions, a spectrum provides an analogous measure, allowing individual observations to be compared to a predetermined standard (Brian et al., 2019). Examples of the use of this type of scale include frameworks employed in the mapping of psychological characteristics or in the diagnosis of neurological traits that, despite their differences, share common characteristics (Adam, 2013). The use of spectrums also seems to be common in the comparison of a series of continuous measurements (Sütő, 1989), such as solar irradiance levels (e.g., University of Colorado, 2022) or average temperatures for certain regions (Ljungqvist et al., 2019). More recently, spectrums have also been used in sports management, in the analysis of the performance of football players. The adoption of heat maps has become increasingly common, with shade variations indicating the regions of the field where a particular athlete plays most frequently (Oddi, 2014). The same principle is often applied in the examination of human mobility in large-scale events (Xavier et al., 2013).

It might be said that among the benefits associated to the use of spectrums is their power to present measures in a graphic and relatively simple way (Aupperle et al., 2020). The combination of different dimensions seems to favour the communicative potential of the most different types of spectrums, with the use of colours and positions being an important ally in the indication of frequencies or variations (Veverka et al., 1996; Hughes and Williams, 2010). The value of spectrums also rests in the fact that they allow the consideration of intermediate positions, with the fluidity of continuous measures denoting the dynamics that lead to a certain result. The evolution of a red dot to a yellow one, for example, will not be done in a discreet way. Instead, a well-constructed spectrum should show the slow and gradual transformation of red tones, with an orange colour appearing as the view moves away from the initial observation point. Likewise, this orange tone should, little by little, metamorphose into a more intense yellow, so that its dynamics of splendour and decay indicate the way through which the transition from red to yellow occurs.

DOI: 10.4324/9781003124719-5

These characteristics guarantee a high applicability to spectrums, mainly with regard to human behaviour and thinking (Guan et al., 2012). In face of the multitude of possibilities offered by the mind (Malle, 2006), the consideration of transition points allows for more elaborate classifications, so that individuals do not have to be necessarily fitted into a grid that does not fully correspond to their nature. These possibilities can be particularly useful in the examination of multifaceted and complex aspects such as political positions (Van Hiel and Mervield, 2003) and ideological views (Hargittai et al., 2008), as classifications in rigid blocks (e.g., right, centre, and left) do not appear to provide the necessary flexibility for more realistic indications. In general, political and ideological positions that are found between these basic groups represent a hybrid form, in which it is possible to identify a mixture of the premises of the block coming immediately before and the one appearing immediately after (e.g., centre-right, centre-left).

Given the complexities of things (basically all things), rigid classifications seem unlikely to be accurate, with the focus on transition phases being, in some cases, more revealing. In this sense, the considerations of 'grey zones' – or 'orange zones', to cohere with the illustration provided above – can be understood as closer to reality, as rigid ideological premises are contested. This gains relevance as the political and ideological spectrums becomes progressively more complex (Maddox and Lilie, 1984), with the most diverse configurations proposed. As societies and public debate evolve, ideas are reformed and often adapted. As discussed throughout the book, the sustainability debate seems to be strongly influenced by societies' dynamics, representing, perhaps, one of the many transformations of ideological thinking. This means that, just as one may investigate the continuous possibilities of ideological views, the fluidity of positions in terms of social and environmental matters must not be ignored. Differently put, a *sustainability spectrum* would be possible.

Despite being focused on a specific phenomenon, the sustainability debate cannot be understood as something isolated from other spheres of public thought. On the contrary, the different ideas that compose it seem to be heirs of long transitions that mainly include aspects of philosophical (Hedlund-de Witt, 2013), political (Hess and Maki, 2019), and economic thinking (Neumayer, 2004). Thus, before entering the *sustainability spectrum* per se, a discussion of its main political and economic origins is necessary.

The Political-economic Spectrum

The proposition of a basic political-economic spectrum (Figure 4.1) is guided by the discussions presented in the previous chapters, mainly concerning the origins of right and left thinking. Consideration of more philosophical questions about beliefs in human nature (i.e., is man naturally good, or naturally evil?) (Morgan, 2005) are important in this sense, just like the understanding of ideal models (e.g., planned economies [Ellman, 2014] and the free market [Carrier, 2020]). The role assigned to individual responsibilities as a means of achieving prosperity (i.e., meritocracy) (Young, 2017) complete these developments. Given that these issues have already been addressed in previous chapters – and are also approached in the following ones – these important points will not be taken up here, except occasionally. Priority will be given to more objective aspects that contribute to the understanding of the characteristics of social thought, at least in terms of worldviews on politics and economics. About these points, it is necessary to remember that they are interspersed, one arguably inseparable from the other. Although many economists refuse to comment on political aspects (e.g., Marcos Lisboa 1964–) – often because they understand that these are too complex, or cannot be predicted in a minimally reliable way – the fact is that politics usually have a great influence on economic decisions, and vice versa. Discussing the two together therefore seems to be the most realistic option.

The Carnivorous Left (Extreme Left)

Positioned at one of the extremes of ideological visions, the carnivorous left (Rachewsky, 2019) concentrates the essence of leftist thinking, combining perceptions and orientations that are focused on collectivism (Hayek et al., 1935), on the notion of equality between individuals (Marshall, 1996), and on the determination of a grandiose role of a central power (Grzymala-Busse and Luong, 2002). More than a simple ideal way of designing societies, however, far-left thinking may have a strong tendency towards authoritarianism (Van Hiel et al., 2006), with the concentration of means in the State dismantling the pillars of the division of powers proposed by Montesquieu (1689–1755) (Krause, 2000). The impact of this movement can be profound, as the allocation of attributions between the legislative, the executive, and the judiciary form the basis of the rule of law (Shklar, 1987). Countries that have experienced extreme left-wing governments have observed either an immediate or gradual erosion of institutions (Latouche, 2019).

This process of centralization can occur in diverse ways, with the weakening of legislative houses and the judiciary generally taking place through corruption (Maya, 2018), co-optation (Reuter and Robertson, 2015), or intimidation (Vreeland, 2008). The result of these processes is the maintenance of a 'democracy of appearances', despite its internal corrosion (Gaona, 2018). In more advanced cases, the extreme left assumes totalitarian tendencies, with state control extending to all spheres of citizens' lives (Geyer and Fitzpatrick, 2009). Contradictorily, repression may be at the origin of popular movements that seek to overthrow totalitarian governments, with individuals rising up against the constituted powers to regain their freedom (Frank and Fuentes, 2022). Tolerance towards left-wing dictatorships, however, varies across societies, with some being more refractory than others.

The extreme left's perception of the functions and capacities of the state also seems to have greatly contributed to the development of these processes. As discussed throughout the book, socialist and communist regimes that have already been installed around the world were characterized by a high degree of secularism (Zrinščak, 2004), with religions often persecuted and even banned (Yang, 2011). The elevation of the state to the highest rank in the lives of citizens would be among the main reasons for this mechanic. Regardless of the restrictions on freedom that extreme leftist thinking tends to promote, its discourse still seems to be quite seductive, especially among the young. It is not uncommon to see teenagers and early adults declaring themselves revolutionary leftists, associating with the most diverse currents of thought (e.g., Marxism, Trotskyism, Leninism). The image of young people dressed in T-shirts bearing the face of guerrilla leader Ernesto 'Che' Guevara (1928–1967), for example, is common in universities around the world. In general, these groups ignore atrocities attributed to Guevara, such as the persecution and murders of a massive number of people identified as obstacles to his goals (James, 2001).

As discussed by Constantino (2021a), the communist utopia would have seduced both average people and intellectuals, the latter being the most responsible for its longevity. Referring to the famous phrase of French thinker Jean-François Revel (1924–2006), '*Si le fascisme et le communisme n'avaient séduit que des imbéciles et des canailles, il eût été plus simple de s'en débarrasser*' (Le Figaro, 2008) ('If fascism and communism had not only seduced fools and scoundrels, it would have been easier to get rid of them'; our translation), the author draws attention to the intelligence of many who advocate the implementation of authoritarian ideas as the path to paradise on earth. Although appearing in different concentrations and formats, these ideas seem to be common to most radical views. A brief debate on the main currents of thought originating in Marxism shall provide a better understanding of the motivations conditioning radical leftist thinking today.

Trotskyism

Often depicted as a romantic figure by his biographers (Mavrakis, 2014), Leon Trotsky (1879–1940) defended the argument that an economic system could not exist in isolation, with a world scheme – instead of a national one – being necessary. In this sense, the success of the Russian Revolution would depend on the victory of subversive processes in other countries. By this means, his perspective of permanent revolution (Trotsky, 2019) differed from that of Stalin, as the latter believed that the new state of things would succeed alone (i.e., independently of rebellion processes in other countries) (Daniels, 1998). As pointed out by Mavrakis (2014), however, Trotsky would be incapable of performing concrete analysis, having among his failures the economism he shared with Stalin.

It is possible to identify in Trotsky's search to export the Russian model a connection with the modern idea of globalism, as this perspective subsidizes the emptying of national identities to the point where borders between countries practically cease to exist (Rohac, 2019). This process would result in the transfer of power from a local sphere (i.e., within countries) to an international and centralized one. As observed by Alexander (1991), the Third International (formally known as the Communist International, and co-organized by Trotsky and Lenin) had 'the ambitious objective of being *the* party of world revolution, an international party with national "sections" ' (p.1). This seemingly bold goal denotes Trotsky's appetite for a global government.

For some, transnational organizations (e.g., European Union, United Nations) would be the embryos of a bureaucracy intended to support regional and world authorities whose possibilities and powers would find no immediate limits (Rochester, 1990; Longo, 2003). Framing this vision in the basic precepts of Trotskyism, the creation of a government hierarchically superior to local powers would be the only way to guarantee that there would be no resistance or threats to the implementation of the intended revolution. For Alexander (1991), Trotskyism might be understood as the world movement led Trotsky by himself after his exile from the Soviet Union. As pointed out by the author, the focus on this path would be justified, as the Trotkyist tendencies in the USSR would have been emptied before and during the Great Purges (late 1930s, Schuman and Corning, 2000). It may be argued, then, that although it originated at the fulcrum of the Russian Revolution, Trotskyism as we understand it today flourished abroad, as it found no space under Stalin's rule. The persecution of ideas and of Trotsky himself also did not respect the borders of their origins, with the Bolshevik leader persecuted in exile.

Synthetizing much of the events that led to the origin of Trotskyism, Alexander (1991) states that

> at the beginning of 1929 Leon Trotsky was exiled from the Soviet Union on the orders of his mortal enemy, Joseph Stalin. From then until his murder by an agent of Stalin's GPU eleven and a half years later, Trotsky spent most of his time and energy trying to organize an international political movement in his own image and reflecting his own evolving ideas. For nearly five decades since his death, Trotsky's followers have continued to attempt to set up such an organization.
>
> (Alexander, 1991, p.1)

Leninism

As pointed out by Wallerstein (1990), Leninism – often referred to as Bolshevism – emerged in 1902, as Vladimir Lenin (1870–1924) produced a counter-draft to Georgy Plekhanov's (1856–1918) text for the 1903 Unification Congress (i.e., Second Congress). From the division of the Party, Lenin would have gained strength, taking control of the Bolshevik portion. The stream of thought arising from this would be inherently pragmatic, representing a set of principles intended to guide social transition from capitalism to communism (Britannica, 2007). Accordingly, that would be due to the chronic lack of practical instruction within Marxism. Broadly, it may be argued that probably no other school is closer to Marx's ideas than what originated in Lenin's views. In his work *The Foundations of Leninism*, Stalin (2020) himself points to the influence of Marxism in the formation of the thought of his predecessor. Originally published in 1924 (right after Lenin's death), the volume condenses a series of lectures delivered by Stalin, in which his views on the historical development of Leninism are presented, as well as its methods, strategies, and main theoretical characteristics. Still, on the influence of Marxism on Lenin's thinking, Stalin stresses that they may not be confounded, as the origination of Leninism would represent a significant contribution to Marx's reasoning.

On the common idea that Leninism would not be more than the application of Marxism in the context of Russia, Stalin shows only partial agreement. While confirming the idea that Lenin would have applied Marxism in terms of the Russian peculiarities of the time, he points to the exemplary and brilliant way in which this would have been done. In addition, he highlights the fact that Leninism does not represent just a Russian phenomenon – as would be expected if it were just an adaptation of Marxism. In resolving these issues, Stalin proposes that Leninism is Marxism applied in the era of imperialism and the proletarian revolution, meaning that, in a general view, it would represent the theory and practices of the proletarian revolution. Within a narrower perspective, in turn, it would be the theory and practice of the dictatorship of the proletariat.

Stalinism

In the same way that Trotskyism and Leninism are associated with the thoughts of historical figures (Trotsky and Lenin respectively), Stalinism also has an essentially personalist character, being largely based on the practices of the government led by Joseph Stalin (1878–1953). For Geyer and Fitzpatrick (2009), Stalinism must be located at the extreme left of the political spectrum, representing a fierce opposition to what the authors call Western liberal traditions. Accordingly, the set of beliefs created around the figure of Stalin would be embedded in ideology, which may explain its study within the perspectives of political religion and political theology (Sollner, 1993). This coheres with the idea of political thinking assuming the role traditionally exerted by religions. Beyond favouring the valorization of the state to the highest social status possible (i.e., origin, reason, and destiny of all social actions), such perspectives seem to subsidize more radical views, from both those who adhere to and those who oppose them. For Bernstein (1984), the Stalinist period in the Soviet Union was characterized by a high degree of administrative incompetence and mismanagement. This would be mainly based on the failed decision to extract rural resources as a way to push industrialization, among the main reasons for the 1932–33 famine.

In face of these discussions, it may be argued that idealistic views of society often result in a high degree of inflexibility on the part of those identified with ideological thinking (Zmigrod, 2021), with far-leftists – as well as those in the far-right – appearing particularly affected. Among other consequences, this can lead to the development of a sort of moralism, in which the behaviour, expressions, and even thoughts of individuals are somehow monitored. In this sense, arguments contrary to the prevailing economic and political models would not be tolerated (Peffley and Sigelman, 1990). Within socialist and communist governments (e.g., Eastern Germany, Cuba, North Korea), this would materialize in reports from state agents censoring what they perceive as potentially problematic

(Vianu, 1998). The surveillance usually extends throughout social life, including the work of writers, economists, philosophers, and artists in general. This dynamic would have been responsible for a considerable drop in the quality of artistic production in the former Soviet Union, with the restriction of freedom of thought having important impacts on content production (Pondé, 2021). The quest for implementation of an artificial society often leads far-left governments to very high levels of control and surveillance.

The Herbivorous Left (Centre-Left)

Despite in essence agreeing with the premises of the carnivorous left (i.e., an orientation towards collectivism, the notion of equality between individuals, and the determination of a grandiose role for the State), the herbivorous left seems to bend to the force of reality, making certain concessions to market economies and democracy (Baker and Greene, 2011). Thus, it can be said that, from an ideological point of view, the herbivorous left maintains great similarities with its 'carnivorous brother', differing from the latter, however, by a greater pragmatism (Danish, 2015). Typically, this translates into a worldview that seeks to focus state activities on the redistribution of value generated by society, leaving most economic activities – and consequently value generation – under the responsibility of private actors (Przeworski, 1986). In general, redistribution is made through the collection of high tax rates (Beramendi and Rueda, 2007) and the granting of various social benefits to the less favoured strata (Klitgaard, 2007). This is the basic mechanism of the so-called social democracy. Summarizing this view, Barbieri (2017) defines social democracy as 'the marriage of free market capitalism with some form of social safety net'. The development of an understanding that the state should play a more modest role in the organization of society may not have occurred through a profound change in ideological convictions. Instead, this more moderate stance seems to reflect the perception that the State as an economic agent is, in general, inefficient (Pierson, 2012), with the private sector the natural holder of adequate incentive mechanisms for value creation (Hicks, 2018). In other words, the greater tolerance that the herbivorous left has towards capitalism would be an expression of its pragmatism, largely based on the various previously unsuccessful experiences that put the state as the engine of the economy (Petrakov, 1993).

This greater openness to the idea of a free market is accompanied by a greater tolerance for the bases of democracy (Jackson, 2013). Often the herbivorous left seeks to participate in electoral disputes and accepts the alternation of power. This tolerance, however, seems to be greater when the actors who take turns are also members of the left, even if more radical. In some cases, power struggles between carnivorous and herbivorous left seem to take the form of a power division in which members of the centre and the right are excluded from the political stage. One of the best-known mechanisms in this sense is what came to be called the '*estratégia das tesouras*' (scissors strategy; our translation), in which radical and moderate leftists simulate an antagonism with each other, with the latter even labelling themselves – and labelled by the radical left – as representatives of the right (Oliveira, 2020). Within this logic, the tolerance of social democrats towards free market mechanisms and democratic precepts is intentionally confused with the ideas that form the basis of right-wing thinking (i.e., liberalism from the economic point of view and conservatism in the sphere of mores) (Constantino, 2021a).

Thus, the exclusion of the right from public debate would take place by classifying the arguments of liberals and conservatives – as well as all possible nuances and combinations between these two points – as something of a fascist (Gentile, 2018) and, at times, even of Nazi nature (Menezes, 2020). The application of the 'scissors strategy' is one of the factors exploiting the historical hegemony of the left in many countries, with the extreme left typically classifying social democrats as neo-liberals, especially when they (i.e., social democrats) seek to advance the efficiency of public services or to resize the role of the State in the economy (Cariello, 2005). The privatization processes of public companies are typically representative of this debate (Boito Jr., 2007). Brazil is perhaps one of the best examples of the application of the scissors strategy, where the extreme left and social democrats have governed the country for decades. As they alternated in power, they accused each other as if they were not the fruit of the same ideological root (Constantino, 2021b).

Still, the moderate left is associated with the so-called Fabian socialism (Dorrien, 2019), which, contrary to the revolutionary methods advocated by the extreme left, aims at a slow and gradual implementation of leftism (Cole, 2013). In this sense, the continuous extension of social benefits and the progression of taxes on the private sector would, in the long run, result in a society where everyone either depends on or works for the State.

The Centre

Typically, people who identify with the centre stance claim to be relatively equidistant from the extremes (Schlesinger, 1950), rejecting ideologies and presenting themselves as essentially pragmatic (SIC, 2021). This would include a screening of ideas, incorporating what is positive, regardless of their origin (i.e., right or left). Likewise, centrists would seek to reject views seen as negative, especially the most radical ones. It can be said that the centre is, perhaps, the position that most easily fits the democratic game (Machado, 1987), with its representatives – at least in theory – tending to be more open to dialogue (Tavares, 2021). The lack of ideological purpose sometimes ends up characterizing a physiological behaviour on the part of parties and centre politicians (Venaglia, 2020). Among the main consequences of this physiologism is excessive utilitarianism, which leads centrists to associate themselves with the occupants of power, regardless of their political and economic orientations. This dynamic seems to be particularly common in classical presidential regimes that end up configuring coalitional systems (Abranches, 2018). Thus, the search for support in parliament and, therefore, for governability often leads to processes of exchanges and concessions in which the executive power needs to divide its attributions, distributing positions in the public administration by criteria other than competence (Pessôa, 2015). These processes show signs of being ingrained in democracies and seem, at times, to be unavoidable (Santos, 2007). As a result, the efficiency of the public machine and the credibility of political agents end up being even more harmed.

If, on the one hand, centrist parties are often labelled as physiological, they can also play an important role in maintaining the rule of law. In this sense, the lack of adherence or of a dogmatic agreement more deeply rooted in ideologies makes centre parties function as a natural barrier to totalitarian advances and radicalisms in general (Cunha and Cunha, 2021). Interestingly, the inexistence of an ideal worldview shall work as an important mechanism of checks and balances, especially when the dilution of the legislative and judicial powers is at a more advanced stage. In these cases, one may justly recognize a democratic essence in the centre. It is also true that this noble posture is rare and usually manifests only when centrists perceive that the advance of authoritarianism threatens the continuity of their physiological schemes. In a way, it can be said that the democratic spirit is awakened in this group when the 'goose that lays the golden eggs' is in danger.

The Herbivorous Right (Centre-Right)

In the same way that the herbivorous left combines its collectivist ideals with a greater openness to market practices and democratic mechanisms, the so-called herbivorous right represents a kind of middle ground between radical liberalism/conservatism and an organized life in society. As Gidron (2022) puts it, centre-right parties 'may find themselves increasingly torn between welfare chauvinists and market cosmopolitans' (p.147). The quote stresses the often-uncomfortable position assumed by those managing antagonistic worldviews, with the hybrid possibilities of the right side of the political spectrum presenting similar challenges (although inverted) to those observable on its equivalent on the left side. This means that those more closely identified with a centre-right perspective may be willing to make certain concessions regarding individual freedoms in the name of some collective interests.

As with the interpretations of the dynamics of its equivalent on the left, a more precise analysis of the behaviour of the herbivorous right can prove to be complex, precisely because it is in a kind of grey zone. If it is true that its characteristics reflect much of the thinking of liberals and conservatives, its members' conceptions may end up clouding the premises on which they are based. In this set, the flexibilization of more defined ideologies eventually brings together groups of different tonalities (Codato et al., 2018). For Gidron and Ziblatt (2019), centre-right parties would fulfil the important function of promoting the stability of the political system, with the weakening of these positions being among the causes of the argued recent increase in radicalism. Other authors, however, identify similarities between the centre-right and more radical positions (i.e., far-right) in some European countries (e.g., Hess and Renner, 2019), which may come to fuel radicalization.

Regardless of the many forms that the centre-right can take and the complexities that may arise as its representatives seek their space, the fact that it places itself between such different perspectives contributes to diametrically opposed ideologies finding a space for debate. As with the centre-left, conditioning the value of ideal worldviews to their applicability gives a special value to the pragmatism of the herbivorous right, with these characteristics acting as a kind of filter against the exaggerations and even the delusions that abstractions in their purest forms tend to favour.

The Carnivorous Right (Extreme Right)

Occupying the other end of the political-economic spectrum, the carnivorous right privileges the individual's wants and needs over all world things (Lukes, 1971), with the search for maximizing one's utility serving as the main engine of the social machine. In this process, social dynamics are basically ignored, just as the traditional functions of the state are discredited and, in some cases, rejected outright. From an economic point of view, this issue translates into the protection of the free market and free enterprise, with the collection of taxes being reduced to the minimum necessary. This understanding, that the value generated by the individual must remain with him, has a direct influence on the political vision of this group, especially regarding the size and functions of the State. As discussed by Gusfield (1972), the popularization of terms such as 'radical right' and 'right-wing extremism' are, at least partially, a consequence of republican senator Joseph McCarthy's (1908–1957) career (Lipset and Raab, 1971). Known by the name of McCarthyism, his virulent campaign against communism in the 1949–1950 biennium became famous for accusing various groups of directly or indirectly contributing to the progress of leftist ideology. This included press professionals, universities, the film industry, and even the federal administration of his country (Larrousse, 2022).

In the most extreme cases, one can find a defence of the total and absolute inexistence of public goods and services, as well as of the entire State bureaucracy. In these perspectives, the market should basically be the only rule for the functioning of economies, with all regulations on its functioning eliminated. At the limit, there would only be private properties, with individuals taking responsibility for all spheres of their existence, from education to security. From these views derive the most fervent arguments in defence of the possession and carrying of weapons by

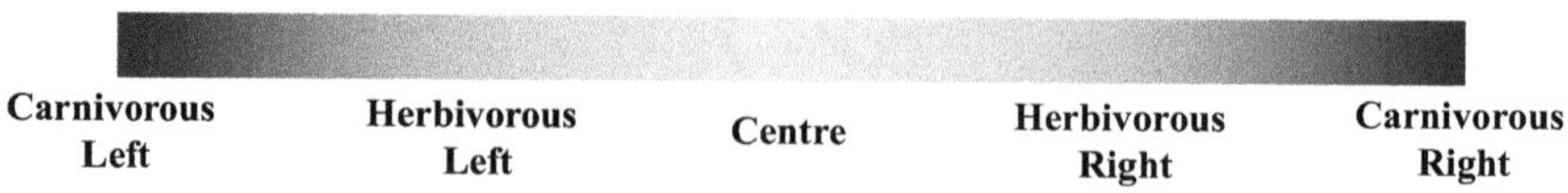

Figure 4.1 The Political-economic Spectrum

ordinary citizens, challenging the principle often adopted in accidental democracies that the state has a monopoly on the use of force. It should be noted, however, that the defence of the right of each individual to protect her/himself with the use of weapons is anchored in not only ideological issues, but also a skepticism built over the centuries under the observation that the State is often unable to provide the necessary security.

In face of these and other discussions conducted throughout the book, it seems plausible that ideologies may be damaging on both sides of the political-economic spectrum. In this sense, just as the search for an egalitarian society seems to be the utopia of the left, exaggerated faith in meritocracy may be seen as the utopia of the right, particularly because those in more advantaged stands are capable of protecting and often do protect their positions. Typically, this translates into distortions of competitive markets, which may make meritocratic dynamics unfeasible.

The Sustainability Spectrum

In the same way that different worldviews on politics and economics can be classified according to their level of adherence to a particular ideology (and consequently to their degree of radicalization), the understanding of issues related to sustainability can be ordered to reflect the degree of acceptance or rejection of the most commonly conveyed ideas in this sense. Given the close connection with ideological developments that debates on sustainable development seem to have, however, it can be argued that this variation does not occur independently, being to a certain extent conditioned to the views that originate or that somehow influence them. The *sustainability spectrum* (Figure 4.2), developed in the following, seeks to present a classification that allows for a better understanding of not only the different perspectives on the subject but also the connections with ideological issues. Based on the political-economic spectrum proposed earlier, this debate will seek to highlight the dynamics and gradations that connect its two extremes.

Eco-Revolutionaries

Generally adopting radical Marxist ideas, this group understands that a revolution either is justified by the deterioration of social and environmental conditions or is the only way to improve them. In the first case, they often point out capitalism as being responsible for both pollution and inequality and preach the destruction of this mode of production as a way of dealing with these problems. In the view of these groups, the search for economic profit would not represent a source of value

Figure 4.2 The Sustainability Spectrum

creation for society, but a vector of accelerated consumption of natural resources and a way of legitimizing relations of oppression, either through the establishment of organizational hierarchies or through the greater economic power that capital accumulation provides to the capitalist.

It is in the group of *eco-revolutionaries* that the greatest influence of leftist-oriented ideologies is perceived, to the point that, in some cases, it may be difficult to distinguish them from their real convictions regarding social and environmental aspects. It can be argued, therefore, that *eco-revolutionaries* instrumentalize sustainability issues in such a way that the apparent concern they show for these matters only serves as a facade for their real political and ideological agendas. This instrumentation is probably the biggest cause of the loss of credibility of issues related to sustainability, since its misuse is, in general, poorly disguised and ends up being easily perceived by other layers of society.

Furthermore, the exaggerations usually committed by *eco-revolutionaries* contribute to the ridicule of their arguments in favour of social and environmental agendas, as if they were liars in their entirety. Once again, the credibility of causes related to sustainability is undermined by their instrumentalization. Finally, the political use of social and environmental issues results in the deepening of the polarization of opinions, with opposing political groups. The difficulty in separating the real intentions of *eco-revolutionaries* from their discourses on sustainability leads opponents to reject everything they say, which often results in the repudiation of themes that are in fact relevant in this sense. In face of these and other issues, it can be said that the instrumentalization of themes linked to sustainability by revolutionaries represents one of the greatest threats to sustainable development.

Social/Environmental Warriors

This group seems generally to be made up of people who developed their convictions not through their own means, but rather through the various influences they suffered in the course of their lives. This includes information received from mass media (i.e., mainstream media), social relationship (e.g., family, friends), and, particularly important in that regard, the educational system. It can be argued, therefore, that *social/environmental warriors* are not, in general, primary thinkers. The long periods that these individuals spend immersed in hegemonic narratives contributes to the consolidation of their convictions, with the lack of access to contrary opinions reinforcing the perception that they belong to the correct side. The feeling that they defend a just cause and therefore deserve to be ardently safeguarded justifies their willingness to present themselves for the fight against opposing views, which can occur in the field of ideas or evolve into physical conflicts.

From this predisposition to confrontation comes the name of the group. Among the most evident characteristics of *social/environmental warriors* is what appears to be a sense of moral superiority in relation to other groups, especially those further to the right of the spectrum. In this sense, the defence of collectivist causes is understood as a necessary counterpoint to the selfishness of collectivists. This idea is diluted in basically all spheres of thought of those belonging to the group, so that they believe they are 'good' people, while those with whom they disagree (in general, individuals identified with the right) are mere propagators of mechanisms of oppression that would be the main cause of inequality. The latter would therefore be enemies of the good, which, in the view of social/environmental warriors, would justify their propensity to fight them.

The fact that they are not, in general, original thinkers favours the instrumentalization of these groups by others, so that they often end up being used as a mere manoeuvring mass. In these cases, they just echo the ideas they receive and, at the same time as they feel ennobled for fighting a fight they consider worthy, they are just being manipulated by political and economic interests. Like puppets or pawns on a chessboard, individuals belonging to these groups seem to be more likely to have their good intentions channelled to the defence of shady causes that, disguised as good intentions, end up attracting people who believe they are morally superior. The behaviour of *social/environmental warriors* also seems to be explained by the social pressure to which they are subjected, with the pillars of what is conventionally called the 'ideology of political correctness' playing an important role in this regard. As discussed, the neo-moralism embedded in contemporary leftist discourse appears to have a great impact on the behaviour and the ways of thinking of this group. With the elevation of the ideology of political correctness to a mainstream position in recent decades, individuals in this group found themselves in the need, even if unconsciously, to embrace certain causes and flags that increasingly came to be defended by their peers, especially in social and environmental issues.

Psychological and emotional aspects have a direct influence on this dynamic, with the search for acceptance and validation from others in their group (i.e., peers) being an important factor in determining individual behaviour, particularly among adolescents and young adults. This quest to adapt to the majority's discourse ends up shaping ways of thinking that can last for decades and even for the entire life of those of the components of this group. This intellectual construction of young people can, therefore, function as an important factor in electoral success, in both the short and long term. The focus of leftist movements on young people is thus justified. In addition to being more easily impressed by illusory, fanciful, and utopian discourses, they are more malleable and subject to the impositions of the environment that surrounds them. Being still vulnerable in several aspects (e.g., emotional, financial), the search for adaptation to group visions seems to be facilitated as a survival strategy, since the dilution of their individualities in a larger group reduces the chances that their weaknesses are exposed, and therefore become in some way targeted by other individuals in their environment. This social behaviour is probably a legacy of more primitive times, when the survival of vulnerable species depended on herd behaviour.

Eco-Moderates

Just as members of the centre of the political-economic spectrum tend to consider themselves equidistant from the extremes represented by the far-right and the far-left, the group of *eco-moderates* includes individuals who do not adhere to the radicalism of either apocalyptic or inflexible skepticism. Among the aspects favouring moderate positions, one can mention a detachment of ideologies, so that the members of this group should not see those who occupy positions further to the right or left of the spectrum as natural enemies. As discussed throughout the book, it is possible that this dissociation between environmental and ideological issues represents the most important condition for the maintenance of a productive dialogue. In this way, it is likely that someone identified as an *eco-moderate* will not feel threatened by pro- or anti-sustainability rhetoric at first, with the lack of any immediate emotion allowing this individual to focus on the real merit of the messages and arguments.

In addition to potentially resulting from greater sobriety and possibly greater emotional/intellectual maturity, *eco-moderate* positions can also be the result of other factors, being in some cases a reflection of a passive attitude towards the environmental debate. In this sense, individuals or groups understood to be indifferent are those who normally have no particular interest in the topic, often ignoring the more technical aspects of the discussions. The causes of this lack of interest can be the most diverse – it is possible, for example, that some individuals consciously seek to distance themselves from discussions on sustainability, precisely because they believe there is a contamination of the topics by political and economic interests. In these cases, the perception that the intentions of those who dedicate themselves to the theme are not genuine may contribute to the discrediting of their speeches, with the classification of these views as hypocritical, establishing a form of division between the interests that in fact deserve attention and those that should be ignored. As is the case with the other members of the silent majority, the *eco-moderate* group is usually important in electoral processes, with their adherence representing, in many cases, a decisive factor for the victory of ideological groups. The fact that they are not radically associated with a pre-defined set of ideas and visions makes them the target of more organized groups that, through narratives, seek to convince them to support certain causes.

Eco-Skepticals

Keeping with the idea that the *sustainability spectrum* descends from its political/economic equivalent, the *eco-skepticals* category bears similarities to the herbivorous right. As discussed, the members of this group are in one of the three intermediate positions of its respective spectrum, being, however, closer to the views of the carnivorous right than the to those of the left. The same occurs with the present category, which, despite being far from the extreme positions most associated with radical environmentalist thinking (i.e., *eco-revolutionaries*), still have a difference with those who maintain a posture that is absolutely contrary to their positions. As may be the case with their political/economical counterparts, *eco-skepticals* only partially identify with members of the most radical groups on the right, which increases their potential to play the role of actors in the dialogue.

As with the other categories, the fact that the members of the sustainability spectrum are not directly included in a dynamic of power can end up attenuating the nature of their relationships with other groups. Like the *eco-moderates*, one cannot initially speak of a physiologism, at least not on its classic manners. However, the power of pressure that *sustainability spectrum* groups can exert on the political class – and on society in general – cannot be ignored. It is not uncommon, for example, for the most radical to end up adhering to political campaigns and even boycotting companies and branding associated with environmental damage. Although these postures are apparently more common in positions closer to the other end of the spectrum, it cannot be said that similar behaviour cannot be assumed at any of the other points. Dynamics that aim to counterbalance the attitudes taken by *eco-revolutionaries* or even *social/environmental warriors* seem to be becoming increasingly common. As these groups organize to attack a particular organization, groups that do not identify with their positions also show signs of being willing not to interact with the organizations that support them.

In this vein, one could argue for the potential of physiological postures among the members of the *sustainability spectrum* as, occasionally, they may exchange their influence for the sake of any punctual interest. Evidently, this is not a 'privilege' of the *eco-skepticals*, with the same rationale being valid for all other positions. However, similarly to what happens in the political-economic spectrum, central positions may be more susceptible to this type of slip, precisely because they do not have ideological convictions, or because they express them in a more diluted way. Thus, it would be natural to assume that physiologism is more likely among *social/environmental warriors*, *eco-moderates*, and *eco-skepticals* than among members of the poles. By this reasoning, *eco-moderates* could be even more susceptible to these issues, precisely because they are at the furthest point from radicalism.

Eco-Refractory

Regarding issues related to sustainability, far-right thinking seems to be reflected in a form of repulsion towards socio-environmental issues, with the perception that these matters were instrumentalized by leftists, fuelling a refractory behaviour. As discussed earlier, in some cases it is possible to perceive a use of themes related to sustainability as a camouflage for totalitarian interests, which, in general, awakens in those who have a particularly dear value in individual freedom a kind of mental alarm that leads to rejecting everything associated with it. Thus, the members of this group seem to be convinced that they need to fight against the advances of communist ideology, which in some cases can explain more aggressive postures. Perhaps the most important feature of the thinking developed in this group is this confusion between environmentalism and ideology, with emotions occupying the space where rationality should reside.

It is possible that, in many cases, *eco-refractory* postures are not the consequence of a genuine contempt for the environment, or even a desire to destroy it. As discussed throughout the book, the appropriation of the environmental theme by politicians ends up contaminating the debate on sustainable development, precisely because the passions that are typical of ideological disputes are imported into this arena. Thus, it can be argued that the more aggressive postures regarding the denial of the environmental cause may be more associated with a fear – albeit unconscious – that the advance of environmental issues represents a threat to values dear to conservatives. This includes the notions of private property, family, and individual freedom. It is possible that the *eco-refractory* group has the most similarities with its equivalent on the political/economical spectrum, since, in the same way that left-wing ideologies mixed with sustainability issues, right-wing ideologies also seem to have advanced beyond their limits. One must also consider that some people may oppose the sustainability discussion for purely economic reasons. As discussed in Chapter 5, millions of people live in the Amazon forest and count on its resources to maintain their subsistence. These people may be more likely to refute claims of environment preservation, even if the damage they cause may end up destroying their means.

Final Considerations

On the limitations of the political-economic spectrum proposed, one must consider that it is based on a traditional classification, meaning that the five macro-groups discussed do not allow for a perception of all the possible variations between them. This may not be a problem in itself, as the purpose of this chapter is not to discuss political and economic ideologies in detail. Instead, the discussion of these questions aims to serve as a reference for the construction of the *sustainability spectrum* presented in the sequence. Just as it seems impossible to disassociate politics and economics, the understanding of positions regarding sustainability also seems to be intrinsically linked to them. The realization of this fact, however, does not generate much enthusiasm. If it is true that social and environmental issues cannot be treated in isolation, their association with financial interests and the search for power seems to be at the root of their fragility.

As denounced across the book, the capture of the sustainable development debate by candidates for elective positions tends to contribute to the radicalization of opposing sustainability positions, as political passions are imported. As a result, the belief in objective data about the use of natural resources and pollution, for example, ends up giving way to ideological convictions, with individuals supporting or refuting this information based on their most intimate worldviews. The result of this process is the favouring of extreme positions, with the exaggeration on the one hand being fought by an inflexible denial on the other. The 'adequacy' of social and environmental issues to the election deadlines also contributes to greater radicalization, while the links between sustainability and the search for gains in profitability contribute to the loss of credibility of the debate. These themes are taken up in later chapters.

It should also be remembered that the proposed debate is not exhaustive. The complexity of the themes does not allow the proper consideration of all its foundations in this space. Once again, it is worth noting that the debate on the political-economic spectrum here does not represent an end in itself, serving as a foundation for the proposition of the *sustainability spectrum* that follows it. Finally, it should be noted that the expression 'carnivorous left' is not a creation of the present authors, in the same way as the equivalents that follow it (i.e., herbivore left, herbivore right, and carnivorous right). These expressions have become popular among political commentators and have been uttered on several occasions. The origins are not known for sure. The same goes for terms such as *social/environmental* warriors that were also employed.

References

Abranches, S. (2018). *Presidencialismo de Coalizão: Raízes e Evolução do Modelo Político Brasileiro*. Editora Companhia das Letras.

Adam, D. (2013). Mental health: On the spectrum, *Nature*, Vol.496, pp.416–418.

Akiskal, H.S., and Pinto, O. (1999). The evolving bipolar spectrum: Prototypes I, II, III, and IV. *Psychiatric Clinics of North America*, Vol.22, No.3, pp.517–534.

Alexander, R.J. (1991). *International Trotskyism, 1929–1985: A Documented Analysis of the Movement*. Duke University Press.

Aupperle, R.L., Paulus, M.P., Kuplicki, R., Touthang, J., Victor, T., Yeh, H.W., Tulsa 1000 Investigators Tulsa 1000 Investigators, and Khalsa, S.S. (2020). Web-based graphic representation of the life course of mental health: Cross-sectional study across the spectrum of mood, anxiety, eating, and substance use disorders. *JMIR Mental Health*, Vol.7, No.1, p.e16919.

Baker, A., and Greene, K.F. (2011). The Latin American left's mandate: Free-market policies and issue voting in new democracies. *World Politics*, Vol.63, No.1, pp.43–77.

Barbieri, P. (2017). The death and life of social democracy. *Foreign Affairs*. Available at http://cf.linnbenton.edu/artcom/social_science/clarkd/upload/The%20Death%20and%20Life%20of%20Social%20Democracy.pdf

Beramendi, P., and Rueda, D. (2007). Social democracy constrained: Indirect taxation in industrialized democracies. *British Journal of Political Science*, Vol.37, No.4, pp.619–641.

Bernstein, T.P. (1984). Stalinism, famine, and Chinese peasants. *Theory and Society*, Vol.13, pp.339–377.

Boito Jr, A. (2007). Estado e burguesia no capitalismo neoliberal. *Revista de Sociologia e Política*, Vol.28, pp.57–73.

Brian, J.A., Zwaigenbaum, L., and Ip, A. (2019). Standards of diagnostic assessment for autism spectrum disorder. *Paediatrics & Child Health*, Vol.24, No.7, pp.444–451.

Britannica. (2007). *Leninism Summary*. Available at https://www.britannica.com/summary/Leninism

Cariello, R. (2005). Para fundação Perseu Abramo, a trasição da gestão FHC é limitada. *Folha de São Paulo*, February 3. Available at https://www1.folha.uol.com.br/fsp/brasil/fc0302200504.htm

Carrier, J.G. (Ed.) (2020). *Meanings of the Market: The Free Market in Western Culture*. Routledge.

Codato, A., Berlatto, F., and Bolognesi, B. (2018). Tipologia dos políticos de direita no Brasil. *Análise Social*, Vol.53, No.229(4), pp.870–897.

Cole, G.D.H. (2013). *Fabian Socialism*. Routledge.

Constantino, R. (2021a). *Uma ameaça Suprema à democracia brasileira*. Available at https://www.youtube.com/watch?v=weV6SDVx7YI

Constantino, R. (2021b). *FHC e Lula: Estratégia das tesouras. Gazeta do Povo*, May 24. Available at https://www.gazetadopovo.com.br/rodrigo-constantino/fhc-e-lula-estrategia-das-tesouras/

Cunha, E., and Cunha, D. (2021). *Tchau, Querida – O Diário do Impeachment*. Matrix.

Daniels, R.V. (1998). Leon Trotsky. *Britannica*. Available at https://www.britannica.com/biography/Leon-Trotsky

Danisch, R. (2015). *Building a Social Democracy: The Promise of Rhetorical Pragmatism*. Lexington Books.

Dorrien, G. (2019). *Social Democracy in the Making*. Yale University Press.

Ellman, M. (2014). *Socialist Planning*. Cambridge University Press.

Frank, M., and Fuentes, M. (2022). In Cuba's poorest neighborhoods, youths could face decades in jail after protests. *Reuters*, January 14. Available at https://www.reuters.com/world/americas/cubas-poorest-neighborhoods-youths-could-face-decades-jail-after-protests-2022-01-14/

Gaona, J.M. (2018). Democratic blending: The new model of dictatorships in Latin America. *Columbia Journal of International Affairs SIPA (June)*. Available at SSRN https://ssrn.com/abstract=3827589

Gentile, F. (2018). A direita brasileira em perspectiva histórica. *Plural*, Vol.25, No.1, pp.92–110.

Geyer, M., and Fitzpatrick, S. (2009). After totalitarism – Stalinism and Nazism compared. In: M. Geyer and S. Fitzpatrick (Eds.). *Beyond Totalitarianism: Stalinism and Nazism Compared*. Cambridge University Press.

Gidron, N. (2022). Many ways to be right: Cross-pressured voters in Western Europe. *British Journal of Political Science*, Vol.52, No.1, pp.146–161.

Gidron, N., and Ziblatt, D. (2019). Center-right political parties in advanced democracies. *Annual Review of Political Science*, Vol.22, pp.17–35.

Grzymala-Busse, A., and Luong, P.J. (2002). Reconceptualizing the state: Lessons from post-communism. *Political Theory*, Vol.30, No.4, pp.529–554.

Guan, Y., Gao, X., Li, F., Pei, S., Chen, F., and Zhou, Z. (2012). Modern human behaviors during the late stage of the MIS3 and the broad spectrum revolution: Evidence from a Shuidonggou Late Paleolithic site. *Chinese Science Bulletin*, Vol.57, No.4, pp.379–386.

Gusfield, J.R. (1972). Book review – the politics of unreason: Right-wing extremism in America, 1790–1970. *American Journal of Sociology*, Vol.78, No.1, pp.252–254.

Hargittai, E., Gallo, J., and Kane, M. (2008). Cross-ideological discussions among conservative and liberal bloggers. *Public Choice*, Vol.134, No.1–2, pp.67–86.

Hayek, F.A., Mises, L., Pierson, N.G., Halm, G., and Barone, E. (1935). *Collectivist Economic Planning*. London: Routledge and Kegan Paul Ltd.

Hedlund-de Witt, A. (2013). Worldviews and their significance for the global sustainable development debate. *Environmental Ethics*, Vol.35, No.2, pp.133–162.

Hess, D.J., and Maki, A. (2019). Climate change belief, sustainability education, and political values: Assessing the need for higher-education curriculum reform. *Journal of Cleaner Production*, Vol.228, pp.1157–1166.

Hess, D.J., and Renner, M. (2019). Conservative political parties and energy transitions in Europe: Opposition to climate mitigation policies. *Renewable and Sustainable Energy Reviews*, Vol.104, pp.419–428.

Hicks, A. (2018). *Social Democracy and Welfare Capitalism*. Cornell University Press.

Hughes, C.W., and Williams, S.D. (2010). The color of sea level: Importance of spatial variations in spectral shape for assessing the significance of trends. *Journal of Geophysical Research: Oceans*, Vol.115, pp.10048–10066.

Jackson, B. (2013). Social democracy. In: M. Freeden, L.T. Sargent, and M. Stears (Eds.). *The Oxford Handbook of Political Ideologies*, pp.348–363. Oxford University Press.

James, D. (2001). *Che Guevara: A Biography*. New York: Cooper Square Press.

Klitgaard, M.B. (2007). Why are they doing it? Social democracy and market-oriented welfare state reforms. *West European Politics*, Vol.30, No.1, pp.172–194.

Krause, S. (2000). The spirit of separate powers in Montesquieu. *The Review of Politics*, Vol.62, No.2, pp.231–265.

Larrousse (2022). Marccartisme. Available at: https://www.larousse.fr/dictionnaires/francais/maccartisme/48297#:~:text=%EE%A0%AC%20maccarthysme&text=Nom%20donn%C3%A9%20%C3%A0%20l'id%C3%A9ologie,de%20sympathies%20pour%20le%20communisme.

Latouche, M. (2019). Venezuela and its labyrinth: Institutional change and authoritarianism in twenty-first-century socialism. *Middle Atlantic Review of Latin American Studies*, Vol.3, No.2, pp.1–26.

Le Figaro (2008). L'hommage de Max Gallo à Jean-François Revel. *Le Figaro*, February 1. Available at https://www.lefigaro.fr/debats/2008/02/01/01005-20080201ART-FIG00001-l-hommage-de-max-galloa-jean-francois-revel.php

Lipset, S.M., and Raab, E. (1971). *The Politics of Unreason: Right-Wing Extremism in America, 1790–1970*. London: Heinemann.

Ljungqvist, F.C., Seim, A., Krusic, P.J., González-Rouco, J.F., Werner, J.P., Cook, E.R., Zorita, E., Luterbacher, J., Xoplaki, E., Destouni, G., García-Bustamante, E., Aguilar, C.A.M., Seftigen, K., Wang, J., Gagen, M.H., Esper, J., Solomina, O., Fleitmann, D., and Büntgen, U. (2019). European warm-season temperature and hydroclimate since 850 CE. *Environmental Research Letters*, Vol.14, No.8, p.084015.

Longo, M. (2003). European integration: Between micro-regionalism and globalism. *JCMS: Journal of Common Market Studies*, Vol.41, No.3, pp.475–494.

Lukes, S. (1971). The meanings of "individualism". *Journal of the History of Ideas*, Vol.32, No.1, pp.45–66.

Machado, E. (1987). O centro democrático do PMDB, enfim o resgate da legitimidade. *O Globo*, August 29. Available at https://www2.senado.leg.br/bdsf/handle/id/127348

Maddox, W.S., and Lilie, S.A. (1984). *Beyond Liberal and Conservative: Reassessing the Political Spectrum*. Cato Institute.

Malle, B.F. (2006). *How the Mind Explains Behavior: Folk Explanations, Meaning, and Social Interaction*. MIT Press.

Marshall, G. (1996). Was communism good for social justice? A comparative analysis of the two Germanies. *British Journal of Sociology*, Vol.47, No.3, pp.397–420.

Mavrakis, K. (2014). *On Trotskyism*. Routledge.

Maya, M.L. (2018). Populism, 21st-century socialism and corruption in Venezuela. *Thesis Eleven*, Vol.149, No.1, pp.67–83.

Menezes, L.M.B.R (2020). *Filosofia política: Perspectivas Pós Covid-19*. Bagai.

Morgan, J.H. (2005). *Naturally Good: A Behavioral History of Moral Development from Charles Darwin to EO Wilson*. Cloverdale Corporation.

Neumayer, E. (2004). Asylum destination choice: What makes some West European countries more attractive than others? *European Union Politics*, Vol.5, No.2, pp.155–180.

Oddi, G. (2014). Mapa de calor: Como atuam os candidatos ao meio-campo ofensivo da seleção de Felipão. *ESPN*, February 10. Available at https://www.espn.com.br/blogs/

gianoddi/388493_mapa-de-calor-como-atuam-os-candidatos-ao-meio-campo-ofensivo-da-selecao-de-felipao

Oliveira, S.A. (2020). A trapaça da esquerda com a 'estratégia das tesouras'. *Jornal da Cidade Online*, November 2. Available at https://www.jornaldacidadeonline.com.br/noticias/24302/a-trapaca-da-esquerda-com-a-equotestrategia-das-tesourasequot

Peffley, M., and Sigelman, L. (1990). Intolerance of communists during the McCarthy Era: A general model. *Western Political Quarterly*, Vol.43, No.1, pp.93–111.

Pessôa, S. (2015). Presidencialismo de coalizão ou de cooptação? *Revista Conjuntura Econômica*, Vol.69, No.1, pp.10–11.

Petrakov, N. (1993). The socialist idea and the economic failure of real socialism. *Problems of Economic Transition*, Vol.36, No.2, pp.6–22.

Pierson, C. (2012). *The Modern State*. Routledge.

Pondé, L.F.C.S. (2021). A indústria do bem. *Linhas Cruzadas*. Available at https://www.youtube.com/watch?v=YBmE_WhB0Qg&t=1142s

Przeworski, A. (1986). *Capitalism and Social Democracy*. Cambridge University Press.

Rachewsky, R. (2019). Entenda a diferença entre a esquerda carnívora e a vegetariana. *Instituto Liberal*, August 6. Available at https://www.institutoliberal.org.br/blog/politica/entenda-a-diferenca-entre-a-esquerda-carnivora-e-a-vegetariana/

Reuter, O.J., and Robertson, G.B. (2015). Legislatures, cooptation, and social protest in contemporary authoritarian regimes. *The Journal of Politics*, Vol.77, No.1, pp.235–248.

Rochester, J.M. (1990). Global policy and the future of the United Nations. *Journal of Peace Research*, Vol.27, No.2, pp.141–154.

Rohac, D. (2019). *In Defense of Globalism*. Rowman & Littlefield.

Santos, W.G. (2007). *Governabilidade e Democracia Natural*. FGV Editora.

Schlesinger, A.M. (1950). *The Vital Center: The Politics of Freedom*. Transaction Publishers.

Schuman, H., and Corning, A.D. (2000). Collective knowledge of public events: The Soviet era from the great purge to glasnost. *American Journal of Sociology*, Vol.105, No.4, pp.913–956.

SIC (2021). *Gouveia e Melo diz posicionar-se num 'centro pramático'*, December 21. Available at https://www.msn.com/pt-pt/noticias/ultimas/gouveia-e-melo-diz-posicionar-se-num-centro-pragm%C3%A1tico/vi-AAS4A0d

Shklar, J. (1987). Political theory and the rule of law. In: A.C. Hutchinson, and P. Monahan (Eds.). *The Rule of Law: Ideal or Ideology*, Carswell. pp.1–16.

Sollner, A. (1993). Totalitarismus: Eine notwendige Denkfigur des ¨ 20. Jahrhunderts. *Mittelweg*, Vol.36, No.2, pp.83–88.

Stalin, J. (2020). *The Foundations of Leninism*. Foreign Language Press.

Sütő, A. (1989). Singular continuous spectrum on a Cantor set of zero Lebesgue measure for the Fibonacci Hamiltonian. *Journal of Statistical Physics*, Vol.56, No.3, pp.525–531.

Tavares, J. (2021). Moro diz que há pessoas boas em todos os partidos, da esquerda ao centrão. *Folha de São Paulo*, November 21. Available at https://www1.folha.uol.com.br/poder/2021/11/moro-diz-que-ha-pessoas-boas-em-todos-os-partidos-da-esquerda-ao-centrao.shtml

Trotsky, L. (2019). *The Permanent Revolution*, pp.285–289. Routledge.

University of Colorado (2022). *Total Solar Irradiance Data*. Available at https://lasp.colorado.edu/home/sorce/data/tsi-data/

Van Hiel, A., Duriez, B., and Kussowska, M. (2006). The presence of left-wing authoritarianism in Western Europe and its relationship with conservative ideology. *Political Psychology*, Vol.27, No.5, pp.769–793.

Van Hiel, A., and Mervielde, I. (2003). The measurement of cognitive complexity and its relationship with political extremism. *Political Psychology*, Vol.24, No.4, pp.781–801.

Venaglia, G. (2020). O que é o centrão, o grupo que domina o Congresso e se aproximou de Bolsonaro. *CNN Brasil*, June 14. Available at https://www.cnnbrasil.com.br/politica/o-que-e-o-centrao-o-grupo-que-domina-o-congresso-e-se-aproximou-de-bolsonaro/

Veverka, J., Helfenstein, P., Lee, P., Thomas, P., McEwen, A., Belton, M., Klaasen, K., Johnson, T.V., Granahan, J., Fanale, F., Geissler, P., and Head III, J.W. (1996). Ida and Dactyl: Spectral reflectance and color variations. *Icarus*, Vol.120, No.1, pp.66–76.

Vianu, L. (1998). *Censorship in Romania*. Central European University Press.

Vreeland, J.R. (2008). Political institutions and human rights: Why dictatorships enter into the United Nations Conventions Against Torture. *International Organization*, Vol.62, No.1, pp.65–101.

Wallerstein, I. (1990). Marx, Marxism-Leninism, and socialist experiences in the modern world-system. *Thesis Eleven*, Vol.27, No.1, pp.40–53.

Xavier, F.H.Z., Silveira, L.M., Almeida, J.M., Ziviani, A., Malab, C.H., and Marques-Neto, H.T. (2013, July). Análise da Mobilidade Humana em Eventos de Larga Escala baseada em Chamadas de Telefones Celulares. In: *Anais do XL Seminário Integrado de Software e Hardware*, pp.272–283. SBC.

Yang, F. (2011). *Religion in China: Survival and Revival Under Communist Rule*. Oxford University Press.

Young, M. (2017). *The Rise of the Meritocracy*. Routledge.

Zmigrod, L. (2021). A neurocognitive modelo of ideological thinking. *Politics and the Life Sciences*, Vol.40, No.2, pp.224–238.

Zrinščak, S. (2004). Generations and atheism: Patterns of response to communist rule among different generations and countries. *Social Compass*, Vol.51, No.2, pp.221–234.

5 Skeptical Views of Sustainability

Skepticism and Denial

Despite having acquired a more negative connotation over the years (i.e., the absence of faith), skepticism represents a fundamental pillar in the development of the scientific process, in addition to acting as an important counterweight to the development of philosophical theories and concepts. In this sense, the fact that skeptics usually refuse to adhere not only to what is new, but to any current of thought, ends up representing a constant challenge to ideas, with the criticisms and objections raised by them functioning as ruthless scrutiny. In its most popular forms, the concept of skepticism is associated with a total or partial lack of belief in something. The skeptic is, therefore, the one who refuses – at least at first – to accept the veracity of ideas, narratives, and even events, if irrefutable evidence of this veracity is not presented to them. This behaviour manifests itself in different contexts, ranging from more every day and banal situations to philosophical debates. In the first group are the doubts of the average citizen about the honesty of politicians or even about the effectiveness of vaccines. In these cases, low levels of transparency, hearsay, or even a lack of scientific consensus can give the skeptic the perception that the matter is dubious. This lack of faith can be decisive for the discrediting of public policies, state institutions, or even systems of government (i.e., representative democracy). In the second group are the confrontations of more complex ideas and premises. Korsgaard (1986, p.5), for example, questions the main pillars of the Kantian approach to moral philosophy. In that regard, the scholar raises 'doubts about the extent to which human action is or could possibly be directed by reason' (i.e., skepticism about practical reason).

Differentiating the different forms of skepticism is fundamental for understanding the different ways in which the term can be applied. In addressing this issue, the *Stanford Encyclopaedia of Philosophy* (2008) distinguishes between ordinary incredulity and philosophical skepticism. Accordingly, ordinary incredulity refers to those cases in which the alleged grounds for doubt are false, or it may be shown that, despite being true, they can be neutralized (Lehrer, 2000). Ordinary incredulity is, then, based on the contrast of something with a background of beliefs, with skeptics not doubting to have knowledge of the world. In this set, the sheer existence of a doubt assumes that there are ways of removing it (Wittgenstein,

DOI: 10.4324/9781003124719-6

1969). In turn, philosophical skepticism seeks to 'render doubtful every member of a class of propositions that we think falls within our ken' (Stanford Encyclopedia of Philosophy, 2008). Yet, the members of the class shall not be confronted with one another, as both the grounds for asserting that one has such knowledge and denying it are such that it is not possible to answer or neutralize them by referring to another member of the class. In opposition to ordinary doubts/skepticism, philosophical doubt, in principle, would not come to an end. Differently put, philosophical skepticism questions the ordinary assumption that there is available evidence that may be useful in one's search to discriminate between the real world and a possible false one.

From the point of view of the history of philosophy, the origin of skepticism dates back to Greek antiquity (Pondé, 2016). Accordingly, the skeptics of this early period – within the Sextus Empiricus tradition – privileged the confrontation of opposing theories, so that they became invalid. The main objective of this opposition of ideas was to establish the impossibility of reaching a final judgement on things, leaving doubt or uncertainty about the nature of issues of great complexity. In this way, the skeptic would assume a position of superiority in relation to all forms of belief, both positive and negative. This state of apathy would free him, therefore, from the suffering common to those who believe in something. So-called academic skepticism (derived from the Platonic academy), in turn, would tend to deny the possibility of knowledge.

Still after Pondé, the evolution of skepticism in the history of philosophy would refer to the contributions of authors such as Michel de Montaigne (1533–1592) in the 14th century and David Hume (1711–1776) in the 18th century. While the former would be associated with a more melancholic or even depressed skepticism, the latter is linked to a distrust of the idea of reason, with a strong questioning of cause and effect relationships. More recently, skepticism has migrated to a form of scientism, with the common understanding that the contemporary skeptic is one who believes in and only in science, which is one of the main meanings of common sense. Hungarian American author Carl Sagan (1934–1996) would be one of the main advocates of the association between skepticism and science.

Pondé (2016) summarizes the debate by pointing out that there is no consensus on what it means to be skeptical, but the attempt by the Greek tradition to transform skepticism into a method of demonstrating the unsustainability of theories is possibly the most interesting path. In this set, the skeptic would be someone distant from both religious beliefs and the idea that science is capable of providing definitive answers. The skeptic's perception that s/he does not enjoy certainty about anything would lead her/him to value established habits, and this dynamic is responsible, at least partially, for the migration of 19th-century English skepticism – personified in Hume's work – to a more conservative political position. In general, this tendency of skeptics towards conservatism would be based on the judgement that proven habits are more valuable than ideas, with skepticism becoming a way of life, or a way of approaching the different situations that present themselves. However, more than a philosophical conviction, the adoption of a skeptical stance would also depend on issues related to the personality of individuals, with the most blasé profiles and/or those who do not need to reach definitive answers to the problems being the most adaptable.

Skepticism and Practice: Impacts on the Sustainability Debate

In addition to the philosophical debate about the nature and evolution of skepticism in the history of thought, consideration of its practical effects is particularly important. The lack of belief in something or the difficulty in trusting the statements or propositions made by others can have a very negative effect, especially in emergency situations. The lack of time to assess a situation can lead the skeptic to develop a kind of paralysis, without being able to take the necessary actions to preserve her/his life or her/his safety in time. This appears to be the case of situations where natural disasters are predicted, including storms and hurricanes. Decision making (e.g., evacuating the places that should be affected) fundamentally depends on the credibility of the sender, with belief in what s/he says being the only parameter sustaining the value of her/his message. On occasions like this, individuals who do not believe in the veracity of the alert may not take the necessary measures in time, which can harm their chances of survival. When this simplistic example is carried over into the sustainability debate, it helps us to understand the dynamics that lead some people to ignore everything or anything that points to deteriorating environmental conditions. As discussed throughout the book, issues related to environmental preservation are not usually treated in an isolated or specific way. In fact, issues such as air and sea pollution, basic sanitation, and global warming are often part of the arguments of politicians, whether they are elected or campaigning. If, on the one hand, the involvement of the political class in the environmental debate can be fruitful in many ways, it is not uncommon for these issues to be used only as a way to garner popular support. The perception that the environmental engagement of some public figures is not sincere can lead to a decrease in the credibility of their messages with the public. In the same way that disbelief in an announcement of an environmental catastrophe will prevent the skeptic from acting on her/his own behalf, distrust in the sincerity of the messenger (i.e., politicians) may lead her/him to consider honest mistakes (i.e., made in good faith) as additional evidence of lack virtue.

The opportunistic use of the environmental cause by the members of the political class can be considered one of the biggest problems for the implementation of a mature and productive debate on sustainable development. This is due to the fact that the association of controversial characters with arguments in favour of sustainability ends up causing a type of deviation of purpose. In this sense, the objective consideration of points relevant to the environment gives rise to a sort of popularity contest in which those who are sympathetic to the politician in question will tend to support what s/he preaches, while those who are opposed to her/him will have to extend their opinion to everything s/he expresses. This confusion between messenger and message is quite pernicious because, in addition to contaminating the environmental debate with the passions that are inherent to politics, it often ends the discussion before it even starts. This dynamic presents a considerable risk for the establishment of a dialogue, favouring the isolation of groups that have different opinions. The lack of contact between opposing views and the consequent absence of contradictory ones increases the chance of radicalization, with contact limited to those who think alike eventually validating radical positions. It can be argued, therefore, that the appropriation of the environmental debate by the political class can be quite harmful, especially when this association has an electoral purpose. However, it is not possible to generalize the behaviour of politicians, since many might identify with issues related to sustainability and seek to participate in the democratic game to contribute to the progress of the preservation of natural resources. Likewise, the association of politics with the environmental agenda should not be automatically condemned, since this is the way in which issues relevant to a society are addressed in representative democracies. What is highlighted here is the need to pay attention to the opportunistic use of the environmental cause, as well as its instrumentalization.

If it is true that the association between sustainable development and opportunistic politicians can undermine belief in the urgency of environmental problems, the ideologization of sustainability can have an even more devastating impact on the credibility of these issues among the population. In this set, the apparent contrast between the preservation of natural resources and economic growth has led many to believe that environmentalism is opposed to the basic mechanisms of functioning of capitalism and is, therefore, a kind of disguise used by leftists to advance their schedule. The arguments defended by more radical environmentalists are particularly important in this direction, with the defence of partial or total interruption of economic activities as a way of protecting the environment fuelling speculation. Discussions about the best ways to promote the preservation of the Amazon rainforest illustrate this point, as many environmentalists argue that the forest should remain in its natural state, with human activity restricted to the subsistence of indigenous peoples. This would be limited to hunting, fishing, and extractive activities, with the sole objective of guaranteeing the survival of the way of life of these groups. Other economic activities, such as mining, wood production, or even the cultivation of crops, would be prohibited.

This radical view seems to be quite common among those who have never visited the Amazon rainforest and who discuss the best way to preserve it thousands of kilometres away in offices, radio and TV studios, and universities in developed countries. In general, those who defend the maintenance of the Amazon rainforest in its raw state ignore that about 29 million people inhabit the Brazilian part of the region (Oliveira, 2020), either in isolated, medium, or large cities. The city of Manaus, for example, has a population of about 2.3 million inhabitants. Located in the heart of the Amazon rainforest, the capital of the state of Amazonas presents basically all the challenges typical of urban areas, including basic sanitation, education, security, mobility, and employment, among many others. Despite being surrounded by the forest, the inhabitants of Manaus have a life very similar to that of those who live in other Brazilian cities and, in a certain sense, to that of the inhabitants of cities in developed countries in Europe and North America. Further

Table 5.1 Largest Cities in the Brazilian Amazon

City	*Estimated Population (2021)*
Manaus	2,255,903
Belém	1,506,420
Porto Velho	548,952
Macapá	522,357
Boa Vista	436,591
Rio Branco	419,452
Palmas	313,349

Source: IBGE (2021a, 2021b, 2021c, 2021d, 2021e, 2021f, 2021g, respectively)

east, the city of Belém (capital of the state of Pará) has similar characteristics, being the second most important urban agglomeration in the region. Its population of about 1.5 million inhabitants faces similar challenges to the population of Manaus, with the same occurring in other cities in the Amazon region. Table 5.1 shows the population of the largest cities located in the Brazilian Amazon.

In terms of territorial extension, the large area over which the Brazilian Amazon extends also contributes to its complexity. The Brazilian part of the forest alone has an approximate area of more than 5 million km², corresponding to about 58.9% of the country's territory (IBGE, 2021h). As discussed earlier, many people ignore the fact that the Amazon has a relatively large population, which favours the formation of unrealistic opinions about the most appropriate ways to protect it. It is unreasonable, for example, to suggest the interruption of economic activities in the region and a full return to its previous state. This proposition seems even more absurd when the history of colonization of the region is taken into account. It must be remembered that the people who live there have needs similar to those presented by citizens from any other region of the world, with economic development being, probably, the most efficient way to guarantee them an improvement in their living conditions. In this sense, one must consider that a significant part of the Amazonian population lives in very precarious conditions, in many cases approaching a situation of misery (G1, 2020). It can be argued, therefore, that the interruption or reduction of economic activities in the region has important practical consequences, dealing a severe blow to the most vulnerable people.

Given this scenario, it is clear that the Amazon region represents, perhaps, the most complete example of the real challenges of sustainable development. This is equivalent to saying that issues related to the region cannot be examined only through the environmental prism, with social and economic issues deserving the same consideration. Once again, Elkington's (1997) triple bottom line draws attention to this need. As discussed, the focus on purely environmental aspects can be harmful to local populations, with reduced economic activities directly impacting the quality of their lives. At the same time, environmental preservation cannot be ignored, leaving the challenge of balancing all these issues. The search for alternatives to generate value that do not compromise environmental preservation continues to be the main objective of those truly concerned with the social aspects of sustainability. From a consequentialist point of view, it could be argued that too much focus on environmental aspects is just as damaging as too much focus on economics. While the latter can in fact compromise environmental preservation when carried out without due care, the search for absolute environmental preservation can result in serious social problems. It is true that this argument may sound too aggressive in the ears of people used to the idea that the defence of nature is an absolute priority, and that the search for economic development is something inherently harmful to this end. These visions are, however, not only innocent but also dangerous, as they can condemn millions of people to a miserable life.

Regarding the impact of these issues on the development of more skeptical views on environmental problems, it should be taken into account that people who know the social reality of places like the Amazon will tend to refute the idea that environmental preservation should be pursued at any cost, precisely because they know the side effects of these measures on the quality of life of local populations. Contrary to what many people may believe, individuals who defend the economic development of forest regions are not necessarily preaching their destruction, but rather seeking to allow the people who live there to sustain themselves in a dignified way. It is not uncommon for those who advocate for the sustainable exploitation of nature to be classified as enemies of the environment and, therefore, deserving of all kinds of censorship and attacks from those who never wanted to have contact with jungle areas or other more remote places. Evidently, people genuinely concerned with social aspects should not be confused with those who only aim to explore the potential for generating wealth in areas such as the Amazon to the detriment of environmental preservation. Efforts in this direction must be fought, so that natural resources are not destroyed or compromised in the name of purely economic aspects. This distinction is fundamental for the re-establishment of the dialogue between environmentalists and those who, despite seeming to want to destroy the planet's forests, are in fact seeking to assert the needs of people who may be impacted by eventual imbalances, among which the search for environmental preservation at the cost of people's quality of life. The solution to these dilemmas involves a greater understanding of the broader meaning of sustainability by all sides involved in the public debate.

Another aspect of this apparent dichotomy between environmental preservation and social development that has been little explored refers to the living conditions of the indigenous people who inhabit areas of native forest in the Amazon. This question introduces an additional component to the debate, with the search for the preservation of the original ways of life of these people and their cultures increasing the complexity of the issues surrounding the economic development of the regions where they live. While many argue that indigenous people should have access to the same possibilities offered to other Brazilian citizens, others argue that their ancestral way of life must be preserved as a manner of perpetuating their beliefs, traditions, and languages, among other cultural aspects. The first group points to the benefits of greater integration of indigenous people into economic and social life, including greater access to education and health care. Furthermore, the possibility for native people to economically exploit forest zones through activities such as agriculture, livestock, and mining would allow them to have access to all the material comforts provided by capitalism such as automobiles, appliances, and electronic equipment (e.g., computers, smartphones, televisions).

The second group, however, argues that this contact with society would lead to a dilution of the culture of these people, representing a threat to their very existence. These arguments seem to be built on the premise that indigenous people do not want to enjoy material goods or have access to wealth – including cultural – created by modern societies. While it is true that many indigenous people wish to maintain their traditional ways of life, others would prefer to integrate, starting with the development of economic activities in the areas they occupy. From a certain point of view, the exclusion of indigenous people from the social system in force in the rest of the country can be understood as cruel for individuals from these groups who would like to live differently. Often, the lack of prospects creates serious problems in the most isolated communities, with cases of alcoholism and violence being relatively common among them.

These are just some of the problems arising from the neglect of social aspects to the detriment of environmental ones. Critics of these more acute forms of indigenous isolationism accuse their defenders of promoting a harmful anthropological experience, in which indigenous people would be kept separate from the rest of the world for observation purposes and, as damning as it may seem, even to training. The terrifying expression 'human zoo' has been increasingly used to describe indigenous isolation. Undoubtedly, the relationship between economic development, environmental protection, and the quality of life of indigenous people represents one of the most complex issues to be addressed in the debate on sustainability. As discussed earlier, the opposition of many environmentalists to the economic development of the Amazon region ends up reinforcing an opposition to their ideas, as they are understood as expressions of their leftism. Among other consequences, that would trigger mistrust from those identified with a right-wing mindset, constituting one of the main causes of environmental skepticism. In addition to understanding that environmentalism serves as a pretext to fight the market economy, many skeptics are convinced that the appeals in defence of the forest are only intended to prevent Brazilians from benefiting from its natural resources, which are reserved for foreign exploration in the future. The demarcation of indigenous lands, for example, is seen as one of the means by which natural resources would be protected from exploitation. The idea that the Amazon will one day be internationalized (i.e., it will cease to be a sovereign territory of Brazil and other Amazonian countries to become a heritage of all nations) also contributes to the opposition to its preservation.

The demarcation of indigenous lands also receives criticism on this issue, with the initiative being understood as an embryo of future sovereign nations (Albert, 1991). According to some skeptics, the division of the Amazon would take place with the various indigenous lands claiming their independence. The purpose of this breach of sovereignty would be to allow these hypothetical nations to negotiate the exploitation of resources present in their territories directly with foreign countries (Medrado, 2011). In addition to finally allowing developed nations to appropriate the wealth of the Amazon, this move would prevent this from taking place through a military dispute with countries in the region, which could be very costly. Still, one of the issues that leads some conservatives to oppose measures to contain the economic and social development of the Amazon is the idea that the many non-governmental organizations (NGOs) operating in the region are representing the interests of foreign groups that seek to access the region's resources. This mistrust is reinforced by the fact that many of these NGOs are directly or indirectly financed by governments, companies, or individuals from other countries (Marcovitch and Pinsky, 2020).

Episodes involving heads of state and authorities from European countries reinforce the theses that the Amazon is at the centre of attention of foreign economic powers, one of the most curious dealing with the discovery of the presence of the king of Norway, Harald V (1937–) in an Yanomami tribe (G1, 2013). More recently, the statements of French President Emmanuel Macron (1977–) rekindled the debate about a possible internationalization of the Amazon, as well as the misuse of the environmental cause as a means to achieve this end. Among Macron's main manifestations in this regard, one of his posts on social media stands out, in which he writes 'Our house is burning. Literally. The Amazon rain forest – the lungs which produces 20% of our planet's oxygen – is on fire' (NPR, 2019), in reference to a specific period when a relatively higher volume of fires was being recorded in the region. The statement was accompanied by a photo of a fire registered at least 16 years earlier by American photojournalist Loren McIntyre (1917–2003) (France 24, 2019). The French president's words caused indignation in many Brazilians, who identified a disrespect for Brazil's sovereignty in his words (Gaier and Stargardter, 2019).

Among the most outraged was Brazilian President Jair Messias Bolsonaro (1955–), who responded firmly, defending Brazilian sovereignty over the entire territory of the country with vehemence (Mazui, 2019). The arguments between the two presidents evolved in a very inelegant fashion, with Macron even accusing Bolsonaro of being a liar (Le Monde, 2019), and the latter claiming that the wife of his French counterpart, First Lady Brigitte Macron (1953–), would be an ugly woman (Nikolic, 2019). The exchange of insults did not cause a diplomatic crisis between the two countries but inaugurated a new type of public relationship between heads of state. Traditionally marked by great courtesy and respect for diplomatic rites, the barter between presidents, prime ministers, and even kings tends to be a friendly contact in which the specific interests of each party are discussed, so that the long-term relationship of nations is ideally strengthened (Lafer, 2018). In the case of the exchange of insults between the presidents of Brazil and France, what was seen was just the opposite. The perception that Macron was not sincerely concerned about forest preservation increased with the circulation of his defence of gold mining in French Guiana, a French Amazon territory that borders Brazil (Farand, 2018). At the time, he declared that the project could be good for Guiana (Marot, 2017). The contradictory stance of the French president is quite harmful to the debate on sustainability, as it reinforces the arguments of those who say they see these efforts as ulterior motives, with the search for the implementation of sustainable development being nothing more than a façade for the advancement of economic goals or power. Furthermore, the excessive involvement of politicians in the discussion of these issues ends up contributing to a polarization of the discussions, with the formation of opposing sides having more to do with the level of sympathy of voters for those who claim to be defenders of nature than with the issues specific to environmental preservation.

Skepticism also seems to be a consequence of companies misusing the environmental cause. In this sense, the perception that messages sent to the public are not sincere can result in the loss of credibility of organizations and, consequently, disbelief in the causes they claim to defend. Particularly important in this regard is the detachment between discourse and practice, with the creation of false social and environmental reputations (Fracarolli Nunes and Lee Park, 2017) being one of the major causes of compromise or destruction of stakeholders' beliefs. In fact, the sources of corporate hypocrisy (Wagner et al., 2009) seem to be abundant in the relationship that companies maintain with environmental causes. The many forms of greenwashing (Ramus and Montiel, 2005), for example, are important factors in this regard, especially when the defence of theoretically sustainable methods is perceived as a mere disguise for the pursuit of profit maximization.

These questions present themselves in the most varied forms, with so-called iceberg strategies (Fracarolli Nunes and Lee Park, 2021) being one of the most common. Accordingly, this refers to practices in which the part of a business that is apparent to stakeholders (e.g., consumers, investors) is sustainable, while the non-sustainable part remains hidden. As with most icebergs, the visible portion is usually relatively small compared to what remains out of sight. A classic example of these strategies is the use of environmentally friendly vehicles (e.g., bicycles, electric cars, trucks powered by biomethane) to deliver products in large urban centres. The use of a sustainable operation in the last mile of delivery would have the objective of camouflaging the entire environmental impact related to the transport process as a whole, usually carried out with traditional vehicles powered by diesel or other fossil fuels (e.g., gasoline, kerosene). This includes planes, ships, and trucks. The issue becomes even more complex due to the long distances travelled by a large number of products, mainly by those that are produced in countries considered as low-labour cost zones and consumed in developed countries (Fredriksson and Jonsson, 2009). It is common for logistics processes in these cases to involve several steps as factories, warehouses, ports, and airports connect. All these factors contribute to the high environmental impact of these alternative business models. More recently, some of the instruments of what is conventionally called green finance (Taghizadeh-Hesary and Yoshino, 2019) have also been included in the category of potential instruments used to create environmental reputations that are inconsistent with the operational practice of companies. Green bonds (Flammer, 2021), for example, have been considered by some stakeholders to be a problematic product in this sense, as their association with a specific project to be financed by them does not eliminate other practices that may be harmful to the environment.

In addition to the feeling that environmental issues serve as a backdrop for the advancement of other interests, many skeptics base their disbelief on scientific data. Contrary to what exaggerated versions and stereotypes might lead you to believe, most skeptics are not flat-earthers, nor do they even question that the temperature in different regions of the planet has been increasing in recent years. For much of this group, global warming is not under suspicion, but rather the extent to which it is caused by human activities (Cook et al., 2016). In many cases, this translates into the argument that the increase in temperature would be part of a natural dynamics of the planet, with issues related to the emission of polluting gases having little or no participation in this process (Whitmarsh, 2009). Among the scientific data supporting this hypothesis is evidence that the planet has experienced a significant variation on its temperatures since a remote past, and long before the very existence of human beings (Frakes, 1986). Another scientific argument widely used by skeptics points to the oscillations of the sun's magnetic activity as a main source of temperature increases on Earth (Parker, 1999). Even some alternatives seen as environmentally superior are considered as potential causes of global warming. This is the case with solar panels that, according to some skeptics, cause the planet's temperature to rise precisely by creating extra shades that, ironically, may cause temperatures to raise (Chen, 2015), or by retaining part of the energy that would naturally be reflected (Lu and Smith, 2021). Likewise, the fact that the most catastrophic environmental predictions of the past (i.e., between the end of the 20th century and the beginning of the 21st century) have proved to be extremely inaccurate (Freeman, 2017) renews the perception that the new predictions also represent exaggerations. The projections of melting polar ice caps and rising sea levels popularized by former US Vice President Al Gore (1948–) were particularly damaging in this regard.

What can be seen is that environmental skepticism results from a series of factors, with the understanding of its origins demanding the consideration of themes that go far beyond the debate on the preservation of nature. The points raised in the chapter aim to offer the reader a better understanding of the reasons why someone assumes a behaviour that is refractory to issues related to the environment. The exposition of these points is important so that prejudiced views are undone, facilitating the reopening of the dialogue. Of particular importance is the understanding that people who think differently are not necessarily unreasonable. As discussed, in many cases environmental skepticism is based on issues that are not directly linked to the preservation of the environment, with repulsion to proposals for the preservation of natural resources and nature in general being a side effect arising from conflicts in other dimensions of social life. Political and ideological disagreements play a particularly important role in this regard. Likewise, distrust of business activities reinforces the idea that environmentalism represents a way of advancing secondary interests. The main contribution of the debate proposed here is, therefore, an alert to the need to know the way of thinking of those who are skeptical, as well as to the urgency of treating environmentalism in a more objective way, ideally dissociated from hidden interests. It is hoped that developments in this direction will facilitate exchanges between environmentalists and skeptics, and that, through the re-establishment of a mature dialogue, sustainable development can be decisively advanced.

References

Albert, B. (1991). Terras indígenas, política ambiental e geopolítica militar no desenvolvimento da Amazônia: A propósito do caso Yanomami. *Amazônia: A Fronteira Agrícola*, Vol.20, pp.37–58.

Chen, S. (2015). Solar panel shade won't cool Earth. *Science*, November 2. Available at https://www.science.org/content/article/solar-panel-shade-won-t-cool-earth#:~:text=Solar%20panels%20fight%20global%20warming,shade%20Earth%20from%20the%20sun.&text=It's%20not%20quite%20that%20simple,actually%20make%20some%20locales%20hotter

Cook, J., Oreskes, N., Doran, P.T., Anderegg, W.R., Verheggen, B., Maibach, E.W., Carlton, J.S., Lewandowsky, S., Skuce, A.G., Green, S.A., Nuccitelli, D., Jacobs, P., Richardson, M., Winkler, B., Painting, R., and Rice, K. (2016). Consensus on consensus: A synthesis of consensus estimates on human-caused global warming. *Environmental Research Letters*, Vol.11, No.4, p.048002.

Farand, C. (2018). Paris to decide fate of 'mega' gold mine in forests of French Guiana. *The Guardian*, April 27. Available at https://www.theguardian.com/environment/2018/apr/27/paris-to-decide-fate-of-mega-gold-mine-in-forests-of-french-guiana

Flammer, C. (2021). Corporate green bonds. *Journal of Financial Economics*, forthcoming. https://doi.org/10.1016/j.jfineco.2021.01.010

Fracarolli Nunes, M., and Lee Park, C. (2017). Self-claimed sustainability: Building social and environmental reputations with words. *Sustainable Production and Consumption*, Vol.11, pp.46–57.

Fracarolli Nunes, M., and Lee Park, C. (2021). Not a "privilege": Environmental fraud beyond the automotive industry. In: M. Fracarolli Nunes and C. Lee Park (Eds.). *Business Ethics and Environmental Fraud*, pp.159–183. Cham: Palgrave Macmillan.

Frakes, L.A. (1986). Mesozoic-Cenozoic climatic history and causes of the glaciation. *Mesozoic and Cenozoic Oceans*, Vol.15, pp.33–48.

France 24 (2019). *Amazon Fires: How Celebrities Are Spreading Disinformation*, August 23. Available at https://www.france24.com/en/20190823-amazon-fires-how-celebrities-are-spreading-disinformation

Fredriksson, A., and Jonsson, P. (2009). Assessing consequences of low-cost sourcing in China. *International Journal of Physical Distribution & Logistics Management*, Vol.39, No.3, pp.227–249.

Freeman, J. (2017). What else did Al Gore get wrong? *The Wall Street Journal*, July 25. Available at https://www.wsj.com/articles/what-else-did-al-gore-get-wrong-1501021804

G1 (2013). *Rei da Noruega passa quatro dias em aldeia yanomami na Amazônia*. Available at https://g1.globo.com/mundo/noticia/2013/05/rei-da-noruega-passa-4-dias-em-aldeia-yanomami-na-amazonia.html

G1 (2020). *Mais de 47% da população do AM vive abaixo da linha de pobreza, aponta IBGE*, November 18. Available at https://g1.globo.com/am/amazonas/noticia/2020/11/18/mais-de-47percent-da-populacao-do-am-vive-abaixo-da-linha-de-pobreza-aponta-ibge.ghtml

Gaier, R.V., and Stargardter, G. (2019). Brazilians support Bolsonaro after Macron's 'offense': Minister. *Reuters*, August 28. Available at https://www.reuters.com/article/us-brazil-politics-araujo-idUSKCN1VI2FE

IBGE (2021a). *Instituto Brasileiro de Geografia e Estatística – Manaus*. Available at https://cidades.ibge.gov.br/brasil/am/manaus/panorama

IBGE (2021b). *Instituto Brasileiro de Geografia e Estatística – Belém*. Available at https://cidades.ibge.gov.br/brasil/pa/belem/panorama

IBGE (2021c). *Instituto Brasileiro de Geografia e Estatística – Porto Velho*. Available at https://cidades.ibge.gov.br/brasil/ro/porto-velho/panorama

IBGE (2021d). *Instituto Brasileiro de Geografia e Estatística – Macapá*. Available at https://cidades.ibge.gov.br/brasil/ap/macapa/panorama

IBGE (2021e). *Instituto Brasileiro de Geografia e Estatística – Boa Vista*. Available at https://cidades.ibge.gov.br/brasil/rr/boa-vista/panorama

IBGE (2021f). *Instituto Brasileiro de Geografia e Estatística – Rio Branco*. Available at https://cidades.ibge.gov.br/brasil/ac/rio-branco/panorama

IBGE (2021g). *Instituto Brasileiro de Geografia e Estatística – Palmas*. Available at https://cidades.ibge.gov.br/brasil/to/palmas/panorama

IBGE (2021h). *Instituto Brasileiro de Geografia e Estatística – Amazônia Legal*. Available at https://www.ibge.gov.br/geociencias/informacoes-ambientais/geologia/15819-amazonia-legal.html

Korsgaard, C.M. (1986). Skepticism about practical reason. *The Journal of Philosophy*, Vol.83, No.1, pp.5–25.

Lafer, C. (2018). *Relações Internacionais, Política Externa e Diplomacia Brasileira. Pensamento e Ação*, Vol.1. Fundação Alexandre de Gusmão.

Lehrer, K. (2000). *Theory of Knowledge*, 2nd edition. Westview Press.

Le Monde (2019). *Climat: Macron accuse Bolsonaro d'avoir « menti » et s'oppose au traité entre l'UE et le Mercosur*, August 23. Available at https://www.lemonde.fr/international/article/2019/08/23/macron-accuse-bolsonaro-d-avoir-menti-sur-le-climat-et-s-oppose-au-traite-entre-l-union-europeenne-et-le-mercosur_5502068_3210.html

Lu, Z., and Smith, B. (2021). Solar panels in Sahara could boost renewable energy but damage the global climate – here's why. *The Conversation*, February 11. Available at https://theconversation.com/solar-panels-in-sahara-could-boost-renewable-energy-but-damage-the-global-climate-heres-why-153992

Marcovitch, J., and Pinsky, V. (2020). Bioma Amazônia: Atos e fatos. *Estudos Avançados*, Vol.34, pp.83–106.

Marot, L. (2017). Emmanuel Macron: Le projet Montagne d'or 'peut être bon pour la Guyane'. *France Info*, October 31. Available at https://la1ere.francetvinfo.fr/guyane/emmanuel-macron-projet-montagne-peut-etre-bon-guyane-527465.html

Mazui, G. (2019). Bolsonaro diz que Macron terá de retirar 'insultos' antes de o Brasil aceitar dinheiro para Amazônia. *G1*, August 27. Available at https://g1.globo.com/politica/noticia/2019/08/27/bolsonaro-diz-que-macron-tera-de-retirar-insultos-antes-do-brasil-aceitar-dinheiro-do-g20-para-amazonia.ghtml

Medrado, V.S. (2011). O meio ambiente à luz dos interesses internacionais no Brasil particularmente na Amazônia. *Revista Paradigma*, Vol.20.

Nikolic, I. (2019). Brazilian government minister calls Brigitte Macron 'truly ugly' just days after the country's president slammed the French First Lady for her looks and its tourism ambassador called her a 'dragon'. *Dailymail*, September 6. Available at https://www.dailymail.co.uk/news/article-7434487/Brazilian-government-minister-calls-Brigitte-Macron-truly-ugly.html

NPR (2019). *Macron Urges G-7 Members to Put Amazon Fires at Top of Agenda*, August 23. Available at https://www.npr.org/2019/08/23/753639869/macron-urges-g7-members-to-put-amazon-fires-at-top-of-agenda

Oliveira, L.H. (2020). População da Amazônia Legal ultrapassa 29 milhoes de pessoas, estima IBGE. *Agência Cenarium*, August 27. Available at https://agenciacenarium.com.br/populacao-na-amazonia-legal-ultrapassa-29-milhoes-de-pessoas-estima-ibge/

Parker, E. (1999). Sunny side of global warming. *Nature*, Vol.399, pp.416–417.

Pondé, L.F.C.S. (2016). *Ceticismo*. Available at https://www.youtube.com/watch?v=-DBTwK1axGs

Ramus, C.A., and Montiel, I. (2005). When are corporate environmental policies a form of greenwashing? *Business & Society*, Vol.44, No.4, pp.377–414.

Stanford Encyclopedia of Philosophy (2008). *Skepticism*. Available at https://stanford.library.sydney.edu.au/archives/win2008/entries/skepticism/

Taghizadeh-Hesary, F., and Yoshino, N. (2019). The way to induce private participation in green finance and investment. *Finance Research Letters*, Vol.31, pp.98–103.

Wagner, T., Lutz, R.J., and Weitz, B.A. (2009). Corporate hypocrisy: Overcoming the threat of inconsistent corporate social responsibility perceptions. *Journal of Marketing*, Vol.73, No.6, pp.77–91.

Whitmarsh, L. (2009). What's in a name? Commonalities and differences in public understanding of 'climate change' and 'global warming'. *Public Understanding of Science*, Vol.18, No.4, pp.401–420.

Wittgenstein, L. (1969). *On Certainty*. Harper Torchbooks.

6 Apocalyptic Views of Sustainability

Apocalypticism

The idea that the world will one day end seems to have accompanied humanity since its first steps, present, perhaps, from the moment human beings became aware of themselves. Just as people wonder about their origins and nature (Long, 2016), concerns about the future seem to fulfil a range of other fundamental philosophical questions. In this sense, the observation of nature often convinces them of the cyclic essence of life, in which sooner or later everything that lives will cease to do so (Shalit, 2011). When transported to a planetary scale, the idea of finitude necessarily flows into the perspective of the end of the world, or a moment when, just like plants and other animals, man himself and everything that lives will no longer exist. Articulating these views, apocalyptic perspectives have been portrayed in various forms of artistic and religious expression (Emmerson and McGinn, 1992).

If, on the one hand, apocalyptic perspectives have been constant, it is possible that the most recent historical events have contributed to the consolidation of these visions. In particular, the two great world wars (1914–1918 and 1939–1945) and the unfolding of the Cold War (1947–1991) that followed them (Schlesinger, 1967; Mason, 2002) seem to have marked the human unconscious in unprecedented ways, with the development of weapons of mass destruction fuelling fears that, from one moment to another, humanity or even the planet could cease to exist (Bendle, 2005). The application of chemical and biological weapons played an important role, as their consequences were not only acute but also extended over large geographic regions (Ekzayez et al., 2020; Pal et al., 2017). The fact that they put the health or lives of large numbers of people at risk (Langford, 2004) may contribute to the understanding that drastic and definitive acts of war can in fact lead to the extinction of populations.

It is likely, however, that no other factor has had a greater impact in this regard than the development and use of nuclear weapons (Daley, 2010). The detonation of atomic bombs in the Japanese cities of Hiroshima and Nagasaki during the final chapters of World War II made it clear that the technology developed during the conflict was capable of causing damage never before imagined (Bernstein, 1991). Furthermore, the fact that the bombs were used demonstrated to the world that

DOI: 10.4324/9781003124719-7

these weapons were not just intimidating. Images of the nearly total devastation caused by the bombs have travelled the world, stamped on the covers of newspapers and magazines and broadcast on television networks (Barnouw, 1982; Torney-Parlicki, 2000). The devastating scenarios of long areas fed the fears of many, with the very form of the atomic explosion becoming synonymous of brutal destruction. The mushroom cloud formed by the detonation of nuclear weapons illustrates this point (Miyamoto, 2012).

Despite the rawness of the images portraying the overwhelming power of atomic weapons, the nuclear attacks at the end of World War II still raise important debates from the viewpoint of their morality. While some judge the use of such disproportionate and unnecessary force as condemnable (Winnacker, 1947), others argue that it was important to avoid the continuation of the conflict, having been a key factor in Japan's surrender (Sodei, 1995). The horror caused by the atomic destruction seems to have really been key in Emperor Hirohito's (1901–1989) decision to lay down arms (Asada, 1998). Proponents of this view argue that, despite their dire side effects, atomic bombs would have actually been an ironic instrument of peace, as their use would have allowed the lives of thousands (or perhaps millions) of soldiers and civilians to be saved (Mohan and Tree, 1995).

In the decades that followed the end of World War II, the possibility of a nuclear apocalypse became quite concrete, with the unfolding of the next conflict stirring the spirits between the two world superpowers (Knoblauch, 2017). On several occasions, the United States and the Soviet Union came close to a direct confrontation, although the retaliatory power of both sides discouraged any concrete action in this regard (Oakes, 1995). Fear of the consequences of a clash between the two largest atomic arsenals in the world led to the establishment of an indirect but constant war dynamic, forming the foundations of what became known as the Cold War. In this context, armed conflicts in the most diverse parts of the world were fought between militarily supported forces by Washington and Moscow, in conflicts that aimed to determine the models of society to be followed (Schmidt, 2013). While the supporters of the capitalist economic model and representative democracies had the support of the American government, those who sought to establish communist dictatorships received arms, ammunition, training, information, and financial resources from communist dictatorships. On the complexity of the situation, Powaski (1997) points out that the struggle for global influence between the United States and the Soviet Union included a variety of methods and strategies, such as the creation of rival alliances, the provision of military and economic aid to foreign countries, propaganda campaigns, espionage, guerrilla warfare, and a massive arms race.

This dynamic resulted in the outbreak of several conflicts around the world, responsible for shaping much of the 20th-century geopolitical scenario. Some of the best-known examples are the various wars on African territory in which armed groups and local armies supported by the superpowers vied for political and economic power (Minter, 1991; Shubin and Tokarev, 2001). Latin America was also affected by ideological disputes (Grandin, 2011), with the establishment of long military dictatorships being one of the results (Kruit, 2001). This seems to be the case in countries such as Argentina (Pion-Berlin, 1985), Chile (Castiglioni, 2001), and Brazil (Skidmore, 1989), which have, at different times, found themselves in the midst of clashes between revolutionary and military groups, with the latter coming to take power. In other situations, there was the direct participation of the United States and the Soviet Union. While the wars in Korea (Park, 1983) and Vietnam (Lunch and Sperlich, 1979) were fought by American troops, conflicts in Afghanistan had intense Soviet participation (Hauner, 2019).

In one of the most remarkable episodes of this period, the American secret service discovered the presence of a significant amount of Soviet nuclear material in Cuba (White, 1995). After flying over the island, spy planes photographed a series of missiles that, if fired, could reach the United States (Brugioni, 2011). The so-called missile crisis triggered one of the most critical periods of the Cold War, when the prospect of a nuclear attack was quite realistic for a significant portion of the American population (George, 2004). After several rounds of tense negotiations, the Soviet Union agreed to withdraw its nuclear weaponry from the region, under the condition that the United States did the same with its missiles in Turkey, which, likewise, threatened Soviet territory (Criss, 1997).

The missile crisis represented the prospect of a nuclear attack, having probably affected the collective unconscious in a decisive way (Stern, 2020). The possibility of a confrontation of such proportions may have generated great anxiety in American society, with the risk of an attack being reflected in the reinforcement of apocalyptic perspectives. The analysis of the real psychological impacts of the Cold War is quite complex and sometimes difficult for individuals who did not live through the period in all its intensity. As Brazilian historian Fernando Novais (2016) warns, the great threat to the accuracy of historical interpretations is anachronism (i.e., 'a temporal incongruity that consists of inserting in a historical period material elements or cultural categories that belong to another, previous or later'; Prieto, 2004, p.250, our translation). Among other factors, it implies the application of ideas, concepts, and views of the world outside their context. Thus, anachronism comprises errors of judgment, with past acts, decisions, and omissions revised according to the moral rules of the present.

In general, this represents a neglect of the contexts in which historical events took place, which can lead to misinterpretations. Furthermore, anachronistic views contain knowledge of the results and consequences of what is being analysed, ignoring that, at the moment they occurred, the main characters were subject to all the uncertainties that affect those who look to the future, which they evidently did not know about. Still, according to Novais (2016), when analysing the past, historians must try to forget that they know the unfolding of the facts (i.e., what happened after what is being investigated) and seek to experience the same doubts as the actors in question. Of course, this configures an extremely difficult task, and one that can probably only be partially successful.

Concerning the present discussion, this is particularly important so that the fears under which the societies of the analysed periods lived are not underestimated by the fact that they did not materialize. It is unreasonable, for example, that the prospect of a nuclear apocalypse should be treated as exaggerated because of the fact that it did not happen. It is curious, however, that these fears have all but disappeared from the popular unconscious, or at least left the top positions among the concerns most commonly expressed by public opinion. This is because, despite the significant calming down of geopolitical moods in recent decades, the technical possibility of a nuclear war remains present.

The number of countries that hold atomic bombs and missiles in their possession has only increased (Hymans, 2002). In this sense, the point that concerns have been considerably reduced – despite the technical possibilities of conflicts being even greater – can be quite revealing of the role played by the media in shaping the public debate. Apparently, the large communication groups (e.g., radio and television stations, newspapers, magazines) have exercised, throughout their histories, a great influence in directing the public debate. Depending on which subjects they decided to focus on, the relevance they attributed to each one, and the nuances they chose to highlight, traditional media directed the focus of their listeners, viewers, and readers. This role of 'gatekeeper' gave them immense power.

It may be argued, for instance, that the media played an important role in several decisive moments of politics in democratic countries, with biases given to certain ideas, parties, or candidates influencing the results of elections (Temin and Smith, 2002). Likewise, the focus given to determined issues (e.g., suspicions of corruption) can decisively contribute to the loss of prestige of elected politicians which, in more acute cases, can lead to resignation or impeachment proceedings. Totalitarian governments seem to have understood very quickly the power of the media to influence public opinion. It is not by chance that these regimes devoted special attention to both the control of third-party production (i.e., censorship) and the creation of their own content that aims to defend their interests (Pandolfi, 1999).

The state propaganda machines were responsible for creating works that had little or no commitment to the truth, but rather were committed to the creation or maintenance of a kind of parallel reality (Remington, 1988) also known as 'official truth'. Thus, embarrassing situations for the representatives did not receive due attention and were systematically neglected or ignored. Possible advances were, in turn, widely publicized and even exaggerated. In view of these and other situations, the so-called free world (i.e., Western democracies) seems to have reached the conclusion that maintenance of a free press is a fundamental condition for maintenance of the rule of law (Brunetti and Weder, 2003; Curtis, 2004). However, the oligopolies formed by the large media groups (Lule, 2018) and the interest games they may come to serve can have exactly the opposite effect if freedom of expression is not actually exercised. The appearance of democratic normality can be even more perverse than an open dictatorship.

Still, regarding the influence of the Cold War on the development of apocalyptic perspectives, it is noteworthy that the debate on environmentalism became more radical during this same historical period. As discussed by Fracarolli Nunes and Lee Park (2021), the argument about the need to adopt urgent and drastic measures to save the planet from environmental collapse gained speed in the early 1970s. In this sense, Basiago (1995) presents such a chronology on more recent developments, with the publication of the article 'A Blueprint for Survival' in *The Environmentalist* pointed out as the first occasion in which the term sustainability was used with the connotation attributed to it today. Promotion of the first global conference on sustainable development by the United Nations in 1972 in Stockholm also represented an important milestone in strengthening environmentally responsible discourse.

The meeting of heads of state (presidents, prime ministers, dictators, kings, and queens) secured political support for the cause and evidently attracted the attention of the media. These initial efforts were joined by others, with the United Nations playing an important role in organizing conferences, forums, and other opportunities to consolidate the environmental discourse. In Basiago's (1995) chronology, the Brundtland Commission in 1987, the Bergen Declaration on Sustainable Development in 1990, and the Earth Summit in 1992 were particularly relevant, having been responsible for the advent of concepts that are still very influential in environmental argumentation today. The concept of futurity, for instance, has been present since its inception (i.e., Bruntland Commission in 1987), preaching that sustainability refers, to a large extent, to the preservation of natural resources for future generations. Likewise, the so-called precaution principle (Bergen Declaration on Sustainable Development in 1990) establishes that discussions on the subject demand a conservative posture, meaning that, even if disagreements on the paths to be followed are admitted, it is necessary for decisions and postures on sustainability issues to be considered while taking into account the most extreme scenarios. In this way, it would ensure that irreversible damage would be avoided, even if some exaggerations – with regard to measures aimed at preventing such damage – were committed. It would thus be preferable to err on account of excess care than lack of care. These ideas often appear in the most commonly employed definitions on the subject.

One way or another, the propositions about sustainability and sustainable development that originated in the 1970s, 1980s, and 1990s seem to suggest that the capitalist mode of production is largely responsible for environmental damage, and that subversion of its pillars would be a fundamental element of environmental preservation. In fact, the debate on sustainability seems to contain a high ideological content, which, as discussed throughout the book, has greatly hampered the advancement of important issues in this direction. The Cold War context seems to have contributed to the politicization of environmental discourse, so that, in many cases, discussion of humanity's interactions with the environment seems to be nothing more than anti-capitalist propaganda pieces. A closer look notices this trend in texts and speeches from the last decades of the 20th century. In reality, contamination of the sustainability debate by economic and political ideologies does not seem to have lost steam in the first decades of the 21st century. Hopefully, the points raised here may contribute, albeit modestly, to a reorientation of these issues so that discussions on social development are just that, for the sake of its noble ends.

Economic crises may also contribute to the development of apocalyptic perspectives, with two factors being fundamental in this regard: the severity of some crises and their potential to generate global damage (Nayak, 2013). Macroeconomic disruptions can impact people's lives in different ways, ranging from a relative deterioration in their purchasing power (in the case of inflation) (Mahdavi and Zhou, 1994), to job losses (Cai and Chan, 2009) and company failures (i.e., bankruptcy) (Nam and Jinn, 2000). In the latter cases, the affected individuals find themselves amid drastic changes in their standards of living. It is not uncommon for people most affected by these issues to interpret their current situation as something permanent, understanding that the world they knew is falling before their eyes. These apocalyptic perspectives can be reinforced when individuals suffering from the most severe consequences of economic crises realize that other people are going through something similar.

In more extreme cases, the perception that economic crises are global may contribute to the idea that a general collapse is underway. In this sense, the media also seems to play an important role, with the constant discussion of the risks of unemployment and bankruptcy being important magnets for viewers, readers, and listeners who seek to assess how serious the risk they are running is or what are their prospects for dealing with the situation that presents itself (Boomgaarden et al., 2011). In general, the apparent success of media coverage in attracting public attention with catastrophic messages works as a mechanism that privileges exaggeration, which, in the case of economic crises, contributes to the development of often unjustified fears.

Sanitary crises are among the situations in which widespread panic and the feeling of chaos lead to the development of pessimistic perspectives, often translated into apocalyptic discourses (Peckham, 2015). Since ancient times, epidemics seem to exert a great influence in this regard, with the lack of knowledge about their causes contributing to them being sometimes interpreted as divine punishment (Stuber, 2003) and, therefore, as a harbinger of the end of time. Evidently, this facet was more accentuated in periods when science contributed little to the determination of the causes of diseases, with ignorance about the existence of microorganisms (e.g., bacteria, viruses, fungi) reinforcing purely metaphysical explanations. Despite all the advances in scientific knowledge over the years, the pandemic caused by Covid-19 from the end of the second decade of the 21st century on showed that humanity is not free to develop apocalyptic perspectives when faced with a threat that it does not fully understand. In this particular issue, the media vehicles seem to have exerted a great influence on the spread of panic, with some companies dedicating a significant part of their programming to discussing the risks arising from contamination (Atri et al., 2021). While, in many cases, these spaces for debate have been of great use in controlling the spread of the pandemic, they have also fuelled distorted views of reality, with some issues apparently being exaggerated.

In addition to the media's direct actions, its evolving reach also contributes to its panic-spreading power. In earlier times, information had limited reach, with few people having access to mass media. The capillarity of current information systems means that media messages have a truly global reach. However, it is also true that the rapid increase in competition has brought about a deterioration in the power of large communication groups, with various social media vehicles presenting their own versions of reality and often contesting those presented by traditional networks (Hermida, 2016). This dynamic seems to have given rise to an ultra-segmentation of the market, in which increasingly specific population niches are served by different communication channels.

It can be argued that this segregation is among the reasons for the development of modern forms of virtual tribalism, in which individuals who share views on certain subjects end up coalescing in electronic environments (Fisher et al., 2018). The global reach of social networks and the internet as a whole allow people from diverse regions to establish contact and develop their conceptions of the world in small clusters that overcome the limitation of geographic proximity. In these environments of individuals sharing similar perspectives, the absence of contradiction ends up reaffirming thoughts and ideas that are in accordance with the views held by the majority, which, in many cases, can lead to radicalization. The validation offered by the constituents of these clusters ends up feeding and sometimes even rewarding the expression of extremist ideas and thoughts.

The level of radicalization may be inversely proportional to their tolerance of the ideas defended in other clusters, especially when these also feature a high degree of radicalization and propagate diametrically opposed worldviews. This seems to be the case for individuals who identify with right-wing thinking and those who, in turn, see themselves represented by ideas classified as left-wing (Lawrence et al., 2010). As discussed throughout the book, the incompatibility of these two perspectives seems to be one of the most relevant factors for the development of what is classified here as extreme sustainability rhetoric. Algorithms developed and applied by social networks, as well as by other big techs (i.e., large technology companies) may play an important role in this direction (Feezell et al., 2021). It can be said, therefore, that the expectation that the internet would lead to greater harmony among people around the world has been largely frustrated, with thought clusters functioning as relevant factors in the development of virtual tribalism.

Despite the difficulties in establishing the real power of influence currently exercised by traditional media outlets, it cannot be denied that they still matter, especially among the poorest and most rural strata. While the wealthier bundle of cosmopolitan societies finds itself increasingly embedded in a kind of virtual life (Diwakar, 2016), lower-income people still have difficulty acquiring the electronic devices needed to ensure a greater level of connectivity. Likewise, access to an internet network itself may be economically unfeasible for the poorest (DW, 2021). Altogether, these factors contribute to these segments of the population being more influenced by traditional communication networks, since they do not need to incur additional costs to access them. Thus, it can be said that the exaggerations and extreme views that may be eventually conveyed by the traditional media usually have a greater impact on the more popular classes, even though this force seems to be decreasing.

Apocalyptic Environmentalism

Regardless of how apocalyptic prospects are generated or disseminated, the idea that humanity holds the power not only to cause apocalypse but also to prevent it seems to reflect an important aspect of the homocentric perspective that has been developing over the past few centuries. The concentration of such power in the human figure can be understood as a transposition of divine attributions to the common citizen, as if it were the author and master of its own destiny. If, on one side, the diagnosis of such a process is relatively simple, the understanding of the reasons why it occurs is, without a doubt, more complex. It is possible to point, for example, to philosophical and historical processes, with the Renaissance, the Enlightenment, and Communism being perhaps the most evident. The alleged elevation of human beings to the category of main actor in their experience, together with the valorization of reason as a source of salvation, must have contributed to a secularization of modern and post-modern societies (Swatos and Olson, 2000). From a more pragmatic point of view, the search to diminish the power of the Catholic Church (Luxmoore and Babiuch, 1999) also seems to have contributed to dynamics through which 'Faith in God' gave space to the belief that individuals could build their own destiny. In short, homocentrism can be understood as a process in which power over the ways of the world would be transferred from the figure of the Creator to the creature.

It is also possible to point to questions of a psychological basis that, in a certain way, derive from these first ones. In this set, the human being's attempt to confront the apocalyptic perspective (i.e., the idea that it is both the cause and the remedy of the apocalypse) can be understood as a search for control and organization of its experience, as a response to chaos resulting from lack of faith in God. Not by chance, the idea that environmental damage caused by human activities will result in the apocalypse seems to be more commonly held by individuals identified with left-wing thinking. Likewise, the realization that humanity has the power to avoid this fate may also appear more frequently in the arguments of those who share a more progressive worldview. The fact that communism attributes to the state the role traditionally occupied by God (Aiello, 2005) might be among the probable causes of this tendency. Allied to this issue of ideological background, the understanding that economic activities are the main triggers of the apocalypse also seems to be more widespread among leftists. As discussed throughout the book, environmentalism sometimes seems to be instrumentalized by those who are really concerned not with the degradation of the planet, but with the advancement of the means of capitalist production.

Reflectively, the repudiation of ideas embedded in apocalyptic environmentalism seems to be stronger among those who identify with right-wing thinking. With regard to the transfer of Divine powers to humans, this resistance can be understood as natural, to some extent, since these groups have never completely strayed from their religious beliefs. Even though they are influenced by the anti-religion ideas defended in recent centuries, the conservative nature of these individuals keeps them linked to their beliefs and religious traditions. The fact that they believe in the existence and power of God and, by contrast, in the insignificance of the creature before its Creator prevents them from accepting the idea that human beings can be masters of their destiny. Among other consequences, the search for control over the apocalypse would not be possible and, from a more orthodox perspective, might even be an affront to God's will. The fact that the end of the world is predicted in the scriptures in the form of a Divine revelation (i.e., Gospel of St. John) classifies it as something inevitable. It can be argued, therefore, that the faith of right-wing individuals works, to some extent, so that they refute the idea that the apocalypse can be both caused and prevented by human beings. On the contrary, power over the existence and destiny of the world would remain reserved to God.

At first glance, the attitude of individuals on the right may seem inconsistent with their beliefs, especially regarding the great value they place on the individual. One would expect, for example, that the understanding that the individual – and not the collective – is the basic unit of analysis of life in society would result in the belief that this is the main agent of all things (including the cause and the solution to the apocalypse). It happens, however, that the valorization of the individual does not oppose Divine sovereignty, since it derives from the belief that God Himself inhabits each one of us. Broadly, it can be argued that the different propensities of the right and the left to develop, accept, or propagate apocalyptic discourses originate, at least partially, in the power that each of these views ascribes to God.

While right-wing individuals tend to treat the apocalypse as a Divine affair, left-wing ideologues may more often see it as likely to be caused or fought by humanity or the institutions it has created (typically, the state). However, all possible gradations of these perspectives cannot be ignored. In this sense, the sustainability spectrum developed in Chapter 4 can be useful in locating the various inclinations that individuals on the right and left may have to base their views of the world on apocalyptic arguments, especially regarding the environmental cause. Quite directly, those closer to the poles are likely to have more radical views, while those in greyer regions are less firm in their convictions and therefore more open to dialogue. Once the possible ideological roots of both the repulsion to and the tendency to adopt apocalyptic discourses have been discussed, their consequences can be addressed in greater detail, as well as the means by which they are most commonly employed.

In this sense, the basic premises placed throughout the book can serve as guides for the discussion, namely: (1) apocalyptic speeches can cause panic; (2) panicked populations are more likely to accept the concentration of power; (3) those who pose as saviours of the world stand to exercise this power; (4) this dynamic can work for the promotion of both personal images and political purposes. Before dealing with how each of these premises applies to extreme environmental discourse, it is important to emphasize that many people are sincerely convinced that environmental damage can lead to the extinction of terrestrial life as we know it, and even to the total destruction of the planet. For them, it is really necessary that the way in which humanity relates to nature undergoes a sudden, radical, and urgent change, which may include the interruption of the current means of production and consumption patterns.

The debate proposed here is not at all intended to question whether the premises on which these people rely are really true. We are more interested in the fact that they believe in what they stand for and, in some cases, apply to themselves the rigor they demand from others. Even if possibly mistaken or under the influence of exaggerated views, individuals in this category deserve the respect of their interlocutors because, despite the inconvenience they may cause, they are not using extreme environmental discourse in a hypocritical or opportunistic way. Thus, the debate that follows has as its object the misuse of extreme environmentalist discourses, especially by those who employ it in an opportunistic and instrumental way, aiming only to obtain personal benefits.

Among the groups that fall into this category, public personalities popularly known as celebrities are perhaps those that have most used environmental alarmism. The fact that many of large communication groups have a progressive (i.e., leftist) bias ends up determining that the space they own will be given preferentially to celebrities who agree, defend, or in some way corroborate their values. Since the economic success of celebrities is often conditioned by their popularity (e.g., invitations to publicity, participation in films), the incentive mechanism that often leads them to join causes with which they do not really agree is clear. This gap between discourse and feelings sets the foundations for hypocritical behaviour, which, as discussed, is highly damaging to the credibility of environmental causes. It is also important to emphasize that the degree of extremism in the environmentalist discourse seems to be proportional to the need that the celebrity in question has to be present in the media showcase. The exaggerations in the messages denote the absolute need that these people have to signal virtues, making it clear – at least for their faithful audience – that they are on the right side, that they are for the good.

Extremist environmental discourse has also been very helpful for those who are still relatively unknown but who are looking to rise in popularity. Defined here as people who are quickly successful in the eyes of the public and who, after an initial gain in popularity, find it difficult to remain in the spotlight (e.g., reality television participants), so-called sub-celebrities also seem to have a tendency to defend notorious causes and radical speeches. Similar to what happens with celebrities, signalling of virtues seems to be a kind of toll that sub-celebrities must pay to be able to be targeted by mainstream media vehicles with a progressive bias. Unlike their more established peers, however, the sub-celebrities need to be even more strident, as, in addition to arousing comparatively lesser interest, they face fierce competition from a host of other sub-celebrities willing to do the same.

In addition to being widespread among those who depend on their public images to develop their professions, extreme environmental discourse also finds an echo among more discreet professionals who, despite also addressing audiences, work in smaller circles. Many professors and researchers, for instance, seem to have rather fanatically embraced the propagation of environmentally revolutionary ideas. Interestingly, these views seem to be more widespread among academics within the humanities (e.g., sociology, economics, political science). The fact that these disciplines offer a generous space for interpretations and subjectivities may be one of the variables that explain this phenomenon. The absence or, at least, the slightest requirement of empirical demonstration in some arguments allows teachers to use extremist speeches to express their ideas, often irresponsibly. It is common, for example, to use environmental causes as a background to defend ideological positions, which usually translates into attacks on the capitalist mode of production.

The defence of extreme views on environmental issues also appears to be relatively commonplace among some non-governmental organizations (NGOs) (Berny and Rootes, 2018). The dynamic seems convenient to them since, in general, NGOs depend on donations to maintain their activities. As such, many NGOs seem to have a constant need to point out serious problems, to which they are the solution. It is interesting to note that, typically, some NGOs are not dedicated to specific issues that can be resolved objectively or even quickly. Instead, they focus their energies on structural and endemic problems, which are difficult to solve. These preferences seem to be in line with the need for external financing, with the existence of the problem working in favour of the continuity of financial resources originating from the financiers. It is also worth noting the apparent inclination towards projects that are difficult to measure in terms of progress or performance. These choices leave room for different interpretations and arguments, which somehow contribute to the continuity of activities. Extreme environmentalist discourse ends up being useful to NGOs, as it reinforces the need for their existence, with the maintenance of their operations sold as one of the many elements that can prevent the apocalypse.

There are also NGOs that seem to have specific purposes and adopt radical environmentalist discourse as a way to defend hidden interests. It is common, for example, for some of these entities to be accused of fighting deforestation or the development of any economic activity in forest regions just to protect areas rich in precious metals, minerals, or any resource of value for future extraction. The defence of the demarcation of indigenous areas would, in some cases, have the same objective, with the aggravation of alienating the sovereignty of countries over extensive regions. This process would aim to enable these territories to give rise to new nations with which interested economic groups could negotiate directly. The latter would even be the financiers of these NGOs. In these scenarios, there is what can be considered one of the most serious cases of manipulation of environmental causes in favour of particular interests. Once again, it is important to emphasize that this part of the chapter is devoted to the misuses of extreme environmental discourse and therefore does not apply to all honest and serious NGOs that actually seek to contribute to sustainable development.

Surprisingly, extreme environmentalist discourse seems to have been very well received by the corporate world, with executives increasingly demonstrating compliance with the demands of radical groups. It is not uncommon, for example, that the directors of large companies make statements in which they acknowledge that the activities they command have a long history of environmental damage, and that important changes throughout the production chain are necessary and urgent. In the case of companies that are really aggressive towards the environment, this attitude can be seen as positive. However, what is observed is that managers from different hierarchical levels are adopting speeches and theses from third parties, which are often invalid or exaggerated. Due to external pressure, or sincere conversion to extremism, these professionals end up validating radical ideas as if they were true, ignoring the need for empirical proof of the hypotheses raised. As discussed throughout the book, this appears to be another dimension of the emerging 'woke capitalism'.

Despite being widespread among different groups, extreme environmental discourse seems to be particularly dear to the political class. In this sense, the very functioning of representative democracy regimes seems to work as an incentive to radicalization, with the determined intervals between elections influencing the temporal dimension of apocalyptic visions. This translates into many politicians describing environmental issues as serious problems, for which they are the solution. This position is aimed at convincing voters that they are worthy of their vote, with the radicalization of the speech functioning as a catalyst for intentions. The fact that elections take place in relatively short cycles (e.g., every four or five years) leads to the transformation – at least, apparently – of long-term issues into immediate ones. Thus, the mismatch between issues related to sustainability and the timing of politics makes politicians exaggerate the urgency of environmental issues, in order to guarantee votes for the next election. In short, the closer we are to the environmental apocalypse, the more necessary is the vote of those who seek to avoid it. This posture is renewed in the attitudes of politicians from different generations. Famous speeches by former US Vice President Al Gore (1948–) already warned of the urgency of measures (Turque, 2000). More recently, Democratic Deputy Alexandria Ocasio-Cortez (1989–) has argued that only 12 years separate us from the end of the world (Cummings, 2019). Once again, it must be remembered that these discussions do not apply to the entire political class, and all those who sincerely and honestly seek to promote sustainable development must be recognized.

In line with the points raised above, it can be argued that the biggest problem brought about by the exaggerated use of apocalyptic views in environmental discourse is the loss of credibility. This process, however, is not limited to those who make use of extreme discourse, extending, to a greater or lesser degree, to the various forms of environmentalism. Furthermore, the perception that the environmental cause is used as a means to achieve personal goals generates resistance among those who are naturally inclined to skepticism. The fact that the apocalyptic environmentalist discourse is apparently more adopted by left-wing politicians collaborates for right-wing individuals to refute it, more out of tribalism than out of an informed opinion on the subject. The processes of politicization and ideologization of the environmentalist discourse only contribute to a greater division between individuals, with apocalyptic themes functioning as additional factors of segregation.

References

Aiello, T. (2005). Constructing 'Godless communism': Religion, politics, and popular culture, 1954–1960. *Americana: The Journal of American Popular Culture*, Vol.4, No.1.

Asada, S. (1998). The shock of the atomic bomb and Japan's decision to surrender: A reconsideration. *Pacific Historical Review*, Vol.67, No.4, pp.477–512.

Atri, H., Kouki, S., and Imen Gallali, M. (2021). The impact of COVID-19 news, panic and media coverage on the oil and gold prices: An ARDL approach. *Resources Policy*, Vol.72, p.102061.

Barnouw, E. (1982). The Hiroshima-Nagasaki footage: A report. *Historical Journal of Film, Radio and Television*, Vol.2, No.1, pp.91–100.

Basiago, A.D. (1995). Methods of defining 'sustainability'. *Sustainable Development*, Vol.3, No.3, pp.109–119.

Bendle, M.F. (2005). The apocalyptic imagination and popular culture. *The Journal of Religion and Popular Culture*, Vol.11, No.1, p.1.

Bernstein, B.J. (1991). Eclipsed by Hiroshima and Nagasaki: Early thinking about tactical nuclear weapons. *International Security*, Vol.15, No.4, pp.149–173.

Berny, N., and Rootes, C. (2018). Environmental NGOs at a crossroads? *Environmental Politics*, Vol.27, No.6, pp.947–972.

Boomgaarden, H.G., Van Spanje, J., Vliegenthart, R., and De Vreese, C.H. (2011). Covering the crisis: Media coverage of the economic crisis and citizens' economic expectations. *Acta Politica*, Vol.46, No.4, pp.353–379.

Brugioni, D.A. (2011). *Eyes in the Sky: Eisenhower, the CIA, and Cold War Aerial Espionage*. Naval Institute Press.

Brunetti, A., and Weder, B. (2003). A free press is bad news for corruption. *Journal of Public Economics*, Vol.87, No.7–8, pp.1801–1824.

Cai, F., and Chan, K.W. (2009). The global economic crisis and unemployment in China. *Eurasian Geography and Economics*, Vol.50, No.5, pp.513–531.

Castiglioni, R. (2001). The politics of retrenchment: The quandaries of social protection under military rule in Chile, 1973–1990. *Latin American Politics and Society*, Vol.43, No.4, pp.37–66.

Criss, N.B. (1997). Strategic nuclear missiles in Turkey: The Jupiter affair, 1959–1963. *The Journal of Strategic Studies*, Vol.20, No.3, pp.97–122.

Cummings, W. (2019). The world is going to end in 12 years if we don't address climate change, Ocasio-Cortez says. *USA Today*, January 1. Available at https://eu.usatoday.com/story/news/politics/onpolitics/2019/01/22/ocasio-cortez-climate-change-alarm/2642481002/

Curtis, M.K. (2004). Democratic ideals and media realities: A puzzling free press paradox. *Social Philosophy and Policy*, Vol.21, No.2, pp.385–427.

Daley, T. (2010). *Apocalypse Never: Forging the Path to a Nuclear Weapon-free World*. Rutgers University Press.

Diwakar, V. (2016). 'It's complicated': The construction of Indian middle-class teens in social media. *Journal of Creative Communications*, Vol.11, No.2, pp.161–182.

DW (2021). *Can Africa Achieve Universal Internet Access by 2030?* Available at https://www.dw.com/en/can-africa-achieve-universal-internet-access-by-2030/a-59729090

Ekzayez, A., Flecknoe, M.D., Lillywhite, L., Patel, P., Papamichail, A., and Elbahtimy, H. (2020). Chemical weapons and public health: Assessing impact and responses. *Journal of Public Health*, Vol.42, No.3, pp.334–342.

Emmerson, R.K., and McGinn, B. (Eds.) (1992). *The Apocalypse in the Middle Ages*. Cornell University Press.

Feezell, J.T., Wagner, J.K., and Conroy, M. (2021). Exploring the effects of algorithm-driven news sources on political behavior and polarization. *Computers in Human Behavior*, Vol.116, p.106626.

Fisher, M., Knobe, J., Strickland, B., and Keil, F.C. (2018). The tribalism of truth. *Scientific American*, Vol.318, No.2, pp.50–53.

George, A.L. (2004). *Awaiting Armageddon: How Americans Faced the Cuban Missile Crisis*. UNC Press Books.

Grandin, G. (2011). *The Last Colonial massacre: Latin America in the Cold War*. University of Chicago Press.

Hauner, M. (2019). *Afghanistan and the Soviet Union: Collision and Transformation*. Routledge.

Hermida, A. (2016). Social media and the news. In: T. Witschge, C.W. Anderson, D. Domingo, and A. Hermida (Eds.). *The Sage Handbook of Digital Journalism*, pp.81–94. Sage.

Hymans, J.E. (2002). Why do states acquire nuclear weapons? Comparing the cases of India and France. In: D.R. SarDesai and R.G.C. Thomas (Eds.). *Nuclear India in the Twenty-First Century*, pp.139–160. Palgrave Macmillan.

Knoblauch, W.M. (2017). *Nuclear Freeze in a Cold War: The Reagan Administration, Cultural Activism, and the End of the Arms Race*. University of Massachusetts Press.

Kruit, D. (2001). Low intensity democracies: Latin America in the post-dictatorial era. *Bulletin of Latin American Research*, Vol.20, No.4, pp.409–430.

Langford, R.E. (2004). *Introduction to Weapons of Mass Destruction: Radiological, Chemical, and Biological*. John Wiley & Sons.

Lawrence, E., Sides, J., and Farrell, H. (2010). Self-segregation or deliberation? Blog readership, participation, and polarization in American politics. *Perspectives on Politics*, Vol.8, No.1, pp.141–157.

Long, P. (2016). *Fire and Stone: Where Do We Come From? What Are We? Where Are We Going?* University of Georgia Press.

Lule, J. (2018). Media industry. In: M. Juergensmeyer, S. Sassen, M.B. Steger, and V. Faessel (Eds.). *The Oxford Handbook of Global Studies*. Oxford University Press.

Lunch, W.L., and Sperlich, P.W. (1979). American public opinion and the war in Vietnam. *Western Political Quarterly*, Vol.32, No.1, pp.21–44.

Luxmoore, J., and Babiuch, J. (1999). The catholic church and communism, 1789–1989. *Religion, State & Society*, Vol.27, No.3–4, pp.301–313.

Mahdavi, S., and Zhou, S. (1994). Purchasing power parity in high-inflation countries: Further evidence. *Journal of Macroeconomics*, Vol.16. No.3, pp.403–422.

Mason, J. (2002). *The Cold War: 1945–1991*. Routledge.

Minter, W. (1991). The US and the war in Angola. *Review of African Political Economy*, Vol.18, No.50, pp.135–144.

Miyamoto, Y. (2012). *Beyond the Mushroom Cloud: Commemoration, Religion, and Responsibility After Hiroshima*. Fordham University Press.

Mohan, U., and Tree, S. (1995). Hiroshima, the American media, and the construction of conventional wisdom. *Journal of American-East Asian Relations*, Vol.4, No.2, pp.141–160.

Nam, J.H., and Jinn, T. (2000). Bankruptcy prediction: Evidence from Korean listed companies during the IMF crisis. *Journal of International Financial Management & Accounting*, Vol.11, No.3, pp.178–197.

Nayak, S. (2013). Great crash and depression: Last economic apocalypse: A relook. In: *The Global Financial Crisis*. Springer. https://doi.org/10.1007/978-81-322-0798-6_8

Novais, F. (2016). *Portugal e Brasil – Antigo sistema colonial*. Available at https://www.youtube.com/watch?v=JsAXNoumgS8&t=1s

Oakes, G. (1995). *The Imaginary War: Civil defense and American Cold War Culture*. Oxford University Press.

Pal, M., Tsegaye, M., Girzaw, F., Bedada, H., Godishala, V., and Kandi, V. (2017). An overview on biological weapons and bioterrorism. *American Journal of Biomedical Research*, Vol.5, No.2, pp.24–34.

Pandolfi, D. (1999). *Repensando o Estado Novo*. Fundação Getulio Vargas.

Park, H.K. (1983). American involvement in the Korean war. *The History Teacher*, Vol.16, No.2, pp.249–263.

Peckham, R. (Ed.) (2015). *Empires of Panic: Epidemics and Colonial Anxieties*. Hong Kong University Press.

Pion-Berlin, D. (1985). The fall of military rule in Argentina: 1976–1983. *Journal of Inter-american Studies and World Affairs*, Vol.27, No.2, pp.55–76.

Powaski, R.E. (1997). *The Cold War: The United States and the Soviet Union, 1917–1991*. Oxford University Press.

Prieto, C.F. (2004). El anacronismo: Formas y funciones. *Actas do colóquio international Literatura e História*, Vol.1, pp.247–257.

Remington, T.F. (1988). *The Truth of Authority: Ideology and Communication in the Soviet Union*. University of Pittsburgh Press.

Schlesinger, A. (1967). Origins of the cold war. *Foreign Affairs*, Vol.46, No.1, pp.22–52.

Schmidt, E. (2013). *Foreign Intervention in Africa: From the Cold War to the War on Terror*, Vol.7. Cambridge University Press.

Shalit, E. (2011). *The Cycle of Life: Themes and Tales of the Journey*. Fisher King Press.

Shubin, V., and Tokarev, A. (2001). War in Angola: A Soviet dimension. *Review of African Political Economy*, Vol.28, No.90, pp.607–618.

Skidmore, T.E. (1989). *The Politics of Military Rule in Brazil, 1964–1985*. Oxford University Press.

Sodei, R. (1995). Hiroshima/Nagasaki as history and politics. *The Journal of American History*, Vol.82, No.3, pp.1118–1123.

Stern, S.M. (2020). *The Cuban Missile Crisis in American Memory*. Stanford University Press.

Stuber, M. (2003). Divine punishment or object of research? The resonance of earthquakes, floods, epidemics and famine in the correspondence network of Albrecht von Haller. *Environment and History*, Vol.9, No.2, pp.173–193.

Swatos, W.H., and Olson, D.V. (Eds.) (2000). *The Secularization Debate*. Rowman & Littlefield.

Temin, J., and Smith, D.A. (2002). Media matters: Evaluating the role of the media in Ghana's 2000 elections. *African Affairs*, Vol.101, No.405, pp.585–605.

Torney-Parlicki, P. (2000). 'Whatever the thing may be called': The Australian news media and the atomic bombing of Hiroshima and Nagasaki. *Australian Historical Studies*, Vol.31, No.114, pp.49–66.

Turque, B. (2000). *Inventing Al Gore*. Houghton Mifflin Harcourt.

White, M. (1995). *The Cuban Missile Crisis*. Springer.

Winnacker, R.A. (1947). The debate around Hiroshima. *Military Affairs*, Vol.11, No.1, pp.25–30.

7 Moderate Views of Sustainability

Introduction and Definition

Except for debates on the intermediate positions of the sustainability spectrum, the previous chapters were basically dedicated to the discussion of the nature, causes, and consequences of extreme speeches or rhetoric. If it is true that extreme attitudes end up drawing more attention and, sometimes, dominating much of the public debate, this seems to be characteristic of select groups that are often not representative of the average thinking of the population. This includes journalists, professors, politicians, and activists, among others. While causes related to sustainability seem to be among the main concerns of these segments, the same is not usually the case for what can be understood as ordinary people (i.e., 'average citizens', 'average public', or any other related form, however imprecise and unfair these ideas may be).

This does not mean that ordinary men and women do not necessarily care about environmental and social causes, or that they are ignorant about these issues. The fact that the most moderate speeches are apparently associated with the average public, however, means that concerns about day-to-day matters occupy an important space in their lives, in such a way that they do not have the time or energy to dedicate themselves to any type of activism. Thus, it is possible that an employed person is more concerned with maintaining their job than melting of the polar caps. Likewise, a parent attentive to raising children may be more occupied with monitoring the child's circle of friends than with the increase in CO_2 emissions in underdeveloped countries. In a certain sense, these majority groups can be compared to the political analysis of the silent majority (Lassiter, 2013). This nickname seems particularly fair mainly because of the noise that extreme views cause, as discussed earlier.

Often, this large volume of people who, apparently, are not aligned with any extreme vision represents an important force in society, in many cases dictating consumption patterns (Gao et al., 2015) and the results of elections (Rieder, 1989). Given the relevance of groups with moderate views, a more detailed discussion of their characteristics may be appropriate. From an evolutionary point of view, it is possible that the adoption of an impartial position is associated with a greater chance of success in certain situations. With extreme sides eventually

DOI: 10.4324/9781003124719-8

seeing themselves as enemies, a neutral position can guarantee those who stand the chance of not being seen as targets by any of the antagonistic sides, hence preventing them from being attacked.

The adoption of neutral or impartial positions seems, in fact, to be associated with the maintenance of dialogue between opposite sides, possibly one of the most important factors to avoid a total degeneration of relations. The stance adopted by Switzerland, for instance, could bring important lessons in this regard (Morris and White, 2011). Historically, the country has remained on the margins of disputes between European nations, serving as a favourable space for negotiations between economic, political, and geopolitical adversaries (Ross, 1989). This role can be seen in some of the most critical moments in recent history. In the development of World War II, for example, the country served as a stage for the continuation of commercial transactions despite the widespread chaos that surrounded it. The maintenance of this neutral environment also served to enable countries directly involved in the conflict to have access to raw materials necessary for the upkeep of their war machines (Reginbogin, 2009).

Among other consequences, the neutrality position allowed Switzerland to consolidate itself as a type of arbitration field (Bersheda, 2012), with several global entities having their headquarters in the country (e.g., FIFA, Panja, 2019). In addition, the country has also come to be seen as a kind of safe harbour for money, with Swiss banks hosting some of the biggest fortunes on the planet (Hirt, 2021).

Causes

Unfamiliarity With Issues

Unfamiliarity with an issue can be one of the main factors that lead individuals to abstain from a given debate. The lack of knowledge can even act as an element of exclusion, as people seem to have a tendency to get involved only with subjects that they know in greater depth or that are at least familiar to them. Not by chance, while simple topics tend to have a greater appeal to mass audiences (Nachbar et al., 1992), complex issues often end up being restricted to a relatively small number of people (Sull and Eisenhardt, 2015). This logic seems to explain the success of television programs such as soap operas (Leal, 1990) and reality shows (Montemurro, 2008). The fact that the audience identifies with the stories and understands the communication serves as an introduction that requires little to no effort for an interaction to unfold. This means that practically any individual – regardless of their cultural or educational level – should be able to follow these programs without any major difficulties, allowing a large part of the population to be classified as a potential consumer. Likewise, sports structured around simple rules seem to appeal to most populations, with football perhaps the clearest example of this dynamic. Based on just under two dozen rules that are relatively easy to understand, the sport has experienced rapid growth since its inception, with the sympathy of the most popular layers serving as the basis for its consolidation. The same seems to apply to car racing or boxing matches.

On the other hand, more complex subjects are usually less accessible, with some even demanding years of study to be minimally understood. Issues related to the development of vaccines, for example, cannot be debated with the same ease with which ordinary citizens discuss the results of the last round of the local football championship. On the contrary, subjects of this type will be restricted to a relatively small group of specialists, with the necessary knowledge to understand the different nuances that make up these themes functioning as a kind of entry barrier that restricts the access of the general public. Similarly, topics related to social dynamics may not allow the participation of lay people, even if they are directly affected. Issues related to the functioning of the economy, for instance, demand a great deal of theoretical knowledge about market relations. In this sense, a qualified debate on the interest rate levels established by the central bank of a given country, or on other structural macroeconomic policies, should not arouse great passion in ordinary citizens, even if their lives are largely impacted by these factors. In many cases, however, complex issues end up escaping their natural habitat (e.g., universities, expert groups) and are artificially brought into popular public debate. This occurs when interest groups see a connection between their goals and the popularization of a given subject.

As discussed throughout the book, this seems to be the case for the sustainability debate. Extremely complex topics such as the interaction between atmospheric air and ocean water (Yu et al., 2017), the greenhouse effect (Kiers, 2020), holes in the ozone layer (Witze, 2020), and the impacts of human activity on the equilibrium of the planet (Xia et al., 2020) were presented to the general public as if most people were capable of not only understanding the seriousness of these issues, but also giving an opinion on the best solutions for each of them. One of the main reasons for this movement is the instrumentalization of discussions related to sustainable development by members of the political classes, with candidates and occupants of elective positions using these discussions to present themselves as possible solutions to the urgent issues they announce.

As a result, the same fanaticism applied by individuals when they support their soccer teams ends up being used in the public debate on sustainability. Among the most visible consequences of this process is the victory of emotional aspects over rational ones, with the use of extremist rhetoric being common. Obviously, this is not about defending an elitist view, according to which only scientists would be able to debate issues related to sustainable development. On the contrary, the main point of the arguments presented here is that public debate can be greatly enriched as more people qualify to take it seriously. In the face of these and other questions, unfamiliarity can be divided into two broad groups. The first refers to the lack of awareness of the very existence of a problem, with the people who suffer from this not even realizing that a certain issue is present or that it can impact their lives. The second type deals with subjects that, despite being relatively well known to people, are embedded in topics that are difficult to understand.

Regarding discussions on sustainability, the first group seems to be increasingly rare, at least in democratic societies. This stems from the intense dissemination of issues related to the environment in both traditional media and new forms of mass communication (e.g., social media). The second group, in turn, seems to be very present in the exchange of ideas, with individuals unprepared or truly aware of the value of their arguments, declaiming them freely. In this sense, it can be argued that the second group will only serve as the basis of a moderate view, when individuals who suffer from this type of unfamiliarity are aware of their low level of knowledge. Ideally, people who fit this classification will seek information before adopting a pre-formatted view.

Disinterest

In the same way that unfamiliarity can lead people not to express extreme views on issues related to sustainability, it is common for the more moderate positions of the sustainability spectrum to be occupied by people who are simply not interested in the topic, or, at least, not interested in it enough to see it as a priority. On the contrary, personal issues may occupy positions of greater relevance in the scale of interest of some individuals, with issues that affect the collective body being to some extent marginalized. This includes concerns about health, education, security, and employment, among many other issues that may come to occupy people's minds. In the case of younger generations, these factors can be particularly important, with those below their 20s, in most cases, immersed in issues specific to the formation of their identities. Children, for example, need to face a series of important challenges for their development, ranging from the most basic learning (e.g., learning to walk and talk – West et al., 2019), to the improvement of their social skills (Kutnick and Manson, 2021), which should allow them to maintain a relationship with society in the future. There are also other important obstacles, such as learning to read and write, as well as the absorption of basic knowledge from other subjects (e.g., mathematics, history, geography).

The fact that they are focused on so many important issues will, in most cases, prevent children from worrying about topics such as global warming or climate change. Added to this is the natural lack of maturity typical of younger people and the consequent difficulty to understand issues that are not only complex but cannot be directly experienced. It is natural, therefore, that a child will not take an extreme position on sustainability, at least not in a genuine way. The exception to this issue is when their positions only reflect the absorbed opinions and views of the adults with whom they have contact, with direct relatives (e.g., parents, grandparents) and teachers likely to be the primary sources of the extreme discourses echoed. It is also possible that children will repeat extreme positions into which they have come into contact through radio and television programs or material produced for the internet. Despite these possibilities, the fact that children are, in general, busy and committed to their own development leaves no room for external interests.

Although the case of children represents a specific situation in the development process, the issues described serve as a basis for understanding the lack of interest in other stages of life. As the individual passes from childhood to adolescence, other personal issues present themselves. In addition to the continuity of matters related to school learning, it is common for adolescents to see themselves within a very active social life, in which affective and friendship bonds are developed (Flynn et al., 2017). In this sense, it is not uncommon for young people aged between 12 and 18, for example, to have a large part of their attention focused on relationships with their peers. A typical young person cannot, therefore, be expected to focus on sustainability discussions in an extremely engaged manner. Of course, there are exceptions to this rule, with the Swedish activist Greta Thunberg (2003–) probably being one of the most notable (Kraemer, 2021). The arguments presented here, however, do not seek to deal with specific cases but rather with what is usually observed most frequently. Thus, it can be said that the interest of young people in their own lives is one of the possible causes of their lack of interest in other topics of great relevance, such as politics, economics, and, particularly relevant to the present debate, sustainability.

In the next stage of life, young adults are usually focused on developing their careers, with the search for their first job usually among their priorities (Wei et al., 2018). In addition, many are starting families, with men and women now marrying and having children Rijken and Knijn, 2009). In this process, several issues tend to demand the attention of couples, such as the purchase of a first property. It is not difficult to assume that these immediate concerns leave little room for issues related to sustainable development, with these topics typically occupying less space. Likewise, sustainability concerns cannot be expected to be treated as a priority in the phases that follow in the life cycle. It is more likely that people's attention is focused on the needs of their children, the development of their careers, their health conditions and that of their relatives, among others, with a similar dynamic appearing in old age.

As the reader may have already noticed, the concerns just listed are typical in the life of an average citizen living in a country that is minimally stable from a social and economic point of view. When other situations are considered, it is possible that the lack of interest in sustainable development is even more pronounced, with the inhabitants of less developed countries having to worry about more urgent matters. Issues related to public security, for example, are often among the main issues that occupy the minds of those living in poor countries (Cardoso et al., 2021). Fear of unemployment can also be important (Castelhano, 2005), as the social security offered in these places is often very precarious or even nonexistent. Problems relating to health and education tend to follow a similar path. These issues can be analysed according to Maslow's pyramid, adapted to social development that is developed in Chapter 9. Among other consequences, the differences between the concerns of the inhabitants of rich and poor countries can help in understanding the reasons for the lesser engagement of the latter, with regard to environmental preservation.

Fear of Reprisals

If, on the one hand, unfamiliarity and disinterest can be understood as genuine reasons for maintaining neutral or moderate positions, other situations denote rational choices, with positions equidistant from the extremes of the sustainability spectrum representing a somewhat artificial posture. It is possible, for example, that some people present themselves as moderates just to avoid being attacked by those who disagree with their real opinions. This prospect becomes even more important when social media interactions are considered. Among other characteristics, these environments allow their users to interact directly in a user-to-user interface. Even if the organizations managing them have been increasingly accused of influencing the content of debates and applying various forms of prior censorship (Moore, 2021), they do not strictly position themselves as content publishers. This means that a user's opinions should not be filtered.

In addition to the possibility of arousing the ire of so-called haters, the fact is that the public nature of opinions expressed on the internet can end up having adverse results for those who issue them. As the patrol of political correctness intensifies (Bock-Côté, 2020), people become afraid to express what may not be in line with 'official opinion'. Depending on the repercussions of a particular position, those who express them may even have their jobs threatened. It is not uncommon for companies to monitor the activities of their employees on social media (Mikkelson, 2010), which, in many cases, ends up putting additional pressure on not freely expressing more extreme opinions. Despite being illegal in some countries, the analysis of the virtual behaviour of the workforce seems to be a well-established reality. Likewise, those who seek to position themselves in the job market (i.e., looking for a job) also need to filter the opinions they disseminate, as the selection processes usually include an analysis of the candidates' activities on the internet. All these factors contribute to people seeking to express neutral or moderate opinions, even if they do not illustrate what they think in reality.

The fear of professional reprisals seems to be even more intense for artists, sportsmen, or anyone who has greater exposure to the public. This is because the opinions they express may be at odds with the views of the organizations that employ them and also with the official positions of their sponsors. In these cases, it is common for expressions of more intense perspectives to be followed by retractions, in which the authors seek to soften the content of their messages. In more critical cases, these remedies may not be enough, with the publication of unwanted opinions resulting in breaches of contract and layoffs.

This dynamic seems to have intensified in recent years, with companies seeking to dissociate themselves from controversial issues and be perceived, as far as possible, as organizations in the service of good (Fracarolli Nunes and Lee Park, 2017). It is common, therefore, that the positions further to the left of the sustainability spectrum are more tolerated, while those further to the right are, in general, opposed. This mechanic takes place through the activities of various organized groups that threaten companies with boycotts or with the destruction of their reputations if they do not take action against those who express opinions considered wrong. The result of this process can represent a severe blow to artists and sportsmen who, in many cases, prefer to hide their real opinions in order to avoid possible reprisals.

Conviviality Issues

As discussed earlier, the consolidation of the internet resulted in wide dissemination of data and opinions to which the general public did not have direct access. Among the most immediate consequences of this new reality is the loss of the role of gatekeepers that was performed by traditional media vehicles. In other words, the direct discussion between users made the circulation of divergent worldviews gain a speed never before experienced in the history of mankind. While the greater distribution of information contributed to the increase in the cultural level of many people, in some cases, this dynamic had the opposite effect. The meeting of individuals who share similar worldviews resulted in the validation of their opinions and the reinforcement of extreme perspectives. In this sense, the grouping of people who share the same opinions gave rise to new forms of virtual tribalism, according to which identification with a group is reinforced through the distinction of others. As discussed in several passages throughout the book, the development of algorithms that aim to make users' experiences on social networks more pleasant has reinforced this process. As opposing opinions are kept at bay, the idea of co-radiation is undermined, resulting in animosities when opposite poles meet.

It is possible that among the main causes of aggression in virtual environments is the fact that there is no possibility of a physical confrontation, with individuals feeling protected by the fact that they are not within reach of those with whom they have clashes. A similar situation seems to explain the tendency of many drivers to show aggressive behaviour when driving. The fact that they are surrounded by a layer of metal gives them a feeling of protection, as if they are wearing armour. It follows that, on many occasions, people usually regarded as peaceful in the relationships they maintain in their daily lives adopt much less friendly behaviour when they are in charge of their cars. This also seems to be the case for some internet users.

However, the same people who express extreme opinions on social networks can adopt a more moderate stance when they are not inserted in virtual environments. Indeed, face-to-face discussions tend to be much less heated, probably because of the possibility of disagreements evolving into a clash of strength. Similar reasoning can be adopted when individual and group behaviours are compared. When they are surrounded by people with whom they share some kind of vision, many people feel comfortable expressing their aggression. The fact that they are in the company of other individuals seems to give them the feeling that they will have their support if a clash starts. This dynamic may underlie the behaviour of many football fans, who can adopt a belligerent posture when among their peers. Interestingly, in some cases the same individual is peaceful when alone.

Another aspect to consider concerns the management of social life more broadly, with people usually seeking to avoid confrontations with others who are part of their daily lives. Disagreeing with neighbours, relatives, co-workers, or other people you need to live with can be a very negative option from the point of view of social harmony. The quest to avoid friction with these groups leads some people to prefer to express themselves through conciliatory attitudes and more diplomatic tones. When it comes to discussions on sustainability, more specifically, this should translate into greater flexibility, with the tone of the arguments adapting to the interlocutor's positions. The more neutral postures, however, do not change the essence of the thinking of those who adopt them, only allowing life to unfold in a less conflicting way. When these and other arguments are considered, it can be said that adopting moderate positions can be a rational choice, typically adopted in the name of conviviality.

On the Usefulness of Moderate Views

Because they are among those who identify with the most extreme perspectives, individuals who share moderate views assume a particularly important value in building or maintaining an environment conducive to dialogue. Among the main factors that can contribute to this role is the potential lack of attachment to a specific set of ideas, which tends to keep those who compose this group protected from the fanaticism that usually characterizes the most radicalized groups. As they are decidedly not convinced of the validity of a particular utopian vision or ideology, this allows moderates not to perceive the views presented by extremists as an offense to their convictions, or something that must be fought fiercely because it is inherently wrong. Softer positions would therefore represent openings not only for the exchange of ideas, but also for radicals to expose themselves, which usually represents an important step towards establishing dialogue and collaboration.

The fact that they are not passionate about a particular way of thinking gives moderates the ability to act as filters or even interpreters of radical views. Evidently, these ideas are based on the premise that individuals located between the poles of thought are more inclined to exercise rationality in their analyses, which is not observed in all cases. It can be argued, for example, that acceptance of an extreme view depends, to some extent, on understanding the logic that connects its various arguments. As much as one disagrees with the premises of conservative thought, one cannot deny that it follows a chain of ideas that lead to a certain conclusion. The same can be said of the theoretical bases that support the other views that escape neutrality. Disagreements with extreme thoughts are therefore much more based on the premises they adopt.

As discussed throughout the book, it is possible to identify, in the different interpretations of human nature, the starting points of the many distinctions of thoughts classified as right and left. While the former tends to be skeptical about the goodness of man, the latter usually understands that individuals are inherently ethical and moral beings. From these basic premises stem the pillars that form conservative thinking, on the one hand, and revolutionary thinking, on the other, with the weight given to individual responsibility perhaps the main explanatory factor of the major differences between them. The skepticism of conservatives leads them to see the individual himself as responsible for his successes and failures. In this sense, the concept of meritocracy links aspects such as innate skills and specific efforts to the results obtained individually by each person. The premise that human beings are naturally good, in turn, favours the leftist logic that the results obtained by individuals (i.e., success or failure) are due to inconsistencies in the environment in which they find themselves. The defence of equality would thus be a way of correcting the harmful effects of an environment that does not operate in the way considered ideal.

It is therefore possible to point to the location of imperfections as an important part of the origins of ideological thoughts. For those who fit into a more right-wing way of thinking, the imperfection would be concentrated in the human being. It is not by chance that conservative currents of thought tend to defend the idea that individual success is, to some extent, a result of the way an individual responds to his or her imperfections. In general, this can be understood as a person's struggle against the many temptations that can lead him to deviate from the path of prosperity. This includes laziness, for example, but also other flaws of moral character such as envy and covetousness. In this set, the search for personal development and the improvement of this imperfect condition would be part of a process of creating value and wealth. On the other hand, perfection would be located in the environment inhabited by imperfect beings, which may explain – at least partially – the idealized constructions of market mechanisms. Once again, the idea of the invisible hand proposed by Adam Smith (1776) in the classic *The Wealth of Nations* illustrates the idea of a perfect market capable of self-stimulating and self-correcting.

From a leftist's point of view, the relationship between perfection and imperfection tends to be opposite, with the individual seen as an infallible part involved in a disorganized and corrupt atmosphere. This vision can be understood as one of the determining factors for the entire logic of left-wing thinking, with the reform of basically all aspects of society becoming an objective of leftists so that it finally adapts to the human being idealized as perfect. This includes changes and planning of diverse natures, such as the concept of family, religion, and, more objectively, market mechanisms. For a classic leftist, these concepts would cause problems for the development of a full life, with these hypothetical social constructions being nothing more than expressions of an unjust society that seeks to maintain inequality between men as a way of guaranteeing the mechanisms of exploitation in force.

Among the main consequences of the development of these views in their extreme forms is the attachment of individuals to their convictions, which in many ways leads them to classify opposing views as heresies. In the case of leftists, this mechanism tends to be intensified, precisely because of the religious function that some of its expressions assume. Marxism, for example, can be understood as an illustration of this issue, with its lack of empirical basis and projections about the future often classified as fantastic or metaphysical thinking. Marxism seems to fulfil some of the functions typically attributed to religions, especially with regard to explaining reality and providing meaning for life itself. The first issue is typically approached from a materialist point of view, with economic factors taking a central role that basically overshadows all others.

The understanding of reality would thus be limited to an attempt to explain the different levels of wealth among individuals, with the mechanisms of oppression and exploitation being, according to this view, the main sources of inequality. The reversal of these corrupt mechanisms and the establishment of a new order would give meaning to life, with revolution the means by which justice among men would be established. The promise of a post-revolutionary earthly paradise is very close to traditional religious thought, with the difference that the leftist believes s/he deserves to experience the perfection of paradise in her/his lifetime. The predictions about the future of capitalism and the projection of its inevitable collapse would represent another facet of the messianic aspect that Marxism tries to assume, with Karl Marx (1818–1883) himself representing the figure of a prophet. These characteristics can explain the success of the radical visions of the left and the need they have to fight religions, since both seek to occupy the same space in the psyche of individuals. The status of religion that leftism assumes would explain, therefore, the vehemence of its defence, as well as the repulsion of those who adopt it as their orientation in life to any idea that opposes it.

For individuals who identify with right-wing thinking, however, the influence of religious aspects in the formation of their way of thinking would not be guided by the replacement of their religiosity by ideologies. Instead, the imperfections attributed to human beings can be related to more widespread religious beliefs in the West, with the expulsion of Adam and Eve from paradise probably representing the initial illustration of the flaws inherent in men and women. The biblical texts make a number of other warnings about the potential of human beings to do evil, which must have influenced the characteristic skepticism of the right about the human condition. The superiority of the environment would be associated with the perfection of divine creation. Thus, contrary to what leftists think, human failures would be the main reasons why human beings do not live in paradise, which results in the idea that each individual must assume responsibility for his or her own condition.

Like leftists, those who identify with right-wing thinking can understand that views contrary to their deepest beliefs must be repelled. From this fundamental debate stems the idea that, while equality is the utopia of the left, this role is played by meritocracy on the right. Along with being based on reasonably logical reasoning, what makes these convictions particularly strong is the fact that they are based on religious thought and, therefore, fundamental for those who believe in it. While providing additional elements that allow a better understanding of the reasons leading extremists to repel each other, the discussion of these points reinforces the idea that moderate thinking can play a fundamental role in maintaining minimum levels of civility and dialogue. The lack of adherence to extremes allows moderates to be classified as the true skeptics as they remain equidistant from the more radical views.

Moderate views can be understood as an ideal to be achieved. It is paradoxical, however, that they are precisely the result of disinterest, or even unfamiliarity, with the search for study usually pushing people to extremes. This seems to occur as individuals find, in authoritarian views, reinforcements for their deepest convictions, many of which they themselves were unaware of. The reading of ideological texts can have an important intellectual impact, bringing to the surface ideas that perhaps would not manifest otherwise. In this sense, ideological texts seem to function as a kind of concatenator that, by filling previously empty spaces with previously developed reasoning, puts into contact the different ideas that make up the psyche of the one who studies them. When these processes occur, the person who comes across a radical text may have the feeling of having finally found something that not only explains reality as s/he perceives it but also gives meaning to her/his own existence. As previously proposed, this can be understood as one of the many origins of attachment to ideologies, with the defence of something so valuable being, perhaps, the great motivator of a refractory attitude against everything that opposes its supposedly perfect vision.

Moderates, however, would have a harder time falling in love with ideas, tending to see more flaws than virtues in what they read. It is possible that this is the result of greater understanding of the complexities of the world and the impossibility of solving them in a simplistic way. Thus, the contact with a radical vision should arouse skepticism in these individuals in such a way that the exaggerations contained in these texts call their attention. The result of this process would be non-adherence to ideas that preach an accurate diagnosis of complex issues, or that propose infallible remedies for the problems they identify. In this sense, the greater stability they enjoy would place them in a privileged position, as they would not necessarily be in search of ideas that offer them comfort or even meaning in their lives. Emotional balance reinforces their intellectual protection system, helping moderates to see the reality of what they read and not a fantasy version that gives them something they lack.

With regard specifically to sustainability issues, the skeptical view of moderates seems to be the main means by which a productive dialogue can be maintained. The fact that they do not surrender to apocalyptic visions allows them to evaluate the proposed solutions with greater tranquillity, without an exaggerated sense of urgency leading them to defend alternatives that do not have the proper scientific evidence. Likewise, the lack of a direct association between the defence of sustainable development and the progress of leftist agendas should contribute so that individuals considered moderates can assess environmental issues more objectively, evaluating them for what they actually are and not for what radicals understand them to be. Moderate views are therefore very valuable and should receive more attention from those who aim to contribute to the advancement of environmental protection and a healthy relationship between economic and social agents and the world around them.

However, moderate views tend to be less attractive to the masses, precisely because of their greater complexity. Unlike radical views, understanding more balanced perspectives often requires analysing different types of arguments, with the ability to filter out exaggerations being an additional difficulty. Because of their often more elaborate nature, moderate views cannot be simplified or turned into streamline slogans that can be communicated quickly. These characteristics contribute to the lack of popularity of less radical views, which reinforces the need to be encouraged and supported.

References

Adam, S. (1776). *The Wealth of Nations* (E. Cannan, Ed.). Modern Library, 2000.

Bersheda, T. (2012). Is arbitration-friendly Switzerland also trust-arbitration-friendly? *Trusts & Trustees*, Vol.18, No.4, pp.348–357.

Bock-Côté, M. (2020). *O Império do Politicamente Correto*. É Realizações Editora.

Cardoso, M.H.S.A., Santos, T.F., and Silva, M.A.V.D. (2021). Violence in public transport: An analysis of resilience and vulnerability in the city of Rio de Janeiro. *Revista Brasileira de Gestão Urbana*, Vol.13, pp.1–14.

Castelhano, L.M. (2005). The fear of the unemployment and the new corporation. *Psicologia & Sociedade*, Vol.17, No.1, pp.14–20.

Flynn, H.K., Felmlee, D.H., and Conger, R.D. (2017). The social context of adolescent friendships: Parents, peers, and romantic partners. *Youth & Society*, Vol.49, No.5, pp.679–705.

Fracarolli Nunes, M., and Lee Park, C. (2017). Self-claimed sustainability: Building social and environmental reputations with words. *Sustainable Production and Consumption*, Vol.11, pp.46–57.

Gao, G., Greenwood, B.N., Agarwal, R., and McCullough, J.S. (2015). Vocal minority and silent majority. *MIS Quarterly*, Vol.39, No.3, pp.565–590.

Hirt, O. (2021). German millionaires rush assets to Switzerland ahead of elections. *Reuters*, September 24. Available at https://www.reuters.com/world/europe/german-millionaires-rush-assets-switzerland-ahead-election-2021-09-24/

Kiers, C. (2020). The dynamics of the greenhouse effect. *The College Mathematics Journal*, Vol.51, No.3, pp.182–194.

Kraemer, D. (2021). Greta Thunberg: Who is the climate campaigner and what are her aims? *BBC*, November 5. Available at https://www.bbc.com/news/world-europe-49918719

Kutnick, P., and Manson, I. (2021). Social life in the primary school: Towards a relational concept of social skills for use in the classroom. In: A. Campbell and S. Muncer (Eds.). *The Social Child*, pp.165–187. Psychology Press.

Lassiter, M.D. (2013). *The Silent Majority*. Princeton University Press.

Leal, O.F. (1990). Popular taste and erudite repertoire: The place and space of television in Brazil. *Cultural Studies*, Vol.4, No.1, pp.19–29.

Mikkelson, K. (2010). Cybervetting and monitoring employees' online activities: Assessing the legal risks for employers. *The Public Lawyer*, Vol.18, p.3.

Montemurro, B. (2008). Toward a sociology of reality television. *Sociology Compass*, Vol.2, No.1, pp.84–106.

Moore, J. (2021). Assaults on freedom of speech: Why social studies must defend the first amendment. *The Social Studies*, Vol.113, No.1, pp.1–20.

Morris, K., and White, T.J. (2011). Neutrality and the European Union: The case of Switzerland. *Journal of Law and Conflict Resolution*, Vol.3, No.7, pp.104–111.

Nachbar, J., Nachbar, J.G., and Lausé, K. (Eds.) (1992). *Popular Culture: An Introductory Text*. Popular Press.

Panja, T. (2019). Fifa quietly considering plan to leave Switzerland. *The New York Times*, July 31. Available at https://www.nytimes.com/2019/07/31/sports/soccer/fifa-headquarters-zurich.html

Reginbogin, H.R. (2009). *Faces of Neutrality: A Comparative Analysis of the Neutrality of Switzerland and Other Neutral Nations During WW II*, Vol.31. LIT Verlag Münster.

Rijken, A.J., and Knijn, T. (2009). Couples' decisions to have a first child: Comparing pathways to early and late parenthood. *Demographic Research*, Vol.21, pp.765–802.

Rieder, J. (1989). The Rise of the 'Silent Majority'. In: S. Fraser and G. Gerstle (Eds.). *The Rise and Fall of the New Deal Order, 1930–1980*, pp.243–268. Princeton University Press.

Ross, J.F. (1989). *Neutrality and International Sanctions: Sweden, Switzerland, and Collective Security*. Greenwood Publishing Group.

Sull, D.N., and Eisenhardt, K.M. (2015). *Simple Rules: How to Thrive in a Complex World*. Houghton Mifflin Harcourt.

Wei, X., Yu, J.W., Wagner, M., Hudson, L., Roux, A.M., Shattuck, P., and Blackorby, J. (2018). Job searching, job duration, and job loss among young adults with autism spectrum disorder. *Journal of Vocational Rehabilitation*, Vol.48, No.1, pp.1–10.

West, K.L., Leezenbaum, N.B., Northrup, J.B., and Iverson, J.M. (2019). The relation between walking and language in infant siblings of children with autism spectrum disorder. *Child Development*, Vol.90, No.3, pp.e356–e372.

Witze, A. (2020). Rare ozone hole opens over Arctic – and it's big. *Nature*, Vol.580, No.7801, pp.18–20.

Xia, C., Liu, G., Meng, Y., Wang, Z., and Zhang, X. (2020). Impact of human activities on urban river system and its implication for water-environment risks: An isotope-based investigation in Chengdu, China. *Human and Ecological Risk Assessment: An International Journal*, Vol.27, No.5, pp.1416–1439.

Yu, L., Jin, X., Josey, S.A., Lee, T., Kumar, A., Wen, C., and Xue, Y. (2017). The global ocean water cycle in atmospheric reanalysis, satellite, and ocean salinity. *Journal of Climate*, Vol.30, No.10, pp.3829–3852.

Part II

The Causes of Extreme Sustainability Rhetoric

8 The Psychology of Extremism

Initial Thoughts

Before entering the discussions of the psychological factors supporting extremist behaviours, it is necessary to consider some caveats regarding the complexity of the topic, the scope of the proposed debate, and its limitations. First, it must be recognized that the human mind is one of the greatest mysteries we need to deal with, as centuries of study have allowed us to make only modest progress on understanding its structure and functioning. Despite the knowledge issued from disciplines such as psychiatry, psychology, and neuroscience, the lack of answers to fundamental questions suggests that comprehension of the intricate mechanisms of the mind is still in its infancy. It is not clear, for example, why the behaviour of some people is close to that of the majority of the population, while that of others deviates enormously from the standards. Simplistically, this issue frames the little intelligence we have about the notions of normality and abnormality, with the very definitions of normal and abnormal behaviours being problematic.

For practical purposes, the concept of normality adopted here considers a statistical perspective, with the normal distribution proposed by the German mathematician Carl Friedrich Gauss (1777–1855) in 1809 serving as the basis for this definition. In this way, relatively normal behaviours are understood as those that lie around the mean (i.e., the closer to the mean, the more normal a behaviour will be). Likewise, the more a behaviour deviates from the mean, the more abnormal it may be considered. Unlike easily measurable quantities (e.g., mass, distance), however, the assignment of numerical values to behaviours might yield considerably irregular results. It should be noted, then, that the classification of a behaviour as normal or abnormal will necessarily be imprecise, with the authors not intending to present any definitive conclusion on the issue. Instead, the reasoning proposed only aims to facilitate the discussion in the chapter, having absolutely no methodological claim.

The use of a statistical normality reinforces the idea that a direct relationship between normality and something positive should not be automatic. Indeed, the definition of a mean and the fact that most observations rest around it refers only to a measure of frequency. Thus, the behaviours considered normal (or close to this) are, a priori, nothing more than the ones most commonly observed, making

DOI: 10.4324/9781003124719-10

it perfectly possible that an abnormal behaviour has greater value. The latter is generally marginalized, however, as it usually affronts social customs. It may be argued that, at the same time that typical behaviours tend to generate feelings of predictability, behaviours considered abnormal add instability and uncertainty, which increases their chances of being rejected.

One must also remember that the same person can present a normal behaviour in one given dimension and an abnormal one in others. Also, it is possible that classifications within the same dimension vary over time, changing from both normal to abnormal, and vice versa. These and other questions denote the great practical difficulty in classifying individual behaviours, with a definitive classification of individuals as normal or abnormal being even less likely. In addition to all the complexity related to the functioning of the human mind, its interaction with the physical body is also poorly understood. Among other things, there still seems to be no certainty about the extent to which thoughts affect biological functioning, nor how body functionalities impact mental health. Likewise, it is not possible to precisely identify all the impacts of the environment on the way of thinking of individuals, which makes the debate about psychological aspects even more difficult.

Despite all the misunderstandings about the psychological factors that can trigger extremism, the discussions learned earlier in the chapter support its classification as an abnormal behaviour. Seeking to provide elements that contribute to the debate on psychological aspects related to the development of extreme thinking, the following discussions address the most diverse aspects that are somehow related to this issue, including political, historical, and philosophical processes. However, it is not sought here to treat them in an isolated and meticulous way. The biggest interest rests exactly in how these aspects are related, influencing each other. For this and other reasons, the most important elements of each of these themes will be presented in a contextualized manner. The aim is not to go into the more technical aspects of the psychology literature itself, but rather to offer the reader a contextualization of the various influences and manifestations of extreme views of the world.

General Thoughts

'Why do people vary in their views of human nature and their visions of the good society? Why do many people categorize themselves as "liberal," "conservative," "libertarian," "socialist," and so on?' With these questions, Haidt et al. (2009, p.110) open their debate on the moral foundations that support ideological narratives. These questions seem not only to be pertinent for those interested in the complexities of the human mind but are also at the heart of the study of political inclinations. They unfold a dialogue around some of the most important factors that separate human beings from each other. As discussed throughout the book, different worldviews are among the main sources of animosity in the political arena, with people who identify with leftist thought often unwilling to exchange with their counterparts on the right side (and vice versa).

Among the reasons for such repulse may be the degree to which each side believes they are correct. Beyond that, the perception that those on the opposite side may somehow represent a threat to their existence increases the chances that the dialogue between these groups will be established. The progressive segmentation of these two macro divisions into increasingly atomized sub-groups results in fierce disagreements, even among those who theoretically share most of their structural beliefs. The extrapolation of these views to sustainability positions (see the *sustainability spectrum* developed in Chapter 4) makes them also central for the debate on sustainable development.

Before further discussing the psychological issues associated with the most prominent categories of political-economic thought, it must be noted that these classifications are not at all rigid. Instead, they have been used in reference to different ideas throughout history, with sometimes radically distinct views being referred to as if they belonged together. This semantic instability certainly contributes to the confusion among these themes, deserving serious attention from those seeking to interpret how the meaning and scope of the referred labels evolve through time. The best example of this phenomenon is probably the transformation of the term liberal. Traditionally associated with those who praise individual freedom above basically any other societal value and defend the benefits of free market economies, the label has been kidnapped by radical leftists in the United States in the last decades. While a discussion of the actual reasons driving this movement are beyond the scope of the book, it seems that it intends to offer camouflage for communists and socialists, as they have long been despised in America.

In addressing this issue, one must consider the tortuous relations that the United States has kept with leftism through its history. As the so-called founding fathers (e.g., George Washington (1732–1799), John Adams (1735–1826), Thomas Jefferson (1743–1826), James Madison (1751–1836), Alexander Hamilton (1755–1804), James Monroe (1758–1831), Benjamin Franklin (1706–1790), John Jay (1745–1829), Samuel Adams (1722–1803), Patrick Henry (1736–1799), John Marshall (1755–1835), and George Mason (1725–1792)) rested the foundation of the new country on the respect for liberty (Hollis, 1990) and the praise of the individual (Meacham, 2007), US society developed values that are incompatible with any sort of Marxist mindset. The valorization of personal merit as the way towards wealthiness (Herrnstein and Murray, 1994), for example, does not leave much space for the defence of economic equality among citizens. Likewise, the protection of free speech (Rabban, 1999) and the defence of citizens' right to own private property (Nedelsky, 1994) are incongruent with the totalitarism of non-democratic leftism. These ideas have practical consequences, such as the typical opposition of US society to taxes (Shlaes, 2012). Understood as one of the main ways through which governments may redistribute wealth (Atkinson, 1971), this mechanism has encountered great resistance among voters, and this is often one of the main issues discussed during election processes and political debates in general (Norquist, 2020).

These views on taxes are part of an even larger orientation regarding the role and the size of the State. In fact, the foundation of the country is, to a large extent, based on the idea that power must be decentralized and remain as close to citizens as possible. This is reflected in the federalism over which the country operates (Beer, 1978). At the base, that means that, despite forming a single country and under a single constitution, each US state has the autonomy to approve many of its own laws and govern itself according to the will of its people (Rose-Ackerman, 1981). Once more, one must refer to the historical roots of the United States to make sense of such arrangement. Among other things, this reflects the fact that the country was formed by the union of 13 separate British colonies, which desired to keep their autonomy once they got their independence (Kincaid, 2010), which led to important debates regarding the birth of the new nation, as citizens were skeptical about a central government.

Much of the discussion referred to the possibility of a common president being not much more than a substitute to the monarchy that used to govern them. The autonomy of each state in relation to a central government appeared as an important condition to any form of agreement. The result of these important debates can be inferred from the very denomination of the country, which reaffirms the fact that it represented the gathering of several independent entities. Despite maintaining much of their independence, the unification demanded a considerable effort from each federal unit. The implementation of a single currency, for instance, represented an important step in that direction as each state had its own (Grubb, 2003). As the country expanded towards the West, the creation and incorporation of new states to the country followed the same logics.

Thus, the historical process of formation of the United States appears as one of the main reasons why US society seems to oppose the worldviews defended by leftists. More specifically, the fact that the country was founded based on the decentralization of power represents an important obstacle to the creation of a strong and grandiose state. On the contrary, traditional US values preach that the state should be as small as possible, limiting itself as to not interfering with the individual's life. Unlike the classic view defended by the left, the State would not represent the solution to the problems of life in society, being, at best, hypothesized as a necessary evil.

The origins of this revulsion towards the concentration of power seem to be associated with a skepticism regarding human nature. While leftists tend to perceive the human being as naturally good (Breines, 1988), individuals who identify with the right are generally less generous with the human condition. It is not by chance that the latter tend to see virtues in democratic systems, especially concerning alternating power. In this sense, the fact that the mandates have predetermined terms would work as a supplementary guarantee so that tyrants would not perpetuate themselves in power. For the leftist, however, the concentration of force in the hands of a few individuals would not necessarily be problematic, mainly because those chosen to occupy the highest positions in the state bureaucracy would be superior human beings and therefore free from the passions common to all others.

In addition to the practical consequences discussed previously, these opposing views are also reflected in a number of other structural issues in the US society. Defence of the possession and carriage of weapons, for example, would work as an additional guarantee that power would remain diluted in society (O'Connor and Barron, 1998). In this set, the most common convictions of the society would be at odds with the Weberian concept of the monopoly of the use of force, according to which the State would be the only holder of the right to impose its directives on society. In the view of a typical right-winger, abdication of the right to defend oneself, one's family, and one's property would be very risky, as it would depend on the goodwill of those in positions of power in the structures of the state. This is one of the main reasons that US society has defended their right to own weapons. Leftists, for their part, are often fervent supporters of a monopoly of force and are usually in favour of disarmament campaigns (Shepherd and Kay, 2018). Once again, the belief that those in power may be higher human beings makes them assume that not abdicating the right to self-defence is not a risk in itself. Some rightists argue that, in addition to representing an innocent or romantic view of human nature, the defence of disarmament would have the objective of preventing the population's resistance in the case of a left-wing revolution.

Far beyond historical curiosities, this quick and modest analysis of the development of basic values in US society provides essential concepts for understanding the influence of culture in shaping a particular political-economic mindset. The dissemination of the values discussed earlier are, to a large extent, responsible for creating the most prosperous nation on the planet, both economically and in terms of respect for individual freedoms. The solidity of the US belief in these values can be seen in the country's determination to fight against the advance of totalitarian regimes. This includes the participation of the United States in the two great world wars of the 20th century, with their intervention having been particularly important in the fight against the Nazi regime in World War II (Casey, 2001).

Likewise, the country's extremely firm stance throughout the period known as the Cold War proved to be essential to curb the advance of communist dictatorships (Powaski, 1997). In addition to the actual armed conflicts, the confrontation of leftist totalitarian ideas also took place through an intense cultural war, in which everything that made mention of leftist ideologies was condemned in television programs, films, music, and other forms of cultural expression (Leab, 1998). Given the incomparability of communist and socialist authoritarian systems with democracy (Wydra, 2007), in many cases these interventions did not even need to strive to create a negative impression on these government alternatives, with the mere representation of their nefarious realities being sufficient to create an extremely negative impression with the public. Faced with these issues, it is not difficult to conclude that US society has developed a strong resistance to leftist ideas throughout its history, which is the probable reason for the radical left presenting itself under the label of liberal. It is because of these and other rhetorical devices that it is necessary to treat the classifications of political and economic views very carefully. Before delving into the discussion of the psychological roots of extremism, however, a discussion of the ways in which the radical left has managed to gain a foothold in US politics may be helpful. This process dates back to the creation and expansion of the infamous Frankfurt School.

Initially formed by a group of young *bourgeois* who believed that they had identified flaws in the Marxist project (i.e., Neo Marxists, Max et al., 2017), the Frankfurt School projected and implemented a vision of total destruction of society's values, according to which the communist paradise would only be implemented after the overthrow of the pillars of Western civilization. This included subversion of the concept of family and severe attacks on religions and anything that, in any way, contributed to what they understood to be the basis of a mechanism of oppression. The very idea of beauty was questioned, with creations of very low technical appeal coming to be classified as art. Many identify in the Frankfurt School the origins of the various radicalisms that dominate public debate today.

After a period of development of their worldviews, the group dissipated with the arrival of Adolf Hitler (1889–1945) to power in Germany, with many members taking refuge in the United States (Minnicino, 1992). Columbia University was one of the main gateways to the Frankfurt School members on US soil (Wheatland, 2009). The ideas imported from Germany also spread to the country's biggest universities (e.g., Princeton, University of California – Berkeley) (Atkinson, 1999), which helps to understand why such radical ideas became mainstream in the space of a few decades. Generation after generation, a legion of opinion makers has been shaped by what seems to have been instrumental in the spread of the subversion of traditional values in the US society. This includes journalists, artists, and teachers, among many other professional categories that tend to maintain a great interface with the public. This influence was reflected in increasingly consistent electoral results, to the point that some analysts argue that the United States can no longer be considered a legitimately conservative country.

From a broader perspective, it can be said that the Frankfurt School seeks to question the concept of truth, promoting a worldview supported by a form of extreme relativism (Gunderson, 2016). It is possible, therefore, that the search for the destruction of Western values is at the root of what North American psychiatrist Lyle H. Rossiter Jr. (2006) calls 'political madness'. In his book, *The Liberal Mind*, the author analyses what he understands to be unreasonable behaviour on the part of left-wing radicals. Accordingly, the policies adopted by those on the extreme left of the political-economic spectrum and the damage they cause to freedom have led many people to question their mental sanity. Still, per Rossiter, understanding what would be characterized as a form of 'political madness' would be critical, as these stances would jeopardize the US goal of creating a society governed by a civilized liberty (which the author classifies as the West's greatest achievement). The capture of the term liberal by the US extreme left becomes even clearer when these perspectives are compared with those presented in the homonymous book written by Kenneth Minogue (2012). In a work also entitled *The Liberal Mind*, Minogue makes a historical and psychological analysis of the origins of the term, focusing on those who argue for the original liberal ideas in defence of individual freedoms.

From a philosophical point of view, the basic difference between individuals who identify with right-wing thinking and those who recognize themselves in left-wing ideas can be summarized in the different beliefs that these two groups have about the concept of reality. While rightists typically believe in the existence of an objective reality, leftists tend to privilege the idea of interpretations. From this initial divergence, the basic ontological views of objectivism and subjectivism are formed. From a broader perspective, the belief in the existence of a reality that is independent of the way it is perceived forms the basis for accepting the idea of truth, and hence the existence of God. This can be considered one of the main reasons why many individuals identified with right-wing thinking – especially conservatives – are also religious (Lienesch, 1982). Reflexively, the fact that many leftists disagree with the possibility that there is an objective reality makes it difficult for them to accept the idea of truth and, consequently, the existence of God. This would explain, at least in part, the lack of religiosity of many leftists (Thrower, 2011).

In addition to issues related to a lack of spirituality, the fact that leftists, in general, do not recognize God as the creator and centre of the universe (Zrinščak, 2004) seems to create a void of meaning in their lives, which may be at the origin of degenerative behaviours such as abuse of alcohol (Knight et al., 2007), cigarettes, and illicit drug use (Hayward et al., 2016). It cannot be said that leftism is the absolute cause of involvement by individuals with this type of substance, nor that contact with them is limited to leftists. The fact is, these issues are complex, with addiction to chemical substances being the product of a variety of causes. It is possible, for example, that a person seeks the consumption of alcohol as a way to alleviate the negative feelings they are experiencing, whether referring to a momentary situation or painful memories of the past.

As discussed by clinical psychologist Jordan B. Peterson (1962–), in many of his interventions, alcohol consumption would allow the individual to lower his level of consciousness, giving him quick relief, as if the suffering inherent in the human condition could be forgotten for some time (e.g., Aerial View, 2019). Other drugs act in a similar way, which explains their 'success', despite all the harm they cause. In fact, the abundance of suffering favours the search for escapes from reality, regardless of each person's political-ideological orientation. Given all the possibilities and nuances that can lead someone to seek relief from their pain in chemical substances, it is not possible to point to a single cause for this behaviour, with an analysis of each case being probably the most indicated.

However, the lack of religious values may favour the search for alternative answers (Gordon, 1983). Throughout human history, belief in God has provided not only hope but comfort in difficult times. Issues that are difficult to understand or accept, such as the death of relatives, for example, tend to be better absorbed by individual believers, with their religious bases – including the communities that make them up – offering the necessary support to face these challenges. Sacred texts serve as guides in moments of great difficulty, breaking down reason. This contact with the sacred is, in many cases, the only thing capable of making individuals accept the great dramas of their lives.

More broadly, it can be said that belief in the Creator resolves the most basic philosophical questions of all, offering the means to recognize the meaning of life, the origin of all that is known, and the fate after death. Resolving these issues saves the faithful from immense existential anguish. Considering the importance of faith, it is not difficult to assume that people who do not believe in God are more likely to seek comfort from their drug problems, whether legal or illegal. The fact that leftism is, in general, incompatible with religious thought (Raines, 2011), excludes many leftists from all the benefits that belief in God offers. This may be one of the reasons why they uselessly seek in chemical substances what they lack. Once again, it is stressed that drug use is not limited to leftists, with many individuals from the right, the centre, or any part of the political spectrum also resorting to these subterfuges. What is argued here is that the closer link between conservatism and religion offers more ways for those who identify themselves as rightists to endure the anxieties of existence, increasing the chances of not getting involved in drugs.

Still, in the consequences of the vacuum created in the minds of those who do not believe in God, it is possible to identify in the lack of faith the origins of many of the leftist agendas, especially concerning the role of the State in society. In this sense, the state bureaucracy would assume the role of God, responsible for both organizing any and all human relationships, and giving meaning to existence itself. Without referring to the latter, one can point to a type of functional tautology in which the State becomes an end and a means. Within this perspective, the individual's reason for existence would come down to serving the state, accepting being treated as a form of resource to be allocated wherever necessary. This would be the basic functioning of forced labour mechanisms in communist regimes, where workers do not have the right to choose their activities according to their individual capacities, talents, or desires. On the contrary, the lack of freedom that is characteristic of these models is represented in the transfer of decisions to a higher level (i.e., the State), which will – according to collective need – determine the way in which each citizen should contribute to the whole. This form of social organization is based on the premise that those who control the state machine are able to manage economic activities more efficiently than the free market, with their decisions being more precise than those defined by the complex mechanism of incentives mainly represented by price variation in a free economy (Richman, 1974).

In other words, the belief that the state will be able to manage economic life better than the free market represents the quest to replace the 'invisible hand', as discussed by Adam Smith (baptized 1723–1790) in his classic *The Wealth of Nations*, with the hand of the State. Evidently, this task requires the State to be omniscient and omnipresent, which, to some extent, explains the tendency of socialist and leftist regimes toward totalitarianism and, therefore, their incompatibility with representative democracy. The other explanatory factor for the search for concentration of State control is less noble, with the thirst for power being one of the main motivators for the construction of an absolute State. Thus, the concentration of power in the state bureaucracy prevents the organization of political opposition or even armed resistance. The architecture of communist politics around a single party illustrates the intolerant aspect of far-left regimes, which do not admit the existence of alternative or contrary views to the official ones.

Regarding the maintenance of a society incapable of rebelling against the current system, the alienation of citizens' right to own and bear arms seems to be one of the most important points. In general, the prohibition of access to firearms by ordinary citizens appears as one of the most important agendas of left-wing parties around the world, appearing most of the time diffracted in an argument in favour of peace, according to which the withdrawal of circulation weapons would prevent unprepared civilians from ending up using them in problematic situations that present themselves in their daily lives, such as traffic disputes and other common misunderstandings. From a conceptual point of view, the prohibition of the use of weapons by the population is inserted in the Weberian concept of monopoly on the use of violence, according to which only the State – through its police, armies, and other armed forces – would have the right to employ force as it seeks to maintain social order. In a broader view, this idea would be based on the need for each individual to agree to delegate to the State the function of protecting both their life and their property, with the abdication of the right to self-defence being a fundamental condition for the development of life in society.

It so happens, however, that measures aimed at restricting ordinary citizens' access to firearms can have a very negative effect in terms of levels of violence. In the case of societies unable to prevent bandits, thieves, and criminals in general from continuing to use weapons, they are encouraged to commit crimes, since they are sure that their victims – when civilians – will be unarmed and therefore unable to offer suitable resistance. Analysing criminal activity under the logic of the relationship between risk and return, it can be said that disarmament policies end up encouraging the practice of crimes, with a reduction in the probability of adverse events occurring to the decision-making agent (e.g., reaction of an armed victim) favouring those who act outside the law.

In countries such as Brazil, the disarmament of the population is pointed out as one of the main causes of the significant increase in levels of violence in recent decades. It is worth remembering that the disarmament policy was implemented by the leftist government of the Workers Party during the first term of the then-president and now ex-convict Luiz Ignacio 'Lula' da Silva (Brazilian Senate, 2003). The decision to restrict the possession and carriage of weapons represents one of the greatest anti-democratic acts in Brazilian history, having been conducted against society's will. The Brazilian people were consulted on the issue in a plebiscite, in which it showed them to be against the measure (Macedo, 2015). Ignoring the will of the Brazilians, the government sanctioned the prohibition. The measure finds a parallel in France, upon the application of a referendum for the ratification of the European constitution in 2005. Against French's rejection to the text (Le Monde, 2005), the country's parliament ratified the treaty of Lisbon in 2008 through a revision of the French constitution (French Ministry of Justice, 2008). According to former French president Valéry Giscard d'Estaing (1926–2020), though, the treaty of Lisbon contains the same proposals that were present in the treaty on the European constitution that had been rejected, with the difference between the two texts being limited to a matter of order in which the proposals were presented (Le Monde, 2007). Despite dealing with a distinct issue, it can be argued that both cases are in line with leftist yearnings, with the imposition made on the French people being an important step in the weakening of nationalism at the expense of a globalist worldview.

Even before representing a way to avoid a popular revolt against an eventual leftist totalitarian government, the ban on the possession and carriage of firearms would aim to nullify a possible resistance in the case of a revolution. If it is true that the precepts defended by the founder of the Italian communist party Antonio Gramsci (1891–1937) prefer the slow and gradual evolution of socialism as a way of imposing it (Lears, 1985), armed revolutions were the choices adopted in Russia in 1917 (Wade, 2017), in China (Chen, 2010), and in Cuba in 1959 (Bonachea and San Martín, 2018), as well as on several other occasions in African (Klinghoffer, 2019) and Asian countries (Vu, 2016). In reality, armed revolution seems to have been the choice of several leftist groups that operated in Latin America in the second half of the 20th century (Cardoso, 2016). These movements would be at the origin of counterrevolutionary movements led by the military in countries such as Brazil (Pinto, 2019), Argentina (Rapoport and Laufer, 2000), and Chile (Ruderer, 2012). Relying on the support of important sections of the local population (Cordeiro, 2021), the resistance to the attempts to implement dictatorial leftist regimes in the 1960s, 1970s, and 1980s culminated in governments led by the leaders of the armed forces that installed themselves in power for years (D'Araujo, 2010).

Regardless of the reason or reasons why one might come to defend the highest levels of state control, it can be said that this desire represents what is perhaps one of the most utopian facets of left-wing thought. First, because the idea that power can be concentrated in a small group of people is based on the premise that human beings are naturally good, ethical, and moral, with the absence of the possibility of retaliation not leading to abuse of power and opportunism. Put differently, the defence of concentration of power is based on an unrealistic idea that a set of men and women freed from human passions will be able to govern others fairly and in the best interest of all, even in the absence of a force capable of opposing them should they deviate from this mission.

It is also possible to point to the extremely elitist aspect that leftist views seem to have, with the determination of a ruling elite based on the perception that, due to a lack of knowledge or a kind of chronic ignorance, people are unable to decide for themselves or are unreliable. In both cases, the solution would be the concentration of power around those who would somehow be enlightened by knowledge, being, therefore, a few steps above the popular mass. It is interesting to note that the apparent naivety of left-wing thinking regarding human nature does not seem to apply in this case, with the possibility of average individuals acting opportunistically and at odds with the collective interest (i.e., privileging their individual needs) revealing some degree of skepticism. As discussed earlier and throughout the book, the distrust of man's virtues that characterizes this philosophical current forms the basis of conservative thought, which makes its application by left-wing theorists even more incoherent. Apparently, employing a skeptical view reflects nothing less than pragmatism, supporting whatever argument is needed in constructing a justification for creating a ruling elite that places itself above other 'incapable' or 'untrustworthy' citizens.

This perspective is also at the origin of the defence of technocracies, in which a government of specialized bureaucrats is proposed as the best solution for managing social life. Once again, the supposed ignorance of the common citizen would serve as a reason for the concentration of power around those who were able to guide them in the direction understood as right by those who assume the positions of command. The premise of 'popular ignorance' falls into two basic categories – the first deals with the lack of technical knowledge in the most diverse spheres. This includes the idea that the common citizen is incapable of understanding what is best for himself in terms of economics, security, health, and education, among others. Delegating their power of choice to an elite that thinks itself aware of the general best interests and capable of pursuing them would thus be a rational choice from the point of view of those who take the premise of ignorance as true. The second category in which the premise of 'popular ignorance' manifests refers to the belief that the average citizen is not a fervent supporter of communism – often even opposing it – just because of their lack of understanding of the benefits that this system would supposedly offer you. Thus, the imposition of an authoritarian government against the will of those who will have to submit to it would be justified.

When the many practical difficulties arising from a total planning of social functioning are considered, the leftist belief in the efficiency of the centralization of power in the state seems even further from anything that can actually be applied. Considering the economic aspects alone, the idea that state bureaucrats can organize the production, distribution, and consumption of goods and services more efficiently than market mechanisms may be enough to convince the most attentive reader of the character of the utopian ideas defended by the radical left. The replacement of incentive mechanisms guided by demand and supply, and objectively translated by the price formation system (i.e., the invisible hand) by planning efforts, can be understood as an expression of a certain arrogance on the part of those who consider it possible to manage such complexity. In this, the notion of the invisible hand must be interpreted as an appeal not to try to interfere in something natural and that has the property of self-regulation (i.e., the market). This idea becomes even clearer when the famous phrase *laissez-faire, laissez passer* is used to express this idea.

A parallel for the contrast between these two diametrically opposed views can be drawn from the fact that there is no need to manage a forest that, despite all its complexity and eventual imbalances, tends to self-regulate, without human intervention being necessary. Right now, the most diverse events are taking place in the heart of the Amazon rainforest. As each plant and each animal – however small – fights for its own survival, complex interactions naturally develop (e.g., symbiosis, predation). The lack of human intervention is probably the most important factor for the good functioning of the forest, and this is precisely the argument defended by most environmentalists. In the specific case of the example discussed, non-intervention in the functioning of the forest resembles the precepts of the invisible hand, typically associated with classical liberal thought (not what is classified as current liberal thought, which, as discussed earlier, is much closer to a radical leftism in countries like the United States). In the totalitarian and centralizing vision of a communist, however, the functioning of the forest would be better if it were managed, with each of its processes being meticulously planned and controlled. Thus, issues as different as the volume of rain, the amount of sunshine, and the timing of flowering would be optimized if they were under the authority of an omniscient and omnipresent elite. Without a doubt, the example of forest management is just an allegory, not far from the communist ambition to control all economic processes. For a classical liberal, the idea of controlling the market sounds as absurd and inefficient as the quest to control nature itself.

The discussion about the different understandings regarding the role of the State in social life is fundamental for a more detailed understanding of the psychology of right and left. As pointed out before, lack of faith and belief in God are of particular importance, with the psychological vacuum created in the minds of atheists in many cases being filled by a larger entity capable of giving them meaning. In addition to the State itself, it is possible that this search points to the defence of other values, with nature appearing as one of the main elements in this direction. The development of Charles Darwin's (1809–1882) views on species' evolution through natural selection can be understood as one of the starting points for the elevation of nature to a superior status, in which – in the psyche of those who do not believe in God – it assumes the role of Creator. Likewise, the defence of nature would represent a noble cause, conferring a type of moral superiority to those who engaged in it, even if only in appearance. The replacement of roles traditionally linked to God by environmentalism would, therefore, be at the origin of the most radical forms of the environment speech and rhetoric.

In conjunction with the dimensions discussed previously, it can be argued that the leftists' worldviews and the behaviours that flow from them are also a result of their belief that society is based on mechanisms of domination and oppression, in which human relations will be expressed basically on account of an imbalance of power between the parties (Nelson and Grossberg, 1988). Thus, a leftist will tend to agree that the destruction of Western society's values is the way in which inequality can be more quickly eliminated. In this view, the fall of the 'pillars of oppression' would allow a new society – in theory, just and equitable – to be built upon its rubble. This belief that destruction precedes creation forms the basis of revolutionary thinking, according to which a *tabula rasa* is necessary for an idealized version to be built. The perspective represents the opposite of what is advocated by conservatives, who argue that social evolution must be slow and gradual (Scruton, 1980). The punctual and systematic correction of deviations would prevent the various advances obtained over centuries and even millennia of civilization history from being abruptly destroyed and without due consideration of their value. Edmund Burke's (1729–1797) classic text *Reflections on the*

Revolution in France presented severe criticisms of the way in which the French Revolution unfolded and is considered one of the most important works for the development of conservative thought as known today (Jones, 2017). Among the many points raised by Burke was his concern with the abrupt abolition of institutions built over centuries, as this could open space for the development of dangerous alternatives. The chaos that ensued in France in the years immediately after the revolution took place (Gough, 2010) shows that many of Burke's arguments were correct, with the spread of the crisis across the European continent (Lyons, 1994) reinforcing this perspective.

From a more objective perspective, it can be argued that the quest for the destruction of Western values fulfils a dual role in the psyche of a radical leftist. In addition to removing possible resistance to the construction of a new society, this movement would also have an even more calculating aspect, according to which the weakening of common values (e.g., religion, family) would have the objective of creating a collective disorientation that, instead, would facilitate the establishment of a totalitarian regime. In its essence, the destruction of a society's values and beliefs, as well as any kind of moral ruler, would aim to create a chaotic state in a way that those who see themselves without parameters beg for the implantation of a totalitarian regime that can give them back a sense of security and control over their lives. This dynamic would be expressed in different ways, with the questioning of the idea of art, for example, being one of the most evident. Similarly, opposition to an ideal of beauty and the notion that there is a hierarchy of values (Blaug, 1994) would contribute to this same end. More recently, some analysts have pointed to what they understand to be one of the main attempts to distort reality, with the denial of the existence of two biological sexes (i.e., male and female) being responsible for a very important state of mental confusion, especially between the younger ones.

Another expression of this search for the installation of a state of chaos that would precede the implantation of a totalitarian dictatorship is sometimes identified in the inclination that many leftists have to show sympathy for those who act in violation of the law. In respect of the logic, according to which states of chaos, disorganization, and panic favour the popular demand for a strong, centralized government capable of giving people back a sense of security, the defence of criminals, thieves, drug dealers, and any group of criminals would have as ultimate goal the nourishment of this process. Thus, the false signs of virtue in the form of defending human rights would be another strategy aimed at implementing a communist dictatorship. Similarly, the defence of groups that violate social norms would also be welcomed by radical leftists precisely because individuals who fall into this category would already present a tendency not to conform to the current system, thus giving evidence of their potential character revolutionary.

Recently, the mechanism of installation of chaos as a pretext for adopting authoritarian measures seems to have manifested itself quite successfully. The panic generated by the rapid spread of the Covid-19 pandemic (Nicomedes and Avila, 2020) provided the conditions for an important part of the world population not only to accept the imposition of measures that restricted their own freedom but also to call for them. In several countries, this was reflected in the imposition of lockdowns (McKie, 2022), creating a scenario of social control never before experienced in history. In addition to this, vaccination (Brice-Saddler et al., 2021, p.xi) and the use of face masks (Katz, 2021) became mandatory in many places. These policies extended the power of governments, allowing mayors, governors, presidents, judges, and other authorities to exert greater control over citizens' lives.

Final Thoughts

Considering the various points addressed in the previous discussions, it is clear that extremist thinking is the product of a series of factors, with the different relationships that individuals form with their environment and with each other influencing their views of the world. In the first part of the chapter, the purpose of the proposed discussions is not to provide a review of the psychology literature but rather to approach this issue from a more holistic perspective, considering the many social and philosophical issues that can influence the development of extreme thinking. In this sense, the identification of ideological aspects is particularly important, serving as a basis for the development of utopian ideas of an idealized world (whether on the left or on the right). It can be said, therefore, that the psychology of extreme thinking is based on the extent to which a person believes in the justice and correctness of her/his beliefs. In fact, the individual who is convinced of the morality of what s/he thinks tends to develop a greater attachment to her/his ideas, defending them ardently. In these cases, aggressive behaviours become justifiable from the perspective of individuals embedded in a rationale that they consider superior, since, in the extreme, they would represent the defence of truth and ethics.

In addition to issues related to the relationship that someone can develop with their own ideas, the triumph of extremist thinking also seems to be linked to people's difficulty in understanding the reasoning developed by other people. The lack of understanding of the rationale through which a different thought develops can contribute to its classification as incorrect and, therefore, not worthy of attention. This inability to absorb the ways of thinking of others can be linked both to a real cognitive difficulty and aspects related to conformism, with the individual refusing everything that somehow bothers him/her, or questioning the premises that make up his/her comfort zone. The impact of these factors should be amplified as those who are radicalized maintain behaviours that disfavour their contact with different perspectives. This includes the unique and exclusive interaction with people who demonstrate similar thinking, with the lack of contradictory arguments contributing to the validation of extreme views through positive reinforcement.

Another important aspect refers to the classification given to those who do not share the same opinions. While some people have no problem facing contrary views, others may show aggressive reactions from a psychological point of view, classifying those who disagree with them as enemies. The dehumanization processes of those who think differently end up playing an important role in this direction. In a sense, it can also be argued that extreme thinking is the result of a limited understanding of the complexity of human relationships, and the world more generally, with extremists usually reducing hard-to-understand problems to a relatively small number of inflexible assumptions. It is possible that this process represents a frustrated attempt to understand something of great intricacy, or even a defence mechanism adopted by those who cannot support the idea of being involved in an unknown and misunderstood environment. Extremist thinking can also be adopted as an instrument in the search for a type of social distinction, in which those who identify with views of the world more distant from common sense claim to belong to some kind of special or unique group.

Understanding the ways in which extremist thinking translates into radical views about sustainability is particularly important for the purposes of this book. Generally speaking, it can be said that the exaggerated passion for environmentalism is not necessarily different from the issues discussed here. Likewise, the development of radical views in the opposite direction can also be understood in light of the proposed debate. Thus, the ideas discussed in the chapter serve as a basis for considering the extreme thinking linked to sustainability that develops throughout the book.

References

Aerial View (2019). *Professor Jordan Peterson on Alcohol and Partying.* Available at https://www.youtube.com/watch?v=rUQFxYje4fU

Atkinson, A.B. (1971). Capital taxes, the redistribution of wealth and individual savings. *The Review of Economic Studies*, Vol.38, No.2, pp.209–227.

Atkinson, G.L. (1999). What is the Frankfurt school? *We the People*. Vol.10, pp.1–6.

Beer, S.H. (1978). Federalism, nationalism, and democracy in America. *American Political Science Review*, Vol.72, No.1, pp.9–21.

Blaug, R. (1994). Habermas's treatment for relativism. *Politics*, Vol.14, No.2, pp.51–57.

Bonachea, R.L., and San Martín, M. (2018). *The Cuban Insurrection, 1952–1959.* Routledge.

Brazilian Senate (2003). *Lula sanciona estatuto do desarmamento*, December 21. Available at https://www12.senado.leg.br/noticias/materias/2003/12/22/lula-sanciona-estatuto-do-desarmamento

Breines, W. (1988). Whose new left? *The Journal of American History*, Vol.7, No.2, pp.528–545.

Brice-Saddler, M., Weil, J.Z., and Portnoy, J. (2021). D.C. to require coronavirus vaccination to enter restaurants, gyms and other businesses. *The Washington Post*, December 22. Available at https://www.washingtonpost.com/dc-md-va/2021/12/22/dc-covid-vaccine-business-requirement/

Cardoso, T. (2016). *O cofre do Dr. Rui: Como a Var-palmares de Dilma Rousseff Realizou o Maior Assalto da Luta Armada Brasileira.* Editora José Olympio.

Casey, S. (2001). *Cautious Crusade: Franklin D. Roosevelt, American Public Opinion, and the War Against Nazi Germany.* Oxford University Press.

Chen, J. (2010). *Mao's China and the Cold War.* University of North Carolina Press.

Cordeiro, J.M. (2021). A Marcha da Família com Deus pela liberdade em São Paulo: Direitas, participação política e golpe no Brasil, 1964. *Revista História*, Vol.180, pp.1–19.
D'Araujo, M.C. (2010). Militares, democracia e desenvolvimento – Brasil e América do Sul. Fundação Getulio Vargas.
French Ministry of Justice (2008). *Loi constitutionnelle ouvrant ratification du Traité de Lisbonne*. Available at http://www.textes.justice.gouv.fr/lois-et-ordonnances-10180/loi-constitutionnelle-ouvrant-ratification-du-traite-de-lisbonne-14134.html
Gordon, J. (1983). Is the existence of God relevant to the meaning of life? *The Modern Schoolman*, Vol.60, No.4, pp.227–246.
Gough, H. (2010). *The Terror in the French Revolution*. Macmillan International Higher Education.
Grubb, F. (2003). Creating the US dollar currency union, 1748–1811: A quest for monetary stability or a usurpation of state sovereignty for personal gain? *American Economic Review*, Vol.93, No.5, pp.1778–1798.
Gunderson, R. (2016). Environmental sociology and the Frankfurt School 2: Ideology, techno-science, reconciliation. *Environmental Sociology*, Vol.2, No.1, pp.64–76.
Haidt, J., Graham, J., and Joseph, C. (2009). Above and below left – right: Ideological narratives and moral foundations. *Psychological Inquiry*, Vol.20, No.2–3, pp.110–119.
Hayward, R.D., Krause, N., Ironson, G., Hill, P.C., and Emmons, R. (2016). Health and well-being among the non-religious: Atheists, agnostics, and no preference compared with religious group members. *Journal of Religion and Health*, Vol.55, No.3, pp.1024–1037.
Herrnstein, R.J., and Murray, C. (1994). *The Bell Curve: Intelligence and Class Structure in American Life*. Free Press.
Hollis, D.W. (1990). Religious liberty and the founding fathers. *Journal of Interdisciplinary Studies*, Vol.2, No.1–2, pp.87–102.
Jones, E. (2017). *Edmund Burke and the Invention of Modern Conservatism, 1830–1914: An Intellectual History*. Oxford University Press.
Katz, A. (2021). Paris makes masks mandatory outdoors starting December 31. *Bloomberg*, December 29. Available at https://www.bloomberg.com/news/articles/2021-12-29/paris-makes-masks-mandatory-outdoors-starting-dec-31
Kincaid, J. (2010). Democracy versus federalism in the United States of America. In *Federal Democracies*, pp.133–155. Routledge.
Klinghoffer, A.J. (2019). *The Angolan War: A Study in Soviet Policy in the Third World: A Study in Soviet Policy in the Third World*. Routledge.
Knight, J., Sherritt, L., Harris, S., Holder, D., Kulig, J., Shrier, L., Gabrielli, J., and Chang, G. (2007). Alcohol use and religiousness/spirituality among adolescents. *Southern Medical Journal*, Vol.100, No.4, pp.349–355.
Leab, D.J. (1998). Introduction: The cold war and the movies. *Film History*, Vol.10, No.3, pp.251–253.
Lears, T.J. (1985). The concept of cultural hegemony: Problems and possibilities. *The American Historical Review*, Vol.90, No.3, pp.567–593.
Le Monde (2005). *29 mai 2005: Le non gagne en France, la ratification du traité continue en Europe*, May 30. Available at https://www.lemonde.fr/europe/article/2005/05/30/le-non-gagne-en-france-la-ratification-du-traite-continue-en-europe_655955_3214.html
Le Monde (2007). Valéry Giscard d'Estaing et 'la boîte à outils' du traité de Lisbonne. *Le Monde*, October 26. Available at https://www.lemonde.fr/idees/article/2007/10/26/la-boite-a-outils-du-traite-de-lisbonne-par-valery-giscard-d-estaing_971616_3232.html

Lienesch, M. (1982). Right-wing religion: Christian conservatism as a political movement. *Political Science Quarterly*, Vol.97, No.3, pp.403–425.

Lyons, M. (1994). *Napoleon Bonaparte and the legacy of the French Revolution*, Vol.1. Macmillan.

Macedo, A. (2015). Em 2005 63% dos brasileiros votam em referedum a favor do comercio de armas. *O* Globo, October 15. Available at https://acervo.oglobo.globo.com/em-destaque/em-2005-63-dos-brasileiros-votam-em-referendo-favor-do-comercio-de-armas-17786376

Max, H., Theodor, W.A., Zoltán, T., and Michael, L. (2017). *The Frankfurt School.* Routledge.

McKie, R. (2022). Britain got it wrong on Covid: Lockdown did more harm than good, says scientists. *The Guardian*, January 2. Available at https://www.theguardian.com/world/2022/jan/02/britain-got-it-wrong-on-covid-long-lockdown-did-more-harm-than-good-says-scientist

Meacham, J. (2007). *American Gospel: God, the Founding Fathers, and the Making of a Nation.* Random House.

Minnicino, M. (1992). The Frankfurt school and 'political correctness'. *Fidelio Magazine*, Vol.1, No.1, pp.1–13.

Minogue, K. (2012). *The Liberal Mind.* Liberty Fund.

Nedelsky, J. (1994). *Private Property and the Limits of American Constitutionalism: The Madisonian Framework and Its Legacy.* University of Chicago press.

Nelson, C., and Grossberg, L. (Eds.) (1988). *Marxism and the Interpretation of Culture.* University of Illinois Press.

Nicomedes, C.J.C., and Avila, R.M.A. (2020). An analysis on the panic during COVID-19 pandemic through an online form. *Journal of Affective Disorders*, Vol.276, pp.14–22.

Norquist, G. (2020). Trump vs. Biden on taxes. *Horizons: Journal of International Relations and Sustainable Development*, No.17, pp.160–173.

O'Connor, K., and Barron, G. (1998). Madison's mistake? Judicial construction of the second amendment. In: J.M. Bruce and C. Wilcox (Eds.). *The Changing Politics of Gun Control.* Rowman & Littlefield Publishers.

Pinto, J.C.R. (2019). Apogeu, ruptura e ocaso do intervencionismo armado no brasil. *Revista da Escola Superior de Guerra*, Vol.34, No.71, pp.132–165.

Powaski, R.E. (1997). *The Cold War: The United States and the Soviet Union, 1917–1991.* Oxford University Press.

Rabban, D.M. (1999). *Free Speech in Its Forgotten Years, 1870–1920.* Cambridge University Press.

Raines, J. (2011). *Marx on Religion.* Temple University Press.

Rapoport, M., and Laufer, R. (2000). Os Estados Unidos diante do Brasil e da Argentina: Os golpes militares da década de 1960. *Revista Brasileira de Política Internacional*, Vol.43, pp.69–98.

Richman, B. (1974). Implementing competition policy in communist countries. *California Management Review*, Vol.16, No.4, pp.104–111.

Rose-Ackerman, S. (1981). Does federalism matter? Political choice in a federal republic. *Journal of Political Economy*, Vol.89, No.1, pp.152–165.

Rossiter Jr, L.H. (2006). *The Liberal Mind: The Psychological Causes of Political Madness.* Free World Books.

Ruderer, S. (2012). Cruzada contra el comunismo: Tradición, Familia y Propiedad (TFP) en Chile y Argentina. *Sociedad y Religión: Sociología, Antropología e Historia de la Religión en el Cono Sur*, Vol.22, No.38, pp.77–106.

Scruton, R. (1980). *The Meaning of Conservatism*, Vol.21. Penguin Books.
Shepherd, S., and Kay, A.C. (2018). Guns as a source of order and chaos: Compensatory control and the psychological (dis) utility of guns for liberals and conservatives. *Journal of the Association for Consumer Research*, Vol.3, No.1, pp.16–26.
Shlaes, A. (2012). *The Greedy Hand: How Taxes Drive Americans Crazy and What to Do About It*. Random House.
Thrower, J. (2011). *Marxist-Leninist 'Scientific Atheism' and the Study of Religion and Atheism in the USSR*. Mouton Publisher.
Vu, T. (2016). *Vietnam's Communist Revolution: The power and limits of ideology*. Cambridge University Press.
Wade, R.A. (2017). *The Russian Revolution, 1917*, Vol.53. Cambridge University Press.
Wheatland, T. (2009). *The Frankfurt School in Exile*. University of Minnesota Press.
Wydra, H. (2007). *Communism and the Emergence of Democracy*. Cambridge University Press.
Zrinščak, S. (2004). Generations and atheism: Patterns of response to communist rule among different generations and countries. *Social Compass*, Vol.51, No.2, pp.221–234.

9 Sustainability, Politics, and Money

Sustainability and Politics

As pointed out throughout the book, themes related to sustainability have been particularly dear to candidates for elective positions, being among the most discussed subjects in electoral disputes. In the same way, many elected politicians seem to seek to associate their image with the advancement of the environmentalist agenda, with this alternative replacing, to some extent, the traditional forms of populism. It is not uncommon, for example, for mayors of large cities to devote a large part of the budgets they manage to the construction of bicycle lanes. This is the case in Paris, which saw many of its streets and avenues become space for lanes entirely dedicated to bicycle traffic (Paris City Administration, 2022). A very similar process was also observed in Latin American cities, among which São Paulo stands out (Mengue, 2021). It is worth mentioning that, in both cases, the acceleration of the opening of cycle paths took place in governments that are recognized as left-wing.

The classification of initiatives such as the opening of cycle paths as populist lies in the fact that these measures allow voters to make a direct association between the politician in question and a concrete and objective achievement. This characteristic of engineering works contrasts with most administrative activities that, despite having important impacts on the lives of citizens, often remain invisible. In addition, such openings are often widely publicized by the press, especially when the politician responsible for them is ideologically aligned with the media. An additional factor in categorizing these measures as populist refers to the longevity of their effects, with the works being associated with the politic throughout the period of their existence. This means that they can not only yield positive electoral effects in the election subsequent to their inauguration, but also generate electoral dividends among the next generations of voters.

The contrast between the cities of Paris and São Paulo can offer some important reflections on the adequacy of the implementation of pro-environmental measures such as the creation of cycle paths. While Paris is the capital of one of the most developed countries in the world, presenting a relatively high human development index (0.901, ranking 26th – United Nations Development Program, 2022), the city of São Paulo is the scene of serious social problems, with a significant part

DOI: 10.4324/9781003124719-11

of its population living in poverty (Carta Capital, 2018). Despite being the most developed city in Brazil (Graça, 2021) and, in some of its neighbourhoods, presenting conditions comparable to the richest regions of the globe, the great economic inequalities are reflected in the different realities faced by its inhabitants.

Some of the difficulties faced by its poorest populations are the lack of access to quality education, health treatments and medicines, exposure to high levels of violence, the precariousness of public transport, and the lack of a basic sanitation system, with many citizens not having access to potable water and sewage networks (Gomes et al., 2021). Among the many consequences of this situation is the increase in risks to the health of the population and the pollution of rivers that receive untreated sewage. The contamination of the city's rivers is historical, with the two large specimens that cross it in alarming conditions. The Tietê (Andrade and Melo, 2018) and Pinheiros (Pereira et al., 2021) rivers present a very different sanitary situation from that found on the French Seine. Likewise, garbage collection and treatment are often precarious, or even non-existent in outlying areas (Ferreira, 2017). This situation favours the creation of clandestine garbage dumps, where all types of waste are discarded. Added to this are several other problems such as a significant homeless population (Betim, 2021), structural unemployment (Margarido, 2018), domestic violence (Machado et al., 2020), alcohol and illicit drug abuse (d'Arc, 2018), and numerous cases of early pregnancy (Folha de São Paulo, 2019).

For those who know the reality of the two cities well – as is the case of the present authors – it is easy to see that the challenges faced by São Paulo are very different from those imposed on Paris. If, on the one hand, the French capital also presents some of the problems just listed, its incidence is significantly lower and less acute than that observed on the other side of the Atlantic Ocean. It is therefore noteworthy that cities with such different social realities have treated the opening of bike lanes with the same attention. It would be reasonable to suppose that, in face of its numerous problems, the financial resources of a city such as São Paulo were primarily intended to solve them, or, at least, to minimize their effects. Once again, it is not a question of demeaning the opening of cycle paths as a valid alternative for improving environmental conditions. What is questioned here is whether the investment dedicated to this option actually represents the best choice for a city with so many problems. It is likely that the improvement in the collection and treatment of urban waste or the implementation of sewage networks would have an even more important environmental impact than the replacement of cars with bicycles provided by bicycle paths.

However, works aimed at improving the living conditions of the poorest populations do not seem to be so interesting for politicians, perhaps because they do not usually generate the same media impact. It is worth noting that most of the bike lanes implemented in São Paulo are located in its noblest neighbourhoods, thus favouring the richest populations (O Estado de São Paulo, 2020). This factor may help to explain the greater impact of cycle paths when compared to sanitation works and improvement of garbage collection in the periphery, since opinion formers (e.g., teachers, journalists, liberal professionals) usually work and/or live in these areas. The perception that São Paulo's scarce financial resources could be better applied to solving serious problems from an environmental point of view (e.g., garbage collection and treatment, implementation of sewage and basic sanitation networks, depollution of rivers and streams) favours the conclusion that the creation of cycle paths is probably conducted due to electoral interests and pretensions. Altogether, these questions support the argument that the promotion of the environmental cause by politicians can be, in some cases, just a modern form of populism.

Given these perspectives, it is possible to argue that in some cases the environmental cause is used by politicians in a frivolous and even dishonest way. The main support for this perception lies in the fact that many initiatives that appear to contribute to alleviating the pressures of human activities on the environment are nothing more than instruments and devices used in the construction of public images of politicians. In these cases, the construction of 'green facades' ends up functioning as a great service to the progress of sustainable development. In the first place, merely cosmetic and superficial attitudes act against the objectives of improving the environmental situation for the simple fact that their impact is usually marginal, if not null. This is grounded in the concept of opportunity cost (Buchanan, 1991), which basically argues that the benefits of alternatives to the one adopted must be considered. Thus, the serious problems faced by São Paulo and that could have received the resources destined to the construction of bicycle lanes greatly increase the cost of this last option, to the point of making it counterproductive in many ways.

Once again, it is important to make it clear that this conclusion does not represent a direct criticism of the construction of cycle paths per se. It is recognized that they can be an important alternative for not only reducing pollutant emissions from cars but also issues related to urban mobility. What is at issue here is the prioritization of this choice over others in relatively poor cities that, as discussed, could present a much more interesting environmental result. An important part of this position is the perception that the choices for cycle paths in many cases seem to aim at building positive images for politicians, regardless of the high prices paid by the population. When viewed from this angle, the defence of these and other measures is harmed, as they suggest the misuse of the environmental cause as a support for hidden interests.

Under this point, three other caveats are necessary. The first seeks to remember that the city of São Paulo does not seem to be an exception, with similar practices being observed in several other equally poor South American capitals. The second draws attention to cases in which incorrect investments are made with good intentions, with managers actually seeking to contribute to the improvement of environmental conditions. While no less harmful, these 'sincere mistakes' might be more ethically acceptable. Finally, the third caveat aims to point out that, in the case of economically and socially developed countries, investments in cycle paths can in fact be an important alternative, since other problems with high potential to cause environmental damage (e.g., garbage collection and treatment) are relatively well balanced. In these cases, investment in lower impact measures can be understood as a fine-tuning of sustainability strategies. Of course, this does not exclude cases of construction of bicycle lanes as a form of populism in rich countries. However, it is necessary that the cases be analysed individually in order to avoid hasty and unfair conclusions.

Sustainability Pyramid

Although it was developed to address other issues, the idea of Maslow's pyramid (Bridgman et al., 2019) illustrates the reasoning developed earlier. According to this view, the basic needs of human beings respect a kind of hierarchy according to which passage to a higher level is conditioned to the satisfaction of the need corresponding to the previous level. Adapting the concept, it can be argued that, following this reasoning, an individual would only care about showing off luxury watches once s/he had, for example, her/his hunger and need for housing satiated. When applied to the debate on the use of environmental causes as an electoral instrument, the idea of Maslow's pyramid suggests that more sophisticated issues such as the construction of bicycle lanes should only be considered when more basic needs have already been fulfilled. The fact that the resources of relatively poor cities are not primarily allocated to the issues that are specific to the base of the pyramid of needs corroborates the idea that many of the initiatives adopted by politicians in fact do not aim to maximize benefits for the societies they govern, but rather increase their popularity and, consequently, their chances of success in the elections. Figure 9.1 proposes an adaptation of Maslow's pyramid to issues related to sustainability, in which the order of priority should be read from bottom-up.

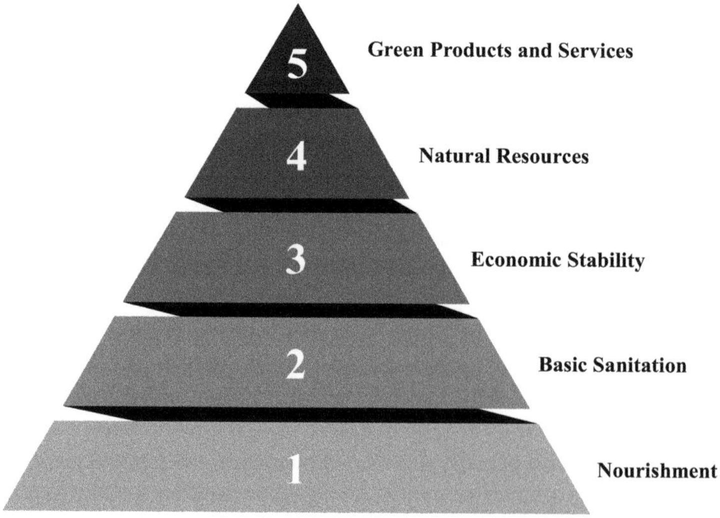

Figure 9.1 The Sustainability Pyramid

Paradoxically, the perception of the importance of themes related to sustainable development in electoral disputes (Nunes and Peña, 2015) can contribute to the understanding of the lesser attention that these issues seem to receive in countries dominated by dictatorial regimes. In general, these countries refuse to commit to reducing their environmental damage (e.g., deforestation, CO_2 emissions, changes in the energy matrix) (Piper and Volcovici, 2021), probably because they understand that these objectives would be counterproductive to their social development. The fact that many countries dominated by authoritarian regimes deny signing international treaties or memoranda of intent that set goals for their environmental policies validates this perspective. On the other hand, discussions about the environment seem to be particularly relevant in countries based on systems of representative democracy, with many of these nations leading the debate on sustainability. Unlike their peers, governed by unelected leaders, Western European countries such as Norway, France, Spain, the United Kingdom, and Germany are often among the first to agree to increasingly stringent environmental targets, with its presidents, prime ministers, kings, and queens proudly communicating their commitment to their people, often elevating the signing of these international agreements with an air of great achievements (United Nations, 2022). Furthermore, the importance of environmental issues in these countries can be inferred from the growing participation of so-called green parties in their electoral disputes (Van Haute, 2016). As the name implies, these political associations have sustainable development as their main banner (Burchell, 2014).

The different realities observed between countries ruled by democratic regimes and those led by dictators suggest not only that sustainability is a demand of a part of society, but also that the pressure exerted by this part has the potential to influence political behaviour. In this sense, an even more direct relationship between environmental policies and marketing strategies can be identified. In a very summarized way, it can be said that the objectives of gaining or maintaining market segments depend on the ability of companies to identify the desires and needs of consumers. Second, they need to develop goods and services that can respond to the previously identified desires and needs, offering them under conditions that are attractive to their targets (e.g., price, convenience). This mechanism seems to work particularly well with so-called green products, as discussed in more detail later in the chapter.

When this logic is used in the analysis of the dynamics between sustainability and politics, it can be argued that, to some extent, the presentation and implementation of environmental plans by candidates and elected representatives denote a product or service developed to meet a desire of or a need for voters or, at least, from those who influence them. The importance of opinion makers should be highlighted as, while they contribute to the formation of public opinion, they seem to act as intermediaries or spokespersons for ordinary citizens (even if no one officially grants them this function). A more comprehensive discussion of the origins and dynamics of environmental demands may be relevant. As discussed by Fracarolli Nunes and Lee Park (2021a), the development of the 'age of green' – 'a *zeitgeist* (i.e., spirit of the time) in which issues related to sustainability acquire a high status in society' (p.87) – would not have taken place in a bottom-up sense, with the will of the people being echoed by the elites. On the contrary, the consolidation of the idea that issues related to the environment should assume a priority role in the definitions of public and private policies would have taken place in the opposite direction (i.e., upside down), with academics, politicians, businessmen, artists, and other personalities putting the environmental agenda among the most important to be observed. Based on the chronology developed by Basiago (1995), the authors discuss the influence of elites in shaping and defending environmentalism. In the face of these observations, they argue that, regardless of a judgement on its justice, the environmental cause would not be the result of a genuine demand from citizens around the world, having been artificially implanted by those who occupy the top of the social pyramid at the international level. The reasons for this position, however, would be uncertain and could combine both a genuine desire to protect the planet from what is perceived as a threat and a way of advancing political, ideological, and economic projects.

In any case, the fact that discussions around sustainability are, in general, more advanced in developed countries corroborates the idea of Maslow's pyramid adapted for sustainable development offered earlier. In this sense, two dimensions seem to intersect, with countries under dictatorial regimes being almost entirely economically underdeveloped or in stages of development prior to those observed in countries considered to be rich (regardless of the absolute values of GDP generated by these nations). Thus, these societies have not yet overcome their basic economic problems (first dimension), which thus prevents them from dedicating resources to ends that are higher up in the pyramid. In many cases, this is reflected in the refusal of dictatorial governments to seek more sustainable alternatives for their energy matrices, as a relatively low cost of energy is a critical factor for the country's economic progress. This would explain, at least in part, the continuity of energy generation sources that rely on long-outdated technologies such as coal-fired thermoelectric power plants.

The second dimension refers to the failure to establish a democratic regime, which, as discussed, seems to be important in conditioning political proposals. Applying the logic of Maslow's pyramid adapted for sustainable development, the consolidation of democracy can be understood as conditioned to the fulfilment of a series of previous social demands and can be even understood as an indicator of the degree of a society's maturity. Evidently, this argument is based on the premise that democratic regimes represent forms superior to all others, precisely because they allow – at least in theory – that power remains with the citizens. In its representative form, democracy would make it possible for the popular will to be expressed when delegating that power to those chosen to represent it. In its direct form, the citizens themselves would be in charge of deliberating on matters that affect their destiny, eliminating the need to elect representatives. This last alternative, however, is closer to a utopian vision and is not observed in practice.

Despite the recognition of the superiority of democracy in relation to all other possibilities of government (e.g., dictatorships), its flaws cannot be ignored. The democratic system has received several criticisms over the centuries, with the most common pointing to the psychological profiles of those who are attracted to the possibilities of power it offers. Individuals who suffer from deviances such as those linked to narcissistic personalities, for example, would find in politics a way to vent their megalomaniac delusions (Underberg et al., 2020). The fact that narcissists tend to be highly self-centred (Miller et al., 2017) would cause a natural deviation in democratic functioning, with candidates affected by these ills ignoring the needs of their voters to the detriment of their own goals when they are elected.

Another quite common practice refers to an alleged inability of the common citizen to adequately choose those who will receive its vote. For the defenders of this view, the people would not be able to choose what is best for themselves, either out of ignorance or lack of political awareness. These perspectives are usually defended by members of intellectual, political, and economic elites, who believe they have a mission to guide citizens towards a better world. In addition to denoting considerable arrogance, these understandings usually result from an ideological view that opposes the distribution of power in society, advocating for its concentration around a few. In many cases, this translates into the defence of a greater participation of the State in the society's life management, which, in some extreme cases, means the defence of socialist and even communist dictatorships. While these perspectives are widespread in intellectual and political circles, attention is drawn to their popularity among economic elites. As discussed later in the chapter, the roots of this seemingly contradictory combination lie in the desire to protect the gains made, with free market sabotage presenting itself as an alternative to avoiding the inherent challenges of competition.

A third source of criticism of democracy refers to the possibility of it enabling a type of dictatorship of the majority. Basically, this refers to the non-fulfilment of the desires and needs of minority groups, simply because they add up to a smaller number than the majority groups. The idea that the votes of all citizens have the same value is at the origin of this question. One of the best-known means of dealing with this possibility was the establishment of the so-called electoral colleges in US elections. As discussed by George (2021), this system would guarantee greater relevance to the votes of citizens of less populous states (e.g., Wyoming), in order to prevent the entire country from being subjugated to the opinions, desires, and needs expressed by the inhabitants of the most populous states (e.g., California). Still, the electoral college system obliges presidential candidates to run a comprehensive campaign, taking into account the different issues relevant to the different regions. Thus, the contrast between cosmopolitan life on the two coasts of the country (i.e., east coast and west coast) and the other realities found further inland would not result in the imposition of the will of the citizens of the first region over those of the second. However, according to the author, the electoral college is one of the biggest factors in the classification of the US government system as a republic, with the rebalancing of the voting power defined by its so-called founding fathers, moving them away from pure democratic models, despite keeping much of its features.

The points made here serve as a basis for the idea that the implementation of a democratic system can be understood as evidence of a society's degree of maturity. The inherent complexity of this model requires a greater openness to dialogue and a greater degree of tolerance to opposing views, which, to some extent, suggests a more elaborate functioning of social mechanisms. Dictatorial regimes, on the other hand, disregard this development, with conflicts (when existent) being resolved through the use of brute force. In what concerns the debate on the association between sustainability and policy, these discussions support the development of Maslow's pyramid adapted to social development. Specifically, they corroborate the hierarchy of social needs proposed in the model. Despite all the criticisms presented and others that were not dealt with here, it is necessary to remember that among the characteristics of democracy is the possibility of correcting errors, represented mainly in the potential systematic and periodic exchange of representatives of the people when in electoral processes that renew. The understanding that, despite imperfect, democracy deserves to be defended can be summarized in the famous phrase uttered by former British Prime Minister Winston Churchill (1874–1965):

> Many forms of Government have been tried, and will be tried in this world of sin and woe. No one pretends that democracy is perfect or all-wise. Indeed it has been said that democracy is the worst form of Government except for all those other forms that have been tried from time to time.
>
> (International Winston Society, 2016)

Another characteristic that favours the use of environmentalist discourse by politicians is its ability to influence crowds, with younger generations being particularly sensitive to the issue. Little experience, combined with a natural naivety, makes teenagers and young adults, in general, more easily seduced by politicians who promise to advance environmental causes (Sloam, 2016). As discussed in greater detail in Chapter 10, this process of presenting politicians as a solution is embedded in a larger dynamic in which fears are generated through extremist discourses. Thus, a very powerful emotional component is combined, making young people even more susceptible to the promises of demagogic politicians. It is not possible, however, to generalize, since many young people have great emotional maturity and are not easily deceived. It turns out, however, that those who end up being convinced that a candidate or party deserves their trust to save the planet will likely exercise that choice for decades, which makes them very valuable from the point of view of political demagogues.

Finally, the relationship between sustainability and politics has been expressed in the radicalization of candidates' speeches, which often exaggerate their arguments in order to increase their convincing power. This includes not only a greater focus on environmental catastrophes but also the propagation of the idea that they must occur in an extremely short time frame. As discussed in Chapter 10, these strategies can be understood as modern forms of the denominated 'panic marketing', in which artificial pressure is built around a theme with the aim of influencing the decision-making of counterparties. In the case of the use of these devices by politicians in the debate of issues related to sustainable development, this strategy tends to point to increasingly shorter deadlines for the alleged environmental apocalypse, precisely because it tries to adapt the debate to the deadlines of the elections.

As also debated in Chapter 10, one of the greatest examples of the use of panic marketing linked to environmentalism is the various pessimistic predictions pointed out by politicians such as the former vice-president of the United States, Al Gore, according to whom the planet's temperatures will rise to unimaginable levels within a few years (Gore, 2006). In the same way, younger politicians seem to have quickly learned the value of the techniques used by older ones. US congresswoman Alessandra Ocasio Cortez, for example, is not shy about saying that the deadline to save the planet is only 12 years (Cummings, 2019). In addition to undermining the credibility of the environmentalist discourse, its political misuse seems to be behind the constant changes in the denominations used by extremists. In this sense, the migration from global warming to climate change would aim to offer an honourable exit to those who preached a rapid increase in global temperatures, in addition to increasing the scope of phenomena that can be pointed out as a consequence of human activity. Based on these questions, it can be said that, while the relationship between sustainability and politics can be an important path to sustainable development, the opportunistic use of the theme by politicians can represent a great risk for advances in this direction.

Sustainability and Money

If the relationships between sustainability and politics are already complex, the links between environmental issues and money are perhaps even more complicated. The boundary between politics and money is unclear, as the two represent dimensions of power. Adding sustainability-related topics to this equation makes them even more troubled. According to the discussions presented earlier in the chapter, unfortunately issues related to sustainable development are more commonly used as instruments by opportunistic politicians. When it comes to money, this utilitarian view of sustainability also seems to be quite common. These aspects can be identified in the great growth in the offer of so-called green products (Arli et al., 2018).

It is difficult to imagine a company that somehow does not rely on the alleged ecological attributes of its products. This can vary from the way the inputs are grown to the destination given to the waste. Considering that, in general, the development of products with greater environmental performance demands significant volumes of investment in the form of research and development, it is possible to argue that, somehow, they end up representing important industries' entry barriers (Porter, 1980). A more skeptical analysis of companies' intentions in their efforts in this direction indicates that it is possible that their interest in the development of green products is related to the protection they offer against new competitors. These issues are discussed in more detail in Chapter 14. To some extent, the rapid growth of companies such as Tesla Motors (Boudette, 2022) illustrates the power of sustainability-centric corporate strategies. The electric car company has a market value around one trillion dollars as of January 18, 2022 (Yahoo Finance, 2022a), which is greater than the sum of the market value of many of its main competitors in the same date. This includes traditional automakers like General Motors (USD 85.4 billion, Yahoo Finance, 2022b), Volkswagen (EUR 116.7 billion, Yahoo Finance, 2022c), Ford (USD 97.4 billion, Yahoo Finance, 2022d), and Toyota (USD 292.3 billion, Yahoo Finance, 2022e), just to name a few.

From a business strategy point of view, the relationship between sustainability and money can also be analysed from the unfolding of the globalization process in recent decades. This refers to the geographic relocation of production processes, with the transfer of factories and jobs in the search for economic efficiencies. Typically, the dynamic known as strategic outsourcing (Quinn and Hilmer, 1994) occurred through the concentration of companies around their greatest competencies, and the search for external alternatives for activities that could be performed more efficiently by other organizations. This quest for operational efficiencies resulted in a series of social developments around the world. Among the most obvious consequences is the economic growth of countries capable of offering more advantageous production conditions (Lei, 2007). In particular, the offer of less expensive labour proved to be an important factor in the decision-making processes of companies that sought to reduce their costs. Critics of this system point to the loss of jobs in developed countries, with the transferring of their production capacity to distant geographic zones leaving waves of unemployed workers (Drezner, 2004).

In addition to lower wages, other conditions allowed many economically underdeveloped countries to be able to attract world production. Investments in transport infrastructure (Rahman and Wu, 2011), for example, also contribute to reducing operating costs, with the construction of roads, railways, ports, and airports being critical in this regard. Likewise, the development of a quality education system allows an increasingly skilled workforce to be formed, which can be particularly important for industries more linked to technology. One of the most important aspects for keeping production costs low, however, is the ability of a country to offer electricity at competitive condition, since this input represents a relevant portion of the costs of many products (Cole et al., 2021).

It is precisely at this point that the conflicts between sustainability and money become particularly relevant. The production of electric energy has received great attention from the environmental point of view, as one of the sectors that most benefited from technological advances. The development of wind energy generation technology, for example, is the result of significant investments in research and development (Wiser and Millstein, 2020), having consumed large resources from universities, companies, and individual researchers. Along with the financial volumes dedicated to the creation and implementation of technically viable systems, the development process also demanded important intellectual resources, with many professors and engineers focusing on the task of enabling a new energy source. In a similar way, the development of technologies for the generation of solar energy are the result of many years of coordinated efforts, mainly regarding the selection of the most appropriate materials to maximize the efficiency of this alternative (Mofijur et al., 2019).

It is necessary to remember that, far beyond the technological challenges inherent in the development of new technologies, the individuals and organizations involved in these processes need to develop solutions from an operational point of view. Among other things, this means mapping potential suppliers and developing relationships with the ones capable of ensuring the maintenance of a minimally stable raw material flow. The dynamics of relationships in supply chains are often quite complex, involving the development of aspects such as trust between the parties, which can be quite time consuming (Kwon and Suh, 2004). Typically, the creation of relational assets occurs after a series of interactions, so that a relatively large stock of past experience allows each party to generate expectations about each other's future behaviour. Furthermore, the principles of transaction cost economics (Coase, 1937; Williamson, 1989) also preconize that such relationships are ruled by behavioural influences, such as opportunism and bounded rationality, which set the need for governance mechanisms.

Along with these issues, a number of other factors must be considered that can contribute to a significant increase in the risks to be assumed by those seeking to develop new sources of energy generation. In the specific case of raw materials used in solar panels and electric batteries, these issues are particularly sensitive, with many of the inputs used in their manufacture coming from mines located in conflict zones, where armed groups dispute local power (Sovacool, 2019). This means that, in many cases, the purchase of these materials sometimes needs to be negotiated with the leaders of such organizations, which not only can be dangerous for those more directly involved in these contacts, but also represents a direct source of funding for conflicts (Schouten, 2019). Likewise, it is not uncommon for cases of modern slavery (Gold et al., 2015) and child labour (Hofmann et al., 2018) to be reported in mineral extraction. When analysed both individually and together, these issues point to a very questionable social performance, with the various ethical issues included in the purchase of these raw materials representing additional sources of instability for the companies involved.

From a commercial point of view, those looking to develop new technologies may have to face equally important challenges, especially in the first few years when their products are introduced to the market (Padmanabhan et al., 1997). The introduction of new technologies can be quite complex, mainly due to the high investment costs associated with the purchase of equipment. In addition, the lack of adequate infrastructure can play a fundamental role in the choice of those responsible for purchasing decisions, which can often lead them to favour equipment already installed. These barriers can demand large investments in the creation of sales teams that, in the case of technology equipment, tend to be highly specialized and consequently expensive.

On top of all these matters, individuals or organizations interested in developing new technologies have often had to dedicate themselves to securing funding for their projects. In some countries, public banks have the mission of helping the nation's technological development by offering subsidized rates for related activities (Rezende, 2010). However, these lines of financing are usually quite limited and end up not supplying all the demand for cheap credit. In these cases, it will be up to the entrepreneur to seek financing from other sources, which usually offer very high-cost options (Breznitz et al., 2018). The very nature of research and development activities qualifies it as a risky activity, since there are no guarantees that the efforts will be rewarded with new products (McAlister et al., 2007). In this way, financing for the development of new technologies often ends up being conditional to the sale of part of the project within what is called venture capital, where the discount rates used in evaluating the value of projects are usually quite high due to uncertainties calculated (Zider, 1998).

Alternatively, funding sources can be obtained from commercial banks, but the fees required for these cases are often prohibitive. Only entrepreneurs and companies that have a high volume of financial resources and can finance their own projects escape these predatory dynamics (e.g., Apple, Leswing, 2019). This does not mean that financing costs are not high, as under the cost of opportunity concept, the value of alternative uses of money must be accounted for (Buchanan, 1991). This debate about the difficulties inherent in the development of new technologies supports the argument that the creation of new sources of energy generation is a tortuous and expensive process. Even if the scaling gains from higher current production volumes have allowed a significant reduction in operating costs, the high initial investments still need to be adequately remunerated. Among other consequences, this means the prices of these products tend to be pressured.

When the high costs of replacing equipment and the instability of energy generation based on climatic aspects (Fracarolli Nunes and Lee Park, 2021b) are also considered, the factors influencing the decision of many countries to maintain their energy generation mainly based on polluting but cheap and relatively more stable sources (e.g., coal, Braun, 2021) become clearer. According to the arguments raised earlier, the maintenance of conditions that allow production costs to remain lower is essential for the continuity of economic growth in countries that, today, host a large part of the world's production. If they are not able to offer these conditions, it is expected that international investments and commercial relations will migrate to other locations, with an eventual de-industrialization that could cause serious social problems. The maintenance of cheap energy generation can be understood, therefore, as *sine qua non* for the maintenance of dictatorial regimes in power, since people dissatisfied with their ability to maintain or increase their consumption levels can become less tolerant of the impositions of those in power.

In this sense, it is clear that these countries opted to prioritize economic aspects to the detriment of environmental ones. As discussed by Fracarolli Nunes et al. (2020), these dynamics configure what has come to be called sustainability trade-offs (i.e., the sacrifice of one sustainability dimension for performance in another). These choices are also observed in the fact that the geographical relocation of industrial activities has created a great distance between the production and consumer poles, with the international movement of raw materials and finished products requiring the consumption of large amounts of fossil fuels. It is necessary to recognize, however, that the responsibility for these decisions needs to be shared with the companies that chose to outsource their productions to distant places and with the final consumers who end up financing this whole model.

References

Andrade, D.E.O., and Melo, K.C. (2018). Recuperação do rio Tietê: Histórico de projetos, custos e problemas socioambientais. *Atas de Saúde Ambiental* (São Paulo, online), Vol.6, pp.151–167, January–December, ISSN: 2357-7614.

Arli, D., Tan, L.P., Tjiptono, F., and Yang, L. (2018). Exploring consumers' purchase intention towards green products in an emerging market: The role of consumers' perceived readiness. *International Journal of Consumer Studies*, Vol.42, No.4, pp.389–401.

Basiago, A.D. (1995). Methods of defining 'sustainability'. *Sustainable Development*, Vol.3, No.3, pp.109–119.

Betim, F. (2021). Pandemia leva famílias para as ruas de São Paulo e acelera mudança de perfil da população sem-teto. *El País*, June 2. Available at https://brasil.elpais.com/brasil/2021-06-02/pandemia-leva-familias-para-as-ruas-de-sao-paulo-e-acelera-mudanca-de-perfil-da-populacao-sem-teto.html

Boudette, N. (2022). Tesla reports 87% increase in 2021 deliveries. *The New York Times*, January 2. Available at https://www.nytimes.com/2022/01/02/business/tesla-sales.html

Braun, S. (2021). Coal: The end is nigh – or is it? *DW*, November 30. Available at https://www.dw.com/en/coal-the-end-is-nigh-or-is-it/a-59929238

Breznitz, D., Forman, C., and Wen, W. (2018). The role of venture capital in the formation of a new technological ecosystem: Evidence from the cloud. *MIS Quarterly*, Vol.42, No.4, pp.1143–1170.

Bridgman, T., Cummings, S., and Ballard, J. (2019). Who built Maslow's pyramid? A history of the creation of management studies' most famous symbol and its implications for management education. *Academy of Management Learning & Education*, Vol.18, No.1, pp.81–98.

Buchanan, J.M. (1991). Opportunity cost. In: J. Eatwell, M. Milgate, and P. Newman (Eds.). *The World of Economics*. Palgrave Macmillan. https://doi.org/10.1007/978-1-349-21315-3_69

Burchell, J. (2014). *The Evolution of Green Politics: Development and Change Within European Green Parties*. Routledge.

Carta Capital (2018). *Mais de 2 milhões de paulistanos ainda moram em favelas*, November 30. Available at https://www.cartacapital.com.br/blogs/32xsp/mais-de-2-milhoes-de-paulistanos-ainda-moram-em-favelas/

Coase, R.H. (1937). The nature of the firm. *Economica*, Vol.4, No.16, pp.386–405.

Cole, M.A., Elliott, R.J., Okubo, T., and Zhang, L. (2021). Importing, outsourcing and pollution offshoring. *Energy Economics*, Vol.103, p.105562.

Cummings, W. (2019). 'The world is going to end in 12 years if we don't address climate change', Ocasio-Cortez says. *USA Today*, January 22. Available at https://eu.usatoday.com/story/news/politics/onpolitics/2019/01/22/ocasio-cortez-climate-change-alarm/2642481002/

d'Arc, H.R. (2018). Une radiographie de la violence dans les métropoles du Sud: Le cas de São Paulo. *Revue Internationale et Strategique*, Vol.4, pp.149–157.

Drezner, D.W. (2004). The outsourcing bogeyman. *Foreign Affairs*, Vol.83, No.3, p.22.

Ferreira, I. (2017). Estudo mapeia condições das favelas em São Paulo. *Jornal da USP*. Available at https://jornal.usp.br/ciencias/ciencias-humanas/estudo-mapeia-condicoes-das-favelas-em-sao-paulo/

Folha de São Paulo (2019). *Cresce proporção de bebês nascidos de adolescentes na periferia de SP*. Available at https://fotografia.folha.uol.com.br/galerias/1634618769774204-cresce-proporcao-de-bebes-nascidos-de-adolescentes-na-periferia-de-sp

Fracarolli Nunes, M., and Lee Park, C. (2021a). The age of green. In: M. Fracarolli Nunes and C. Lee Park (Eds.). *Business Ethics and Environmental Fraud*, pp.87–104. Palgrave Macmillan. https://doi.org/10.1007/978-3-030-73800-6_4

Fracarolli Nunes, M., and Lee Park, C. (2021b) Not a 'privilege': Environmental fraud beyond the automotive industry. In: M. Fracarolli Nunes and C. Lee Park (Eds.). *Business Ethics and Environmental Fraud*, pp.159–184. Palgrave Macmillan. https://doi.org/10.1007/978-3-030-73800-6_7

Fracarolli Nunes, M., Lee Park, C., and Paiva, E.L. (2020). Can we have it all? Sustainability trade-offs and cross-insurance mechanisms in supply chains. *International Journal of Operations & Production Management*, Vol.40, No.9, pp.1339–1366.

Gold, S., Trautrims, A., and Trodd, Z. (2015). Modern slavery challenges to supply chain management. *Supply Chain Management: An International Journal*, Vol.20, No.5, pp.485–494.

Gore, A. (2006). *An Inconvenient Truth: The Planetary Emergency of Global Warming and What We Can Do About It*. Rodale.

George, R. (2021). The difference between a democracy and a republic. *Prager U*, October 6. Available at https://www.youtube.com/watch?v=wbsfpeMELGE

Gomes, A.C., Veloso, L., and Bernardo, J. (2021). Ratos fizeram ninhada debaixo da cama das crianças', diz moradora de favela sem saneamento em SP. *Folha de São Paulo*, September 6. Available at https://www1.folha.uol.com.br/cotidiano/2021/09/ratos-fizeram-ninhada-debaixo-da-cama-das-criancas-diz-moradora-de-favela-sem-saneamento-em-sp.shtml

Graça, E. (2021). Cidade mais rica do país, São Paulo tem 66 mil pessoas sem teto aponta ONG. *O Globo*, October 21. Available at https://oglobo.globo.com/brasil/cidade-mais-rica-do-pais-sao-paulo-tem-66-mil-pessoas-sem-teto-aponta-ong-25231502

Hofmann, H., Schleper, M.C., and Blome, C. (2018). Conflict minerals and supply chain due diligence: An exploratory study of multi-tier supply chains. *Journal of Business Ethics*, Vol.147, No.1, pp.115–141.

International Winston Society (2016). *The Worst Form of Government*, February 25. Available at https://winstonchurchill.org/resources/quotes/the-worst-form-of-government/

Kwon, I.W.G., and Suh, T. (2004). Factors affecting the level of trust and commitment in supply chain relationships. *Journal of Supply Chain Management*, Vol.40, pp.4–14.

Lei, D. (2007). Outsourcing and China's rising economic power. *Orbis*, Vol.51, No.1, pp.21–39.

Leswing, K. (2019). Apple is spending more than ever on R&D to fulfill the Tim Cook doctrine. *CNBC*, August 3. Available at https://www.cnbc.com/2019/08/03/apple-rd-spend-increases-fulfilling-tim-cook-doctrine.html

Machado, D.R., Kimura, M., Duarte, Y.A.D.O., and Lebrão, M.L. (2020). Violência contra idosos e qualidade de vida relacionada à saúde: Estudo populacional no município de São Paulo, Brasil. *Ciência & Saúde Coletiva*, Vol.25, pp.1119–1128.

Margarido, M.A. (2018). Elasticidade PIB e desemprego no estado de São Paulo: Uma aplicação do modelo Vetorial de Correção de Erro (VEC). *Revista Teoria e Evidência Econômica*, Vol.24, No.50.

McAlister, L., Srinivasan, R., and Kim, M. (2007). Advertising, research and development, and systematic risk of the firm. *Journal of Marketing*, Vol.71, No.1, pp.35–48.

Mengue, P. (2021). Ciclovias se espalham por mais 158 km da cidade de São Paulo. *Terra*, March 15. Available at https://www.terra.com.br/noticias/brasil/cidades/ciclovias-se-espalham-por-mais-158-km-da-cidade-de-sao-paulo,97ae9b9d4e24b82f01482ac8ca4a9a4d2s18oluv.html

Miller, J.D., Lynam, D.R., Hyatt, C.S., and Campbell, W.K. (2017). Controversies in narcissism. *Annual Review of Clinical Psychology*, Vol.13, pp.291–315.

Mofijur, M., Mahlia, T.M.I., Silitonga, A.S., Ong, H.C., Silakhori, M., Hasan, M.H., Putra, N., and Rahman, S.M. (2019). Phase change materials (PCM) for solar energy usages and storage: An overview. *Energies*, Vol.12, No.16, pp.3167–3186.

Nunes, J., and Peña, A.M. (2015). Marina Silva and the rise of sustainability in Brazil. *Environmental Politics*, Vol.24, No.3, pp.506–511.

O Estado de São Paulo (2020). *Ciclovias nas periferias de SP poderiam gerar economia ao trabalhador*, March 21. Available at https://mobilidade.estadao.com.br/mobilidade-para-que/ciclovias-nas-periferias-de-sp-poderiam-gerar-economia-ao-trabalhador/

Padmanabhan, V., Rajiv, S., and Srinivasan, K. (1997). New products, upgrades, and new releases: A rationale for sequential product introduction. *Journal of Marketing Research*, Vol.34, No.4, pp.456–472.

Paris City Administration (2022). *Le Plan vélo de Paris (2015–2020)*. Available at https://www.paris.fr/pages/paris-a-velo-225

Pereira, M.C.S., Martins, J.R.S., Nogueira, F.F., Magalhães, A.A.B., and Silva, F.P.D. (2021). Melhoria da qualidade da água de rios urbanos: Novos paradigmas a explorar – Bacia hidrográfica do rio Pinheiros em São Paulo. *Engenharia Sanitaria e Ambiental*, Vol.26, pp.577–590.

Piper, E., and Volcovici, V. (2021). Obama tells COP Obama tells COP26 to help poor nations, chides China and Russia. *Reuters*, November 9. Available at https://www.reuters.com/business/cop/focus-turns-climate-finance-after-flurry-cop26-pledges-2021-11-08/

Porter, M.E. (1980). *Competitive Strategy. Techniques for Analyzing Industries and Competitors*. New York: Free Press.

Quinn, J.B., and Hilmer, F.G. (1994). Strategic outsourcing. *MIT Sloan Management Review*, Vol.35, No.4, pp.43–55.

Rahman, S., and Wu, Y.C.J. (2011). Logistics outsourcing in China: The manufacturer-cum-supplier perspective. *Supply Chain Management: An International Journal*, Vol.16, No.6, pp.462–473.

Rezende, S.M. (2010). Brazil: Challenges and achievements. *Issues in Science and Technology*, Vol.26, No.3, pp.61–68.

Schouten, P. (2019). Why responsible sourcing of DRC minerals has major weak points. *The Conversation*, April 22. Available at https://theconversation.com/why-responsible-sourcing-of-drc-minerals-has-major-weak-spots-115245

Sloam, J. (2016). Youth political participation in Europe: A new participatory landscape. In: A. Furlong (Ed.). *Routledge Handbook of Youth and Young Adulthood*, pp.303–310. Routledge.

Sovacool, B.K. (2019). The precarious political economy of cobalt: Balancing prosperity, poverty, and brutality in artisanal and industrial mining in the Democratic Republic of the Congo. *The Extractive Industries and Society*, Vol.6, No.3, pp.915–939.

Underberg, J.E., Gollwitzer, A., Oettingen, G., and Gollwitzer, P.M. (2020). The best words: Linguistic indicators of grandiose narcissism in politics. *Journal of Language and Social Psychology*, Vol.39, No.2, pp.271–281.

United Nations (2022). *The Paris Agreement*. Available at https://www.un.org/en/climatechange/paris-agreement

United Nations Development Program (2022). *Human Development Reports – France*. Available at http://hdr.undp.org/en/countries/profiles/FRA

Van Haute, E. (Ed.) (2016). *Green Parties in Europe*. Routledge.

Williamson, O.E. (1989). Transaction cost economics. *Handbook of Industrial Organization*, Vol.1, pp.135–182.

Wiser, R., and Millstein, D. (2020). Evaluating the economic return to public wind energy research and development in the United States. *Applied Energy*, Vol.261, p.114449.

Yahoo Finance (2022a). *Tesla, Inc. (TSLA)*. Available January 19, at https://finance.yahoo.com/quote/TSLA/?guccounter=1&guce_referrer=aHR0cHM6Ly93d3cuZ29vZ2xlLmNvbS8&guce_referrer_sig=AQAAAM_9_Hlmp0MojmhU1QZq_X66wpfuB2bWYjbu6Tjcpz20ei95KkcZ6L8YRA9OhurcYrKDYBg5kSVYL39cq0oy9e3yo8KL9FUaA-Hhq2EmoKS4CxQaILlB-lqK21xEH-R5q-GCta0vnNr5TcSfzQFY-bH3Nd6b_htY0vrfahlCu2z0

Yahoo Finance (2022b). *General Motors Company*. Available January 19, at https://finance.yahoo.com/quote/GM/

Yahoo Finance (2022c). *Volkswagen AG*. Available January 19, at https://finance.yahoo.com/quote/vow.de/

Yahoo Finance (2022d). *Ford Motor Company*. Available January 19, at https://finance.yahoo.com/quote/F/

Yahoo Finance (2022e). *Toyota Motor Corporation*. Available January 19, at https://finance.yahoo.com/quote/TM/

Zider, B. (1998). How venture capital works. *Harvard Business Review*, Vol.76, No.6, pp.131–139.

10 Panic, Sustainability, and Marketing

Consumer Behaviour

At large, panic marketing refers to the idea that it is possible to influence consumers' decisions by exerting some type of additional pressure. Typically, this materializes in the form of windows of opportunity, in which consumers are led to believe that they need to take advantage of a certain circumstance to acquire something, since the conditions presented there have limited validity. This appears to be the dynamic of many of the practices used by sales and marketing professionals. Among them, we can highlight 'flash sale promotions', in which an important discount on the product or service's price is announced, together with its validity period (usually short) (Sendpulse, 2021). This configures a scenario in which the consumer is faced with a new and surprising situation in which a decision needs to be made quickly.

From a psychological point of view, windows of opportunity have the power to increase the importance given to the products or services they refer to, positioning them at the front lines of consumers' priorities (Lades, 2014). As pointed by Ayadi et al. (2013), purchasing temptations may demand considerable efforts from consumers, as they seek to resist them. If, from the companies' perspective, this situation seems to be positive – as it increases the probability of sales – it can be quite harmful to consumers (Ben-David and Bos, 2021). It is common, for example, that unplanned purchases end up causing regret (Atalay and Meloy, 2011) as, among other things, they may consume the budget previously allocated to other important matters. This can include health, food, and housing expenses (e.g., rent, mortgages). In some cases, the psychological pressure exerted by panic marketing mechanisms ends up leading consumers to make decisions that are not in their best interest.

In this sense, it can be argued that the emotional aspects contained in these sales strategies aim to undermine the assumptions of rationality of economic agents (Brocas and Carrillo, 2003), diverting them from the search for maximizing their well-being and leading to a spiral of decisions in which they are nothing more than passengers of their own emotions. In addition to the issues discussed above, consumers most affected by these points (i.e., those who end up giving in to pressures and buying items impulsively) may end up getting into debt processes

DOI: 10.4324/9781003124719-12

that they may have great difficulty getting rid of (Achtziger et al., 2015). One of the best examples of the application of panic marketing is the sales strategy adopted on what is popularly known as 'Black Friday' when, typically, products are offered at significantly reduced prices when compared to other periods of the year (Lee et al., 2019). The specificity of this day, however, lies in the fact that the duration of the promotions is quite short, usually extending for just one day (Simpson et al., 2011).

Of course, the entire responsibility for the situation cannot be attributed to the companies that make use of these strategies. Adult and responsible consumers should assess their possibilities and act accordingly. It so happens, however, that this expectation is realistic only when applied to psychologically healthy consumers who present a relative degree of emotional balance (Lee and Böttger, 2017). In these cases, consumers are expected to be able to resist both the temptations that generous price reductions pose and the time pressures that are placed on them (Baumeister, 2002), as they seem to be generally less likely to give in to their impulses. On the other hand, consumers who find themselves in a state of emotional imbalance can be more easily convinced to make purchasing decisions when placed in pressured situations (Shi et al., 2017). These states include situations in which the individual suffers from low self-esteem (chronic or occasional) and sees in the act of buying an opportunity to exercise a type of power or to convince himself that he has some value (Dhandra, 2020). In these cases, consumption far exceeds the needs satisfied by the product's features, with consumers seeking to purchase items as a way to deal with their underlying emotional issues. From the point of view of psychoanalysis, impulsive behaviours can be interpreted according to the functions traditionally attributed to what is conventionally called id, ego, and superego (Rennison, 2015).

When discussing the different relationships between consumers and their consumption targets, Sheth et al. (1991) propose five value categories that can be attributed to products and services: functional, social, emotional, epistemic, and conditional values. Hence, the functional value of a product is that arising from its intrinsic value, or from the functions it can perform. The functional value of a bag would be to allow the one who uses it to be able to transport objects inside it. Tools such as screwdrivers can also be understood as examples of products with high functional value. They are acquired because of practical results and clearly observable for those who use them. Social value, in turn, would be associated with their impact on the way their users are perceived by other individuals they live with, or by any member of the society to which they belong. In general, this is associated with a position in the social hierarchy with some products signalling the economic power of those who can afford them. Luxury items are particularly strong in this regard, with their possession and use serving as an indication of their consumers' financial status. Thus, in addition to the functional value of enabling the transport of items inside, bags manufactured by luxury brands also give their users greater social status. In contrast, the same is not true for tools, the possession of which does not signal economic power. Similarly, possession or use of a particular product can affect an individual's perception of themselves. The ability to afford luxury items, for example, can reinforce in the consumer the feeling that they are successful, at least financially.

Emotional value relates to how consumers feel whenever purchasing a determined product or service. In this sense, it corresponds to the impact of such product or service on the way their users are perceived by themselves. This can be the case for new clothes, which can positively impact a consumer's self-esteem. Epistemic value is linked to the idea of curiosity, with some products arousing the interest of those who observe them. Products that have been recently launched and that are equipped with new technologies still unknown to the general public can be included in this category. Finally, conditional value refers to the worth assigned to a given item depending on the context. A flashlight, for example, will be of greater value in the event that the electricity supply is interrupted. Table 10.1 presents the definitions of the five types of values as proposed in the literature.

Table 10.1 Types of Value

Type of Product/ Service Value	*Definition*
Functional	'The perceived utility acquired from an alternative's capacity for functional, utilitarian, or physical performance. An alternative acquires functional value through the possession of salient functional, utilitarian, or physical attributes. Functional value is measured on a profile of choice attributes' (Sheth et al., 1991, p.160).
Social	'The perceived utility acquired from an alternative's association with one or more specific social groups. An alternative acquires social value through association with positively or negatively stereotyped demographic, socioeconomic, and cultural-ethnic groups. Social value is measured on a profile of choice imagery' (Sheth et al., 1991, p.161).
Emotional	'The perceived utility acquired from an alternative's capacity to arouse feelings or affective states. An alternative acquires emotional value when associated with specific feelings or when precipitating or perpetuating those feelings. Emotional value is measured on a profile of feelings associated with the alternative' (Sheth et al., 1991, p.161).
Epistemic	'The perceived utility acquired from an alternative's capacity to arouse curiosity, provide novelty, and/or satisfy a desire for knowledge. An alternative acquires epistemic value by questionnaire items referring to curiosity, novelty, and knowledge' (Sheth et al., 1991, p.162).
Conditional	'The perceived utility acquired by an alternative as the result of the specific situation or set of circumstances facing the choice maker. An alternative acquires conditional value in the presence of antecedent physical or social contingencies that enhance its functional or social value. Conditional value is measured on a profile of choice contingencies' (Sheth et al., 1991, p.162).

Sustainability and Panic Marketing

As discussed in previous chapters, creating a sense of urgency and need has seemed to accompany the sustainability debate since its inception. It is true, however, that these characteristics seem to have gained strength from the second half of the 20th century onwards, a period in which themes related to sustainable development took on a form closer to what we know today (Fracarolli Nunes and Lee Park, 2021). In addition to the political and ideological reasons discussed previously, it is possible that the adoption of extreme discourses – and the consequent spread of panic that they cause – will also serve the economic interests of companies that intend to offer solutions to a current demand. The plethora of products marketed as environmentally friendly items over the past few decades seems to support the idea that the prospect of an environmental apocalypse is good for business (Laroche et al., 2001). In this sense, the belief that the consumption of traditional products (i.e., non-green goods) contributes to the destruction of the environment is fundamental to boost the acceptance of alternatives considered to be environmentally correct (Moser, 2016).

If the ethicality of using panic marketing for commercial purposes is questionable, the application of this strategy through issues related to sustainability can be considered a serious offense, mainly because of its consequences. As discussed throughout the book, the use of exaggeration as a form of persuasion is one of the main reasons why people are suspicious of arguments pointing to the need to preserve natural resources or to take actions that aim to contribute to the reduction of temperatures of the planet. The lack of credibility ends up resulting in a natural repulsion for the arguments of environmentalism, with the perception that these do not correspond to reality being potentially as harmful as their association with political and ideological issues (which also lead to the deterioration of credibility). In this sense, a brief, more in-depth analysis of creating an atmosphere of panic through doomsday predictions may be helpful.

One of the most common ways of creating environmental panic is the idea that rising temperatures on the planet will lead to the melting of the polar layers and, consequently, the rise in ocean levels (Lomborg, 2020). While many scientists point to the veracity of this prediction, the fact that it has already been presented to the public in the past and has not been confirmed – at least not in the way it was presented – causes the impression that it is unrealistic. Ocean levels have remained relatively stable and even where they have risen, cities have not disappeared, as was often predicted in the not-so-distant past. According to the arguments raised in Chapter 5, this disconnection between the discourse of some environmentalists and the reality observed by the general population ends up fuelling environmental skepticism.

The role played by the political use of the environmental cause should be pointed out as an important factor in the deterioration of its credibility. It is possible, for example, that many candidates for elected office adopt a strategy of generating fear in voters in the expectation of presenting themselves as a solution. According to this calculated reasoning, exaggerators in the environmental discourse would increase their chances of being successful in electoral processes, in addition to providing a cause to be defended throughout their term of office (if they are elected). In this sense, two factors are particularly important for understanding the reasons that lead candidates to exaggerate the gravity of their arguments. The first refers to the undue adaptation of environmental issues to election deadlines, preferring that long-term forecasts such as the melting of the polar layers be presented as urgent and immediate. The panic caused by statements in this sense should ideally generate, in the voter, the feeling that drastic actions need to be taken immediately, with the vote for the candidate who presents himself as a fighter for the good cause being the first of them. This dynamic is discussed in more detail in Chapter 9. The second question refers to the difficulty, or even impossibility, of accurately measuring environmental impacts. Thus, it is difficult for those who are elected based on environmental pessimism to be confronted with the errors of their catastrophic predictions, and they can always argue that they are being confirmed in some part of the world or that they should be confirmed in the near future. In the case of politicians more adept at using evasive tactics, it is common to say that the issues are even more complex than initially anticipated and that their consequences are likely to be even more serious. The lack of objective criteria and the general inability of the public to analyse scientific studies that seriously address the issues contribute to the political use of predictions about the negative consequences of environmental damage.

Ultimately, the ways in which environmental panic is created seem to change over time. While the melting of the polar layers was one of the most common expressions of environmental panic between the late 20th century and the first decades of the 21st century, the depletion of the ozone layer used to dominate debates about its sustainability in the 1970s and 1990s. At the time, the argument was common that the emission of CFC gases used in various products was responsible for creating a hole in the ozone layer responsible for filtering the sun's rays. Thus, the intensity of solar radiation reaching the planet would be much more intense, causing not only the melting of ice at the poles, but also greatly increasing the incidence of health problems related to people's exposure to sunlight, with the prospect of an increased, exponential rate of skin cancer cases being among the main consequences of this scenario. The image of children completely swathed in sun cream and protected by several layers of clothing playing on the beaches must come to the minds of those who lived through that time. The adoption of these and other measures was common as people sought to protect themselves from the various harms associated with the higher level of radiation received due to the lack of protection previously offered by the ozone layer.

What draws attention is the almost disappearance of this debate, to the point that many young people – even those most engaged in themes related to sustainable development – are unaware of the relevance that was attributed to this issue a few decades ago. In some cases, the younger ones are even completely unaware of the subject, believing that the public debate on sustainability has always been reduced to themes of global warming or climate change. Even though the depletion of the ozone layer is related to these issues in many ways, the rationale attributed to the mechanics of the greenhouse effect seems to have completely replaced the previous argument. It remains to understand the reasons why the focus of the discussions so clearly changed. The fact that the themes have been replaced suggests the existence of some type of coordination, or at least a subordinated relationship in which some categories that participate in the public debate as opinion makers agree to follow the guidelines of some other group, even if this alignment takes place involuntarily.

Proponents of the view that sustainability debates are managed in a way that favours specific interests usually point to commercial and ideological issues as possible causes for this phenomenon. It is common, for example, for environmental skeptics to speculate that the focus on the emission of CFC gases as the probable cause of the destruction of the ozone layer was aimed at replacing this product with other industrial solutions developed by companies linked to innovation, which would result in considerable financial gains. The most developed hypotheses in this regard point to the end of the patent validity of CFC gases, which would lead to the loss of exclusivity for their use by the company holding the rights. The replacement by new products whose patents would guarantee exclusive application in the future would appear, therefore, as a way to get around the problem. The prospect of a large increase in the company's profits, or at least the maintenance of its dominant position, would have motivated the coordination of the environmental agenda, with the alleged impact of CFC gases on the growth of the hole in the ozone layer being insistently presented by vehicles of the traditional media of the time (e.g., newspapers, magazines, television, radios). Speculation also occurs about the ways in which the definition of the subjects to be dealt with by the media would be given, with the offer of undue payments to the executives of these companies or even to the editors and presenters being one of the most commonly considered possibilities. The purpose of this articulation would be to influence public opinion so that it not only favoured the consumption of products that used the alternative to the CFC, but also created additional pressure on the political class to create laws, rules, and regulations that favoured the replacement of products. The achievement of commercial goals would be the cause of the virtual abandonment of the debate about the hole in the ozone layer, since it was simply no longer useful. Once more, it must be noted that these points are no more than speculations fuelling discussions in blogs, internet forums, and other informal discussion outlets.

These ideas tend to circulate easily in virtual groups, as well as in circles of friends and acquaintances who share similar views. We do not seek here to ratify any of these possibilities, but the discussion is important for understanding the way of thinking of those who defend them and, consequently, tend to develop radical forms of environmental skepticism. Individuals that are more attentive to these issues have difficulty understanding the reasons a subject so debated during a certain period of history practically disappears from public debate. In addition to considering possible economic and political interests, other issues are often considered. Among the most discussed is the solution to the problem, the discovery that it was not as serious as expected, and the lie by those who defended it. In all cases, the credibility of the environmental debate can be expected to be seriously impacted, which could have important consequences for the development of skeptical views in the future.

Understanding the issues that made up the environmental debate in the past is important for a better understanding of the dynamics of public debate in the present. Once the connection between them becomes evident, the idea that environmental skepticism is a notion built up over the years becomes clearer, with the development of refractory views that can be understood as a legacy of mistakes or exaggerations made in the past. It should be remembered that many of the opinions about sustainability are based on information received from teachers and relatives, which can decisively influence young people's beliefs. With regard to individuals who suspect the veracity of the debate about the hole in the ozone layer, for example, this can translate into the development of a chronic lack of belief in their family members (e.g., children, nephews, grandchildren), transmitting the distrust acquired in past decades for generations. The same is true for unconfirmed predictions about the consequences of global warming, especially in what concerns about rising sea levels and the flooding of entire cities that they would cause. It is possible, therefore, that a statement by those who failed to promulgate a certain environmental issue would help to dispel doubts about the honesty of their previous statements. It would be very important, for example, for journalists who devoted a considerable part of their time to pointing out the dangers of depleting the ozone layer to explain in a very transparent way the reasons that led them to abandon this topic. Likewise, the debate would be greatly enriched if the scientists who endorsed the most catastrophic projections in this regard explained the reasons why they no longer devote the same attention to the topic. Perhaps an acknowledgment of any errors or exaggerations would be less damaging to one's credibility than one's silence. In reality, the lack of explanation makes room for the most diverse speculations, including the most elaborate conspiracy theories.

In addition to issues related to the possible benefits of environmental alarmism for the business of specific companies, maintaining a state of alert has great economic potential for several sectors. Similar to the mechanism adopted by politicians who claim to defend environmental causes, many companies have specialized in positioning their products as a solution to immediate environmental problems. As discussed throughout the book, 'green products' end up benefiting from maintaining an apocalyptic perspective. In addition to ensuring market share for companies that offer them, environmentally superior products can also act as a vector of income concentration and social inequality, since only large companies would be able to bear the high costs of research and development necessary for the level of innovation they demand. Likewise, public investment in the form of university research is usually restricted to developed countries, precisely because they are the only ones able to allocate a larger portion of their budgets for this purpose. These and other side effects that are often overlooked in the green product development debate are covered in more detail in Chapter 14.

Just as there is great suspicion about the real reasons that led to the promotion of a state of alert about the hole in the ozone layer, arguments about the dangers of the greenhouse effect are not spared by the skeptics. In general, the idea of global warming is linked to ideological issues, with the hypothesis that movements in this direction represent veiled attacks on the capitalist system and on individual freedoms being relatively common. In particular, the fact that the use of automobiles is considered one of the main factors responsible for the increase in temperatures on a global level usually generates discomfort in those who understand that their vehicles are important instruments in maintaining the autonomy of individuals. Furthermore, the attack on automobiles is also understood as an effort to undermine the mode of production adopted in most parts of the world, precisely because the automobile industry concentrates a non-negligible part of private capital.

Maintaining a permanent state of environmental panic is, hence, not only favourable to companies interested in promoting their products, or to politicians seeking to be elected in the next elections. Unexpectedly, this situation ends up being advantageous for a number of industries and professional categories, even if indirectly. Among the most evident are the various forms of media, including both traditional and social. In the case of the former, it is quite common for television news to end up keeping the attention of viewers interested in understanding the seriousness of environmental issues, in order to somehow become aware of the level of risk to which they are exposed, with individuals who believe they are facing some sort of danger seeking to increase their chances of survival through greater knowledge of the enemy being faced. The same mechanism extends to other media, with newspapers often seeking to print front-page stories in which environmental issues are presented as a threat to be closely monitored. Magazine covers are also no exception to this pattern, with the image of characters linked to the defence of environmental issues being relatively common. This includes activists from all walks of life, with the election of these figures as personalities of the year being commonplace. Radio programs also end up benefiting from long debates in which opposing views are often confronted. Typically, these programs have the participation of specialists, almost always in the condition of university professors, researchers, and authors of books and articles on the topics covered. Consulting these professionals establishes another category of beneficiaries of environmental extremism and the associated panic marketing, as discussed later in the text.

When it comes to social media and other more recent formats, the use of strategies that aim to generate a greater degree of apprehension about the urgency of environmental issues can also be very fruitful. In the case of professional networking apps, for example, it is possible to imagine that the exposure of controversial topics should generate greater user interaction, which should be reflected in a greater number of comments and, consequently, in a longer time of use of the product. The success of this process should result in revenue growth for companies that may see an increase in the number of advertisers interested in having their brands exposed to their users or will have the possibility of increasing the price of ads. One of the operational possibilities for the use of panic marketing in these environments is the calibration of algorithms used by different applications that offer these services, so that these tools increase the probability of confrontations due to the users' exposure to controversial issues. On video platforms, valuing the most sensationalist aspects should result in an increase in views of the content presented, as well as a greater interaction of viewers through 'comments', 'likes', and 'shares'. Similar to what happens with social networks, this greater engagement by the audience should translate into increased revenue for companies that manage these processes. This could be due to either a greater number of advertisers interested in relating their brands to videos of this type, or the natural increase that can be expected in the prices of advertisements. Recently, the success experienced by the podcast format has brought together some of the elements of radio and new digital media, with debates about sustainability resembling the type of program shown in traditional forms of communication.

Among the most important conclusions of this debate is the perception that the use of panic marketing strategies to address sustainability can be very attractive for a number of industries, presenting an important potential for generating profits. As previously mentioned, the attractiveness of these devices is not restricted, however, to legal entities, with many individuals also benefiting from the maintenance of a permanent state of tension. This seems to be the case for a large number of academics devoted to the topic of sustainability, many of whom build entire careers based on the discussion of purely abstract issues (i.e., without any practical application or commitment to reality). The privileged position they occupy allows them to criticize basically any economic activity, which they usually do through a survey of purely theoretical environmental impacts and, in most cases, without presenting any alternative.

As discussed in Chapter 5, it is not uncommon for people who are unaware of the reality of environmentally important regions (e.g., the Amazon) to focus their attention almost exclusively on aspects related to the preservation of natural resources, ignoring social issues of the highest relevance. While attitudes in this direction are regrettable, the reasons why they occur can be understood when perpetrated by laypeople. In these cases, the superficiality of their knowledge or ignorance of reality end up explaining the serious evaluation errors. It so happens, however, that very similar mistakes are made by professors, intellectuals, and many who consider themselves experts in sustainability.

Inappropriate behaviours or those that demonstrate excessive poverty in terms of analytical capacity end up being very harmful, for both the environmental cause and the specialists who propagate them. The perception that those who express strong opinions on complex issues do not have a knowledge of the subjects they deal with ends up undermining their credibility, especially among those who analyse their speech more objectively. The result is almost always a compromise of the trustworthiness of these specialists, and, at the limit, of the very science they represent. This issue is discussed in more detail in Chapter 11. This erosion of reputational capital seems to be nevertheless concentrated in academic circles, with the general public lacking the necessary knowledge to understand the real lack of value of what pseudo-specialists preach. In this sense, the use of extreme rhetoric and panic marketing to address sustainability issues ends up being useful to those who just want to stay in social shop windows, appearing periodically as guests on radio and television programs.

The reasons for promoting panic marketing by those who should be the first to propose a more balanced perspective can be motivated by several factors. In addition to ignorance itself, it is also possible to point to an eventual laziness or self-indulgence that leads many academics to remain in their offices, congresses, and classrooms discussing subjects they know only through books instead of visiting the various realities *in loco*. Chapter 5 discusses the fact that many of those who present themselves as profound experts on issues related to sustainability in the Amazon have never been there and, in general, ignore the serious social problems faced by the region. However, it is likely that, in addition to these issues, vanity is the main reason why uninformed and often ignorant academics take radical positions, as this increases the chances that they will continue to be invited to participate in debate programs. Media exposure gives them some social status with their families, colleagues, and students, which ends up working as a powerful attraction for them to continue talking about what many media outlets expect them to say, that is, controversial speeches that attract the attention of viewers, as well as the validation of a climate of panic that, as discussed earlier, tends to increase the time that the viewer remains attentive. In addition to causing great damage to the public debate, the limited attitude of many academics ends up having a long-term impact, precisely because they are constantly in contact with the legions of students who will make up the workforce in the near future.

The notoriety that extreme discourses ensure to those who disseminate it seems to be even more attractive to members of the artistic class. The ratification of panic marketing strategies by singers, actors, painters, and performers in general seems to guarantee them greater exposure, with the replication of their speeches in all forms of media contributing to the consolidation of their careers. In addition to yielding immediate dividends in the form of advertising contracts and box office sales, the increased placement of artist images seems to give them access to a select group of notables who claim to defend the environmental cause. This includes politicians and multibillionaires who, with the support of the artistic class, manage to spread the idea that they are agents of good fighting against the forces that relentlessly seek to destroy the planet's forests and seas. These relationships seem very convenient, especially for businessmen who run controversial businesses from the point of view of social or environmental development, as well as for politicians who seek to improve the contact they maintain with voters.

In general, it can be said that the use of typical panic marketing strategies to address issues related to sustainability is extremely harmful to the construction of a mature and balanced debate. The search for the creation and maintenance of a permanent state of tension is only useful for those who somehow wish to benefit from discussions on sustainable development, without actually being committed to real and simultaneous progress in social, environmental, and economical areas. In this sense, communication companies seem to have specialized in the application of constant alarmism, being more concerned with capturing the public's attention than proposing solutions to the problems they talk about. The distortion of facts, together with the selection of subjects with the potential to cause greater commotion with the public, ends up generating too much focus on some issues, while at the same time contributing to others being ignored.

This dynamic largely explains why the majority of the lay public does not take into account many of the social and economic issues that, according to the triple bottom line concept (Elkington, 1997), should receive equal attention. Too much focus on environmental issues is not a problem in itself, but it generates biased discussion when it is not accompanied by minimal consideration of the other spheres that influence and are influenced by it. The result is the creation of entire generations that repeat what they hear from opinion makers, without being aware of the great complexity of the themes they deal with. It is sad to note that despite good intentions, many of those who engage in the environmental debate are actually serving as a ploy for manipulative agents to achieve their hidden goals. Young people seem to be especially exposed to this possibility, with the innocence and lack of experience that are typical of them, allowing the exaggerated and biased messages that are conveyed through panic marketing to reach them even more strongly. Added to this is the fact that students represent a captive audience for their teachers. The fact that they do not have the option of not attending certain classes, not attending seminars, or not reading the books indicated in the biography that make up the literary basis of their training makes them end up absorbing the messages without the possibility of contradictory. The result is the creation of many professionals who will not have the minimal analytical skills that are necessary to develop an open and constructive dialogue with those who have different views. Thus, the use of panic marketing represents one of the main factors responsible for the radicalization of public debate, with the cultivation of radical views preventing an understanding from being reached between all parties that make up the public debate, including environmental skeptics.

Given these and other issues discussed, it is clear that combating the indiscriminate use of panic marketing represents a duty for all those who wish to interrupt the instrumentalization of the environmental debate. In this set, this chapter sought to present elements that facilitate the identification of both the causes and consequences of the use of these strategies, so that their identification is facilitated. These themes are taken up in the following chapters, so that the understanding of the need to rationalize discussions on sustainable development becomes even clearer. In particular, the need to adopt a holistic view is reinforced, with the consideration of social aspects that are often neglected being emphasized. One of the most relevant issues to achieve this goal is the provision of basic elements that allow the average citizen to identify the malicious use of panic marketing, thus preventing it from being manipulated by those who do not hesitate to use it unscrupulously.

References

Achtziger, A., Hubert, M., Kenning, P., Raab, G., and Reisch, L. (2015). Debt out of control: The links between self-control, compulsive buying, and real debts. *Journal of Economic Psychology*, Vol.49, pp.141–149.

Atalay, A.S., and Meloy, M.G. (2011). Retail therapy: A strategic effort to improve mood. *Psychology & Marketing*, Vol.28, No.6, pp.638–659.

Ayadi, N., Giraud, M., and Gonzalez, C. (2013). An investigation of consumers' self-control mechanisms when confronted with repeated purchase temptations: Evidence from online private sales. *Journal of Retailing and Consumer Services*, Vol.20, No.3, pp.272–281.

Baumeister, R.F. (2002). Yielding to temptation: Self-control failure, impulsive purchasing, and consumer behavior. *Journal of Consumer Research*, Vol.28, No.4, pp.670–676.

Ben-David, I., and Bos, M. (2021). Impulsive consumption and financial well-being: Evidence from an increase in the availability of alcohol. *The Review of Financial Studies*, Vol.34, No.5, pp.2608–2647.

Brocas, I., and Carrillo, J.D. (2003). Information and self-control. *The Psychology of Economic Decisions*, Vol.1, pp.89–104.

Dhandra, T.K. (2020). Does self-esteem matter? A framework depicting role of self-esteem between dispositional mindfulness and impulsive buying. *Journal of Retailing and Consumer Services*, Vol.55, p.102135.

Fracarolli Nunes, M., and Lee Park, C. (2021). The age of green. In: M. Fracarolli Nunes and C. Lee Park (Eds.). *Business Ethics and Environmental Fraud*, pp.87–103. Palgrave Macmillan.

Laroche, M., Bergeron, J., and Barbaro-Forleo, G. (2001). Targeting consumers who are willing to pay more for environmentally friendly products. *Journal of Consumer Marketing*, Vol.18, No.6, pp.503–520.

Lades, L.K. (2014). Impulsive consumption and reflexive thought: Nudging ethical consumer behavior. *Journal of Economic Psychology*, Vol.41, pp.114–128.

Lee, J.S., Chun, S., and Choi, J. (2019). South Korean consumers' experiences and underlying shopping mechanism of Black Friday. *The Journal of Distribution Science*, Vol.17, No.11, pp.63–72.

Lee, L., and Böttger, T.M. (2017). The therapeutic utility of shopping: Retail therapy, emotion regulation, and well-being. In: *The Routledge Companion to Consumer Behavior*, pp.38–61. Routledge.

Lomborg, B. (2020). *False Alarm: How Climate Change Panic Costs Us Trillions, Hurts the Poor, and Fails to Fix the Planet*. Hachette.

Moser, A.K. (2016). Consumers' purchasing decisions regarding environmentally friendly products: An empirical analysis of German consumers. *Journal of Retailing and Consumer Services*, Vol.31, pp.389–397.

Rennison, N. (2015). *Freud and Psychoanalysis: Everything You Need to Know About Id, Ego, Super-Ego and More*. Oldcastle Books.

Sendpulse (2021). *What Is a Flash Sale: Ideas and Tips*. Available at https://sendpulse.com/support/glossary/flash-sale

Sheth, J.N., Newman, B.I., and Gross, B.L. (1991). Why we buy what we buy: A theory of consumption values. *Journal of Business Research*, Vol.22, No.2, pp.159–170.

Shi, H.Y., Jing, F.J., Yang, Y., and Nguyen, B. (2017). The concept of consumer vulnerability: Scale development and validation. *International Journal of Consumer Studies*, Vol.41, No.6, pp.769–777.

Simpson, L., Taylor, L., O'Rourke, K., and Shaw, K. (2011). An analysis of consumer behavior on Black Friday. *American International Journal of Contemporary Research*, Vol.1, No.1, pp.1–5.

Part III

The Consequences of Extreme Sustainability Rhetoric

11 Science and the Erosion of Credibility Capital

Credibility Capital

As proposed by Newell and Goldsmith (2001), corporate credibility can be understood as the union of two sub-constructs, each referring to a different facet: expertise and trustworthiness. While the first refers to the observers' perception that a company is able to deliver on its promises, the second deals with the extent to which the organization is seen as sincere in what it expresses. Based on this differentiation, it is possible to associate the expertise component with the set of resources, competencies, and thus capabilities that the company has. In the case of the development of new equipment or a new application for a pre-existing technology, the statements of a company that holds innovation as an important part of its business model should have more credibility than those made by companies that belong to more traditional industries or are based on old practices. Similarly, past experiences also seem to have an important effect on sustaining claims about future behaviour. From this perspective, an organization perceived as having diligently fulfilled its commitments in the past should be perceived as capable of continuing to do so, fostering positive levels of corporate credibility – expertise. This category can include the ability of a supplier to deliver its products to its customers within the previously agreed deadlines and with the desired quality (Seth et al., 2006). Within this perspective, companies that manage to deliver what they promise from an operational point of view should profit from positive future expectations (Yoon et al., 2021). In contrast, frustrated or not so successful experiences tend to generate a kind of distrust in stakeholders, which translates into damage to the belief that the company has the means to honour its promises (Adams et al., 2010).

Corporate credibility – trustworthiness – in turn can be viewed as a parameter or measure of the perception of a company's ethics (Potts and Matuszewski, 2004). In particular, the sub-construct refers to the understanding that the claims coming from the organization are true or, at least, sincere (Lock and Seele, 2016). Unlike the aspects related to its complementary sub-construct (i.e., expertise), the development of trustworthiness is not associated with the company's possession of something (e.g., resources, competencies, or capabilities). Instead, it comes from a behavioural expectation linked to attachment to reality and transparency

DOI: 10.4324/9781003124719-14

(Grimmelikhuijsen and Meijer, 2014). Despite being intrinsically different from expertise, trustworthiness has some similarities with it, especially concerning the processes that give rise to them. In this sense, the perception that a company has a positive history must condition expectations around its future behaviour (Sheth, 1996). Quite simply, organizations perceived as having been sincere and honest on previous occasions should have a credibility capital that could benefit them in the future. This dynamic forms the basis of what came to be known as insurance mechanisms, which might relate to the same dimension of conduct (e.g., corporate social responsibility) (Kang et al., 2016) or interchangeably between dimensions (e.g., corporate social and environmental responsibility), configuring a cross-insurance mechanism (Fracarolli Nunes et al., 2020). Likewise, companies recognized for their dishonesty will have difficulty convincing consumers that they will not commit irregularities again, or that, even if they have acted incorrectly in the past, they will no longer make the same mistake in the future. One of the greatest examples of the destruction of a company's trustworthiness occurred during the case known as Volkswagen Dieselgate (Fracarolli Nunes and Lee Park, 2016, 2021a). Briefly, the German automaker admitted to having rigged emissions tests in the United States, deceiving both local authorities and its consumers. In one of the most remarkable moments of the episode, its then US Chief Executive Officer Michael Horn acknowledged the serious faults committed. In his own words, 'Our company was dishonest with the EPA and the California Air Resources Board, and with all of you' (Ramey, 2015).

Still, on the importance of credibility for companies, Goldsmith et al. (2000) propose that the construct is an important part in the formation of corporate reputation, playing a similar role to that played by other concepts such as corporate image and identity. Among other consequences, this is equivalent to saying that the construction and preservation of credibility is fundamental for the performance of companies (Zhang and Rezaee, 2009). From a strategic point of view, corporate credibility can be considered an intangible resource that can be a source of sustainable competitive advantage (Fracarolli Nunes and Lee Park, 2021b). Applying the criteria proposed by Barney (1991), it is clear that while corporate credibility is valuable, it is also rare and difficult to imitate and replace. Regarding its value, this is linked to the development of trust with stakeholders, as well as its effects on the type of relationship they should maintain with the company (Rao, 2012). In addition to influencing punctual purchasing intentions (Kim and Choi, 2012), the perception that a particular company is (or is not) worthy of trust should influence the propensity of those who exchange with it to develop stronger relationships (Xie and Haugland, 2016; Lee Park et al., 2021). This should translate into better levels of collaboration in the case of relationships between companies (i.e., business-to-business) (Hoejmose et al., 2012) or a greater degree of customer loyalty in terms of the relationship between companies and end customers (i.e., business-to-consumers) (Pérez and Del Bosque, 2015).

On the criterion of rarity, this is associated with the fact that credibility is not something that can be simply acquired. Instead, it needs to be built over time, as the company proves to be trustworthy and to have expertise (Kemp, 2011). Within a perspective more associated with the Industry Structure – more specifically within Porter's (1979, 1980) five forces – corporate credibility can even be understood as a barrier to entry in some cases. The financial services industry is highly dependent on the credibility it has with depositors, with banks probably being the most sensitive to this issue (Ruiz et al., 2014). The high value of credibility can be understood from the fact that, from the moment a customer deposits his money in a banking institution, s/he only counts on her/his belief that the counterparty in question is honest and will return the money when that s/he demands so. In this way, the lack of credibility of a new player can generate great difficulties for its operation and, in extreme cases, even make it unfeasible. The criteria that deal with the impossibility of imitating or replacing corporate credibility refers to the very nature of the concept, mainly its uniqueness (Balmer, 2012). As discussed, corporate credibility should result from interactions between the company and its stakeholders, meaning it is path dependent. Added to this is the very intangibility of the construct, which, along with making it more complex – when compared to tangible resources (e.g., machines, buildings) – prevents it from being examined or understood in its entirety. Strictly speaking, the *locus* of corporate credibility cannot be defined, as it is distributed in the perceptions of each individual. These characteristics mean that credibility cannot be copied or replaced. Altogether, the perception that corporate credibility is valuable, rare, not imitable, and not substitutable qualifies it as a strategic intangible resource (i.e., one that may be source of sustained competitive advantage) within the theoretical frames of the Resource-Based View (Penrose, 1959; Rumelt, 1984; Wernerfelt, 1984; Barney, 1986, 1991).

When analysed together, all these dimensions seem to point to a broader issue, according to which the management of corporate credibility is directly linked to the maintenance of coherence between the messages that a company sends to its audiences and what it actually is or does (Shim and Yang, 2016). Stakeholders' perceptions that there is an alignment between these dimensions reinforces the feeling that the organization is credible, in terms both of the belief that it is really capable of accomplishing what it proposes (i.e., expertise), and in what concerns the sincerity of its manifestations (i.e., trustworthiness). More simply, this coherence is expressed in the variations of the popular expression 'talk the talk, walk the walk'. While the alignment between discourse and practice reinforces the credibility of companies (Urde, 2009), deviations in this direction can, nevertheless, be decisive for the destruction of trust. As gaps between messages sent to the public and organizational practices are detected, perceptions of corporate hypocrisy (Wagner et al., 2009) may emerge. Among the main consequences of this process is the probable deterioration of the quality of the companies' relations with their various publics, since they would develop distrust about both the intentions of the directors in question and their transparency in demonstrating exactly what they practice.

Lessons learned about corporate credibility can be extended to any other level of analysis. Applying the idea of trustworthiness, it is possible to assess, for example, the credibility of a country with regard to the prospects that it will fulfil its commercial or financial commitments (Edwards, 2006). Nations with a good record of respecting the rules that govern international transactions (e.g., incoterms) tend to have a positive expectation regarding their future behaviour. Similarly, countries that over the years have diligently paid their creditors profit from a positive image in terms of their fairness (Rigobon, 2002). These and other attitudes reinforce the feeling that the country is worthy of trust, which, in general, brings numerous benefits. In the case of respect for trade conditions, one can expect a greater propensity of economic agents to do business with the nation in question, which will probably materialize in greater volumes of foreign direct investment, exports, imports, job creation, and collection taxes, among others. When all these factors are considered together, they can indicate a trend towards economic growth, which should not only benefit the population of that country immediately, but also bear fruit in the long term, including better living conditions for future generations (Jaramillo and Tejada, 2011). If, on the one hand, these positive cycles cannot be entirely attributed to the construction of credibility, its influence as an important criterion in the decision of economic agents serves to illustrate its importance (Zheng, 2011). Likewise, the fact that a country pays its creditors not only guarantees access to new sources of financing but also lowers the cost of borrowing (Jaramillo, 2010). The perception that a nation has a high probability of honouring its financial commitments implies a better assessment of the risks of lending money to it. Once again, greater access to financial resources at a lower cost can be decisive for economic growth (Vreeland, 2003). Reflectively, the lack of credibility can prevent the country from taking advantage of these opportunities.

Regarding the credibility dimension that deals with the perception of expertise, positive evaluations can have profound impacts on a nation, including issues related to its internal security. A country perceived as capable of developing war weapons or of implementing effective defence strategies will be able to exert great deterrent power over its enemies, preventing them from attacking them for fear of retaliation (Press, 2005). Credibility expertise can also be an important factor when it comes to economic development, as long-term foreign investments are often decided on the basis of the belief that a country will be able to successfully perform certain tasks. Among them may be the development of the necessary infrastructure to create a favourable environment for the operations of companies (Khadaroo and Seetanah, 2010), such as the opening of roads, the construction of ports and airports, and the implementation of high-speed internet networks. Expectations about the capacity or expertise of countries can extend to more complex issues that do not necessarily involve tangible aspects. The belief that the country is capable of achieving significant improvements in its educational system, for example, may represent a critical factor in this regard, since the development of skills and knowledge levels of those who will make up the economically active population in the future can be fundamental for the proper functioning of some industries (Akin and Vlad, 2011). It is also likely that the belief that nations are capable of maintaining democratic environments with due alternation of power between political groups favours the interest of international investors in investing their resources (Asiedu and Lien, 2011). As discussed earlier, the maintenance of the so-called rule of law and the corresponding institutional stability that derives from it seems to be a fundamental factor for social and economic development (Haggard et al., 2008). It must be argued, then, that the fact that a product carries a 'made in' brand may significantly contribute to its performance as, to some extent, it incorporates the reputation attributed to its country of origin (Fracarolli Nunes and Lee Park, 2021a).

Scientific Credibility

The credibility attributed to scientists plays an important role in validating basically all issues present in public debate (Jensen, 2008). It is not uncommon, for example, for experts to be consulted on their opinion about specific subjects, especially those that are both relatively unknown and of great interest to the public (Maier et al., 2016). In these cases, professors and researchers are commonly invited to participate in radio and television programs, exposing their views to those who follow traditional media vehicles. More recently, this phenomenon has also started to happen in a virtual environment, with experts starring in podcast interviews, as well as in other internet communication channels. This dynamic was intensified throughout the period of the pandemic caused by the new coronavirus (Covid-19) (Hart et al., 2020). Faced with the novelty of the problem and all the panic spreading in populations on a global scale, doctors, biologists, and pharmacists – as well as a series of other categories of health professionals – were consulted about both the real seriousness of the challenges that the disease presented and the best ways to fight it. Discussions regarding the need or effectiveness of the use of surgical masks, the possibility of treatment with existing drugs, and strategies for the development and application of effective vaccines occupied a particularly important space.

Despite presenting several positive aspects, the popularization of the scientific debate in such a troubled moment ended up producing results that may not favour the credibility of specialists with lay populations. The typical uncertainties of the first moments of a pandemic (Chater, 2020), combined with the high degree of media coverage (Haroon and Rizvi, 2020), favoured the dissemination of various hypotheses and projections by experts, many of which proved to be incorrect some time later (Holmdahl and Buckee, 2020). This dynamic seems to have affected the most different categories of scientists and organizations, including study centres and universities (Kreps and Kriner, 2020). If, on the one hand, this speculative period is common in the scientific process, it seems to have not been well understood by the public. In fact, ordinary citizens expected to obtain answers to their anxieties from specialists, and as they were faced with contradictory information in some cases, they began to distrust their abilities (Safford et al., 2021).

It can be said, therefore, that the pandemic ended up triggering a process of erosion of the reputational capital not only of the scientists, but even of science itself as a supposedly superior entity, from which the truth is expected to emerge. Once again, it is important to highlight that the missing information and the elaboration and subsequent falsification of hypotheses on the various topics related to the pandemic do not represent a problem in themselves. As previously stated, this experimental phase is, to a certain extent, expected in the initial moments of the study of a new phenomenon, with the posing of questions and the raising of doubts being typical of the scientific method – and perhaps even more than the provision of answers. The damage caused to the credibility of scientists, research institutions, and more broadly to the natural steps of the development of science came not from the lack of uniformity of opinion or the many mistakes made, but from the fact that this initial phase of the process was excessively explored by the media, with the exposure of a relatively fragile and confused moment of the researchers, perhaps not being understood as something normal by the lay population and, therefore, not accustomed to the difficulties common to the processes of knowledge development.

At this point, a brief discussion of the origin of scientific credibility may be helpful. The search for truth through science seems to be the result of a long historical process that has developed in Western civilization over the last few centuries (Weaver, 1991). In a very simplistic way, this process can be understood as the progressive replacement of religious perspectives by others. If, on the one hand, many continued to attribute the source of truth to God, others began to see this virtue in other instances. Among the most common, politics and science can be highlighted, with this being, perhaps, some of the most important results of complex social phenomena such as the French Revolution and the Enlightenment (Hazen, 2000; Doyle, 2018). Despite presenting eminently different 'solutions', the connection, association, and even cause and effect relationships between these two movements denote their objectives of replacing religious thought. Evidently, the discussion about the real influence of historical processes of such importance cannot be summarized in a simple objective, nor in direct associations. The debate proposed here is only intended to offer the reader a somewhat broader perspective on the dynamics that result in scientific credibility, with a more detailed approach to these topics resting beyond the scope of the book.

Another aspect that seems to be important in the development of scientific credibility refers to the longevity of universities and the perception that these institutions are perennial. Some universities have many centuries of history, having harboured in this period some of the most brilliant minds that humanity has ever produced. In particular, some of the oldest European universities seem to meet these requirements. Established in the Middle Ages, institutions such as the University of Bologna in Italy (founded in 1088, Università di Bologna, 2022), the University of Paris ('La Sorbonne') in France (founded in 1257, Université de Paris 1 – Pantheon Sorbonne, 2022), and the University of Salamanca in Spain (founded in 1218, Universidad de Salamanca, 2022) illustrate this dynamic. Universities created in the transition periods between the Middle Ages and the Renaissance period also made important contributions. Among them, the University of Seville (founded in 1505, Universidad de Sevilla, Sanchez Mantero and Serrera Contreras, 2005), can be highlighted. To these are added the many renowned universities that emerged in the new world in the course of the following centuries. Exemplary of this category is Harvard University (founded in 1636, Harvard University, 2022). The immense services rendered to humanity by these and other institutions throughout their existence contributed to their being perceived as centres of excellence and providers of human capital for society. Far beyond the offer of academic training and the consequent creation of professional categories, the research activities carried out by universities represented, perhaps, the greatest source of knowledge generation, which made it possible not only to alleviate much of human suffering, but also to offer the conditions for technological development. Thus, it can be argued that universities are probably the institutions that have had the greatest impact on shaping life in society, having fulfilled this role since their inception. The motto of the University of Seville translates this vision: '*Cinco siglos impulsando el conocimiento*' (Five centuries pushing knowledge; Universidad de Sevilla, 2022, our translation). In a way, the credibility acquired by universities due to the long years of service to humanity is passed on to their scientists. Thus, anyone who makes up the faculty of an educational institution ends up acquiring part of its reputation as well.

Science, Politics, and Economics

Although they have not experienced the same intensity as the discussions on the new coronavirus pandemic, topics related to sustainability have been the subject of analysis by experts in recent decades, being equally disseminated in the most diverse communication channels (Holt and Barkemeyer, 2012). In addition to the issues discussed previously, some aspects of the way in which the reputational capital of scientists and universities can be eroded demand some additional consideration. As discussed in Chapters 5, 6, and 8, the development of radical views can be intensively impacted by emotional needs, contributing to individuals not only accepting extreme arguments more easily but also defending them as if they represent an absolute truth. This mechanism seems to be based on the attachment that extremists would have to some certainties, which would fulfil the function of protecting them from the psychic chaos arising from doubts about fundamental issues. In this way, the radical thoughts would bring them comfort through the diagnoses they present of the prescriptions. The simplicity with which complex themes are approached would also characterize radical thinking, serving as a magnet for intellects of lesser analytical capacity. In the face of these and other issues, the adherence of scientists to radical thinking can reveal their weaknesses, especially for those who have a slightly closer look at the nature and dynamics of academic activities. In the first place, one can point to the inability of some scientists to admit the excessive ambition of extremist thoughts, in terms of both understanding complex realities and proposing remedies to correct any identified dysfunctions. Starting from the premises that scientists are, in general, endowed with deeper knowledge to the average population (Magnus, 2013) and that they seek to know the truth (Richardson and Slack, 2005), it would be natural to suppose that they were the first to refute simplified views, especially with regard to more complex issues such as those related to sustainability and sustainable development.

Thus, after a first moment in which opinions are formed based on the superficial and even aesthetic aspects of speeches, lectures, public positions, and production in general (e.g., articles, reviews, books), it is likely that the one who analyses the positioning of scientists who defend extreme points of view develop a vision that is unfavourable to them. The appeal of extreme views stems from, among other things, the ease of being absorbed, being accessible to all types of intelligence. The translation of issues that are difficult to understand into the form of direct and absolute arguments works as an invitation for less prepared people to engage in public debate. The fact that they understood the messages offered to them seems to guarantee the radicals a high degree of confidence, accelerating the adoption of more aggressive and refractory postures to everything that appears to be contrary to their beliefs. The adhesion of academics to extreme discourses can simply contaminate their image, in a way that they start to be confused with the different profiles that accompany them. Obviously, it is not a question here of defending simplistic views as essentially incorrect for the simple fact that they are accessible to the general public. However, those who have an academic background and are directly engaged in scientific research tend to deal more with doubts than with certainties, mainly because they understand the fragility of the methods used in the constitutive process of science. The characteristic limitations of scientific research tend to occupy an entire section of the articles in which they are presented, in such a way that all the fragility of the announced conclusions are recognized (Jensen, 2008). Depending on the area of study and the type of question being investigated, this usually includes a debate on the problems related to the construction of the sample used, the problems of application of the methods used, potential bias, and the limited capacity of generalization, among many other issues likely to be presented.

It is not uncommon, therefore, for scientific research to result in new questions, not even answering the research question that initially motivated it. While this can be difficult to understand for a layman and to a certain extent disappointing, this process is part of everyday life for the vast majority of scientists. While this routine seems unproductive and slow, it is inserted in what can be understood as the classic scientific rhythm (Stengers, 2018). Even when the results of an investigation are encouraging, its exposure to the scientific community will serve as a very rigorous test, with the scrutiny of other scientists acting as a powerful filter of radicalism. In this sense, it can be said that, in addition to its additive aspects, the construction of knowledge is also residual. Among other things, this means that most conclusions end up being discarded, not because they are necessarily false, but because they lack a foundation to support their acceptance as probable. The very process of publishing an academic article follows this logic, with the submitted research being analysed by a group of scientists who were not directly involved in the conduct of the work (i.e., the peer-review process) (Rowland, 2002). This usually includes the editor-in-chief of the outlet in question (e.g., journal, review) and at least two reviewers who, anonymously, will assess the quality of the evaluated work. An important part of this task is the search for methodological or theoretical flaws that may somehow compromise the quality of the results. This step can turn into a rejection of the article, or a review process, depending on the editor-in-chief's perception that the flaws can or cannot be corrected. This dynamic can be repeated until the article reaches a level of quality that justifies its publication. Even after this initial filter, the results continued to be questioned by the academic community. If flaws are detected, they will be pointed out in both the form of direct criticisms and counterarguments to be published as an integral part of future articles. In some more extreme cases, studies understood to be faulty are even ratified after publication.

This whole process usually contributes to scientists developing great humility in the face of their inability to construct absolute truths (Hoekstra and Vazire, 2021). If it is true that some end up harbouring an apparently arrogant posture (Schoenfeld, 1984), most tend to recognize their insignificance, which seems to have a direct relationship with the development of greater skepticism towards any idea that preaches the understanding of complex realities or the proposition of means to change it. In view of these reflections, it can be argued that, in principle, scientific thinking is incompatible with extreme worldviews and, in particular, with ideologies. It is possible, therefore, to defend the idea that a scientist who is too favourable to an extreme view probably has not yet reached the level of maturity necessary for the proper exercise of her/his role, leaving doubts as to whether this will ever be able to be reviewed. As discussed throughout the book, extreme views often occupy the space traditionally dedicated to religions, which can make it difficult for those who identify with them to develop a more critical stance.

The lack of prudence and skepticism of academics often ends up denoting a misunderstanding of the nature of science, which, among other things, can lead to questioning the very capacity of the scientist in question. With universities being largely composed by the academic production of these individuals, it is not difficult to imagine that they could have their reputational capital contaminated by the adoption of more radical postures, even when their reputations – often built over centuries, as mentioned earlier – point in the opposite direction. Quite broadly, a scientist's conviction on a given subject (i.e., lack of doubt) usually suggests that s/he is too taken up with human passions, and is, therefore, subject to all the natural consequences of this condition. In the case of those who enjoy the prestige that academic titles and positions confer, this issue is particularly dangerous, as the use of authoritative arguments tend to spread through society, ending many debates in an undue way.

In the case of discussions on sustainability, this can be reflected in serious difficulties for the development of dialogues between the dissenting parties. In this sense, the ballast provided by extreme positions defended by scientists can work as a kind of shield behind which people disinterested in opposing arguments hide. This dynamic can be even more pernicious when the extreme points of view are used in electoral campaigns, or as a way to justify a certain political action (Mareš, 2008). In these cases, what is observed is the incorrect use of the belief that society has in scientific work, with this being often distorted to adapt to the calendar and agenda of politicians, businessmen, or any other interest group that may benefit from some form of an extreme argument. For politicians, this is often expressed as an opportunity to communicate with a large number of voters through a message that addresses a problem common to all.

Likewise, the creation of an apocalyptic scenario allows the proposition of a kind of dichotomy between good and evil, according to which those who question their views on the environment are seeking the destruction of the planet, representing, therefore, enemies that must be fought. Evidently, the solution to environmental problems involves voting for candidates who present themselves as defenders of the environment, which suggests a high level of instrumentalization of academic opinions and views. The defence of extreme views by scientists ends up favouring the creation of childish narratives, in which the environmental issue is treated as a disputed issue between villains and heroes. The extreme simplification that is applied to such a complex topic tends to cause great harm, mainly due to the validation of obscure interests. From an economic point of view, the defence of extreme perspectives usually translates into the use of strategies that somehow aim to influence the behaviour of stakeholders, with environmental issues often used as a way to facilitate the commercialization of products and services (Fracarolli Nunes and Lee Park, 2017).

The association of academics with these issues can be very harmful to their credibility, precisely because the eventual lack of commitment to the truth on the part of greedy politicians and businessmen can increase the risk of exaggerating messages, and consequently of their radicalization. One can point to the different interests of these groups as the probable cause of the inadequacy of their relationship (Friedman, 2002). In fact, the focus on power and money does not seem compatible with the search for truth that should guide scientific work. While contact between these worlds can be essential for the progress of sustainable development, it can also be extremely dangerous. It can be assumed that it will be beneficial in terms of the search for truth if it takes precedence over other goals (e.g., power and money). In these cases, politicians and businessmen would contribute to the development of better diagnoses and solutions for environmental issues. Nevertheless, when the search for the truth is subordinated to the interests of power and money, this is a disastrous combination that, in addition to compromising the credibility of scientists and the institutions they represent, works as an important catalyst in the consolidation of extreme views.

References

Adams, J.E., Highhouse, S., and Zickar, M.J. (2010). Understanding general distrust of corporations. *Corporate Reputation Review*, Vol.13, No.1, pp.38–51.

Akin, M.S., and Vlad, V. (2011). The relationship between education and foreign direct investment: Testing the inverse U shape. *European Journal of Economic and Political Studies*, Vol.4, No.1, pp.27–46.

Asiedu, E., and Lien, D. (2011). Democracy, foreign direct investment and natural resources. *Journal of International Economics*, Vol.84, No.1, pp.99–111.

Balmer, J.M. (2012). Corporate brand management imperatives: Custodianship, credibility, and calibration. *California Management Review*, Vol.54, No.3, pp.6–33.

Barney, J.B. (1986). Strategic factor markets: Expectations, luck, and business strategy. *Management Science*, Vol.32, pp.1231–1241.

Barney, J.B. (1991). Firm resources and sustained competitive advantage. *Journal of Management*, Vol.17, No.1, pp.99–120.

Chater, N. (2020). Facing up to the uncertainties of COVID-19. *Nature Human Behaviour*, Vol.4, No.5, pp.439–439.

Doyle, W. (2018). *The Oxford History of the French Revolution*. Oxford University Press.

Edwards, M.S. (2006). Signalling credibility? The IMF and catalytic finance. *Journal of International Relations and Development*, Vol.9, No.1, pp.27–52.

Fracarolli Nunes, M., and Lee Park, C. (2016). Caught red-handed: The cost of the Volkswagen Dieselgate. *Journal of Global Responsibility*, Vol.7, No.2, pp.288–302.

Fracarolli Nunes, M., and Lee Park, C. (2017). Self-claimed sustainability: Building social and environmental reputations with words. *Sustainable Production and Consumption*, Vol.11, pp.46–57.

Fracarolli Nunes, M., and Lee Park, C. (2021a). Your fraud, our country: Impacts on national brands and reputations. In: M. Fracarolli Nunes and C. Lee Park (Eds.). *Business Ethics and Environmental Fraud: Improper Competitive Advantage in the Age of Green*, pp.207–228. Palgrave Macmillan. https://doi.org/10.1007/978-3-030-73800-6_9

Fracarolli Nunes, M., and Lee Park, C. (2021b). The intangible costs of environmental fraud: Impacts for brands, trust, corporate identity, image, credibility, and reputation. In: M. Fracarolli Nunes and C. Lee Park (Eds.). *Business Ethics and Environmental Fraud: Improper Competitive Advantage in the Age of Green*, pp.185–206. Palgrave Macmillan. https://doi.org/10.1007/978-3-030-73800-6_9

Fracarolli Nunes, M., Lee Park, C., and Paiva, E.L. (2020). Can we have it all? Sustainability trade-offs and cross-insurance mechanisms in supply chains. *International Journal of Operations & Production Management*, Vol.40, No.9, pp.1339–1366.

Friedman, P.J. (2002). The impact of conflict of interest on trust in science. *Science and Engineering Ethics*, Vol.8, No.3, pp.413–420.

Goldsmith, R.E., Lafferty, B.A., and Newell, S.J. (2000). The influence of corporate credibility on consumer attitudes and purchase intent. *Corporate Reputation Review*, Vol.3, No.4, pp.304–318.

Grimmelikhuijsen, S.G., and Meijer, A.J. (2014). Effects of transparency on the perceived trustworthiness of a government organization: Evidence from an online experiment. *Journal of Public Administration Research and Theory*, Vol.24, No.1, pp.137–157.

Haggard, S., MacIntyre, A., and Tiede, L. (2008). The rule of law and economic development. *Annual Review of Political Science*, Vol.11, pp.205–234.

Haroon, O., and Rizvi, S.A.R. (2020). COVID-19: Media coverage and financial markets behavior – a sectoral inquiry. *Journal of Behavioral and Experimental Finance*, Vol.27, p.100343.

Hart, P.S., Chinn, S., and Soroka, S. (2020). Politicization and polarization in COVID-19 news coverage. *Science Communication*, Vol.42, No.5, pp.679–697.

Harvard University (2022). *The History of Harvard*. Available at https://www.harvard.edu/about-harvard/harvard-history/

Hazen, C. (2000). *The Village Enlightenment in America: Popular Religion and Science in the Nineteenth Century*. University of Illinois Press.

Hoejmose, S., Brammer, S., and Millington, A. (2012). 'Green' supply chain management: The role of trust and top management in B2B and B2C markets. *Industrial Marketing Management*, Vol.41, No.4, pp.609–620.

Hoekstra, R., and Vazire, S. (2021). Aspiring to greater intellectual humility in science. *Nature Human Behaviour*, Vol.5, No.12, pp.1602–1607.

Holmdahl, I., and Buckee, C. (2020). Wrong but useful – what covid-19 epidemiologic models can and cannot tell us. *New England Journal of Medicine*, Vol.383, No.4, pp.303–305.

Holt, D., and Barkemeyer, R. (2012). Media coverage of sustainable development issues – attention cycles or punctuated equilibrium? *Sustainable Development*, Vol.20, No.1, pp.1–17.

Jaramillo, L. (2010). *Determinants of Investment Grade Status in Emerging Markets*. Working Paper. International Monetary Fund.

Jaramillo, L., and Tejada, M.M.M. (2011). Sovereign credit ratings and spreads in emerging markets: Does investment grade matter? *International Monetary Fund*, No.044. https://doi.org/10.5089/9781455218981.001

Jensen, J.D. (2008). Scientific uncertainty in news coverage of cancer research: Effects of hedging on scientists' and journalists' credibility. *Human Communication Research*, Vol.34, No.3, pp.347–369.

Kang, C., Germann, F., and Grewal, R. (2016). Washing away your sins? Corporate social responsibility, corporate social irresponsibility, and firm performance. *Journal of Marketing*, Vol.80, No.2, pp.59–79.

Kemp, E. (2011). Healthy brands: Establishing brand credibility, commitment and connection among consumers. *Journal of Consumer Marketing*, Vol.28, No.6, pp.429–437.

Khadaroo, A.J., and Seetanah, B. (2010). Transport infrastructure and foreign direct investment. *Journal of International Development*, Vol.22, No.1, pp.103–123.

Kim, S., and Choi, S.M. (2012). Credibility cues in online shopping: An examination of corporate credibility, retailer reputation, and product review credibility. *International Journal of Internet Marketing and Advertising*, Vol.7, No.3, pp.217–236.

Kreps, S.E., and Kriner, D.L. (2020). Model uncertainty, political contestation, and public trust in science: Evidence from the COVID-19 pandemic. *Science Advances*, Vol.6, No.43, p.eabd4563.

Lee Park, C., Fracarolli Nunes, M., and Ishizaka, A. (2021). End-to-end sustainability: Trade-offs, consumers' perceptions and decisions beyond B2C interfaces. *Supply Chain Management: An International Journal*, forthcoming.

Lock, I., and Seele, P. (2016). The credibility of CSR (corporate social responsibility) reports in Europe: Evidence from a quantitative content analysis in 11 countries. *Journal of Cleaner Production*, Vol.122, pp.186–200.

Magnus, P.D. (2013). What scientists know is not a function of what scientists know. *Philosophy of Science*, Vol.80, No.5, pp.840–849.

Maier, M., Milde, J., Post, S., Günther, L., Ruhrmann, G., and Barkela, B. (2016). Communicating scientific evidence: Scientists', journalists' and audiences' expectations and evaluations regarding the representation of scientific uncertainty. *Communications*, Vol.41, No.3, pp.239–264.

Mareš, M. (2008). Environmental radicalism and extremism in postcommunist Europe. *Journal for the Study of Radicalism*, Vol.2, No.1, pp.91–107.

Newell, S.J., and Goldsmith, R.E. (2001). The development of a scale to measure perceived corporate credibility. *Journal of Business Research*, Vol.52, No.3, pp.235–247.

Penrose, E.T. (1959). *The Theory of the Growth of the Firm*. John Wiley.

Pérez, A., and Del Bosque, I.R. (2015). An integrative framework to understand how CSR affects customer loyalty through identification, emotions and satisfaction. *Journal of Business Ethics*, Vol.129, No.3, pp.571–584.

Porter, M.E. (1979). How competitive forces shape strategy. *Harvard Business Review*, pp.21–23.

Porter, M.E. (1980). *Competitive Strategy: Techniques for Analyzing Industries and Competitors*. Free Press.

Potts, S.D., and Matuszewski, I.L. (2004). Ethics and corporate governance. *Corporate Governance: An International Review*, Vol.12, No.2, pp.177–179.

Press, D.G. (2005). *Calculating Credibility: How Leaders Assess Military Threats*. Cornell University Press.

Ramey, M. (2015). Volkswagen US CEO on diesel emissions fiasco: 'We totally screwed up'. *Autoweek*, September 22. Available at https://www.autoweek.com/news/a1877321/volkswagen-us-ceo-our-company-was-dishonest/

Rao, R. (2012). Brand credibility and brand involvement as an antecedent of brand equity: An empirical study. *Asia-Pacific Journal of Business*, Vol.3, No.1, pp.17–28.

Richardson, M., and Slack, G. (2005). *Faith in Science: Scientists Search for Truth*. Routledge.

Rigobon, R. (2002). The curse of non-investment grade countries. *Journal of Development Economics*, Vol.69, No.2, pp.423–449.

Rowland, F. (2002). The peer-review process. *Learned Publishing*, Vol.15, No.4, pp.247–258.

Ruiz, B., Esteban, Á., and Gutiérrez, S. (2014). Determinants of reputation of leading Spanish financial institutions among their customers in a context of economic crisis. *BRQ Business Research Quarterly*, Vol.17, No.4, pp.259–278.

Rumelt, R.P. (1984). Towards a strategic theory of the firm. In: B. Lamb (Ed.). *Competitive Strategic Management*, pp.556–570. Prentice-Hall.

Safford, T.G., Whitmore, E.H., and Hamilton, L.C. (2021). Follow the scientists? How beliefs about the practice of science shaped COVID-19 views. *Journal of Science Communication*, forthcoming.

Sanchez Mantero, R., and Serrera Contreras, R.M. (2005). La Universidad de Sevilla – 1505–2005. *Colección: Historia de la Universidad De Sevilla*, No.9. ISBN: 978-84-8455-139-3

Schoenfeld, R. (1984). Are scientists arrogant? *Accounts of Chemical Research*, Vol.17, No.12, p.409.

Seth, N., Deshmukh, S.G., and Vrat, P. (2006). SSQSC: A tool to measure supplier service quality in supply chain. *Production Planning & Control*, Vol.17, No.5, pp.448–463.

Sheth, J.N. (1996). Organizational buying behavior: Past performance and future expectations. *Journal of Business & Industrial Marketing*, Vol.11, No.3, pp.7–24.

Shim, K., and Yang, S.U. (2016). The effect of bad reputation: The occurrence of crisis, corporate social responsibility, and perceptions of hypocrisy and attitudes toward a company. *Public Relations Review*, Vol.42, No.1, pp.68–78.

Stengers, I. (2018). *Another Science is Possible: A Manifesto for Slow Science*. John Wiley & Sons.

Universidad de Salamanca (2022). *Historia*. Available at https://www.usal.es/historia

Universidad de Sevilla (2022). *Universidad*. Available at https://www.us.es/taxonomy/term/16

Università di Bologna (2022). *La nostra storia*. Available at https://www.unibo.it/it/ateneo/chi-siamo/la-nostra-storia

Université de Paris 1 – Pantheon Sorbonne (2022). *Historie de l'université*. Available at https://www.pantheonsorbonne.fr/universite/presentation/histoire-luniversite

Urde, M. (2009). Uncovering the corporate brand's core values. *Management Decision*, Vol.9, No.4, pp.616–638.

Vreeland, J.R. (2003). *The IMF and Economic Development*. Cambridge University Press.
Wagner, T., Lutz, R.J., and Weitz, B.A. (2009). Corporate hypocrisy: Overcoming the threat of inconsistent corporate social responsibility perceptions. *Journal of Marketing*, Vol.73, No.6, pp.77–91.
Weaver, W. (1991). Science and complexity. In: *Facets of Systems Science*, pp.449–456. Springer.
Wernerfelt, B. (1984). A resource-based view of the firm. *Strategic Management Journal*, Vol.5, pp.171–180.
Xie, C., and Haugland, S. (2016). Formation of reputation in business markets. *Journal of Business-to-Business Marketing*, Vol.23, No.1, pp.25–45.
Yoon, Y.L., Yoon, Y., Nam, H., and Choi, J. (2021). Buyer-supplier matching in online B2B marketplace: An empirical study of small-and medium-sized enterprises (SMEs). *Industrial Marketing Management*, Vol.93, pp.90–100.
Zhang, R., and Rezaee, Z. (2009). Do credible firms perform better in emerging markets? Evidence from China. *Journal of Business Ethics*, Vol.90, No.2, pp.221–237.
Zheng, Y. (2011). Credibility and flexibility: Political institutions, governance, and foreign direct investment. *International Interactions6*, Vol.37, No.3, pp.293–319.

12 Eco-Anxiety and Other Psychological Outcomes

Extremism and Emotions

Building on the premise that extremist thinking represents an acute response to an exaggerated view of reality (Githens-Mazer, 2012), it can be argued that those who suffer from it have, to some extent, their capacity for observation compromised. Among other things, this is tantamount to saying that individuals more likely to adopt extremist rhetoric have ceded an important space of their rationality to their emotions and instincts (Gerodimos, 2015; Zembylas, 2021). As discussed in previous chapters, emotions do seem to play an important role in conditioning human behaviour (Elster, 2009). While some can inhibit the action at specific moments or even for longer periods, others can trigger disproportionate reactions, often explosive (Fonseca, 2021). Below, some of the emotions most common to humans are briefly discussed, with their potential influence on the development of extreme sustainability rhetoric discussed in greater detail.

Fear

Among all human emotions, fear is perhaps the one with the most contradictory effects. While it can lead to a total or partial paralysis of the person who feels it (Craske et al., 1986), it can also provoke strong attack reactions against what causes it (Lockwood, 2013). Depending on the degree of danger recognized in the threat and on the identification of the possibilities of success in a confrontation, the frightened individual takes a path that, in her/his opinion, maximizes her/his chances of survival. In some cases, standing still and waiting for the threat to dissipate may be the best alternative, or running to safety may be preferable. In other circumstances, facing the threat directly may present itself as the most viable alternative, or even the only alternative (Milosevic, 2015). The mechanism by which decisions around these possibilities are made are quite complex and depend on how each individual interprets the threat in question (Bracha, 2004). Furthermore, your ability to accurately assess your own conditions and those of the threat can decisively impact the quality of your judgement and therefore the effectiveness of your decision.

DOI: 10.4324/9781003124719-15

While the neuro-cerebral mechanisms through which these decisions are made are beyond the scope of this book, it is important to emphasize that fear-based reactions do not appear to be subordinate to the rationality of individuals and are probably closer to instinctive reactions (Wrenn, 2014). It follows that the search for a logical understanding of actions and decisions based on this emotion can be frustrating, with the understanding of automatic and pre-programmed behaviours being, perhaps, more indicated. In some ways, it could be argued that fear is one of the strongest manifestations of our wild heritage, representing one of the many pieces of survival mechanisms in hostile environments (Kazanas and Altarriba, 2017). The fact that our evolution as a species took place under conditions radically different from those present today seems to contribute to the perception that fear-based reactions are sometimes inadequate. The acceleration of the growth of cities from the 19th century (Puga, 1998) and the consequent mass migration of rural populations to large urban centres (Antrop, 2004) represented a major change in the types of danger to be faced by those who underwent this migration. A farm worker, for example, is more likely to encounter wild animals (e.g., jaguars, wolves, snakes) much more often than a factory worker. The patterns that generate fear mechanisms in rural workers (e.g., recognition of threats) must, therefore, be calibrated to their own reality, perhaps proving inadequate when they migrate to an urban concentration.

Long before the social changes of the last centuries, however, humanity had already experienced important changes in its way of life and in the way it relates to its surroundings. In general, it can be said that the emergence of the civilizing process itself appears as one of the main factors in this dynamic, with the development of agriculture and cattle raising decisively changing the characteristics of the risks faced by individuals (Maisels, 2003). The transition from a nomadic to a sedentary way of life has reconditioned the dynamics of survival and competition between members of the species, with the physical dangers arising from a greater degree of human insertion in nature giving way to new challenges. Typically, these refer to the products of social relations, which, although apparently less violent – at least on the surface – can be significantly more complex and even harmful in the medium and long term. In other words, it is possible to identify in the civilizing process the fundamental bases of what, to some extent, summarizes an important part of the thinking of English philosopher Thomas Hobbes (1588–1679). His discussion around the expression, 'man is man's wolf' (*Homo homini lupus*) seems to illustrate the transition from dangers from nature to those that would be typical of relationships between human beings, with politics probably being one of the most accomplished expressions of this process.

More broadly, fear can be pointed out as one of the main architects of the development of ways of life in society. This perspective is perhaps even clearer for those who have already had the opportunity to visit well-preserved medieval cities in countries such as France or Spain. It is common for these ancient communities to be surrounded by self-enclosed walls and have their access restricted by large gates (Kibler et al., 2013). Likewise, the castles of the time do not look so much like the buildings illustrated in fairy tales, being more like fortresses and strongholds (Coulson, 2004). All these protective measures were intended to spare the inhabitants of cities from invasion and looting by enemies and rival peoples. Fear of these occasions would be the main element in defining the organization of society, at least as regards the design and implementation of its physical structures.

Regarding the relationship between fear and extreme sustainability rhetoric, more specifically, it is possible to draw an analogy between the construction of walls around cities and the different levels of resistance that the most skeptical ones develop towards the most alarmist discourses. It is possible, for example, that positions that associate environmental issues with the development of extreme situations (e.g., melting polar ice, rising sea levels, floods and disappearing cities, droughts, famine) end up generating too much fear, which may sometimes be larger than the interlocutors can handle (Clingerman and Ehret, 2013). In these cases, it seems natural that the most sensitive individuals go through a process of denial as a way to protect the sanity of their mental processes (Cramer, 2008). The refraction to everything that refers to the environmental cause would therefore be the emotional equivalent of the walls around medieval cities and castles. In addition to the alleged protection they offer to those who build these psychological barriers, the trenches created between skeptics and alarmists end up contributing to the interruption of the dialogue and, consequently, to the radicalization of the views shared by those who occupy the opposite sides. Thus, as approached in Chapter 5, the strongest environmental discourses can be important factors in the development of various forms of environmental skepticism. These and other issues are discussed later in the chapter, in the subsection dealing with the relationship between emotions and development in the many forms that environmental denial can take. A second factor to be considered refers to the use of hyperbolic language as a means to attract the public's attention (Taylor and Nathan, 2002). In addition to compromising the credibility of the messages, the exaggerations contained in them contribute to a greater difficulty in assessing the real dimensions of the problems. Among the most common results is the rise of conservatism to fight what is not understood. Another possible outcome is the encouragement of disproportionate reactions as a natural consequence of the fear generated by the inability to obtain a more accurate assessment of the issues that arise (Lomborg, 2001; Besley and Shanahan, 2004).

Envy and Frustration

Objectively, envy can be understood as a negative feeling, usually arising from the perception that the person who is envied has something that the person who is envious lacks (Vecchio, 2000). This dynamic can originate in the most diverse of things, including material goods, as well as talents and virtues. Generally speaking, the envious person feels wronged for not having been blessed in the same way as the envied person, with the feeling that they have fewer resources or opportunities than the latter. Among the possible consequences of the feeling of envy is a tendency to seek the destruction of what originates it, as an attempt to end the suffering of the one who suffers. Among all the circumstances capable of triggering envy, it is possible that the possession of material goods is the most obvious (Zheng et al., 2018). In these cases, it is common for the envious person to fail to see their own responsibility for their financial failure, even as an ego protection mechanism. The recognition that your past attitudes and choices are probably the biggest causes of your lack of success in the present can be painful and even unbearable. The most common defence mechanism seems to be the search for a scapegoat, or, usually, for the determination of an external culprit, often pinpointed as the greed of successful people, tax rates considered excessively high, and even the prevailing economic system in some countries (i.e., capitalism), to name a few.

Of all the short-sightedness that afflicts the envious, her/his understanding of economics as a zero-sum game is likely to be the most serious. These simplistic views defend that the financial success of an individual implies the failure of another or, as popularly expressed, for one to win, the other must lose. These misguided ideas fuel feelings of injustice and even hatred against those who manage to build fortunes, usually blamed for not only everything the envious lacks, but also all the misery that falls upon the world. These conclusions ignore essential factors of wealth generation, which ultimately benefit society as a whole. It should be noted, for example, that in a free market environment, the accumulation of capital is associated with the generation of value to society. Thus, individuals who are able to offer products and services that meet the population's demands must appropriate the profits from their activities. Capital accumulation must be understood as the result of a benefit generated and offered to everyone. In this set, the possibility of obtaining financial dividends (i.e., profits) would be the basis of the incentive mechanism that drive economic activity.

Similar to envy, frustration is associated with a feeling of injustice (Steil et al., 1978), with individuals believing they deserve something they do not have. The perception of failure can generate negative feelings (Donnelly et al., 2016), especially when a person understands that s/he is entitled to something s/he lacks. This seems to be quite common among people in organizations structured in hierarchical ways, with those at the base of the pyramid often not realizing the merits of those in higher positions. The lack of understanding of the reasons or causes of this situation can reinforce feelings of revolt, which usually leads to excessive sentimentality and the loss of space for rationality (Tai et al., 2012). Attempts to subvert established structures may end up being one of the manifestations of those who see their ambitions frustrated.

The same rationale can be applied in the analysis of various social dynamics. With regard specifically to the impact of these emotions on the development of extreme speeches, envy and frustration combined can result in a very harmful combination. It is possible, for example, that the individual who finds her/himself suffering from this 'combo' develops destructive attitudes, as s/he seeks to restore a minimum level of justice (according to her/his own criteria). This could be translated into the use of extreme environmental discourses as a pretext for this individual to cause harm to the lives of others, evidencing an improper use of the environmental cause.

Denial and Emotions

As anticipated in the discussion of the influence of fear on the development of extreme environmental discourses, the intensity of the negative emotions that these processes cause can lead individuals who experience them to develop processes of denial, in which they basically refuse to believe in the causes of their feelings as a way to avoid them. It can be said, therefore, that while the high intensity of emotions can be a determining factor for the development of extreme pro-environmental discourses, they can also have the opposite effect, subsidizing the more aggressive forms of denial of problems environmental issues. In both cases, it is clear that the reactions – on both one side and the other – have little to do with the facts or with the reality that presents itself, but rather how these are perceived and interpreted by the observers (Gifford and Sussman, 2012).

Fear can also exert considerable influence given the association made by many between the spread of extreme sustainability reports and the enactment of hidden ideological agendas (Fracarolli Nunes and Lee Park, 2021). In particular, it is common for individuals who identify with a more right-wing political-economic thinking to perceive in the defence of environmental causes a way to increase the state's power over the lives of ordinary citizens (Harring and Sohlberg, 2017). The idea that more laws (Ashford and Caldart, 2008) and more taxes are needed to achieve sustainable development is often understood as an advance by the state machine over individual freedoms. Likewise, arguments pointing to the legitimacy of the suppression of citizens' rights in the name of a collective good tend to reinforce the notion that the environmentalist discourse is, in some cases, used as a smokescreen for the deterioration of the capitalist mode of production and, consequently, for its gradual replacement by economic and social models that come closer to communism.

Once again, a brief discussion of the origins of the current form of the environmental movement may be helpful in understanding its association with ideas perceived as left-wing. As discussed by Fracarolli Nunes and Lee Park (2021), and also throughout the book, the debate on sustainable development as we know it today is, to a large extent, the result of the efforts of supranational entities. In particular, the United Nations played a very important role in this process, promoting or supporting various efforts in this direction. The Stockholm conference in 1972 and the Brundtland Commission in 1987 illustrate this commitment. Similarly, events sponsored by other supranational entities helped to shape the discussions, with the European Union offering important contributions in that direction (Wurzel and Connelly, 2011).

From a historical point of view, it is necessary to remember that these initial efforts took place in a period of high geopolitical tension, with the ideological clash between communities and capitalists fuelling the period that became popularly known as the Cold War (Whitfield, 1996). This question is relevant to the development of perceptions about the environmentalist discourse, since the antagonism inherent to opposing worldviews was probably in its most acute state (Kramer, 1999). It is possible that the high degree of polarization that was observed contributed to greater distrust on both sides, so that any new ideas that arose were quickly classified as being from the right or from the left (Medhurst et al., 1997). The fact that the sustainability debate has been driven by supranational entities reinforces the understanding that it serves the interests of leftists. In addition, the supranational nature of communism itself – at least in some of its strands (e.g., Trotskyism, Daniels, 1998) – contributes to the strengthening of these associations.

These initial tensions can be understood as the origin of many forms of denial, with the link between sustainability and ideology contributing to the progress of refractory views. It can be argued, therefore, that the association between sustainable development and politics is quite harmful for the former, as it often entails an immediate rejection by those who have opposing views of society. Thus, fear of communism would be one of the main causes of environmental denial. In this set, the confusion between leftism and environmentalism (Neumayer, 2004) would function as one of the biggest triggers for the rejection of the idea of sustainable development, with the perspective of the suppression of individual freedoms, a typical idea within communism (Županov, 1996), pushing the individuals more identified with the right out of fear. The intensive and sometimes exaggerated use of environmentalist discourse by left-wing politicians (Carter, 2013) does not contribute to this process being reversed. On the contrary, the instrumentalization of environmental causes only serves to further alienate those who distrust their use as a means of advancing ideologies.

Eco-Anxiety

Anxiety can be defined as a feeling of acute apprehension in which uncertainties about the future cause suffering and, often, exaggerated reactions (Eysenck, 2006). To some extent, anxiety can prove beneficial, leading the individual to prepare to deal with something unknown (Clarke et al., 2008). Dysfunctions occur when projections about events or situations to come are very far from what is usually observed in practice. In these cases, distortions and unreasonableness can trigger a series of adverse reactions from both physical and psychological points of view (Litz and Keane, 1989). Expectations that something very negative is approaching can lead those who suffer from high levels of anxiety to adopt defensive behaviours that, in addition to being inappropriate, can result in serious damage to their sociability (Loudin et al., 2003). Among other things, overly anxious individuals may choose to minimize their interactions with the world as an attempt to control what they perceive to be an overly complex and dangerous reality (Lim et al., 2016). It is not uncommon, for example, for people suffering from high degrees of anxiety to isolate themselves and lead more self-centred lives (Ennis et al., 2008).

These processes of exaggerated anxiety can manifest themselves in the most diverse issues, including those associated with more structural matters. In any case, the development of feelings of anxiety seems to be linked to the way people deal with their emotions (Izard, 2013). As discussed earlier, fear is a particularly important emotion in conditioning human behaviour and appears to be directly related to anxiety (Chambless and Gracely, 1989). From an ordinary life perspective, the relationship between feelings of fear and anxiety can be seen in people suffering from phobias, such as those who, at all costs, avoid flying in a plane (Rothbaum, and Hodges, 1999). The expectations that something extremely serious might happen (e.g., a plane crash) leads them in many cases to avoid this alternative as a way to manage the risks they deem too high. In situations where they cannot avoid what they fear (i.e., they have to travel in an airplane), extreme reactions can be observed, with those who suffer from anxiety even experiencing serious physical reactions (e.g., panic attacks, De Houwer et al., 2020). An interesting point in this analysis is the fact that, in situations like these, people tend to ignore the probabilities that something negative could actually happen. Statistical data pointing to the high degree of safety in air transport (Rose, 1992) seem to have no effect on those afflicted by fear. This dynamic points to a relative abandonment of rationality, which can have serious consequences.

Anxiety processes linked to fear can be repeated in other circumstances of everyday life (Räikkönen et al., 1999). It is common to see people having great difficulty getting into elevators (Botella et al., 2000). Similar to what happens with those who prefer to avoid transportation by planes, some people see an enormous potential for malfunctions and accidents in the equipment, which often lead them to seek other alternatives. Likewise, some people develop severe anxiety processes before a visit to the physician or dentist (Hauge et al., 2021). The expectation of physical suffering or even that they may receive adverse news about their health condition can cause great anguish (e.g., health anxiety, Kőszegi, 2003). These processes also seem common among students as their final exams approach, with the lack of predictability about the questions they will need to answer often leading them to imagine catastrophic scenarios, in which they are faced with only the unfavourable questions (von der Embse et al., 2018). In addition to all the suffering that precedes taking the test, in some cases, students find themselves paralysed when they finally face the questions, even those for which they know the answers. From a physiological point of view, the lack of mental performance at these times may be associated with the use of working memory resources by anxiety-related thoughts in such a way that they (i.e., working memory resources) may not be employed for test-related processes (e.g., information retrieval and problem solving) (Mavilidi et al., 2020). This may be also linked to our most primitive stress management mechanisms, with blood being directed to the muscles in order to increase the chances of success in an eventual confrontation of a threat, or in the escape from it (Debiec and LeDoux, 2004). It so happens, however, that these survival mechanisms were adapted to the dangers common to the wild man, which includes animals (e.g., wolves, bears) or members of rival tribes. If, on the one hand, these threats are still present to some extent, the civilizing process and the migration of populations to urban centres have changed the sources of problems.

These more general discussions about the nature, the causes, and the effects of anxiety serve as the basis for a more focused debate on the association between the various views on sustainability currently disseminated and the development of exaggerated views about the future of the planet and of life as we know it. As discussed in more detail in Chapter 6, one of the most common perspectives in discussions about sustainable development is that of apocalyptic forecasts. In addition to the harmful effect caused by these projections on the credibility of pro-environmentalist arguments, the high degree of responsibility they place on the common individual can also be highlighted. In extreme cases, this can result in feelings of guilt (Culiberg et al., 2022) that make a productive life unfeasible, with the perception that any form of consumption contributes to the apocalypse. While individual consumption decisions can, in fact, have an important impact on a number of aspects of sustainable development (Michaelis, 2003) (e.g., use of natural resources, need for energy production, amount of waste generated), the belief that all and any action in this sense has an immediate impact and is a direct cause of environmental degradation can be quite harmful to the mental health of those who find themselves totally immersed in these issues. It is possible, for example, that these more extreme understandings result in acute feelings of culpability which, in turn, can trigger rigorous processes of self-censorship and self-punishment (Nelissen and Zeelenberg, 2009). The idea that basically every human action can be understood as an additional piece of a scenario of total destruction can even make life in society unfeasible, leading those in these mental states often to isolate themselves in an attempt to avoid these alleged damages. Coupled with the feeling of guilt, the apprehension caused by the idea that the world might actually go into environmental collapse can generate great anguish. In these cases, individuals more sensitive to apocalyptic discourses also turn their concerns to the activities and behaviour of others, as they realize that controlling their own environmental impact will not be enough to change the fate of total destruction in which s/he believes (Upton, 2020).

In addition to a debate about the individual psychological processes that affect people in these situations, a discussion about their interaction with society can add to the understanding of the impacts of these feelings on social dynamics. First, one can highlight the tendencies that these groups apparently hold to become propagators themselves of the extremist discourses they have been victims of. Mental states of conviction that the environmental apocalypse is approaching, allied to the idea that the adoption of aggressive and urgent measures is the only possibility to remedy it, should favour the propagation of radical messages as a mechanism for convincing those who – according to the criteria of the defenders of apocalyptic ideas – show themselves little affected by the catastrophic situation in which the planet finds itself. Added to this is the perception that changes in the behaviour of everyone are necessary to alter the path of imminent destruction on which the planet is believed to be. Again, the words of Swedish teenage activist Greta Thunberg illustrate this dynamic. Phrases such as 'I want you to panic' seem to express her intention to bring those who listen to her into her own universe, in the expectation that they will feel the same way she does (The Guardian, 2019).

New Forms of Authoritarianism

The points raised earlier draw attention to the need to decouple the debate on sustainability and extreme emotions. In addition to allowing social, environmental, and economic issues to be observed objectively, the rationalization of discussions seems to be a fundamental condition for establishing – or re-establishing – the dialogue between the dissenting parties. Individuals absorbed by feelings such as fear, frustration, or even envy tend to respond to stimuli giving vent to their most primitive instincts. As discussed throughout the previous chapters, the development of these emotions is favoured by the misuse of extreme communication, with strategies such as panic marketing potentiating the creation of negative emotions based on apocalyptic visions. Likewise, the instrumentalization of the debate about sustainable development by politicians, businessmen, artists, and all those who somehow seek to obtain personal gains through the adoption of an environmental discourse detached from reality feeds the perception that these attitudes are manifestations of a structural hypocrisy.

Among the main outcomes of these postures is the strengthening of environmental skepticism, with more and more individuals showing that they do not believe in the arguments of environmentalists (Lomborg, 2001), mainly because they believe that they carry hidden interests. The possibility of defending the environment to serve ideological interests associated with leftist thinking, for example, tends to cause revulsion on the part of all those who understand that the defence of individual freedoms in a context formed by the union of the market economy with a representative democratic regime is non-negotiable (Åslund, 2009). In addition to bringing a greater understanding of the dynamics responsible for the construction of environmental skepticism, understanding the emotions that these processes cause can be important for those who seek to dialogue with individuals who take positions that are refractory to environmental arguments. It is possible, for example, that the association between environmentalism and leftist positions arouse feelings of fear, or even panic, among those who identify with rightist thinking. In these cases, emotions would be one of the main factors explaining the low tolerance or the lack of openness that many of these people demonstrate to have. That seems to have a particular effect against arguments pointing to the need to implement policies aimed at reducing the consumption of natural resources, or the emission of pollutants, as well as at any other type of alternative understood as important in advancing environmental preservation. Once again, the lack of rationality seems to play a fundamental role in interrupting the debate, or even in creating psychological barriers that close it before it even starts.

These processes favour the arguments pointing to the potential that the association between sustainability and political-ideological interests has to harm sustainable development. It can be discussed, therefore, that this association ends up being responsible for the creation of another type of eco-anxiety in which concerns are not related to the imminence of an environmental apocalypse, but to the end of the models of society in which skeptics wish to live. In other words, the confusion between environmentalism and communism tends to frighten those who understand that the capitalist system is the ideal, bringing back feelings that have perhaps been dormant since the end of the Cold War period. Importantly, those who oppose the arguments in favour of sustainability (or at least who they appear to be) are not necessarily aware of the reasons for adopting such positions, probably acting automatically against what they perceive to be a threat to social functioning.

It can be said, therefore, that eco-anxiety is one of the most harmful side effects that exaggerations in environmental discourse can cause. In addition to generating great suffering in individuals most affected by projections of a bleak future (Grose, 2020), the most radical positions end up providing arguments for the development of an increasingly consolidated environmental skepticism. The natural result of this dynamic ends up being the distancing of groups that have opposing views, with the possibility of re-establishing a healthy and productive dialogue becoming increasingly reduced. Just as the separation of two people will require them to raise their voices to communicate, the distance between the poles of the debate tends to make speeches even more radical. Attempts to sensitize those who are convinced of their positions can favour emphasis on issues that aim to generate panic, renewing the cycle of rejection of environmental messages understood as exaggerated and, at the limit, lies.

From the point of view of the individual who suffers the effects of eco-anxiety more acutely, efforts to re-establish dialogue may seem like threats to those who, according to their overly sensitive view of reality, are precisely seeking to promote environmental apocalypse. These perceptions fuel the idea that environmental skeptics not only think differently but are also enemies to be fiercely fought. This perception is particularly dangerous, as the feeling that opposition to these groups is fair and urgent can justify extreme takes, including attempts to stop their actions through aggressive acts. This includes the invasion of farms and the destruction of property in general. In an apparently more subtle but no less dangerous way, the certainty that they are dealing with an agent who deliberately seeks to destroy the planet could lead many eco-anxiety sufferers to promote acts of censorship and freedom of expression for those with different views. The certainty that they are fighting the good fight seems to be one of the main elements in the development of authoritarian postures that aim to silence or intimidate those who think otherwise. In the case of those who suffer from the development of various forms of eco-anxiety, the incentives for the development of these attitudes can be even greater, because in addition to the issues related to the moral judgement of opposing positions, individuals who take a stand in a refractory way to their ideas can be understood as those directly responsible for their suffering. In these cases, the elimination of the sources of the anguish they suffer becomes, in their understanding, not only fair but also necessary. As time goes by and eco-anxiety sufferers continue to absorb radical messages, their feelings tend to become even more intense, making them more likely to assume aggressive postures.

It is essential, therefore, that all those who use strategies such as panic marketing or any other form of instrumentalization of the environmental discourse are aware of the consequences of their actions. One must consider the long-term effects that radical narratives have on people's subconscious and, as they consolidate, on the development of societies. As discussed throughout the book, the division of people between groups in favour of and against sustainable development does not aid the search for the evolution of issues related to environmental protection. On the contrary, the segmentation of society and the creation of well-defined stereotypes nurture the flourishing of tribal aspects. Among the main consequences of this process is the interruption of contact between those who see themselves as different and the inevitable destruction of the possibilities for dialogue. Furthermore, the formation of tribes can lead to warfare, with one group seeking to arm themselves and fight the other. Maintaining this dynamic is quite harmful, as the complexity of environmental challenges requires collaboration. The enhancement of eco-anxiety through the enactment of extreme ambient features acts in the exact opposite sense.

References

Antrop, M. (2004). Landscape change and the urbanization process in Europe. *Landscape and Urban Planning*, Vol.67, No.1–4, pp.9–26.

Ashford, N.A., and Caldart, C.C. (2008). *Environmental Law, Policy, and Economics: Reclaiming the Environmental Agenda*. MIT Press.

Åslund, A. (2009). *How Ukraine Became a Market Economy and Democracy*. Columbia University Press.

Besley, J.C., and Shanahan, J. (2004). Skepticism about media effects concerning the environment: Examining Lomborg's hypotheses. *Society & Natural Resources*, Vol.17, No.10, pp.861–880.

Botella, C., Baños, R.M., Villa, H., Perpiñá, C., and García-Palacios, A. (2000). Virtual reality in the treatment of claustrophobic fear: A controlled, multiple-baseline design. *Behavior Therapy*, Vol.31, No.3, pp.583–595.

Bracha, H.S. (2004). Freeze, flight, fight, fright, faint: Adaptationist perspectives on the acute stress response spectrum. *CNS Spectrums*, Vol.9, No.9, pp.679–685.

Carter, N. (2013). Greening the mainstream: Party politics and the environment. *Environmental Politics*, Vol.22, No.1, pp.73–94.

Clarke, P., MacLeod, C., and Shirazee, N. (2008). Prepared for the worst: Readiness to acquire threat bias and susceptibility to elevate trait anxiety. *Emotion*, Vol.8, No.1, pp.47–57.

Clingerman, F., and Ehret, V.M. (2013). Hope and fear: The theological side of framing environmental change. *Ethics, Policy & Environment*, Vol.16, No.2, pp.152–155.

Chambless, D.L., and Gracely, E.J. (1989). Fear of fear and the anxiety disorders. *Cognitive Therapy and Research*, Vol.13, No.1, pp.9–20.

Coulson, C. (2004). *Castles in Medieval Society: Fortresses in England, France, and Ireland in the Central Middle Ages*. Oxford University Press on Demand.

Cramer, P. (2008). Seven pillars of defense mechanism theory. *Social and Personality Psychology Compass*, Vol.2, No.5, pp.1963–1981.

Craske, M.G., Rachman, S.J., and Tallman, K. (1986). Mobility, cognitions, and panic. *Journal of Psychopathology and Behavioral Assessment*, Vol.8, No.3, pp.199–210.

Culiberg, B., Cho, H., Kos Koklic, M., and Zabkar, V. (2022). The role of moral foundations, anticipated guilt and personal responsibility in predicting anti-consumption for environmental reasons. *Journal of Business Ethics*. https://doi.org/10.1007/s10551-021-05016-7

Daniels, R.V. (1998). Leon Trotsky. *Britannica*. Available at https://www.britannica.com/biography/Leon-Trotsky

Debiec, J., and LeDoux, J. (2004). Fear and the brain. *Social Research*, Vol.71, No.4, pp.807–818.

De Houwer, J., Tackett, J., and Carter, J. (2020). Conditioning is more than association formation: On the different ways in which conditioning research is valuable for clinical psychology. *Collabra: Psychology*, Vol.6, No.1, p.2.

Donnelly, G.E., Ksendzova, M., Howell, R.T., Vohs, K.D., and Baumeister, R.F. (2016). Buying to blunt negative feelings: Materialistic escape from the self. *Review of General Psychology*, Vol.20, No.3, pp.272–316.

Elster, J. (2009). *Strong Feelings: Emotion, Addiction, and Human Behavior*. MIT Press.

Ennis, E., Vrij, A., and Chance, C. (2008). Individual differences and lying in everyday life. *Journal of Social and Personal Relationships*, Vol.25, No.1, pp.105–118.

Eysenck, M., Payne, S., and Santos, R. (2006). Anxiety and depression: Past, present, and future events. *Cognition & Emotion*, Vol.20, No.2, pp.274–294.

Fonseca, C. (2021). *Emotional Intensity in Gifted Students: Helping Kids Cope with Explosive Feelings*. Routledge.

Fracarolli Nunes, M., and Lee Park, C. (2021). The age of green. In: M. Fracarolli Nunes and C. Lee Park (Eds.). *Business Ethics and Environmental Fraud: Improper Competitive Advantage in the Age of Green*, pp.87–104. Palgrave Macmillan. https://doi.org/10.1007/978-3-030-73800-6_4

Gerodimos, R. (2015). The ideology of far left populism in Greece: Blame, victimhood and revenge in the discourse of Greek anarchists. *Political Studies*, Vol.63, No.3, pp.608–625.

Gifford, R., and Sussman, R. (2012). Environmental attitudes. In: S.D. Clayton (Ed.). *The Oxford Handbook of Environmental and Conservation Psychology*, pp.65–80. Oxford University Press. https://doi.org/10.1093/oxfordhb/9780199733026.013.0004

Githens-Mazer, J. (2012). The rhetoric and reality: Radicalization and political discourse. *International Political Science Review*, Vol.33, No.5, pp.556–567.

Grose, A. (2020). *A Guide to Eco-Anxiety: How to Protect the Planet and Your Mental Health*. Watkins Media Limited.

The Guardian (2019). 'Our house is on fire': Greta Thunberg, 16, urges leaders to act on climate. *The Guardian*, January 25. Available at https://www.theguardian.com/environment/2019/jan/25/our-house-is-on-fire-greta-thunberg16-urges-leaders-to-act-on-climate

Harring, N., and Sohlberg, J. (2017). The varying effects of left – right ideology on support for the environment: Evidence from a Swedish survey experiment. *Environmental Politics*, Vol.26, No.2, pp.278–300.

Hauge, M.S., Stora, B., Vassend, O., Hoffart, A., and Willumsen, T. (2021). Dentist-administered cognitive behavioural therapy versus four habits/midazolam: An RCT study of dental anxiety treatment in primary dental care. *European Journal of Oral Sciences*, Vol.129, No.4, p.e12794.

Izard, C.E. (2013). *Patterns of Emotions: A New Analysis of Anxiety and Depression*. Academic Press.

Kazanas, S.A., and Altarriba, J. (2017). Did our ancestors fear the unknown? The role of predation in the survival advantage. *Evolutionary Behavioral Sciences*, Vol.11, No.1, pp.83–91.

Kibler, W.W., Zinn, G.A., and Earp, L. (2013). *Medieval France: An Encyclopedia*. Routledge.

Kőszegi, B. (2003). Health anxiety and patient behavior. *Journal of Health Economics*, Vol.22, No.6, pp.1073–1084.

Kramer, M. (1999). Ideology and the cold war. *Review of International Studies*, Vol.25, No.4, pp.539–576.

Lim, M.H., Rodebaugh, T.L., Zyphur, M.J., and Gleeson, J.F. (2016). Loneliness over time: The crucial role of social anxiety. *Journal of Abnormal Psychology*, Vol.125, No.5, pp.620–630.

Litz, B.T., and Keane, T.M. (1989). Information processing in anxiety disorders: Application to the understanding of post-traumatic stress disorder. *Clinical Psychology Review*, Vol.9, No.2, pp.243–257.

Lockwood, J. (2013). *The Infested Mind: Why Humans Fear, Loathe, and Love Insects*. Oxford University Press.

Lomborg, B. (2001). *The Skeptical Environmentalist: Measuring the Real State of the World*. Cambridge University Press.

Loudin, J.L., Loukas, A., and Robinson, S. (2003). Relational aggression in college students: Examining the roles of social anxiety and empathy. *Aggressive Behavior: Official Journal of the International Society for Research on Aggression*, Vol.29, No.5, pp.430–439.

Maisels, C.K. (2003). *The Emergence of Civilization: From Hunting and Gathering to Agriculture, Cities, and the State of the Near East*. Routledge.

Mavilidi, M.F., Ouwehand, K., Riley, N., Chandler, P., and Paas, F. (2020). Effects of an acute physical activity break on test anxiety and math test performance. *International Journal of Environmental Research and Public Health*, Vol.17, No.5, p.1523.

Medhurst, M.J., Ivie, R.L., Wander, P., and Scott, R.L. (1997). *Cold War Rhetoric: Strategy, Metaphor, and Ideology*. MSU Press.

Michaelis, L. (2003). The role of business in sustainable consumption. *Journal of Cleaner Production*, Vol.11, No.8, pp.915–921.

Milosevic, I. (2015). Fight-or-flight response. In: I. Milosevic and R.E. McCabe (Eds.). *Phobias: The Psychology of Irrational Fear*. Greenwood.

Nelissen, R., and Zeelenberg, M. (2009). When guilt evokes self-punishment: Evidence for the existence of a Dobby effect. *Emotion*, Vol.9, No.1, pp.118–122.

Neumayer, E. (2004). The environment, left-wing political orientation and ecological economics. *Ecological Economics*, Vol.51, No.3–4, pp.167–175.

Puga, D. (1998). Urbanization patterns: European versus less developed countries. *Journal of Regional Science*, Vol.38, No.2, pp.231–252.

Räikkönen, K., Matthews, K.A., Flory, J.D., Owens, J.F., and Gump, B.B. (1999). Effects of optimism, pessimism, and trait anxiety on ambulatory blood pressure and mood during everyday life. *Journal of Personality and Social Psychology*, Vol.76, No.1, pp.104–113.

Rose, N.L. (1992). Fear of flying? Economic analysis of airline safety. *Journal of Economic Perspectives*, Vol.6, No.2, pp.75–94.

Rothbaum, B.O., and Hodges, L.F. (1999). The use of virtual reality exposure in the treatment of anxiety disorders. *Behavior Modification*, Vol.23, No.4, pp.507–525.

Steil, J., Tuchman, B., and Deutsch, M. (1978). An exploratory study of the meanings of injustice and frustration. *Personality and Social Psychology Bulletin*, Vol.4, No.3, pp.393–398.

Tai, K., Narayanan, J., and McAllister, D.J. (2012). Envy as pain: Rethinking the nature of envy and its implications for employees and organizations. *Academy of Management Review*, Vol.37, No.1, pp.107–129.

Taylor, N., and Nathan, S. (2002). How science contributes to environmental reporting in British newspapers: A case study of the reporting of global warming and climate change. *Environmentalist*, Vol.22, No.4, pp.325–331.

Upton, R. (2020). The decade of environmental panic. *Planning Theory & Practice*, Vol.21, No.1, pp.3–6.

Vecchio, R.P. (2000). Negative emotion in the workplace: Employee jealousy and envy. *International Journal of Stress Management*, Vol.7, No.3, pp.161–179.

von der Embse, N., Jester, D., Roy, D., and Post, J. (2018). Test anxiety effects, predictors, and correlates: A 30-year meta-analytic review. *Journal of Affective Disorders*, Vol.227, pp.483–493.

Whitfield, S.J. (1996). *The Culture of the Cold War*. JHU Press.

Wrenn, M.V. (2014). The social ontology of fear and neoliberalism. *Review of Social Economy*, Vol.72, No.3, pp.337–353.

Wurzel, R., and Connelly, J. (Eds.) (2011). *The European Union as a Leader in International Climate Change Politics*. Routledge.

Zembylas, M. (2021). The affective dimension of far right rhetoric in the classroom: The promise of agonistic emotions and affects in countering extremism. *Discourse: Studies in the Cultural Politics of Education*, Vol.42, No.2, pp.267–281.

Zheng, X., Baskin, E., and Peng, S. (2018). The spillover effect of incidental social comparison on materialistic pursuits: The mediating role of envy. *European Journal of Marketing*, Vol.52, No.5–6, pp.1107–1127.

Županov, J. (1996). The social legacy of communism. *Drustvena Istrazivanja 5*, Vol.2, No. 22, pp.425–455.

13 Dialogue and Collaboration

Segregation and Polarization

Among the many consequences of extreme sustainability rhetoric is the segregation of society, with individuals gathering around those with whom they share similar beliefs. With the 'clusterization' of views, this process seems to favour the generation of animosities among groups, pushing them into constant states of polarization. As discussed on several occasions throughout the book, the instrumentalization of the environmental cause by politicians seems to play an important role in the development of these dynamics. Perhaps the greatest support for this argument rests in the fact that the misuse of environmental discourse by politicians ends up importing their rivalries into the discussions on sustainable development. These associations may be even more harmful as they lead those who identify with a certain type of thinking (e.g., liberals, conservatives, socialists) to refute basically everything that is defended by others.

It is possible, therefore, to classify these processes as modern forms of tribalism, in which the members of a group not only coalesce among themselves but also seek to combat everything that is defended by groups they perceive as rivals. Since the instrumentalization of the environmentalist cause seems to be at the origin of this question, a brief discussion about political tribalism (North et al., 2021) becomes necessary. In this sense, it is possible to identify in the antagonism between the values of freedom and equality (Berggren, 1999) the probable cause of the conflicts. A society formed by free individuals cannot be expected to be equal from an economic point of view (Anderson, 2018). As citizens express their unique talents, act on their own motivations, are willing to sacrifice momentary benefits for future gains, and are able to make better decisions, they will generate different levels of value for society. With money being the socially agreed form of expression of this generated value (Walsh, 2004), it is natural to expect that individuals who fit the above description will obtain greater wealth than those who fail in one or all of the proposed factors (Agarwal and Holmes, 2019).

The reasoning is based on the idea that people are mostly remunerated by the value they produce, and not by other factors such as the time or the energy necessary to obtain an outcome (Neale and McElroy, 2004). Another relevant element in that regard refers to the extent to which the outcomes are rare, with those

DOI: 10.4324/9781003124719-16

ranking higher in this category being often more appreciated (Farrell, 2005). Within this view, it would be natural to expect a specialized physician to make more money than a cab driver, or a shoes seller. Regardless of the importance and nobility of these two activities, the fact that they require less training, less investment (of time, energy, and money), and less skills would justify their more modest remunerations. That is basically due to the fact that these characteristics result in more individuals capable of performing them. With respect to the economic law of demand and supply (Yang et al., 2002), this may lead to lower equilibrium prices when compared to the value generated by the specialized physician. With the passage of time, these differences result in the establishment of different levels of capital accumulation between the categories and, consequently, in the establishment of a social hierarchy (Zou, 1998).

Although quite simplistic, the preceding example illustrates how social inequality can be, at least in part, explained by the freedom of individuals (de Soysa and Vadlamannati, 2021), with the different remunerations attributed to each of the professions reflecting the choices made by them throughout their lives. Nevertheless, several other factors can influence whether a person pursues a higher paid position. This includes issues that have little or nothing to do with their natural talents or willpower, such as the country in which they were born (Ferreira et al., 2012), the economic and social conditions of their families (Salgado and Ortiz, 2020), or the various adversities they may have faced over the years. Despite the potential of these and other issues to impact individuals' economic successes, they may be argued to be often secondary, possibly being outweighed by the factors discussed earlier. Stories of people who overcame extreme difficulties and became very successful, for instance, are not rare. Likewise, cases in which initially favourable conditions were wasted are also common.

It can be argued that capitalism represents the ideal stage for the development of inequalities (Hodgson, 2003), with the free market offering the conditions for the different values generated by individuals to be remunerated in an equally different way (Piketty, 2015). Price formation sends important signals to economic agents (Arrow, 1973), representing a very powerful incentive mechanism. In this way, the better-paid professions or activities should naturally attract a greater number of people. According to the mechanism of the laws of supply and demand, however, as the number of individuals capable of performing a certain function increases, the value of their remuneration decreases, precisely because it becomes less rare. The multiplication of alternatives on the supply side ends up triggering a process of price-based competition with the absence of differentiation between the possibilities, raising price to the status of the most important factor for purchasing decisions (Porter, 1996).

This process puts additional pressure on the remuneration of these activities, which would partly explain the reasons why a cab driver or a shoe salesman usually makes less money than a specialist physician. Despite fitting into the basic functioning of the law of supply and demand, some considerations are relevant for a better understanding of the nature of remuneration. First of all, it is necessary to take into account that, in practice, the choice of a profession is not based only on the remuneration it offers (Sharif et al., 2019). If, on the one hand, this can be an initial factor in creating a desire to practice a profession, interested individuals will have to go through a harsh journey before they can practice the activity they want and finally have access to the desired remuneration. The difficulties inherent to these routes may end up having a direct influence on the rarity of activities and, consequently, on the value of the remuneration attributed to them. In general, the better-paid professions tend to demand a more tortuous path than the less rewarding ones. For the purpose of comparing the examples used earlier, the person who wishes to obtain the remuneration of a specialist physician must prepare her/himself to walk a long path that includes important aspects of her/his personality and ger/his financial capacity to bear the various costs of this choice. This includes factors as diverse as a previous academic performance that allowed the individual to join a medical school (Lynagh et al., 2018), the willingness to attend classes and dedicate intensively to studies for many years, the sacrifice of part of the personal life (e.g., meeting with friends, romantic relationships, going to the movies), and in general, less sleep.

From an economic point of view, this individual should seek ways to finance their studies, with regard to both the payment of tuition fees charged by the college (in the case of private institutions) and the purchase of teaching materials (e.g., books, equipment). In the case of students from more affluent families, these costs may be covered with the financial resources of the parents or any relative who wishes to collaborate. In some cases, however, the medical student comes from humble families and needs to finance the studies on her/his own. This means that, in addition to all the sacrifices discussed above, s/he will have to work to bear all the expenses necessary for the good progress of her/his studies. In these cases, it can be said that the merits of those who finally manage to obtain their diplomas are even greater. In fact, even after graduating from the faculty of medicine, the path to the position of specialist will still be difficult, with the young physician having to work long shifts (Tyssen and Vaglum, 2002) and dedicating to the study of the area in which s/he intends to specialize. In some cases, the total journey between the beginning and the end of the training of a specialist physician can take more than a decade.

Once again, it is necessary to consider that all these difficulties will have an important effect on the rarity of specialist physician and, consequently, on career remuneration. Another important aspect to consider is that those who decide to take this course assume a considerable risk since, at the beginning of their studies, they have no guarantee that they will be able to reap the fruits of their efforts. The temporal distance between investments (e.g., time, energy) and returns (i.e., remuneration) makes things even more complex in this sense. According to basic finance reasoning, individuals will be willing to accept higher levels of risk only if they expect higher levels of return (Campbell, 1996). The same logic used in studying the behaviour of investors in assets such as stocks and derivatives can be applied to any other circumstance. In this way, the high degree of uncertainty characteristic of a professional career also contributes to the understanding of the reasons that result in its higher valuation in terms of remuneration (i.e., higher return). In the case of a cab driver or a shoe seller, the requirements for exercising the profession are considerably lower than that of the specialist physician. None of these two careers require, for example, a good academic performance. For cab drivers, a driver's license and a public authorization are usually sufficient. In the case of shoe sellers, not even that will be needed. Obviously, there are difficulties in obtaining the necessary requirements for a person to become a cab driver and some effort will be necessary to fulfil the required obligations. What is interesting for the present discussion is the comparison of these levels of difficulty with those required of a specialist physician. Analogously to the previous example, it can be said that easier access to the professions of cab driver or shoe seller is an important aspect in understanding the lower remuneration attributed to these activities. In addition to the lower rarity of the offer and the consequent price-based competition that may be established, the lower risks taken by those who seek these professions (compared to what they are oriented in the career of specialist physicians) also explain the lower level of returns in the form of remuneration.

In light of these and other issues, it can be argued that social inequalities are an inevitable result of not only the typical conditions of the free market but also all the choices that individuals make throughout their lives. This means that, despite the various conditions that can affect people's financial prosperity, an important part of one's ability to generate value – and to be remunerated for doing so – comes from the way s/he uses her/his natural talents. This view encompasses four factors that seem to be complementary in the process of capital accumulation: the first deals with structural circumstances, over which individuals have little or no control. This includes matters such as the educational level of her/his parents, the characteristics of the neighbourhood where s/he grows up, the socioeconomic level of the people s/he lives with, her/his networks, values accumulated by ancestors that are received in the form of inheritance. Likewise, the individual will have little autonomy over the events s/he encounters in her/his life, with some of them being able to be decisive in his destiny. This second category includes unexpected circumstances that present themselves, for which there is no advance planning, and that can be both positive and negative. A third category refers to a person's natural talents, such as intelligence, eloquence, charisma, and beauty. If, on the one hand, some of these attributes are innate, others can be developed (Gannett and Brereton, 2016). Finally, the fourth category refers to the attitude of individuals in the face of circumstances. In addition to the topics discussed earlier, such as the dedication to the pursuit of success, the willingness to accept greater levels of risk, the capacity for long-term planning, and, more generally, the way the individual deals with adverse events of life. While some people seem to be victims of circumstances, others seek to absorb the blows, aiming not only to survive the countless difficulties but also to prosper.

This last category is particularly important for the argument developed here, because it shows how an individual can respond to the different situations presented to her/him by life and thus shape her/his destiny. In particular, this denotes that, to some extent, individual success depends on the attitudes that each one has. In this sense, a reflection on the 'distribution' of human suffering is necessary.

Contrary to what many apparently think, the pains of life are not reserved for individuals who occupy the lowest layers of the social hierarchy. Those who have more favourable financial situations are not free from anguish, anxieties, frustrations, disappointments, worries, or illnesses. Despite having material resources that allow them to alleviate the suffering arising from some of these evils, one cannot ignore the fact that the rich are also human beings and, as such, are likely to feel everything that is natural to the species. Of course, it can be argued that the poorest in general suffer the most. However, this principle cannot be taken as a rule, since the pains of human experience be analysed cannot according to the social segment that the individual in question occupies, but rather case by case. The influence of Marxist ideas is notable in the most simplistic arguments in this sense (i.e., poor suffer more than rich), especially those that treat the so-called class struggles, which, among other factors, encourages the misappropriation of material goods of superior social classes for the sake of the collective (Freitas et al., 2020). Beside obvious, the remembrance that those occupying superior classes are also human beings should be constant, once the dehumanization of these people (i.e., processes through which they are argued to lose basic human rights) may favour barbaric and violent attitudes against them, mainly in the course of revolutions. This seem to have been the case of the Russian Revolution in 1917 (Fitzpatrick, 2017).

From the debate over the potential origins of social inequality emerge the fundamental ideas of responsibility and meritocracy (Young, 2017), which seem to be at the heart of the disagreement between those who privilege freedom and those who place equality as a superior value. As discussed through simple examples and illustrations, the remuneration of individuals largely depends on themselves, with their financial success being justly deserved. The concept of freedom has a fundamental importance in this sense because, at all times, we are faced with the sacrifices necessary to seek a better position in this hierarchy. The power to choose which path to follow (e.g., study *versus* rest, work *versus* leisure, savings *versus* spending) represents a dimension of free will and will have important consequences in the form of financial results. The understanding makes it possible to attribute, at least in part, responsibility to individuals who, due to their personal choices, should deserve the remuneration they pursue. In this set, inequality would be a natural consequence of individual freedom, with differences in the choices of each one being reflected in their accumulation of capital.

These concepts make up the basic idea of the more straightforward worldviews of the political-economic spectrum, being common in the discourses of classic liberals and conservatives (Son Hing et al., 2011). In general, these understandings defend that the individual is the driving force of her/his own success (Saunders, 1995), with free enterprise being the means by which this success should be achieved. According to these perspectives, welfare visions should be avoided, reserved for moments of calamity. This means that resources should not be offered to those who need it on a permanent basis, but only at times when these people are truly unable to seek their own sustenance (Likki and Staerklé, 2015). This does not mean that there is a desire on the part of those who defend this position that people in shortage do not have access to what they need. Instead, the idea would be more coherent with the argument that everyone who has a material necessity should seek to satisfy it themselves, through their work and the creation of value for society (Suzuki and Hur, 2021). For them, a better alternative than meeting the needs of someone who has all the possibilities to achieve success on their own would be to ensure that this person can, in fact, generate value. This can range from defending the conditions inherent in a free market to the provision of training and education (Bukodi and Goldthorpe, 2018).

The possibility of increasing the remuneration received by increasing the value generated to society would be one of the main guarantors of social mobility, with the development of their capacities offering individuals the possibility of moving towards more privileged situations. In this sense, the social pyramids would not be immutable and could be redefined. This plasticity can be seen in notorious cases of enrichment, with some of the richest men and women on the planet coming from relatively humble backgrounds. This seems to be the case for famous American tech entrepreneurs such as Steve Jobs (1955–2011) (Independent, 2011), Jeff Bezos (1964–) (Cox, 2019), and, more recently, Elon Musk (1971–) (Blystone, 2021). The three owe their fortunes to the great value they generated through solutions to, hitherto, unmet market demands. In a more comprehensive analysis, the rise of these and other characters seems to confirm that social inequalities are an inevitable result of freedom of choice, with the path adopted and the choices made by each individual impacting their financial performance. What draws the most attention in these cases is the fact that none of the three received their fortunes out of necessity, but rather out of merit for the value they generated for a large number of people. Developing the skills needed to create the products and services they created appears to have been the single most important factor in building their respective successes.

This idea has been expressed over time in the form of an allegory, in which it is argued that it is preferable to teach someone how to fish rather than offer the fish. This perception is embedded in the idea that merit, and not necessity, is the justification for access to what is needed. For defenders of right-wing thinking, enabling individuals to work at the expense of simply meeting their needs would be the most ethical choice, since the acquisition of skills would allow a person to eat for a lifetime, while offering what it lacks would be only a momentary relief, which must be constantly renewed. This dynamic would create weakened individuals, increasingly dependent on others to have their basic needs met.

In any case, overcoming the dichotomy between the classic views of the left and the right on these and other issues seems to be a critical point in the maintenance of productive and constructive dialogues. With regard specifically to issues related to sustainable development, this reinforces the idea that the debate on sustainability should ideally be decoupled from political and ideological views. As discussed throughout the book, the importation of the basic premises of these arenas ends up contaminating the discussions about the best ways to pursue environmental performance. Disagreements about the real role of meritocracy, for example, should be left out of attempts to implement a truly sustainable development. The fact that discussions about sustainability are embedded in ideology, however, ends up putting those who disagree with these and other issues on opposite sides, even if they concur with matters directly related to the social or environmental debate.

On Healthy Dialogues

Among the many benefits of maintaining the dialogue for sustainable development is the most appropriate direction of public policies, so that the financial resources used for this purpose are applied for a real impact. This question seems to be particularly important when the social aspects of sustainability are considered. As discussed in Chapter 9, it is not uncommon for the search for environmental preservation to take priority over improving the living conditions of people who inhabit a region of interest. The case of the Amazon rainforest is one of the most representative of this phenomenon, with many experts ignoring that about 20 million people inhabit the region. The lack of knowledge of data as relevant as this seems to result both from a genuine lack of interest and from a lack of dialogue with local representatives.

The exchange of information with Brazilian, Colombian, Venezuelan, and Peruvian academics and researchers who are dedicated to the study of social issues in the Amazon region could be quite fruitful in this regard. In addition to accessing primary data, exchanges with these groups can offer a more realistic perspective to European and North American specialists, so that the most common stereotypes about the situation of the Amazon rainforest are debunked. Although there are a good number of academics from developed countries who actively seek contact with their South American colleagues, others seem to form their opinions solely on the basis of television news and the exchange of ideas with their colleagues, who are equally isolated in their cognitive bubbles. The future of the Amazon forest is often discussed from the top of these 'ivory towers' (Bok, 1982) by people who have never visited the region. In addition to drawing attention to the existence of problems that go beyond environmental issues, the dialogue with local experts should allow the application of resources destined to the preservation of the Amazon biomes to be more effective. This is because social problems are often the source of environmental degradation. It is very common, for example, that the lack of professional prospects leads the inhabitants of forest regions to engage in harmful activities, as a way of seeking to support their families. Among the most common activities is deforestation aimed at selling wood or raising cattle (Barreto et al., 2006). Likewise, mining activities end up being one of the most sought-after alternatives, representing a very important potential for water and soil pollution, with heavy materials that are used in gold separation (e.g., mercury) being particularly problematic (Gonzalez et al., 2019). It is therefore necessary to consider that economic, social, and environmental issues are interdependent and cannot be treated in isolation.

Evidently, the issues related to the Amazon rainforest are not the only ones that need to be reconsidered, with the arguments presented here applying to almost all of the most targeted regions in terms of environmental preservation. This includes

African (Aleman et al., 2018) and Asian rainforests (Onder et al., 2021), coastal regions, and the poles, as well as all urban areas that tend to have many of their environmental and social problems neglected. Concerning the latter, strengthening dialogue with the poorest populations is essential so that their real needs are met. Chapter 9 addresses some of these issues, discussing how, in many cases, significant amounts of public resources are destined for the creation of cycle paths in neighbourhoods inhabited or frequented by the urban *bourgeoisie*, while garbage collection or basic sanitation in peripheral regions remains abandoned. This scenario is very common in large metropolises located in underdeveloped countries. It can be argued that the dialogue with the most popular classes will only really be established when they have some kind of active voice. The fact that the basis of the social pyramid is mostly made up of individuals with low social power tends to relegate the participation of these people in public debate to a secondary position, often being completely ignored. The exception exists in the periods leading up to the elections, when politicians from the most varied ideological currents repeatedly visit poor areas in the hope of winning votes. Candidates for elective positions – in many cases endowed with an extinct populist – manage to make their interlocutors feel heard, even going so far as to believe the promises made to them. If, on the one hand, it cannot be said that this behaviour is characteristic of all politicians, it ends up being observed frequently. This usually results in not meeting the needs of the poorest population, which, in different ways, could end up negatively impacting the environment.

In the context of supply chains, maintaining a healthy dialogue between all the actors involved in the production process seems to be one of the main factors that explain the success of strategies that aim to improve the social or environmental performance of the extraction, transformation, and distribution of goods and services. The acceleration of cost-based competition in recent decades (Christopher, 2016) has favoured the geographic redistribution of production processes, with many companies choosing to transfer their industrial operations to so-called low-labour cost zones. Defined as places where the cost of labour is significantly lower when compared to regions of traditional industrialization (e.g., Europe), these alternatives turned out to be very attractive, as the low wages paid to workers allowed companies to survive international competition in some cases and yield great financial returns in others. However, changes in industrial geography reflect quite complex movements that include an increase in the number of participants throughout the processes. Far beyond the simple transfer of operational activities to low-labour cost zones, these changes reflect important organizational reengineering in which companies seek to focus on a few activities – usually those in which they excel – while transferring others to companies that have the ability to execute them more efficiently. This industrial reorganization and the consequent reduction of the organizational scope that it represents became popularly known by the name of strategic outsourcing (Quinn and Hilmer, 1994). Based, to some extent, on the popularization of the value chain concept (Porter, 1985), the strategic outsourcing process refers to the identification of main and auxiliary activities, with the first being the one in which the company manages to generate value. Once this distinction is made, the decision follows as to which activities will be carried out internally (i.e., by the company itself) and which activities will be acquired from suppliers. This dynamic is popularly known as the 'do-or-buy decision'.

As previously mentioned, one of the main consequences of this dynamic refers to the increase in the number of actors involved in the production of goods and services. Added to this is the fact that many are located in distant regions, in terms of both physical and cultural distances. This increase in the complexity of production processes is reflected in a greater complexity in coordination of activities. In addition to demanding greater alignment of the processes of physical movement of raw materials and finished products (e.g., inventory management, logistics), the specialization of companies around precise and well-defined activities requires an advance in governance and control mechanisms, with flaws resulting, in some cases, in significant losses of social and environmental performance. It is common, for example, for various types of human rights offenses to occur in the operations of small local suppliers that make up the early stages of large supply chains. Situations in which workers have their freedom restricted (Davidson, 2015), are not adequately remunerated (Crane, 2013), suffer physical punishment (Machura et al., 2019), or are forced to work for longer periods than permitted by law (Wang, 2020) constitute situations classified as modern slavery. Trafficking of workers also makes up the list of this category of practices (Ikeora, 2017).

Another very common social problem concerns the employment of children and adolescents as labour. In addition to posing risks to the safety and health of young people, the employment of child labour can have an important impact on the development of those who are victims of these processes. This issue is particularly important when it comes to education, with children who are forced to work usually having serious intellectual development problems. In many cases, these children do not even attend school, remaining on the fringes of the educational system. The lack of development of basic skills, such as reading or writing, will have important consequences on the living standards of these people throughout their adult lives, representing additional difficulties for a successful insertion into the labour market. It can be said, therefore, that child labour greatly increases the possibility that generations of workers will not be able to ascend socially, being to some extent destined to remain at the base of the social pyramid.

Cases of modern slavery and child labour seem to be a consequence of business models based on strategic outsourcing. In this sense, the constant search to reduce production costs ends up exerting additional pressure on the entire production chain, which, in many cases, ends up working as an incentive for suppliers to adopt illegal and immoral practices. This dynamic tends to be even more common in industrial operations carried out in underdeveloped countries, with the situation of poverty or misery faced by local populations increasing the chances that they will submit to extremely harsh working conditions, in exchange for a salary that allows them to have access to minimal amounts of food and comfort. Added to this is the fact that, in economically underdeveloped countries, it is common for state structures to be inefficient (Leff and Heidenheimer, 2017), meaning that ordinary citizens do not usually count on the support of institutions such as the police or justice structures. This situation ends up favouring the occurrence of the aforementioned problems, with those who break the laws having the conviction that they will remain unpunished.

The deficiencies of the State apparatus are also reflected in the almost non-existence of inspection, or any measure aimed at curbing the practices of modern slavery and child labour. These flaws add to the responsibility of large companies that have chosen strategic outsourcing as a business model, since they seem to be the only ones capable of preventing the proliferation of offenses. In this sense, maintaining a healthy dialogue with all members of the supply chains seems to be the only way to promote collaboration and, ideally, eliminate these issues from the production process. As discussed by Fracarolli Nunes (2018, 2019), however, many companies struggle to combat these abuses, with cases of modern slavery and child labour being relatively common in industries such as electronics and fast fashion. Cases involving the employment of under-aged workers in production lines or the maintenance of very poor working conditions have been reported in these two industries. Authors have also pointed to similar cases in other economic activities, mainly those related to mining (Hilson, 2012) and agriculture (Gold et al., 2015).

From an environmental point of view, the challenges are quite similar, covering a large number of industries. The atomization of production processes – especially in the early stages – leads many companies to ignore the origin of the products they use and, therefore, ignore their impacts on the environment. This situation seems to be more common when using commodities, with the characteristics of these products making it difficult to identify their origins. The fact that, in general, they do not present any distinction or characteristic that allows their differentiation, when mixed, products originated in an environmentally correct way cannot be separated from those originated by means of pollution, deforestation, or any other form of aggression to the environment. It can be seen that the lack of transparency of modern supply chains reflects the absence of dialogue between the many parts that compose it.

In a comprehensive way, the arguments proposed here reinforce the idea that the maintenance of dialogue represents one of the main aspects of the search for sustainable development. The consideration of the relevance of this theme in the quality of the interaction of the most diverse groups of stakeholders aims to demonstrate the complexity of the issue, as well as to support the idea that a joint and organized effort is necessary for the treatment of the discussed problems. In this sense, building and maintaining favourable conditions for dialogue appears as a fundamental factor in the development of collaborative relationships. It is necessary to remember, nevertheless, that the economic aspects discussed in these last paragraphs do not overshadow the relevance of the political and ideological issues discussed in the previous passages, and with greater focus later on in the book. Despite being, in some cases, even more important from a pragmatic point of view, economic issues tend to be easier to deal with, with the pressure exerted by consumers, investors, governments, and other agents with whom companies maintain interfaces acting in this sense. The overcoming of the political-ideological aspects, however, seems to be a more difficult solution, with the evolution in this direction being, probably, the fundamental question in the advancement of dialogue and collaboration as instruments of sustainable development.

References

Agarwal, R., and Holmes Jr, R.M. (2019). Let's not focus on income inequality. *Academy of Management Review*, Vol.44, No.2, pp.450–460.

Aleman, J.C., Jarzyna, M.A., and Staver, A.C. (2018). Forest extent and deforestation in tropical Africa since 1900. *Nature Ecology & Evolution*, Vol.2, No.1, pp.26–33.

Anderson, E. (2018). Freedom and equality. In: D. Schmidtz and C.E. Pavel (Eds.). *The Oxford Handbook of Freedom*, pp.90–105. Oxford University Press.

Arrow, K.J. (1973). *Information and Economic Behavior*. Harvard University Press.

Barreto, P., Souza Jr, C., Noguerón, R., Anderson, A., and Salomão, R. (2006). *Human Pressure on the Brazilian Amazon Forests*. World Resources Institute.

Berggren, N. (1999). Economic freedom and equality: Friends or foes? *Public Choice*, Vol.100, No.3, pp.203–223.

Blystone, D. (2021). Qui est Elon Musk? *Investopedia*, August 23. Available at https://www-investopedia-com.translate.goog/articles/personal-finance/061015/how-elon-musk-became-elon-musk.asp?_x_tr_sl=en&_x_tr_tl=fr&_x_tr_hl=fr&_x_tr_pto=sc

Bok, D.C. (1982). *Beyond the Ivory Tower*. Harvard University Press.

Bukodi, E., and Goldthorpe, J.H. (2018). *Social Mobility and Education in Britain: Research, Politics and Policy*. Cambridge University Press.

Campbell, J.Y. (1996). Understanding risk and return. *Journal of Political Economy*, Vol.104, No.2, pp.298–345.

Christopher, M. (2016). *Logistics & Supply Chain Management*, 5th edition. Pearson.

Cox, J. (2019). From humble beginnings to master of the universe: How did Jeff Bezos make his billions? *Independent*, February 25. Available at https://www.independent.co.uk/news/long_reads/jeff-bezos-amazon-how-rich-billions-tech-national-enquirer-washington-post-a8777201.html

Crane, A. (2013). Modern slavery as a management practice: Exploring the conditions and capabilities for human exploitation. *Academy of Management Review*, Vol.38, No.1, pp.49–69.

Davidson, J.O.C. (2015). *Modern Slavery: The Margins of Freedom*. Springer.

de Soysa, I., and Vadlamannati, K.C. (2021). Free market capitalism and societal inequities: Assessing the effects of economic freedom on income inequality and the equity of access to opportunity, 1990–2017. *International Political Science Review*, forthcoming. https://doi.org/10.1177/01925121211039985

Farrell, D. (2005). Offshoring: Value creation through economic change. *Journal of Management Studies*, Vol.42, No.3, pp.675–683.

Ferreira, F.H., Messina, J., Rigolini, J., López-Calva, L.F., Lugo, M.A., Vakis, R., and Ló, L.F. (2012). *Economic Mobility and the Rise of the Latin American Middle Class*. World Bank Publications.

Fitzpatrick, S. (2017). *The Russian Revolution*. Oxford University Press.

Fracarolli Nunes, M. (2018). Supply chain contamination: An exploratory approach on the collateral effects of negative corporate events. *European Management Journal*, Vol.36, pp.573–587.

Fracarolli Nunes, M. (2019). The impact of negative social/environmental events on the market value of supply chain partners. In: L. De Boer and P.H. Andersen (Eds.). *Operations Management and Sustainability: New Research Perspectives*, pp.151–178. Palgrave Macmillan.

Freitas, A.A., Saludjian, A., and Pinto, E.C. (2020). Apontamentos acerca da origem do debate sobre heranças na visão da economia política clássica e de Marx. *Revista da Sociedade Brasileira de Economia Política*, No.57, pp.114–142.

Gannett, C., and Brereton, J. (Eds.) (2016). *Traditions of Eloquence: The Jesuits and Modern Rhetorical Studies*. Fordham University Press.

Gold, S., Trautrims, A., and Trodd, Z. (2015). Modern slavery challenges to supply chain management. *Supply Chain Management: An International Journal*, Vol.20, No.5, pp.485–494.

Gonzalez, D.J., Arain, A., and Fernandez, L.E. (2019). Mercury exposure, risk factors, and perceptions among women of childbearing age in an artisanal gold mining region of the Peruvian Amazon. *Environmental Research*, Vol.179, p.108786.

Hilson, G. (2012). Family hardship and cultural values: Child labor in Malian small-scale gold mining communities. *World Development*, Vol.40, No.8, pp.1663–1674.

Hodgson, G.M. (2003). Capitalism, complexity, and inequality. *Journal of Economic Issues*, Vol.37, No.2, pp.471–478.

Ikeora, M. (2017). *Bilateral Cooperation and Human Trafficking: Eradicating Modern Slavery Between the United Kingdom and Nigeria*. Springer.

Independent (2011). Steve Jobs: From humble start to game changer. *Independent*, October 6. Available at https://www.independent.co.uk/news/world/americas/steve-jobs-from-humble-start-to-game-changer-2366290.html

Leff, N.H., and Heidenheimer, A.I. (2017). Economic development through bureaucratic corruption 1. In: A.I. Heidenheimer and M. Johnston (Eds.). *Political Corruption*, pp.307–320. Routledge.

Likki, T., and Staerklé, C. (2015). Welfare support in Europe: Interplay of dependency culture beliefs and meritocratic contexts. *International Journal of Public Opinion Research*, Vol.27, No.1, pp.138–153.

Lynagh, M., Horton, G., Nair, B.K., Walker, M., Kelly, B., and Powis, D. (2018). Student selection for medicine: Still a 'thorny' issue. *Archives of Medicine and Health Sciences*, Vol.6, No.1, pp.147–151.

Machura, S., Short, F., Hill, V.M., Suddaby, C.R., Goddard, F.E., Jones, S.E., Lloyd-Astbury, E.L., Richardson, L., and Rouse, C.A. (2019). Recognizing modern slavery. *Journal of Human Trafficking*, Vol.5, No.3, pp.201–219.

Neale, B., and McElroy, T. (2004). *Business Finance: A Value-Based Approach*. Pearson Education.

North, S., Piwek, L., and Joinson, A. (2021). Battle for Britain: Analyzing events as drivers of political tribalism in Twitter discussions of Brexit. *Policy & Internet*, Vol.13, No.2, pp.185–208.

Onder, S., Erbaugh, J.T., and Kosmidou-Bradley, G.C. (2021). Economic issues related to Asian deforestation. In: *Oxford Research Encyclopedia of Environmental Science*. Oxford University Press.

Piketty, T. (2015). *The Economics of Inequality*. Harvard University Press.

Porter, M.E. (1985). *Competitive Advantage. Creating and Sustaining Superior Performance*. The Free Press.

Porter, M.E. (1996). What is strategy? *Harvard Business Review*, Vol.74, No.6, pp.61–78.

Quinn, J.B., and Hilmer, F.G. (1994). Strategic outsourcing. *Sloan Management Review*, Vol.35, No.4, pp.43–55.

Salgado, C.D., and Ortiz, V. (2020). Mexican Americans and wealth: Economic status, family and place. *Journal of Ethnic and Migration Studies*, Vol.46, No.18, pp.3855–3873.
Saunders, P. (1995). Might Britain be a meritocracy? *Sociology*, Vol.29, No.1, pp.23–41.
Sharif, N., Ahmad, N., and Sarwar, S. (2019). Factors influencing career choices. *IBT Journal of Business Studies*, Vol.15, No.1, pp.33–46.
Son Hing, L.S., Bobocel, D.R., Zanna, M.P., Garcia, D.M., Gee, S.S., and Orazietti, K. (2011). The merit of meritocracy. *Journal of Personality and Social Psychology*, Vol.101, No.3, pp.433–450.
Suzuki, K., and Hur, H. (2021). Revisiting the old debate: Citizens' perceptions of meritocracy in public and private organizations. *Public Management Review*, forthcoming.
Tyssen, R., and Vaglum, P. (2002). Mental health problems among young doctors: An updated review of prospective studies. *Harvard Review of Psychiatry*, Vol.10, No.3, pp.154–165.
Walsh, A.J. (2004). A price on everything? Ethics and the widespread application of the money-metric. *Res Publica*, Vol.13, No.1, pp.14–18.
Wang, J.J. (2020). How managers use culture and controls to impose a '996' work regime in China that constitutes modern slavery. *Accounting & Finance*, Vol.60, No.4, pp.4331–4359.
Yang, H., Wong, S.C., and Wong, K.I. (2002). Demand – supply equilibrium of taxi services in a network under competition and regulation. *Transportation Research Part B: Methodological*, Vol.36, No.9, pp.799–819.
Young, M. (2017). *The Rise of the Meritocracy*. Routledge.
Zou, H.F. (1998). The spirit of capitalism, social status, money, and accumulation. *Journal of Economics*, Vol.68, No.3, pp.219–233.

14 Economic Development and Innovation

Green Products, Innovation, and Inequality

When viewed from a strictly technological point of view, environmentally friendly products are, in most cases, superior to traditional ones (Xie et al., 2019). This is because the latter are usually a legacy of a previous era, in which the preservation of the environment was not among the priorities of consumers or companies. Internal combustion engines are perhaps one of the best examples of this mindset. With the advent of the 'age of green' (Fracarolli Nunes and Lee Park, 2021a), however, sustainability-related issues took on a leading role never imagined before, as the debate on sustainable development permeated practically all spheres of society. As one of the main consequences of this process, the search for operational efficiency has gained great relevance (Kwon and Lee, 2019), with products and services designed to consume fewer and fewer natural resources, as well as having most of their components reused. (Alblas et al., 2014). Furthermore, the 1973 and 1979 oil crises highlighted the value of natural resources, with the skyrocketing fuel prices pushing a transition towards the development of more economical engines (Venn, 2016; Candelo, 2019).

The auto industry appears to have been one of the most affected by this movement, with automobiles incorporating a number of environmental innovations over the years. If, on the one hand, the improvements reflect changes in the geopolitical and macroeconomic spheres, the pressure exerted by different groups of stakeholders accelerated the incorporation of new technologies (Li et al., 2017). Furthermore, the automotive industry is among those that have suffered the most accusations of causing environmental damage, having, in many, cases served as a kind of scapegoat (Fracarolli Nunes and Lee Park, 2021b). Accordingly, it is likely that this focus on impacts arising from both the production and use of automobiles is not entirely motivated by sincere environmental concerns. Instead, the choice of these specific objects seems to be, to some extent, motivated by ideological issues.

One of the factors that most contributes to the strengthening of this argument is the perception that, much more than a simple means of transport, the car would be an instrument of freedom for its users (Berg et al., 2015). The possibility of getting from point A to point B at any time illustrates this issue, because unlike collective means of transport (e.g., buses, trains, subways, planes), private cars are

DOI: 10.4324/9781003124719-17

not restricted to a previously defined scale, being entirely at the disposal of their owners to be used in the way that suits them best. Among other consequences, this means that displacements by car are practically impossible to predict and, consequently, to control. From the point of view of those who are not so fond of individual freedoms, this situation can be uncomfortable, as it diminishes both control over society and the effectiveness of collectivist measures. In addition, automobiles would be an instrument of inequality between people, from both a functional and aesthetic perspective. The different skills of drivers, as well as the many characteristics of each vehicle, can result in very different outcomes. In addition to impacting, for example, the time spent commuting, these differences can lead to different levels of value creation and remuneration. Likewise, automobiles have an impact on the way their owners are perceived in society, with more expensive vehicles typically giving them a higher social status (Diekmann et al., 1996). This reasoning applies the Resource-Based View (RBV) arguments (Rumelt, 1984; Wernerfelt, 1984; Barney, 1991) to everyday life.

As discussed throughout the book, individuals more linked to thought classified as left tend to have as one of their main characteristics a preference for the idea of equality, with values related to freedom being – according to their dogmas – inferior. As discussed by Fracarolli Nunes (2021b), this basic idea seems to translate into a lesser sympathy for automobiles among leftists, with public transport often being scorned by politicians from these groups. In terms of equality, options such as trains, buses, and subways provide each of their users with the same level of service, while offering no increase in the social status of their users. These characteristics are enough for public transport to be classified as more appropriate to the way a leftist thinks a society should work. Despite representing potentially important factors in the left's predilection for collective forms of transport, the 'attack' on individual freedom that the alternative provides is perhaps the biggest reason for this choice. Unlike automobiles, public transport does not allow each user to define the nature of their own journey. It is not possible, for example, to choose a different path or change the destination sought. Likewise, it is not possible to choose what time the trip should start or end.

Still, after Fracarolli Nunes (2021b), the fact that public transport is subject to a very rigid scale and a standardized way of functioning may allow for a great level of control to be concentrated in the hands of those who operate the system. In this specific case, this means greater interference by the State in the lives of ordinary people. Even when offered by private companies, these services are often regulated by public bodies, which also results in a greater concentration of power around those who exercise bureaucratic functions within state structures. In addition to the possibility of a greater level of control in the displacements themselves, the use of public transport ends up providing important information about the routine of its users, which can be very interesting for governments with authoritarian pretensions. Considering that the most extreme forms of leftist thought are incompatible with the idea of democracy (e.g., dictatorship of the proletariat), one can understand, at least in part, the ideological reasons for the attacks that these groups sponsor against automobiles.

Understanding the possible ideological motivations behind the war against the automobile represents an important step in identifying environmentally hypocritical behaviour. In this sense, special attention is needed when analysing the arguments of political groups, with the exception that, in many cases, environmental issues are used only as a smokescreen for the advancement of ideological issues and power projects (often totalitarian). As discussed in previous chapters, the perception of these dynamics can contribute to the loss of credibility of environmental discourses and, in a collateral way, to the reinforcement of skepticism. Once again, the pernicious role that the instrumentalization of environmental discourse plays in the advancement of debates on sustainable development, with the alleged monopoly of virtues, trumpeted by politicians with a leftist bias, being one of the main causes of the refractory and negationist postures adopted by individuals who identify with right-wing thinking.

Using this logic leads many rightists to see communist threats in supporting alternative modes of transport such as bicycles. According to these views, despite not being as restrictive to users' freedom as public transport, bicycles would represent a setback when compared to automobiles, at least with regard to the power of drivers to cross long distances in less time. Just as an understanding of the effects of environmentally hypocritical views helps in perceiving the resistance to eventual environmental solutions, a deeper understanding of the logic developed by the most refractory can lead to a better perception of the real reasons for their attitudes. As discussed, it is likely that, in many cases, environmental denial is not necessarily linked to a desire to prevent the plan from being saved, but is – albeit unconsciously – linked to the defence of freedom. The lack of clarity on this topic is one of the main reasons for the interruption of dialogue between those who present opposing views.

Despite the complex dynamics capable of influencing the supply of environmentally superior products, the fact is that their development usually requires significant investments in the form of research and development (Demirel and Kesidou, 2019). Once again, it is worth remembering that 'green' products are, in general, technologically more advanced than traditional alternatives, which justifies the need for great efforts to develop them. With regard specifically to the need for investments in research and development, this often results in a significant increase in the cost of final products, with the high values necessary for the remuneration of specialized labour (i.e., scientists, engineers, PhDs), the use of materials in experiments, and the construction and maintenance of the physical structures necessary for the development of these activities (i.e., laboratories) explaining a large part of this situation. Added to this is the fact that investments in research and development are essentially high risk, since the degree of predictability of their expected results is usually low. This uncertain nature contributes directly to the high costs of final products, with the only reason for private agents to accept such levels of risk being the expectation of high returns. Thus, the search for a return on invested capital should exert additional pressure on the final price of environmentally superior products. In an even broader way, it must be considered that successful attempts (i.e., developed products and services that are commercialized) must absorb not only their high development costs, but also those related to unsuccessful alternatives.

Among the main consequences of these processes is the potential concentration of the market for environmentally responsible products, since only large companies will have the financial and technological resources necessary for environmental innovation. In the case of research from public universities, one can also discuss the possibility of the ecological transition resulting in a kind of market reserve for rich countries, given that only these will have the financial capacity to bear the high costs of developing clean technologies. It is not to be expected, for example, that great innovations emerge from universities located in underdeveloped countries, when they often have difficulties in keeping students' desks in minimal conditions of use. Their normally tight budgets do not allow for them to invest large amounts in research and development, often resulting in a low rate of patents, for instance. Universities in poor countries still have to deal with the problems resulting from the migration of their professors and researchers, who seek better working conditions in universities in rich nations (Aupetit and Gérard, 2009). This 'brain drain' ends up reducing even more the chances of poor countries in the competition for the market of environmentally responsible products. From a more holistic point of view, the loss of human capital can be considered particularly harmful when researchers who relocate had all their training paid for with public money in their countries of origin. In these cases, the poorest societies end up not having access to the fruits of their investments in the training of professionals capable of developing innovative products and services, which can have an important impact on maintaining their condition of underdevelopment.

Although these and other social consequences result from promoting 'green' products, they are often ignored. Thus, discussions on this topic aim to provide the reader with arguments that often end up not receiving due attention. The relationship between the search for environmental sustainability and social damage is also expressed in other themes, such as the discussion of land use to the detriment of forest preservation. These and other topics are addressed later in the chapter. As discussed in more detail in Chapter 9, the close relationships between sustainability and politics seem to influence the adoption of environmentally sound measures, with the level of advancement of representative democracies being one of the factors with the greatest potential to influence in this direction. If the pressure exerted by voters and support groups can be really beneficial for the advancement of issues on the environmental agenda, they can also contribute to an increase in environmental hypocrisy, as purely economic interests come to be represented through illegitimate environmental concerns. These issues are discussed below, with aspects related to the development of protectionist measures receiving special attention.

Sustainability, Performance, and Protectionism

From a purely commercial point of view, the idea of protectionism can be understood as the set of policies that aim to isolate a certain segment of a country's economy from international competition. This includes various restrictions on the importation of certain products, with the barriers taking the form of explicit limitations on the quantities allowed to enter the national territory, subsidies, and/or tax increases for imported items. While the reasons for adopting such policies can be diverse, the fragility of local economic agents is apparently the most common. In this sense, protectionism acts as a market reserve for national producers, so that economic agents operating in other regions may have their marketing pretensions totally or partially frustrated. These measures are aimed at not only maintaining jobs in the national territory but also achieving long-term economic objectives, with strategies seeking a certain distribution of economic activities being particularly affected.

Likewise, countries may choose to adopt protectionist measures as they see risks to national security. This category includes considerations about food security, i.e., the ability of a nation to guarantee that its citizens have access to a minimum amount of food. This can be a central issue in a government's aptitude in maintaining minimal levels of order and stability within its borders, with food shortages rapidly escalating into violent disputes and, ultimately, even civil war. Faced with this possibility, many governments adopt protectionist measures as a way of encouraging the continuity of food production in the territories under their management, even if this alternative is not the most interesting from an economic angle. An important aspect that can also influence decisions in this sense is geopolitical dynamics. In this context, the close relationship that exists between power and dependence must be considered, with the latter, in many cases, the main reason for the existence of the former. More specifically, it can be argued that the fact that an individual A depends on an individual B causes a power relationship to be established, with B occupying a privileged position. The greater the dependence of A on B, the stronger must be the power exercised by B over A.

This reasoning can be extended to basically any type of relationship, with some of the most famous frameworks in the strategic management literature being particularly successful in capturing this issue (although not explicitly stated). The developments of the so-called *Industry Structure*, for example, devote special attention to power relations in the division of the value generated in exchange relations between companies. In this sense, two of the famous *five forces* developed by Michael Porter (1979, 1980) are directly associated with the different types of relationships that can be established between a focal company, its suppliers, and its customers. Due to a number of factors, the power of one organization over the other would be established so that the most powerful would retain most of the value created. According to Porter (1979, 1980), this process would be due to the different levels of what he calls bargaining power of suppliers and bargaining power of customers. The origins of these forces can be diverse, with the influence of the dependence of one organization on the other being sub-understood.

This dynamic is based on the differentiation between the concepts of value creation and value capture (Lepak et al., 2007). While value creation refers to the value effectively generated in the different phases of an industrial process (e.g., transformation of raw materials into semi-finished products), the concept of value capture concerns the division of this value among the different players that contributed to its creation. In the case of a supplier being the only one capable of offering a certain raw material, for example, it must have a great bargaining power, with the lack of option of the company that needs its raw materials being characterized as a form of dependence. This bargaining power can be exercised in a variety of ways, with raising prices or demanding more stringent payment terms (e.g., advance payment) being the most common. In both cases, the pressure exerted by the supplier should have a positive impact on its profitability; at the same time, the profitability of the company that buys its raw materials will deteriorate. If, on the one hand, the generated value should not be necessarily affected (i.e., value creation), the distribution of this value as a function of the power imbalance between the parties illustrates the idea of value capture. Reflectively, a customer may be too important to a supplier, meaning that it must have favourable bargaining power. This is the case, for example, in situations where a customer accounts for a significant portion of a company's sales volume, so that a dependency relationship is established. Likewise, once the purchasing company is aware of the fragility of its supplier, it will be able to exercise its bargaining power through pressure on the prices of the products it acquires (i.e., demand for lower prices), or through better conditions of payment (e.g., longer terms, payment in instalments). It is also possible that customer bargaining power is established by other factors, such as the level of capillarity and access to the consumer market. This situation appears to be one of the main strengths of some of the largest retail chains in the world, with their large physical presence guaranteeing access from suppliers to end consumers.

While the idea of value capture through price pressure can be more easily understood, understanding the processes that lead to an unequal distribution of the value generated due to agreed payment terms demands greater attention. The indirect ways in which companies can influence their profitability are often ignored, which can make it difficult to understand the real reasons that lead some players to succeed while others may even go bankrupt. In this context, working capital management can play a crucial role, with the bargaining power of buyers and suppliers being among the main factors of influence. In a practical way, the concept of working capital can be understood as the financial volume necessary for the company to be able to develop its activities. By way of illustration, one can think of the different stages of building a hospital. Instinctively, people not used to economic and financial analysis will tend to consider only the amounts to be invested in physical assets as necessary for the hospital to start serving its patients (e.g., building, equipment). They forget, however, that for operations to start, many other expenses must be considered, such as the salaries of doctors, nurses, cleaning staff, and administrative workers. In the same way, it will be necessary that materials for immediate use such as towels and dressings are provided, as well as the expenses of water, electricity, and gas, among many others. This simple (and not exhaustive) example demonstrates the relevance of working capital, although the items discussed here are not fully in line with the academic view of the concept.

Despite the importance of this idea, the amounts needed in terms of working capital are usually poorly dimensioned in budgets and investment projects, probably due to their extremely dynamic nature. In accounting terms, these issues are most directly reflected in three major accounts: inventories, accounts receivable, and accounts payable. The inventory account refers to all the raw material held by the company, as well as the volumes of semi-finished and finished products. Inventory management depends on a number of factors, with the production system adopted being one of the most relevant. In general, these systems can be classified as push and pull. In the first one – also known as make to stock – companies will produce before sale so that the product is readily available to their potential buyers. For some products, high degrees of availability are required, as is the case with some types of food offerings (e.g., fast food chains). The physical presence of the product at points of sale implies a higher level of inventories. In turn, pull production systems – also known as make to order – are those in which companies wait for a manifestation of demand to start the production process. Contrary to what happens with push systems, pull systems will be more suitable for products that do not need to have a particularly high level of availability, or for products for which maintaining availability is economically unfeasible. A classic example of a pull system is found in airplane manufacturing processes. Due to the high costs of this equipment, manufacturers will not be able to anticipate their production, having to wait for a purchase signal. In many cases, the advance payment required from customers works as both a guarantee of future payment and a means of financing production. As such, the low availability of final products should influence the levels of inventories maintained by the companies, pushing them towards lower levels.

In addition to the production systems most adapted to each type of product, the levels of inventories to be maintained also depend a lot on the philosophies adopted by companies in managing their physical flows. In this category, the *Lean* approach (Womack et al., 1990) – also known by several other names, such as *Lean Management* and *Lean Synchronization* – stands out, broadly aiming to minimize any type of waste. As far as the present discussion is concerned, the treatment given to inventories within the *Lean* perspective is particularly important, with these being seen as one of the forms of waste. In this sense, the techniques focused on the idea of *just-in-time* result in the synchronization of production processes so that the need for safety stocks is reduced to the lowest possible levels (Chapman and Carter, 1990). Despite having been developed with the objective of making the operations of Japanese companies viable in periods of great scarcity of resources, the *Lean* philosophy ends up meeting the environmental objectives (Rothenberg et al., 2001), with the fight against waste representing one of the most efficient ways to relieve the pressure on the use of natural resources (Dieste et al., 2019). In practice, the implementation of operating models based on *Lean* approaches has been seen as a possible solution to one of the most important trade-offs involving the simultaneous search for economic and environmental performance. The concept of shared value developed by Porter and Kramer (2011) seeks to portray these and other conjectures by proposing that, far from being mutually exclusive, environmental and financial gains feed back into each other. In addition, the scholars discuss several ways in which the pursuit of environmental performance can represent an important source of competitive advantage for companies dedicated to this objective. The arguments seem to be in line with the strategies of most companies, especially those that seek to express their environmental initiatives more forcefully.

Still, on issues related to working capital management, it can be argued that the relationships of dependence and power between companies will be expressed even more importantly in accounts payable and accounts receivable (Fabbri and Klapper, 2016). As discussed earlier, the power of buyers or suppliers can be exercised in several ways, including demands for payment terms – in the case of buyers – or receipt – in the case of suppliers – more favourable (Cho et al., 2019). Thus, contrary to what one can imagine at first, the fact that a company presents high values in the form of accounts payable does not necessarily represent something negative, even if it denotes a position of indebtedness. This is because the amounts that make up this account represent everything that the company has already received from its suppliers without paying. From a financial management perspective, therefore, it can be said that the company's operations are being financed by its suppliers. Similarly, the amounts that build the accounts receivable account should not be immediately seen in a positive light, even if they relate to the company's receivables rights, as the generating event of these rights is precisely the delivery of products or the provision of services to customers without these being immediately paid. This means that, in addition to financing the operations of their customers, companies in this situation will have to look for additional sources to finance their own expenses (e.g., salaries, rent), which can have an important impact on their profitability.

The application of this logic to the relations between countries allows for the identification of some of the origins of the protectionist movements. In general, it can be said that nations that occupy positions of power will tend to use their strength to capture a greater share of the value generated in their trade relations. However, it is common for this power to be used precisely to protect activities in which these countries are in a position of weakness. One of the typical illustrations of these movements is found in the complex commercial relationships involving countries in South America and Europe. For centuries, exchanges between countries from the new and the old worlds took place in a very similar way to the schemes established in colonial times, with colonies exporting raw materials to their metropolises and importing finished products from them (Ricupero, 2016). In many cases, the colonies were even prohibited from developing more complex activities, with the industrial monopoly reserved for European countries. This type of relationship took place between countries such as Portugal and its colonies, with the territory currently understood as Brazil being an important supplier of commodities such as *pau-brasil*, sugar cane, and gold (Novais, 1995). Spanish colonization was based on a similar mechanism, with low value-added products such as tobacco being exported to the metropolis to be processed there (Baud, 1991). The Real Fabrica de Tabacos (i.e., Royal Tobacco Factory), located in the region of Andalucía, is said to be the first tobacco factory in Europe, with its old building currently serving as the headquarters of the University of Seville (Andalucia.org, 2022).

Although former Iberian colonies such as Brazil (Pereira et al., 2019) and Argentina (Glaeser et al., 2018) have gone through important industrialization processes in the 20th century, the trade relations of these countries with the rest of the world are still largely based on the export of agricultural (Richardson, 2009) and mineral commodities (Vale, 2017). The production of meat for the foreign market, for example, represents an important part of the wealth produced by both Argentina (Moreno et al., 2021) and Brazil (Rodrigues et al., 2021). Likewise, agricultural products such as soybeans (Escher and Wilkinson, 2019; Ramos et al., 2020) and corn (Costa and Ferreira Filho, 2019) make up the export agenda of these two countries. In the case of Brazil, there is also a strong participation in the world production of coffee (Caixeta et al., 2019), sugar (Carvalho and Brandt, 2019), orange juice (Moretti et al., 2019), and cotton (Copetti and Coronel, 2018), among many other products. Still, the export of ores also stands out (Pais et al., 2012). In general, it can be said that these countries are more efficient in the production of these goods than their European counterparts.

Among the various reasons for such superiority is what Joseph Schumpeter (1883–1950) called comparative advantages (Bassanini and Ernst, 2002). Basically, the concept refers to the set of conditions present in a country or region that make it particularly efficient in a given economic activity. In the case of Brazil, its comparative advantage would be a result of factors such as its large territorial extension, the availability of large amounts of water for irrigation, and the fact that the country receives large amounts of solar radiation practically all year round. Taken together, these and other elements would have a positive impact on the country's ability to produce large volumes, which invariably results in lower production costs. One of the direct consequences of these more favourable conditions for food production is greater pressure on European rural producers. Due to the significant differences in the productive capacity of these regions, it can be said that, under normal conditions, European producers would hardly be able to compete with Brazilian agricultural products. At the limit, this competition can lead rural producers on the old continent to almost certain bankruptcy.

As discussed earlier, an eventual decrease in the capacity to produce food can threaten the food security of countries, with European nations being particularly sensitive to this possibility. Aware of this issue, the governments of many countries in the region are accused of offering different types of incentives to their producers, artificially increasing their competitiveness. Among the most common measures is the provision of various forms of subsidy, ranging from direct subsidies to offering advantageous financing. Interest rates lower than those offered by the market or more generous terms act as an important stimulus for economic activities included in this productive sector. Likewise, the increase in taxes for imported products reduces their attractiveness, favouring the marketing of local products.

Evidently, these measures are contrary to the functioning of the free market and can have different consequences for both the countries that adopt them and those whose export capacity is compromised. In this sense, it is necessary to consider that the regulation of a market should have an immediate impact on the formation of prices and, consequently, on the complex mechanism of incentives that governs the propensity to produce. On the demand side, these changes will affect the ability or interest of individuals to consume a certain product, which can make the situation even more critical. In view of these and other consequences, it is clear that the various forms of protectionism tend to be harmful, even for the countries that practice them. If, on the one hand, measures in this sense can guarantee the viability of a given activity in the short term, these conditions are not usually sustained over the years, with protectionist measures needing to be constantly renewed. Among the many possible outcomes is the structural loss of competitiveness, with local producers becoming increasingly dependent on public policies.

In addition to issues related to maintaining minimum levels of food safety, the protection offered to European producers is also motivated by political aspects. Members of the primary sector still appear as one of the main economic segments in some countries in the region, with their influence reflected in the parliamentary composition and in the different layers of the executive and public administration (i.e., deep state). These individuals committed to defending the interests of the category often end up working against the national interest. When all these pressures are considered, the power of lobbying activities carried out by rural producers becomes evident. The pressures exerted by these interest groups are not limited, however, to politicians. With the influence of rural producers extending throughout the food industry, it can be argued that their expectations are often shared with public opinion through the various channels of traditional media.

In recent decades, this protectionism has manifested itself in the discussions on the trade agreement between Mercosur and the European Union. Among other things, these efforts sought to guarantee better access for agricultural products from Brazil, Argentina, Uruguay, and Paraguay to Europe, while at the same time reducing barriers to European industrial products in these countries. The signing of the agreement generated several adverse reactions among rural producers in some European countries, who feared that their activities could not withstand greater market opening. This dispute seems to have contaminated the environmental debate, with South American rural producers – especially Brazilians – being harshly accused of promoting environmental destruction. In particular, it sought to associate Brazilian agricultural activities with the destruction of the Amazon rainforest. This clash was largely carried out by the presidents of Brazil and France, with accusations and inelegance from both sides configuring a regrettable episode in the discussions on the environment. President Emmanuel Macron called the Brazilian government negligent and even complacent with the destruction of the forest. On the Brazilian side, President Jair Bolsonaro accused his French counterpart of being a liar, pointing to several flaws in his arguments (e.g., presentation of photos of old fires taken more than 30 years ago as if they were current). Furthermore, the Brazilian head of state pointed to a kind of neocolonialism, with French meddling in Brazil's internal affairs representing a serious offense to national sovereignty.

References

Alblas, A.A., Peters, K.K., and Wortmann, J.H. (2014). Fuzzy sustainability incentives in new product development: An empirical exploration of sustainability challenges in manufacturing companies. *International Journal of Operations & Production Management*, Vol.34, No.4, pp.513–545.

Andalucia.org (2022). *Antigua Fábrica de tabacos – Universidad de Sevilla*. Available at https://www.andalucia.org/fr/sevilla-tourisme-culturel-antigua-real-fabrica-de-tabacos-universidad-de-sevilla

Aupetit, S.D., and Gérard, E. (Eds.) (2009). *Fuga de Cerebros, Movilidad Académica, Redes Científicas: Perspectivas Latinoamericanas*. IESALC – CINVESTAV – IRD.

Barney, J. (1991). Firm resources and sustained competitive advantage. *Journal of Management*, Vol.17, No.1, pp.99–120.

Bassanini, A., and Ernst, E. (2002). Labour market regulation, industrial relations and technological regimes: A tale of comparative advantage. *Industrial and Corporate Change*, Vol.11, No.3, pp.391–426.

Baud, M. (1991). A colonial counter economy: Tobacco production on Española, 1500–1870. *New West Indian Guide/Nieuwe West-Indische Gids*, Vol.65, No.1–2, pp.27–49.

Berg, J., Levin, L., Abramsson, M., and Hagberg, J.E. (2015). 'I want complete freedom': Car use and everyday mobility among the newly retired. *European Transport Research Review*, Vol.7, No.4, pp.1–10.

Caixeta, G.Z.T., Leite, C.A.M., and de Oliveira, A.M. (2019). Tendências do mercado de café do Brasil. *Revista de Economia e Sociologia Rural*, Vol.27, No.2, pp.173–196.

Candelo, E. (2019). The first oil shock: A turning point in production and marketing. In: *Marketing Innovations in the Automotive Industry*. International Series in Advanced Management Studies. Springer. https://doi.org/10.1007/978-3-030-15999-3_12

Carvalho, F.C., and Brandt, S.A. (2019). Avaliação da política de estabilização de preços no mercado de exportação de açúcar do Brasil. *Revista de Economia e Sociologia Rural*, Vol.25, No.3, pp.357–365.

Chapman, S.N., and Carter, P.L. (1990). Supplier/customer inventory relationships under just in time. *Decision Sciences*, Vol.21, No.1, pp.35–51.

Cho, W., Ke, J.Y.F., and Han, C., (2019). An empirical examination of the use of bargaining power and its impacts on supply chain financial performance. *Journal of Purchasing and Supply Management*, Vol.25, No.4, p.100550.

Copetti, L.S., and Coronel, D.A. (2019). Competitividade das exportações brasileiras e indianas de algodão. *Revista Brasileira de Administração Científica*, Vol.1, No.1, pp.25–46. http://doi.org/10.6008/CBPC2179-684X.2018.003.0003

Costa, S.M.A.L., and de Souza Ferreira Filho, J.B. (2019). Liberalização comercial no Brasil e integração de commodities agrícolas: Os mercados de algodão, milho e arroz. *Revista de Economia e Sociologia Rural*, Vol.38, No.2, pp.41–70.

Demirel, P., and Kesidou, E. (2019). Sustainability-oriented capabilities for eco-innovation: Meeting the regulatory, technology, and market demands. *Business Strategy and the Environment*, Vol.28, No.5, pp.847–857.

Diekmann, A., Jungbauer-Gans, M., Krassnig, H., and Lorenz, S. (1996). Social status and aggression: A field study analyzed by survival analysis. *The Journal of Social Psychology*, Vol.136, No.6, pp.761–768.

Dieste, M., Panizzolo, R., Garza-Reyes, J.A., and Anosike, A. (2019). The relationship between lean and environmental performance: Practices and measures. *Journal of Cleaner Production*, Vol.224, pp.120–131.

Escher, F., and Wilkinson, J. (2019). A economia política do complexo Soja-Carne Brasil-China1. *Revista de Economia e Sociologia Rural*, Vol.57, pp.656–678.

Fabbri, D., and Klapper, L.F. (2016). Bargaining power and trade credit. *Journal of Corporate Finance*, Vol.41, pp.66–80.

Fracarolli Nunes, M., and Lee Park, C. (2021a). The age of green. In: M. Fracarolli Nunes and C. Lee Park (Eds.). *Business Ethics and Environmental Fraud: Improper Competitive Advantage in the Age of Green*, pp.87–103. Palgrave Macmillan, Cham.

Fracarolli Nunes, M., and Lee Park, C. (2021b). The automotive industry under suspicion. In: M. Fracarolli Nunes and C. Lee Park (Eds.). *Business Ethics and Environmental Fraud: Improper Competitive Advantage in the Age of.* Palgrave Macmillan.

Glaeser, E.L., Di Tella, R., and Llach, L. (2018). Introduction to Argentine exceptionalism. *Latin American Economic Review*, Vol.27, No.1, pp.1–22.

Kwon, H.B., and Lee, J. (2019). Exploring the differential impact of environmental sustainability, operational efficiency, and corporate reputation on market valuation in high-tech-oriented firms. *International Journal of Production Economics*, Vol.211, pp.1–14.

Lepak, D.P., Smith, K.G., and Taylor, M.S. (2007). Value creation and value capture: A multilevel perspective. *Academy of Management Review*, Vol.32, No.1, pp.180–194.

Li, D., Zheng, M., Cao, C., Chen, X., Ren, S., and Huang, M. (2017). The impact of legitimacy pressure and corporate profitability on green innovation: Evidence from China top 100. *Journal of Cleaner Production*, Vol.141, pp.41–49.

Moreno, S.F., Paturlanne, J.L., Mariano, R., and Pérez, S.A. (2021). Desempeño exportador de carne bovina en La Pampa (Argentina): 2003–2019. *Estudios Económicos*, Vol.38, No.77, pp.65–81.

Moretti, V.A., Vieira, M.C., Almeida, L.A., Marques, J.F., and Bicudo Neto, L.C. (2019). Demanda de exportação do suco de laranja concentrado congelado do Brasil para países não produtores. *Revista de Economia e Sociologia Rural*, Vol.25, No.4, pp.403–418.

Novais, F. (1995). *Portugal e Brasil na crise do Antigo Sistema Colonial (1777–1808)*, 6th edition. Hucitec.

Pais, P.S.M., Gomes, M.F.M., and Coronel, D.A. (2012). Análise da competitividade das exportações brasileiras de minério de ferro, de 2000 a 2008. *RAM: Revista de Administração Mackenzie*, Vol.13, pp.121–145.

Pereira, L.B., Bruneau, T.C., and Van Dyke, M. (2019). *Development and Crisis in Brazil, 1930–1983*. Routledge.

Porter, M.E. (1979). How competitive forces shape strategy. *Harvard Business Review*, pp.21–38.

Porter, M.E. (1980). *Competitive Strategy: Techniques for Analyzing Industries and Competitors*. Free Press.

Porter, M.E., and Kramer, M.R. (2011). Creating shared value. *Harvard Business Review*, Vol.89, No.1–2, pp.62–77.

Ramos, C.M., Pizaia, M.G., Caldarelli, C.E., and da Camara, M.R.G. (2020). Competitividade e inserção da soja brasileira no mercado internacional. *Revista de Ciências Agrárias*, Vol.43, No.1, pp.74–85.

Richardson, N.P. (2009). Export-oriented populism: Commodities and coalitions in Argentina. *Studies in Comparative International Development*, Vol.44, No.3, pp.228–255.

Ricupero, R. (2016). O estabelecimento do exclusivo comercial metropolitano e a conformação do antigo sistema colonial no Brasil. *História (São Paulo)*, Vol.35.

Rodrigues, L.M.S., and Marta-Costa, A.A. (2021). Competitividade das exportações de carne bovina do Brasil: Uma análise das vantagens comparativas. *Revista de Economia e Sociologia Rural*, Vol.59.

Rothenberg, S., Pil, F.K., and Maxwell, J. (2001). Lean, green, and the quest for superior environmental performance. *Production and Operations Management*, Vol.10, No.3, pp.228–243.

Rumelt, R.P. (1984). Towards a strategic theory of the firm. In: R. Lamb (Ed.). *Competitive Strategic Management*, pp.556–570. Prentice-Hall.

Vale (2017). *Qual a importância da mineração para a economia do país?* Available at http://www.vale.com/brasil/pt/aboutvale/news/paginas/qual-a-importancia-da-mineracao-para-a-economia-do-pais.aspx

Venn, F. (2016). *The Oil Crisis*. Routledge.

Wernerfelt, B. (1984). A resource-based view of the firm. *Strategic Management Journal*, Vol.5, No.2, pp.171–180.

Womack, J.P., Jones, D.T., and Ross, D. (1990). *The Machine That Changed the World*. Harper Perennial.

Xie, X., Huo, J., and Zou, H. (2019). Green process innovation, green product innovation, and corporate financial performance: A content analysis method. *Journal of Business Research*, Vol.101, pp.697–706.

Part IV

Lessons and Practice

15 Extreme Sustainability Rhetoric

Lessons Learned

Based on the discussions held throughout the book, it may be argued that the maintenance of open attitudes to dialogue yields valuable dividends for disagreeing parties, even if their views never converge. Among the potential benefits is the avoidance of conflicts and the waste of costly resources that they often demand (e.g., time, money). By keeping themselves away from harmful disputes, parties focus on advancing their agendas, saving their energies for what they believe to be constructive goals. Although simplistic, the value of this notion also comes from its broad applicability, as it is suitable to nearly all types of controversies. In the case of politicians and their parties, for instance, the preservation of dialogue with opponents may translate into an increased attention on passing bills that are consistent with their voters' ideas. Regarding the minimization of legal expenses, the conservation of interfaces with opponents can be extremely valuable, since the judicial route is usually privileged precisely when the parties are unable or do not wish to reach an agreement on their own. Even though disagreements can prevail in any situation, they seem to be more common in cases where the communication routes are closed. If there is no point of contact between two different groups, resolving their conflicts will be practically impossible without the help of an outside party.

Evidently, the benefits of maintaining dialogue are not limited to politicians and their parties but can be extended to basically any individual or group that takes part in the public debate. The value of communication channels can be deduced from the resistance of most nations to extinguish their diplomatic relations, even with countries with which they have commercial, ideological, and even territorial disputes. In these cases, embassies tend to function as important elements for the resolution of conflicts. Diplomatic efforts may be seen, then, as formal attempts to keep the lines of dialogue open. In some cases, however, countries fail to reach common terms, with the intermediation of a third country (or a group of countries) appearing as a last alternative to the armed conflict. This approach is similar to the search for a judicial solution to conflicts, which, as previously discussed, is quite common in other contexts. With the sovereignty of national states not bowing to any global authority, the role of the nation or nations acting as intermediaries is merely that of facilitating dialogue, with no power to impose anything on either party.

DOI: 10.4324/9781003124719-19

Among the various factors that may hinder the maintenance or development of dialogue is the will or the necessity of divergent parties to stay away. In the case of political actors, the constant reaffirmation of positions is a manner to satisfy electoral bases, increasing their chances of electoral success. It seems relatively common for politicians to behave in close agreement with their voters, often limiting themselves to channelling the voice and ideas of the portion of the population they represent. From the point of view of political survival (i.e., electoral success), adherence to relatively fixed ideas and speeches guarantees to the political actor an identification with a group of people, which can favour their choice as a representative. In a way, it can be said that politicians depend on maintaining these ideas and even on the continuity of certain problems. If the demands of the groups that support them were resolved, the reason for maintaining them as a representative would be emptied. This need for non-problem solving appears as an important factor in obstructing the dialogues. Often this position can be assumed by both parties involved, which helps them not only to remain isolated but also to radicalize the positions they defend.

In general, it can be said that the maintenance or progress of the dialogue depends fundamentally on the will of the parties, as well as on their understanding of the need and the benefits that a more open posture can bring. In the absence of these conditions, the exchange of ideas and arguments becomes very unlikely, especially in conditions of radicalization. As discussed throughout the chapters, closed positions themselves tend to create their own validation mechanics that seem to favour the emergence and reinforcement of the extremes. As individuals have their coexistence limited to groups that share their ideas, they are not faced with contradictory views or direct questions about their positions. In addition to accelerating the radicalization of ideas, this dynamic helps these individuals to develop the certainty of correcting their assumptions, increasingly distancing them from opposition groups and, consequently, from the possibility of an opening for dialogue. This tendency to close positions and the apparent naturalness of ideological tribalism do not mean that the dialogue between antagonistic parties cannot be restored. For that, some measures are necessary to create a favourable environment, in which the antagonistic parts are somehow brought into contact.

Regarding the dialogue on sustainability, disconnecting the environmental agenda from the political debate is perhaps the main issue to be examined. The fact that discussions about sustainable development are now embedded in ideology means that it inherits all the passions that are typical of those who have opposing views of society. As discussed throughout the book, the environmental debate seems to have been hijacked by political agents, precisely because of its great potential for alarmism and mobilization. With the collapse of socialist/communist systems at the end of the Cold War, left-wing parties around the world found themselves defending a kind of lost and credible cause. Thus, the kidnapping of the environmental cause seems to have been the quickest and most efficient way to fill this void, giving leftist parties a cause to defend and a flag to wield. The choice for the environmental cause was quite convenient because, in addition to being able to be used in the direct fight against economic activities typical of a free market environment, it has a kind of varnish of kindness, as well as the search for equality supposedly defended by the left parties. The ideologization of the environmental discourse ends up putting on the opposite sides people they claim as 'good' (i.e., defenders of nature and equality between men) and the others, associating right-wing thinking (i.e., privilege of freedom over equality) with the destruction of nature.

The mix between sustainability and politics issues ends up producing a combination of ideas that are not possible to dissociate from each other. Among other consequences, this implies the almost automatic association of those concerned with environmental issues with leftist thinking, which can repel individuals more inclined to the right from the debate. The impossibility of discussing issues related to sustainability without entering the ideological debate therefore represents one of the most important barriers to the development of dialogue. As anticipated, this association between the left and environmentalism is not a matter of chance; it is inserted in what can be understood as the search for a sort of 'monopoly of virtues'. In a very simplistic way, this is equivalent to the left claiming for itself everything that it positions as morally correct, while transferring responsibility for the evils of the world to the right. Once again, the disconnection of the debate on sustainability of political ideologies seems to be the main condition for the re-establishment of the dialogue between the extremes.

If this diagnosis is relatively easy, executing a separation between sustainability and political ideology can be very difficult. There are those who believe, for example, that this separation should not be pursued, as politics is the instrument by which social changes occur in democratic environments. The disengagement would therefore result in a retrogression of the debate on sustainability for academic environments, away from the materialization of socio-environmental agendas. In general, those who defend this view are convinced of the urgency of implementing measures to 'save the planet', believing that there is no more space or need for discussion on this issue. In other words, they believe that the dialogue phase is over, and that the moment is for action. Evidently, those who share these dogmatic stances have their ears closed to positions to the contrary and usually label those who question their certainties as denialists and enemies of the planet. The re-establishment of the dialogue involves questioning these dogmas and the perception that the phase of conversation may not be over. In this sense, the reopening of the academic debate can be quite salutary, since in the action phase there is usually no room for disagreements. Thus, the political environment would be suitable not for dialogue, but for imposing the vision of those who are convinced of something about those who question them.

The return to this previous phase does not guarantee, however, the independence of the debate on ideologies. With academics often despising science in the name of their ideological convictions, the space that should be devoted to the debate of ideas and the pursuit of truth is, in many cases, just another stage for worldviews to be imposed on students. Untying the themes of sustainability from ideological views would require a greater focus on scientific data and less attention to the search for interpretations that favour certain worldviews. From an epistemological point of view, it can be argued that the treatment of environmental issues through an objectivist prism can be quite beneficial for its ideological decontamination. In fact, subjectivism seems to favour the misuse of data, which is usually inclined to subscribe to political ideas.

This greater focus on scientific data depends on a joint effort by the whole of society. The media, however, seems to play a key role in this matter. It is necessary, for example, that newspapers, magazines, and television programs favour the transmission of the opinions of researchers and scientists on the subject, including those who present contradictory opinions. The opening of this space would contribute not only to providing credible data to the average population but would also replicate the scientific process itself (i.e., a collective construction, based on argumentation and counter-argumentation). What we see today is a large part of the media debate being led by popular figures, including politicians, actors, singers, and activists. In addition to, in general, not having the academic preparation to debate subjects of greater complexity, the transmission of the opinions of these characters can be very harmful, since they tend to have the sympathy of large portions of the public. This ends up spreading simplistic and sometimes wrong views, increasing the chances of polarization and interruption of the dialogue.

The re-establishment of the dialogue on environmental issues also requires an awareness that its many themes and sub-themes are of great complexity, and that they will hardly have the unanimity of specialists. This is equivalent to the recognition that the debate on sustainability will probably be conducted not on the basis of certainties, but rather on doubts and a constant questioning of the various positions presented. The acceptance of this premise avoids the adoption of dogmas that, as previously discussed, inhibit the discussion. The adoption of a humbler posture in the face of the great complexity of the debate may, therefore, nurture the exchange of ideas. Once again, favouring the opinions of researchers and scientists can be very beneficial in this regard, since these dynamics are also characteristic of the scientific method.

Establishing an open and productive dialogue on issues involving sustainable development would also benefit enormously from a better understanding of Elkington's (1997) triple bottom line in business. Although widely disseminated among scholars, the author's conception of sustainability still seems to be largely ignored by the lay public and even by environmental activists. The idea that sustainability resides in the intersection between social, environmental, and economic objectives can be very useful in solving some of the most heated debates regarding environmental preservation. Issues related to the preservation of the Amazon rainforest, for example, could benefit greatly if the three dimensions were considered. Currently, there seems to be an imbalance in favour of the environmental performance of the region, which often translates into the absolute preservation of the forest, ideally without any human intervention other than the activities developed by the indigenous peoples. This includes a practically total opposition to burning and deforestation, as well as to economic activities that, to some extent, are based on such practices as agriculture, livestock, extraction, and mining. It is common for politicians and artists to publicly oppose anything that threatens the absolute integrity of the jungle, often based on half-truths or absolute lies. In the beginning of 2019, France's President Emmanuel Macron demonstrated this on social networks, strongly condemning the burning in the Amazon rainforest. At the time, he published a photo of a fire that dated 1989 as if it portrayed the situation at that moment. In addition to misleading the population, the use of images that do not correspond to reality can be understood as an act of great gravity, either because it is a gross error or because it denotes the dishonesty and bad faith of those who do it.

Supporters of these more radical stances seem to ignore, however, that approximately 29 million people live in the Brazilian Amazon alone (Oliveira, 2020) who, like every human being around the planet, have basic needs in terms of access to a minimal variety of nutrients, sewage treatment, medical care, security, and education, among others. These needs can only be fulfilled through the economic development of the region, which, to some extent, is at odds with those who defend the view that the forest must be kept absolutely intact. In these cases, the prioritization of the environmental dimension will result in the total annulment of social and economic aspects, which, as discussed throughout the book, is the opposite of the assumptions of the triple bottom line in business. It is possible, therefore, to point to the Amazon as an ideal case for the implementation of sustainable development, in which the correct economic exploitation of the forest can guarantee a dignified life for generations of its inhabitants. If done in a truly sustainable way and in full accordance with the environmental legislation in force, the development of economic activities can guarantee the forest's own survival.

The defence of something other than keeping the forest intact usually generates exacerbated reactions, precisely because this view has become a dogma. The repetition of these opinions over decades seems to have shaped public opinion, which, ignoring the real situation in the Amazon, usually echoes these voices without due reflection. It is common, for instance, that worn and long denied by science expressions are used as sensational slogans, both by the masses and by world leaders. Expressions such as 'the Amazon is the lung of the world', for example, are often remembered on these occasions, as if the region was responsible for most of the production of oxygen that the world population breathes. This hypothesis is highly controversial, with many experts arguing that the forest consumes almost all of the oxygen it produces, with a very low or even zero balance. Marine plankton is also often cited as the source of most of the oxygen available on the planet.

Those who advocate a more open debate on the possibilities of sustainable development in the Amazon are, in general, labelled as enemies of the environment, having their opinions treated as a form of scientific denialism. The same occurs with those who question the premises of global warming, especially those that refer to the relevance of human activity in this regard. Simply questioning the ideas taken for granted (e.g., global warming is the result of economic activity) can have serious consequences for the careers of scientists and public figures. It is common, for example, that hypotheses linking global warming to solar cycles (i.e., variation of radiation emitted by the sun) or to the very natural dynamics of the planet are quickly dismissed and treated as denialists. The discrediting of conflicting opinions and the stigmatization of those who defend them work as an important factor in interrupting the dialogue, which, as discussed in Chapter 2, is largely composed of the meeting and eventual confrontation of ideas.

In a practical way, it is necessary that everyone involved in the public debate on sustainability be aware of these forms of dogmatic censorship and, as much as they disagree with the opposite opinions, protect the right of expression of those who defend them. This attitude is a fundamental condition for the maintenance of communication bridges, without which one cannot experience a real evolution towards sustainable development. Unfortunately, to expect this more respectful attitude toward other people's views to appear spontaneously is not reasonable, and this expectation is even a demonstration of innocence. It is difficult to imagine that radicalized people – and therefore convinced of the correctness and fairness of their ideas – will voluntarily make room for intellectual opponents. The belief that they are acting in defence of the right cause gives them a perception of moral superiority that, from an authoritarian point of view, justifies more aggressive attitudes regarding the stifling of contrary views. It is common for this search to eliminate dissenting thinking from public debate to take place through intimidation of the most varied types. In the case of university students, for example, students who defend ideas incongruent with those of hegemonic thinking can be harassed both by their colleagues and by teachers and employees of the institutions they attend. In the first case, peer pressure can occur in the form of total or partial isolation of dissenters, who are now classified as not belonging to the group as an ideological enemy. This discrimination can manifest itself in the exclusion of dissenters from social activities organized by students such as study groups, sports practices, and discussions to improve study conditions, among many others. It is also possible that the disagreement leads to other forms of hostility that can even involve physical confrontations between students.

Regarding the pressure exerted by teachers and professors, the power attributed to them is usually quite effective as a practice of intellectual coercion. As discussed throughout the book, the high degree of subjectivity that sometimes occurs in the processes of evaluating academic performance gives faculty members a great influence on the behaviour of students who, at times, may even come to defend ideas with which they cannot agree for fear of retaliation. Intellectual coercion to dissenting teachers and professors can originate from both students and co-workers, especially other faculty. In the first case, classroom discussions tend to be monitored and combated if they are not in accordance with the dominant ideological position. In the case of pressures exerted by other teachers/professors, it is possible to point to several possibilities, the exclusion of those who do not fit political circles being very common. Another form of coercion refers to limiting access to research funds, which can have a negative impact on the development of the academic career of those who are prevented from developing their investigations in the best way. This mechanism for combating ideas is particularly perverse because it transforms educational institutions – especially universities – into centres for the propagation of ideologies.

In this sense, the interruption of the dialogue removes from academic environments the possibility of really contributing to the advancement of knowledge and to the search for the truth that, as discussed in Chapter 2, depends on the confrontation of ideas. As a result, in many cases educational institutions end up becoming addicted environments and, in general, little open to contradictory, where dogmas are created and defended. The fact that many teachers/professors and students behave in this way is particularly serious, since social elites are generally expected to be aware of the importance of dialogue and to seek to promote it. Once again, the fact that the intellectual elite is largely imbued with ideology seems to contribute to not only being negligent in building bridges between different ways of seeing the world, but often acting deliberately to eliminate the possible communication channels. The same goes for the political elite, which, as discussed earlier, often takes shelter in the defence of extreme positions, especially when they are more accepted by voters. With regard to the economic elite, it often seems to be outside the public debate or aligned with the political elite, including financing the latter's projects. The famous 'I disapprove of what you say, but I will defend to the death your right to say it' (Hall, 1906, p.199), attributed to Voltaire's thinking, illustrates the spirit of tolerance and openness to dialogue that seems to be lacking for those who should be the first to defend them.

From the point of view of classifying the methods employed, the mechanisms of coercion used by social elites against those who seek to express contradictory views can be understood as a new form of fascism, in which a hegemonic view is defended with the use of various types of violence. In addition to the issues discussed previously in the context of the academic environment, it is possible to identify similar initiatives in basically all public spaces. Threats of dismissal to journalists, for example, seem not to be rare, especially when they seek to reveal facts that go against mainstream views. Boycotts of artists who do not profess hegemonic beliefs, whether from a political, economic, or environmental point of view, also seem common. These and other practices seem to be part of what is conventionally called the *culture of cancellation*, which, among other things seeks to eliminate dissenting voices. In a sense, this is similar to the process known as ostracism, in which people who somehow displeased society were forced to withdraw from the city limits, isolating themselves from those who decided to live together. The political practice was especially exercised in the Ancient Greece (Encyclopaedia Britannica, 2021). Regarding the maintenance of the dialogue on issues related to sustainability and sustainable development, the culture of cancellation appears as one of the main destructive elements, preventing dissonant voices from manifesting themselves.

Within its umbrella, it is also possible to identify the dehumanization practices of opponents, something that can be quite harmful even from the point of view of the physical security of those who are victims of this process. In general, the dehumanization process consists of classifying opponents as representatives of everything that is bad or that in some way prevents or hinders the progress of what is understood as correct or necessary. As a consequence, any attack on these people is understood to be fair, with opponents losing rights that would be natural to a human being (e.g., pity, empathy). Despite materializing in the most diverse contexts, dehumanization processes seem to be more common in the clash between progressive and more radical conservatives, with the first group usually dehumanizing the second precisely because they see them as an obstacle to social developments considered as urgent.

Modern forms of censorship are also an important pillar of the culture of cancellation, especially on social media. Blocking posts and even banning users due to the expression of their opinions seems to be increasingly common in these environments. Digital censorship often ends up being accepted and even celebrated by many people who claim to be democrats and defenders of free speech. This permissive attitude seems to be more common when those who are censored are identified as opponents or enemies, and should therefore have their opinions suppressed according to the judgment of those who believe in the correction of such processes of exclusion from the public debate. Both digital censorship and its approval can be understood as authoritarian and contrary to the maintenance of public debate. This behaviour is, in fact, the precise opposite of what is expected of a defender of democracy and freedom of expression, who should be concerned mainly with the possibility of those with whom he disagrees to speak out.

Like individuals, organizations have also been increasingly targeted by attacks and coercions by groups that wish to control them indirectly. Public shaming practices and boycott threats are among the techniques used by activists, NGOs, and radicalized virtual groups that aim to impose their worldviews through the eventual destruction of intangible assets (e.g., brand, corporate image, reputation, credibility), and by potential financial loss that these techniques can cause. Although these proto-fascist initiatives target various types of organizations and state and government institutions (e.g., parliaments, courts, ministries), companies appear to be among the main victims of this type of blackmail. For fear of the possible negative consequences of these attacks, in many cases entrepreneurs and managers end up giving in to the pressures and adapting themselves to the will of those who coerce them. Among other consequences, this is reflected in the annulment of sponsorship to artists and athletes who defend different positions from the political, economic, social, or any other possibly controversial point of view.

Although condemned under the most diverse aspects, it is necessary to recognize the effectiveness of the set of fascist measures that, at the end of the accounts, seek to impose opinions and ideologies through the prohibition of public debate. Due to the immense destructive power of these methods, it is essential that free and democratic societies remain attentive to their use, since the extermination of dissenting voices usually results in the implantation of dictatorships. In this sense, more than a prescriptive measure for the dialogue on sustainability to be strengthened – or even made feasible – the fight against ideological fascism and opinions is a fundamental condition for the maintenance of the democratic rule of law and must be stopped by all those who they understand its essentiality and regard it as an essential condition for a minimally healthy social life.

By now, the reader should be convinced that the book deals with the topic of extreme sustainability rhetoric in a very comprehensive way, with the impacts of this practice on the progress of sustainable development being approached in an interdisciplinary way. In this sense, the 14 previous chapters sought to integrate thoughts from the most diverse areas of knowledge, aiming to highlight how the different views on the subject communicate. While this more general approach can contribute to building a more holistic understanding of the topics covered, it also adds an important degree of complexity to the discussions. In Chapter 1 ('Sustainability Rhetoric'), discussions of rhetorical sustainability are presented, with some of the arguments that form the basis of further discussions introduced. In particular, the concept of rhetoric and its uses over time are approached in greater detail. In this sense, rhetoric is treated as one of the most important instruments used by those who seek to advance political, economic, philosophical, or any other ideas. Among the main contributions of the chapter is the discussion on the importance of rhetoric in the debate on sustainability. More specifically, the pointing out of exaggerations as a source of damage to the environmentalist cause provides the main framework on which the other discussions in the book are based. Starting from this initial idea, the following chapters address, for example, the impact that the misuse of sustainability rhetoric can have on the quality of public debate, with its instrumentalization of discussions on sustainable development by political groups being particularly harmful. Likewise, the discussions presented in the initial chapter support the arguments that issues related to the environment are often used as a facade, with the signalization of virtues hiding hidden interests. Among the most common would be the pursuit of advancing ideologies, the immoral pursuit of profits, and economic protectionism.

In the second chapter ('Sustainability Dialogue'), the concept of dialogue is discussed. Similar to the treatment given to the idea of rhetoric in the previous chapter, the historical origins and different understandings of the topic are presented. The development of the typologies of the dialogue and the discussions about its possible causes, objectives, and forms represent one of the main contributions of the chapter, with the usefulness of these propositions possibly extending beyond the debate on sustainable development. It is possible that these ideas will find use in understanding the role of dialogue more comprehensively, with the insights presented allowing better use of exchanges between stakeholders on other issues. Regarding the development of dialogues directly related to sustainability, discussions on the need to agree on assumptions are particularly useful. In this sense, the chapter opens space for the debate on the impossibility of dialogue between extremists. Parting from the argument that agreement on topics such as the existence of environmental problems and the impact of human activities is essential for the search for solutions, this debate shapes many of the topics covered later in the book. Among them, discussions about the nature and psychology of environmentalist skeptics, as well as those who harbour extreme views of the opposite side.

Considering the premise that positions on sustainability are largely based on political and economic beliefs, Chapter 3 ('Right Thinking, Left Thinking') addresses some of the most relevant issues in the formation of ideological thinking. This discussion introduces the basic concepts for building a political/

economical spectrum in the next chapter. The addition of more specific aspects about the ideological dynamics of the left and the right in their different shades, as well as a more analytical look at the positions considered to be exempt (i.e., centre) complement the reasoning. These and other issues culminate in the development of the *sustainability spectrum*. Thus, the two chapters should be understood as complementary. Among the main take-aways of Chapter 3 is the idea that the creation of an ideal vision of society must result in a natural conflict with reality, with the latter usually proving to be different from what conceptual and theoretical models assume. The chapter serves as a warning so that mistakes made in the development of political and economic debate are not repeated in discussions on sustainability. In addition to allowing for the prescription of eminently practical measures in this direction, the discussions reinforce the urgency of dissociating the environmental issue from other interests. This reinforces one of the book's central arguments, according to which dialogue on sustainability should be favoured, as debates on the topic are 'decontaminated' from an ideological agenda.

Based on discussions on different political, economic, and ideological views, Chapter 4 ('The *Sustainability Spectrum*') develops the framework as a way of helping to locate different public actors in terms of their positioning on issues related to sustainable development. Particularly important in this sense are the discussions about the origin of ideas of thoughts generically classified as right-wing or left-wing. Starting from an analysis of the importance of values referring to the freedom of individuals and equality between them for each of these groups, a political-economic spectrum is constructed as a support for the development of the *sustainability spectrum*. Among the main contributions of the chapter is the proposition of a more detailed discussion on the link between relatively well-established political and economic thoughts with the debate on sustainability still in development. In addition to providing a better understanding of the processes of creation of the proposed classification, this association provides the basis for many of the discussions developed throughout the book. In particular, the association between ideologies and sustainability reinforce the arguments presented in Chapter 2, according to which this connection represents one of the main causes for the interruption or non-development of constructive dialogues on sustainable development.

In Chapter 5 ('Skeptical Views of Sustainability'), the most striking aspects of the right pole of the *sustainability spectrum* are discussed. Through a debate on the main features of the relationship between sustainability and skepticism, the social and psychological dynamics that lead to the most aggressive forms of environmental denial are developed. In addition to considering the philosophical origins and roots of skepticism itself, this includes locating the different currents of thought that can somehow contribute to the development of postures that are refractory to discussions around themes associated with sustainability and sustainable development. According to the arguments presented in the chapter and throughout the book, one of the main causes for the development of extreme forms of environmental denial is the association between sustainable development and the different political and economic visions that have been associated with it throughout the time. In this way, the same repulsion that an individual associated with a thought understood as right-wing feels in relation to left-wing ideologies will be reproduced in her/his relationship with sustainability if s/he is not able to dissociate one from the other. The perception that environmental issues are used for merely electoral purposes or for the advancement of ideologies represents one of the biggest factors in creating opposing views. It can be said that, in a general way, radically skeptical positions are, in many cases, direct consequences of the instrumentalization of the environmental debate by the groups that dispute political power. Among the main contributions of the chapter is the schematization of the processes of construction of environmental skepticism, as well as the way in which it feeds various forms of denial. In this sense, the chapter contributes to a better understanding of one of the most extreme forms of relationship with themes related to sustainability. Discussions aimed at clarifying points still poorly understood about the origins and causes of radical positions, and the proposed perspectives are particularly relevant because of their potential to facilitate the construction or re-establishment of dialogue.

Similar to the discussions on extreme forms of denial proposed in the previous chapter, Chapter 6 ('Apocalyptic Views of Sustainability') addresses some of the most relevant characteristics of those who inhabit the left pole of the *sustainability spectrum*. The discussions presented in the chapter contribute to a better understanding of the nature, causes, and effects of the most extreme views. Regarding the first, it can be said that the proposed debate characterizes apocalyptic discourses as exaggerated and representative of a distorted view of reality. If the understanding that omissions on environmental issues can in fact result in the deterioration of the conditions necessary for sustainable development are valid, the association of these possibilities with progressively shorter deadlines contributes to the environmentalist discourse being viewed with suspicion by the recipients of this message. In this context, the chapter addresses the instrumentalization of the environmental cause by politicians as one of the great vectors of radicalization. Among other issues, this is due to the fact that both candidates and holders of elected positions seek to adjust environmental issues to the deadlines of elections. Thus, the arguments stating that environmental issues resulted in very serious consequences within a relatively short period of time would have as their main objective the presentation of the politicians who propagate them as solutions for the referred emergencies, such that they are deserving of the votes of those who want to save the planet.

Completing the discussions on the different positions that individuals can occupy in the *sustainability spectrum*, the last chapter of the first part of the book (Chapter 7, 'Moderate Views of Sustainability') deals with the more moderate opinions, which are, consequently, relatively equidistant from the poles. In this way, the perspectives of so-called average citizens are discussed, with the reasons why they distance themselves from extreme views being particularly relevant. Even before proceeding with the discussions, it is necessary to point out the limitations of this approach. First, the great variability of possible positions must be considered, so that the determination of an average understanding is, by definition, imprecise. Thus, there is no intention here to present a definitive profile of those who occupy the intermediate layers of public opinion. On the contrary, the chapter seeks to draw attention to the wide variety of perspectives present in this great grey area. The chapter is important because it provides a counterpoint to extreme views, presenting the opinions of those who do not understand the debate on sustainable development as a priority. On the contrary, the individuals that make up this segment tend to be more concerned with everyday aspects and more directly related to their well-being. Aspects related to housing, security, health, employment, and education would receive greater attention. This does not mean, however, that these people are necessarily alienated or that they intentionally ignore discussions about sustainability. Many of them usually exercise a set of good practices, which includes simple everyday attitudes such as the search for reducing their consumption of natural resources (e.g., water) or separating recyclable waste.

The fact that a relatively large portion of the population fits this profile increases the relevance of the discussions, since they can decide elections or determine consumption patterns. From a statistical point of view, it can be assumed that those who make up the positions closest to the centre of the *sustainability spectrum* form the majority of consumers and voters, with their positions expressing, to some extent, their lack of interest in the political and economic. In this sense, the debate of the reasons for their immunities to extreme views is particularly helpful. As discussed in the chapter and throughout the book, while deeper ideological debates seem to be more common among those who, in a certain way, form an intellectual elite (e.g., professors, teachers, students, journalists), the instrumentalization of the environmental debate by political groups may have alienated those less interested in these topics. Continuing the discussions developed in the previous chapters, the consideration of moderate perspectives constitutes an important step in the development of the *sustainability spectrum*. In this set, understanding issues such as the profile of those who hold more neutral opinions, as well as the causes of these positions, can contribute to a greater understanding of extreme positions. From a broader point of view, it can be said that moderate opinions are part of the repertoire of the average citizen.

Chapter 8, 'Psychology of Extremism', discusses the role of emotions in the construction of extremism thinking and behaviour. In particular, the impact of some of the most common human reactions (e.g., envy) in the development of radical attitudes is approached from a holistic perspective. The origins and effects of these issues on the debate around sustainable development are examined, with the contribution of emotions to the distancing of those with opposing views being highlighted. In addition to emphasizing the importance of aspects that are often overlooked in the analysis of the public debate on sustainability, the chapter provides the basis for a better understanding of the reasons why groups considered as rivals behave in a certain way. A better understanding of the psychological issues that shape extreme behaviour can be quite useful for those who seek to re-establish dialogue with groups that oppose dissenting positions. In this sense, the exposure of some of the factors influencing the behavioural profile of individuals most strongly associated with ideological thoughts gains importance.

The main contribution of Chapter 9 ('Sustainability, Politics, and Money') lies in the detailing of the complex relationships that are established between politics and sustainability, as well as the use of these issues for purely economic purposes. In this sense, the chapter can be understood as an analysis of the many deviations of purpose that occur when using environmental discourse. Particularly relevant in this direction are the discussions on the misuse of environmental issues by candidates for elective positions, with these practices being understood as modern forms of populism. Likewise, the debate on the different levels of relevance attributed to environmental debate in democracies and dictatorships allows for a better understanding of the importance of the different forms of pressure exerted by public opinion. In this context, the development of the *sustainability needs* pyramid, adapted from Maslow's framework to sustainable development, represents a possibly relevant addition to the debate, helping to better understand environmental priorities in terms of the different situations faced by societies around the world.

Among the main contributions of Chapter 10 ('Panic, Sustainability, and Marketing') is the discussion of some of the ways in which the discourse on sustainability can be formatted in order to generate extreme sensations and, as a consequence, condition public opinion in a certain sense. The electoral uses of environmental issues are highlighted, with the adequacy of topics related to sustainable development to the electoral calendar being pointed out as one of the main factors of instability in the public debate. Likewise, the chapter points to the main ways in which companies seem to take advantage of the pessimism caused by messages that fuel a sense of urgency, while offering products and services considered environmentally friendly as the most common response. Thus, the chapter offers some warnings for voters and consumers to realize the possible manipulations to which they are subjected, separating messages that actually seek to promote sustainable development from those that only aim to bear fruit to those who propagate them irresponsibly.

In Chapter 11 ('Science and the Erosion of Credibility Capital'), the effects of the association between science and the misuse of environmental discourse are discussed. In particular, the use of the reputational capital of universities and academics as a way of validating radical and targeted discourses is approached as a particularly dangerous practice. While these issues can favour vested interests, they can compromise the way scientists and centuries-old institutions are seen by different stakeholder groups. Thus, the chapter draws attention to the need for decoupling the personal beliefs of scientists from their positions on environmental issues. The importance of separating ideological aspects and increasing objectivity in the analysis is reinforced, configuring the main message conveyed by this discussion.

Chapter 12 ('Eco-Anxiety and Other Psychological Outcomes'), in turn, deals with some of the more immediate consequences of the misuse of exaggerated and hyperbolic speech. With regard specifically to the environmental debate, discussions focus on the harmful effects that the constant projection of apocalyptic scenarios can have on more sensitive people. In addition to increasing the likelihood that these individuals will succumb to radicalism, too much exposure to a pessimistic outlook can have major effects on their physical and emotional health. The reflections presented contribute to a more responsible use of environmental rhetoric as a way of avoiding extremism and contributing to the maintenance of dialogue.

Chapter 13 ('Dialogue and Collaboration') treats the many advantages that maintaining dialogue can offer those willing to accept the sacrifices it demands. In this sense, the search for greater openness to contrary ideas and the development of a degree of tolerance and understanding are proposed as necessary investments to achieve these goals. Thus, the chapter helps those who wish to increase the space for the exchange of ideas and thus contribute to the progress of sustainable development in a productive way, to be able to recognize more quickly the benefits associated with this posture.

Finally, Chapter 14 ('Economic Development and Innovation') deals with some of the aspects linking sustainable development to profit generation, analysing how the economic power of large industrial conglomerates can function as a market concentrating mechanism. The fact that the reduction of environmental impacts often depends on the development of new technologies is discussed as an entry barrier, which ensures that only a relatively small number of economic actors can benefit from the provision of goods and services that will satisfy the demand for green items. Thus, the chapter offers a means for this dynamic to be better understood and, ideally, treated, in order to guarantee the minimum conditions for a greater number of small and medium-sized companies to participate in the market for environmental solutions. This movement is understood as a potentially positive factor, with increased competition increasing the likelihood that more environmental solutions will be developed.

References

Hall, E.B. (1906). *The Friends of Voltaire*. Smith Elder & Company.

Encyclopaedia Britannica (2021). *Ostracism*. Available at https://www.britannica.com/topic/ostracism

Oliveira, L.H. (2020). População da Amazônia Legal ultrapassa 29 milhoes de pessoas, estima IBGE. *Agência Cenarium*, August 27. Available at https://agenciacenarium.com.br/populacao-na-amazonia-legal-ultrapassa-29-milhoes-de-pessoas-estima-ibge/

16 Reconnecting Dialogue in Sustainability

Prescriptive Measures

Introduction

As a result of the discussions conducted throughout the book, ten prescriptive measures are proposed so that the dialogue around sustainability and social development can be resumed, reinforced, or even built. The maintenance of favourable terrain for the confrontation of ideas, however, depends fundamentally on the will of the parties, with external initiatives having modest impacts. This does not mean that those interested in establishing a dialogue should not seek to create an atmosphere that favours it. Yet, openness to contrary ideas seems to be much more conditioned to a gain of personal conscience, according to which the benefits of exchanging ideas and values with those who see reality in a different way are better perceived. Thus, the prescriptive measures discussed next are intended to help those who wish to move in this direction. At the same time, more structural issues are also discussed so that the reasons why many people are averse to contradiction are better understood.

The Bursting of Cognitive Bubbles (Clusters)

As discussed, the almost exclusive coexistence of individuals who share similar views creates a mechanism for validating ideas that favours extremism and the interruption of dialogue. The absence of the contradictory can be understood as the very failure of dialogue, with the creation of hegemonic and dogmatic visions being among the most harmful effects of these dynamics. Despite affecting the most diverse dimensions of society, these issues seem to be particularly important with regard to the debate on sustainability and social development. Thus, the bursting of cognitive bubbles appears to be indeed a fundamental measure for advancing the exchange of ideas.

It is possible to identify some particularly fertile grounds for the creation of these clusters. The most obvious is, perhaps, that of social networks. Despite being often classified as the 'new public square', social networks often end up preventing contradictory ideas and thoughts from crossing. Through their complex algorithms, they seem to control the distribution of ideas, deciding directly or indirectly who will have access to the created content. People who are more

DOI: 10.4324/9781003124719-20

interested in certain topics, for example, tend to receive suggestions for videos and contacts related to what they are most excited about, guaranteeing them potentially more pleasant moments. From a marketing point of view, this kind of shielding of users can be understood as an attempt to maximize the customer experience and, consequently, the profit potential of the companies that manage these platforms. The maintenance of social networks' current business model can therefore be considered a major impediment to the bursting of the cognitive bubbles that were created in these environments, as well as to preventing new bubbles from forming. The cultivation of a 'comfortable' zone (i.e., where the confrontation of ideas is non-existent or minimal) aims to maximize the time users spend connected. In a logic similar to that used by radio and television companies for decades, social networks generally seek to extend their audience to increase their attractiveness to advertisers. This dynamic derives a large part of the profits of companies that manage user-to-user platforms. Given the adverse consequences of ideological clusters, it is possible to argue that the great challenge faced by social networks in terms of social and environmental responsibility is precisely the sacrifice of their profitability in the name of creating healthier environments for the development of dialogue. In this sense, the triple bottom line in business (Elkington, 1997) appears, once again, as the appropriate framework, as discussed later in the chapter.

The idea that the companies that control social networks would be willing to sacrifice their profits to promote dialogue may seem naive at first. However, it is possible that they themselves recognize the need to do so as a way of guaranteeing their long-term survival. Despite currently acting hegemonic, the monopoly of the most consolidated social networks may not be eternal. With thousands of entrepreneurs continually innovating and nascent technology companies receiving huge financial contributions from venture capitalists, the likelihood that competitors will consolidate in the near future seems not to be negligible. New companies can be particularly threatening if they commit to maintaining an absolutely democratic space for dialogue and, consequently, full respect for freedom of expression. These issues seem to be part of the concerns of administrators and investors of current social networks, since the acquisition of potential competitors appears as one of the strategies adopted to protect their business models.

Despite being arguably efficient, this dynamic can have its limits, which is still a source of hope for those who dream of seeing dialogue thrive on social networks. The solution via competition is preferable to all others, especially those that could be given through legal impositions. The emergence of alternatives that pay for the maintenance of dialogue would naturally attract the interested public. It remains to be seen whether the number of people willing to continually face contradictory views would be large enough to guarantee the economic viability of these businesses. Thus, if it is not up to governments to force current social networks to change their functioning to open space for dialogue, they must guarantee the maintenance of a free market environment, which, in turn, can generate alternatives in this sense. The rigorous fight against the formation of oligopolies and cartels is particularly important to achieve this objective. It can be said, therefore, that the guarantee of the conditions inherent to a free market can be configured as an important ally of dialogue on social networks.

While government interventions in the functioning of private companies must be condemned, the same is not true of the institutions that make up the State apparatus. Thus, it is expected that governments act in public universities so that they can in truth fulfil their social function. It is clearly not a matter of pursuing any political or ideological visions, or issues related to sustainability. Government actions should be just the opposite, ensuring that dissenting voices can express themselves freely in the university environment, so that dialogue and the debate of ideas are promoted in a healthy and productive way. In a practical and objective way, it is necessary for governments to combat the fascist methods of coercion described above, which seek to impose worldviews to create or maintain the hegemony of certain ideas among professors, instructors, students, and employees of educational institutions. Regrettably, the fight against university cognitive clusters by governments is, in general, unlikely, precisely because the university public represents important political instruments, both in terms of direct votes and in terms of the influence that the academic community has on society. This issue is linked to the decoupling of sustainability issues from political and economic ideologies, as follows.

Dissociation of the Sustainability Debate From Economic and Political Ideologies

Although probably utopian, dissociating the debate on sustainability from political and economic ideologies would be extremely beneficial for reopening the dialogue on sustainable development. The idealistic character of this separation does not result from a hypothetical natural intersection of the themes, or from the need to support the debate on sustainability on more well-founded theories and concepts. On the contrary, this disconnection is unlikely due to the fact that themes related to sustainability are of great use for the dissemination of political ideas, as well as for increasing the acceptance of these classes among voters. In the same way, many of the measures defended as necessary in the fight against the destruction of the planet are in line with certain ideas about economic planning, in addition to favouring the authoritarianism of rulers through greater control over the lives of citizens and the increase in taxes.

Spotting Hypocrisy

The perception that those who appear to be engaged in the environmental cause behave differently from what they prescribe greatly compromises the credibility of their messages. Recent episodes involving politicians, mega-businessmen, and celebrities illustrate the point. In 2019, several people from these groups gathered on the Italian island of Sicilia to discuss measures to be taken against global warming, in a meeting that attracted famous artists, billionaires, and even members of the British royal family. One of the biggest sources of criticism for the participants stems from the fact that most of them travelled to the event in small and medium-sized private planes. In addition to representing a high cost from an economic point of view, the use of these planes results in significant greenhouse gas (GHG) emissions, even when compared to other alternatives for accessing the event site (English et al., 2019). Given the backlash of the episode, Prince Harry was satirically nicknamed 'Carbon Footprince' (Bryant, 2019; Fracarolli Nunes and Lee Park, 2021) in reference to the damaging impact of his trip on the environment.

Emissions from international travel in the name of the environmental cause do indeed seem to make a bad impression on the general public. Anticipation of this problem and the search for an alternative solution, however, did not save Swedish activist Greta Thunberg from heavy criticism during her transatlantic trip towards a UN summit in New York dedicated precisely to discussions on zero emissions goals. At the time, she opted for a solar-powered boat for the trip, which would apparently guarantee a minimum level of emissions along the way, especially compared to the aerial alternative (Watts, 2019). The motivation for the most scathing criticism came from information that an entire crew would travel by plane to take the boat back to Europe, totalling six round-trip air tickets. Thus, the use of the boat would have multiplied the emissions of the trip, having a significantly greater impact than what would have been observed if the activist had chosen to travel by plane from the first moment (France 24, 2019).

In the face of these and other matters, it is possible to argue that either those responsible for the trip are not able to calculate the environmental impacts of their choices in a holistic way, or they use alternative transport only to sustain an environmentally correct facade, even if the impact for the environment is greater. Whether due to ignorance or bad faith, the fact is that these and other similar episodes contribute to the destruction of the credibility of those who not only say they are concerned but also want to impose their ideas and solutions on other people. The perception of a detachment between discourse and environmental practice is also observed in the consumption habits of many activists, whether famous or not. The consumption of large amounts of clothing, for example, indicates indifference to the social and environmental impacts of the fashion industry, just as the consumption of meat denotes an alienation or even a disdain about the damages of cattle raising and practices such as overfishing for the sustainable development.

The quest to create a better image with the public leads many celebrities to adopt consumption habits that, despite being apparently responsible from an environmental point of view, may not be necessarily less aggressive than traditional alternatives. This seems to be the case with celebrities' general preference for electric cars. Contrary to what one might imagine at first, the environmental impact of electric vehicles is far from zero. The fact that they do not emit CO_2 when in operation often leads consumers to ignore the full impact of their production. A more holistic view of the production of the batteries that equip them, for example, may already be enough to support a more critical view. Among other issues, lithium – the main component of batteries – can be pointed out as the source of a series of environmental and social issues that are usually ignored. First, it is necessary to consider that it is a non-renewable resource that is extracted through mining processes, generally extremely aggressive from an environmental point of view. The social impacts of the exploitation of this material must also be considered. With many of the lithium mines located in poor countries and even in troubled conflict zones, it is not uncommon for children to be employed in them, or for minimum safety conditions to be offered to workers. Likewise, there are several reports of disrespect for the fundamental rights of workers, and even situations classified as modern slavery.

In addition to these issues related to failures from the point of view of social performance, it is also necessary to consider the various environmental problems related to the production of electric energy itself. The production of hydroelectric energy, for instance, usually requires the flooding of large areas, destroying the natural habitat of plants and animals. The creation of dams and the interference in the flow of rivers are associated with several problems for the reproduction of several species of fish, as well as other aquatic animals. The generation of wind energy, in turn, is identified as responsible for the death of birds, mainly because the turbines are positioned to capture air currents that are used by birds, ducks, and other animals as a kind of aerial highway. Likewise, solar energy is seen as an additional element of global warming, precisely because it stores the energy of solar rays, which would be partially reflected. Furthermore, the solar panels are also built on lithium, reinforcing the previously discussed issues regarding the extraction and use of this material. The use of electric energy demands the production of a series of lithium batteries along with those used in automobiles, used as a form of storage.

In the face of all these issues, the argument that electric cars are less problematic than those powered by fossil fuels (e.g., diesel) lose steam. As a result, the perception that the use of electric cars only works as a green facade fuels the notion that the activists who drive them are somewhat hypocritical. In addition to the other points discussed, it is possible to argue that this loss of credibility arising from a discourse incoherent with practice does not contribute to the restoration of dialogue. On the contrary, the impression that one of the parties does not treat the issues with due seriousness usually causes an interruption of exchanges with those really concerned with advancing the sustainable development agenda.

Reinforcement of Objectivism

As discussed in more detail in Chapter 6, the apocalyptic perspectives commonly associated with sustainability issues can be responsible for a number of psychological disturbances, especially in emotionally sensitive people. The idea that the 'end of the world' is fast approaching seems to generate feelings of anguish, anxiety, and fear in those who believe in the most catastrophic predictions. People in these conditions cannot be expected to be open for dialogue. On the contrary, the panic that grips them will likely make them immune to any argument that goes against their most acute beliefs. The sense of urgency will drive them to the action stage, where drastic actions are justifiable. Given the difficulty, or even the impossibility, of establishing an argument with people steeped in negative perceptions of reality, the separation between facts and feelings appears as an essential condition for the construction of dialogue on sustainability.

In a pragmatic way, this is equivalent to a greater focus on data and empirical evidence, which even favours a scientific perspective on the subject. As highlighted earlier, it is possible that, from an epistemological perspective, objectivism is more suitable to address the various issues that make up the debate on sustainability and sustainable development as a whole. It should be noted that an objectivist perspective is ontologically anchored in the belief that reality exists and can be studied (Burrell and Morgan, 1979). The defence of objectivism as a means of promoting dialogue represents an attempt not to diminish the value of subjectivist perspectives, but rather to recognize that these may not be coherent with what is understood by science. Thus, it can be argued that the exaggerated consideration of the infinite individual views and feelings does not contribute to the construction of any solid foundation, on which serious debate can be built. For these reasons, the strengthening of objectivism is defended here as one of the most fundamental prescriptive measures for a real evolution towards truly sustainable social, economic, and environmental dynamics. This greater attachment to data, facts, and empirical evidence may even be a determining factor for the reopening of the academic debate, as discussed next.

Reopening of the Academic Debate

The dissociation of the debate on sustainability from political and economic ideologies, allied to a greater appreciation of objectivity, can greatly favour the reopening of the academic debate. In general, these two conditions should nurture a discussion based on empirical data and, fittingly, free from passions. However, such reopening still demands specific initiatives that can guarantee at least the coexistence of divergent ideas in educational institutions, and in academia as a whole. Among these actions is the redesign of the selection processes for hiring professors, in order to avoid that those who defend views different from those accepted by most scholars who already work in an institution are summarily eliminated from the dispute for a vacancy. It is curious to observe that, in general, the same academics who tend to fight for greater diversity in both public and private environments (i.e., the presence of representatives of the so-called minorities mainly in positions of decision and power) do not extend the same behaviour when it comes to the presence of discordant people in their circles, with the hegemony of ideas often being privileged. Regrettably, for these scholars, diversity issues seem to be limited to factors such as skin colour, sexual orientation, and gender, with variety of thinking not being equally appreciated.

In addition to the issues related to the recruitment of new professors, it is necessary to work so that divergent thoughts have deserved access to academic conferences and congresses. While the vast majority of these events select the works to be presented anonymously (i.e., without the reviewers knowing the name of the authors), in some cases, the opposite is true. In these situations, it is common for those responsible for the selection of articles to give preference to authors who are part of their professional or even personal circle and who, as a consequence, tend to present similar worldviews. As a result, many academic meetings end up not fulfilling their basic function of providing a healthy environment for the confrontation of ideas and for the advancement of science. On the contrary, these addictive environments end up reinforcing similar worldviews and creating and feeding cognitive clusters within the academy.

As discussed earlier in the chapter, these hegemonic views are particularly harmful among professors and researchers, precisely because of the great influence of these figures in society. Something similar also seems to occur with some frequency in the processes of reviewing scientific articles for publication in academic journals. While the blind review process (i.e., maintaining the anonymity of authors for reviewers) is most often imposed, editors of academic publications are usually fully aware of the identity of those who submit research for their evaluation. It is to be expected, therefore, that more radicalized editors tend to pre-select the production of authors according to their political-ideological views, or even according to the usefulness of the evidence and arguments presented for the worldview they deem correct. Given the great power of editors, this possibility becomes even more worrying since it is up to them to make the final decision on whether or not to publish the articles. In this sense, editors end up playing the role of gatekeepers of academic production and what is considered contemporary science. Due to the great pressure on scholars to publish academic articles, they sometimes end up adapting to the editors' worldviews, even when they initially disagree.

It is difficult to imagine how these dynamics can dissolve by themselves. The awareness that they exist, however, represents an important step for those who seek to re-establish dialogue to act in this direction. Objectively, it is necessary that they denounce such situations whenever they come across them, and especially that they do not submit to ideologically biased editorial processes.

Enough With Celebrities

In his speech at the 2020 Golden Globes, English comedian Ricky Gervais called the public's attention to the lack of intellectual preparation of celebrities, especially those who engage in the sustainability debate more intensely. According to him, most of the actors and actresses who are willing to enact solutions to complex issues such as global warming have very low education, and practically zero knowledge of the cause. The argument is reinforced through a comparison of the intellectual capacity of celebrities with that of the Swedish teenager and activist Greta Thunberg, recognized, among other things, for promoting student strikes. Addressing an audience full of celebrity activists, Gervais uttered the following words:

> If you do win an award tonight, please don't use it as a platform to make a political speech, right? You're in no position to lecture the public about

> anything. You know nothing about the real world. Most of you spent less time in school than Greta Thunberg.
>
> (Washington Post, 2020)

Although considered by some to be aggressive, the humourist's words are accurate with regard to the lack of qualifications of most celebrities to deal with complex topics. The lack of knowledge on topics such as politics, economics, and sustainability seems to lead actors, singers, and other public figures to repeat simplistic ideas, including prescribing solutions. With celebrities depending on the approval of the masses, it is common for them to align themselves with the views held by the mainstream, which, in general, can be understood as politically correct discourse. Here lies a particularly important threat to the continuation of the dialogue, as discussed in more detail next.

Greater Skepticism Towards Political Correctness

As discussed throughout the book, the imposition of political correctness represents a rupture in the exchange of ideas, silencing opponents and constituting the basis of the 'cancel culture' (Romano, 2020). Despite being wrapped up in good intentions, political correctness can hide an authoritarian bias used by those who are convinced of their ideas and who wish to impose them upon society, acting as a form of 'perfumed fascism'. The first step to avoid the harm caused by the misuse of political correctness is precisely to become aware of these harmful effects. In this sense, it is essential that intellectuals remain detached from these impositions and that they manage to protect their way of thinking. Otherwise, they will lose their freedom and become simple echoes of official views. In these cases, your contributions are simply worthless.

These measures do not imply the search for a total and complete elimination of politically correct language. The elementary point is that intellectuals remain attentive to their great effectiveness in terms of imposing a certain vision of the world. The form of discourse plays a particularly important role in that the message that one wants to disseminate is wrapped in a series of linguistic elements that shield it from criticism. Positioning those who are somehow opposed to these contents as someone 'evil', political correctness acts as an important instrument for the interruption of dialogue.

Humility: The Topics Are Complex

Recognizing that issues related to sustainable development are essentially complex can help to prevent simplistic solutions from being trumpeted all the time. This involves both the individual search for knowledge and State policies. In the second case, it is essential that governments are committed to the education of the population, with the decoupling of scientific thinking from ideological issues being a critical prerequisite. The average citizen needs to be aware that the cause and the effect relationships usually exposed by the major media vehicles (e.g., CO_2 emissions and increase in the planet's temperature) are far from representing a scientific consensus. The understanding that correlation relationships between variables do not necessarily imply causal relationships between them would be of great value. The consideration of the possibility that human action may not be the only factor responsible for climate change would also be a great advance in dissociating the debate on sustainability from political and economic ideologies. Among other consequences, it is possible that the increase in taxes will no longer be considered an essential instrument in the fight against global warming. As American thinker Henry Louis Mencken (1880–1956) mentions, 'For every complex problem, there is an answer that is clear, simple and wrong'. This seems to be the case with restrictions imposed on economic development as a way of securing what is often thought of as a form of environmental peace. As discussed earlier, the total preservation of the Amazon rainforest could condemn more than 20 million people to a miserable life.

More broadly, it can be argued that the recognition of the complexities of issues related to sustainable development requires an awareness and the adoption of a humbler stance on the part of those who are dedicated to investigating these issues. It would be reasonable to expect this humility to come from scientists, since the scientific method is itself, to a large extent, based on the relentless questioning of premises and the test of hypotheses. It is not uncommon for researchers to dedicate their entire professional lives to the understanding of seemingly simple questions and that, even after many years, energy, and financial resources applied to their studies, do not manage to make a relevant contribution. This process usually imposes a great degree of humility on scientists who are forced to recognize their intellectual limits and, eventually, their impotence in the face of the complexity of a given subject.

It is true that, in some cases, the observed effect may be quite the opposite, with scholars developing psychological processes of denial and self-delusion, which typically fuel arrogant thoughts. Even if this adverse effect is also relatively widespread in academia, it can be argued that Science tends to humiliate – in the sense of making humble – those who live in it, with the recognition of their incapacities being, perhaps, the great learning of those who seek the truth. These questions also seem to be translated into the famous phrase attributed to the Greek philosopher Socrates (470–399 BC), 'The only thing I know is that I know nothing'. As one accesses some knowledge, one has access to more knowledge in an infinite dynamic. The perception of the immensity of the things that are still to be discovered relativizes the knowledge already acquired, which, however great, is minimal compared to all the other things that we do not know. Thus, humility would be an attribute of the wise who, despite not having all the knowledge, are aware of its immensity. Fools, on the other hand, would be at a much earlier stage of intellectual development in which, for not knowing the immensity of things to discover, still believe that the knowledge they have acquired – however small – is absolute.

Development of the Triple Bottom Line

Despite being subject to criticism – among other things due to its idealistic nature and, perhaps, not very applicable – the concept of the triple bottom line in business (Elkington, 1997) has the merit of not prioritizing the dimensions of sustainable development. The fact of considering that sustainability derives from the simultaneity of social, economic, and environmental performance is itself a call to debate, as it forces those who defend more than one point or another to come across arguments to the contrary. In particular, considering economic performance as just as important as other dimensions demands that categories as diverse as radical environmentalists and investors sit at the same table and seek a common theme. The dissemination of these ideas seems to be more easily perceived within the second group, with issues related to ESG (i.e., environmental, social, and governance) gaining strength among those who invest their capital in companies.

Whether out of a real desire to contribute to social and environmental causes, or out of a sheer concern with the protection of its heritage due to the demands of the various stakeholders, the sustainability agenda is taken into account in any investment decision. These issues are also quite present in the development of new green finance instruments, including the already traditional green bonds, and the emerging sustainability-linked bonds. While the former are used in the specific financing of projects considered environmentally sustainable, the latter associate the cost of raising companies (i.e., the interest rate paid on loans taken within this system) to the achievement of pre-established environmental goals.

From the point of view of radical environmentalists, it also seems possible to identify a greater acceptance that economic performance represents an important part of the sustainable development equation, with companies becoming less and less seen as enemies and increasingly understood as important allies in the transition for an ecologically viable world. Evidently, these ideas do not have the same appeal among environmentalists more contaminated by political and economic ideologies, who tend to see companies as the ultimate expression of capitalism and, therefore, something to be fought and eventually destroyed. Once again, the importance of detaching the debate on sustainable development from idealized worldviews, as discussed earlier in the chapter and throughout the book, can be seen.

Less Protectionism

The hijacking of environmental issues by those who intend to justify protectionist measures is extremely harmful to dialogue, with the extinction of this practice representing a fundamental step towards sustainable development. Usually supported by lies and exaggerations, these justifications contribute to the distortion of reality, as well as to the stigmatization of countries and regions as enemies of the environment. In this sense, it is necessary that all those who are interested in the search for the truth delve deeper into their analyses so that they can actually get to know the reality of producing regions classified as environmentally irresponsible. The neglect of more detailed investigations can contribute to good initiatives being abandoned, or not receiving due recognition.

No More Labelling: 'Enemies'

In addition to the initiatives discussed above, ending enemy labelling is probably the measure that has the greatest potential to pay dividends in the short term. The portrayal of opponents as defenders of evil creates a psychological barrier in both the groups qualified in this way and those who promote labelling, which, among other things, hinders any form of exchange. In addition to automatically repelling opposing parties, the Manichean division of groups often justifies the radicalization of discourse and even more aggressive attitudes. Once again, the importance of separating sustainability issues from political and economic ideologies is verified, so that the debate on sustainable development does not inherit the passions and vices that are typical of idealized worldviews.

Particularly important is the perception that the labelling of enemies often translates into an extremely simplistic way of understanding the world, with the rigid division between sides ignoring the nuances that exist between the extremes. As a result, it is possible that those who label opponents more forcefully end up losing opportunities to dialogue with people who, despite presenting discordant views on some points, may come to converge on others. It can also be argued that the simplistic labelling, and the division into groups it entails, favours the annulment of the individual, since s/he must fully adhere to a series of collective decisions, with which s/he may not necessarily agree. This collectivization of the debate favours, in turn, the capture of these groups by politicians who see it as an opportunity to gain votes and, ultimately, power.

Despite the many harms that the labelling of enemies entails, radicalized parties cannot be expected to decide to stop this process by themselves. This role must be exercised by all those who, in addition to being really interested in opening or maintaining dialogue on sustainable development, understand the importance of this measure. Unfortunately, this finding does not imply crediting this mission to the so-called constituted intellectual elites. As discussed earlier, these often fail to fulfil what could be understood as a moral obligation to maintain open dialogue in academic environments, being themselves often agents of radicalization.

References

Bryant, C. (2019). Prince Harry's shaming is bad news for private jets. *Bloomberg*, August 23. Available at https://www.bloomberg.com/opinion/articles/2019-08-23/climate-change-prince-harry-shaming-is-bad-news-for-private-jets

Burrell, G., and Morgan, G. (1979). *Sociological Paradigms and Organizational Analysis*. Heinemann.

Elkington, J. (1997). *Cannibals with Forks: The Triple Bottom Line of 21st Century*. Capstone.

English, R., Allen, V., and Norton, J. (2019). Prince Harry 'flew on a private jet AND helicopter paid for by Google' to get to tech giant's 'hypocritical' Sicily climate change camp (and the prince would need to plant 190 trees just to offset one leg of the trip). *Daily Mail*, August 2. Available at https://www.dailymail.co.uk/news/article-7313843/Prince-Harry-flew-private-jet-helicopter-Google-climate-change-camp.html

Fracarolli Nunes, M., and Lee Park, C. (2021). The age of green. In: M. Fracarolli Nunes and C. Lee Park (Eds.). *Business Ethics and Environmental Fraud: Improper Competitive Advantage in the Age of Green*, pp.87–104. Palgrave Macmillan.

France 24 (2019). *CO_2 Row Over Climate Activist Thunberg's Yacht Trip to New York*, August 18. Available at https://www.france24.com/en/20190818-co2-row-over-climate-activist-thunberg-s-yacht-trip-to-new-york

Romano, A. (2020). Why we can't stop fighting about cancel culture. *Vox*, August 25. Available at https://www.vox.com/culture/2019/12/30/20879720/what-is-cancel-culture-explained-history-debate

Washington Post (2020). Ricky Gervais teaches Hollywood what speaking truth to power really means. *Opinion*, January 7. Available at https://www.washingtonpost.com/opinions/ricky-gervais-teaches-hollywood-what-speaking-truth-to-power-really-means/2020/01/07/be97df72-3185-11ea-91fd-82d4e04a3fac_story.html

Watts, J. (2019). Greta Thunberg sets sail for New York on zero-carbon yacht. *The Guardian*, August 14. Available at https://www.theguardian.com/environment/2019/aug/14/greta-thunberg-sets-sail-plymouth-climate-us-trump

Index

www.ingramcontent.com/pod-product-compliance
Ingram Content Group UK Ltd.
Pitfield, Milton Keynes, MK11 3LW, UK
UKHW020147200926
475702UK00016B/2584
* 9 7 8 0 3 6 7 6 4 4 7 9 6 *